"Mark Coppenger has rendered a great service to the Christian church in the 21st century. *Moral Apologetics* is a special gift to all of those faithful Christians who believe that Christianity brings new life to the mind as well as to the soul. *Moral Apologetics* should be added to every thinking Christian's bookshelf."

Dr. Richard Land
President, Ethics and Religious Liberty Commission
of the Southern Baptist Convention

"Pascal noted that 'the heart has reasons that reason cannot know.' Mark Coppenger in his extraordinary book realizes the mind has positions the brain cannot fathom. Here in poignant argumentation is the case for faith and the natural state of morality. His explanations are breathtakingly persuasive regardless of your religious conviction."

Herbert I. London
President Emeritus, Hudson Institute

"I wish every Christian could have the opportunity of sitting in Mark Coppenger's classroom—a place of constant intellectual exchange, all aimed at developing a consistently biblical worldview. Well, reading this book is as close as many Christians may ever get to sitting in that classroom, but it is an experience not to be missed. This book is a tour de force of apologetic thought, revealing ethical issues to be apologetic opportunities. The book is fascinating on every page. Don't miss this book. Get ready for a guided tour through contemporary culture and Christian apologetics."

R. Albert Mohler Jr.
President, The Southern Baptist Theological Seminary

MARK COPPENGER

Moral

APOLOGETICS for Contemporary Christians

Pushing Back Against Cultural and Religious Critics

ACADEMIC

NASHVILLE, TENNESSEE

DANIEL R. HEIMBACH, *Series Editor*

CONTENTS

SERIES PREFACE

T HE GREATEST CHALLENGE TO the life and witness of the church in our age is widespread moral confusion and denial of moral authority. This condition has been greatly influenced by a number of factors, including postmodern denial of objective truth, secularization of common life, pluralization of worldviews, and privatization of religion—all accompanied by growing hostility toward anything Christian. In fact, claims of objective moral authority and understanding are openly contested by our culture more than any other aspects of Christian faith and witness. Those who are redefining justice, character, and truth are working hard to deconstruct essential social institutions to justify a variety of ends: pursuing sensuality, elevating lifestyle over protecting innocent human life, stealing what others have fairly acquired, ridiculing the rule of law, abandoning the needy for self-fulfillment, and forsaking lifelong commitments. They reject the Judeo-Christian values on which the institutions of Western civilization were erected (i.e., marriage, property ownership, free-market enterprise, justice, law, education, and national security) and without which they cannot endure. Never in the history of the church has there been a more critical need for scholarship, instruction, and application of Christian ethics in ways that equip Christian men and women to engage the surrounding culture in prophetic moral witness.

This series aims to promote understanding and respect for the reality and relevance of God's moral truth—what Francis Schaeffer called "true truth"—in contrast to truth claims that are false or distorted. We hope these books will serve as a resource for Christians to resist compromise and to contend with the moral war raging through our culture and tormenting the church. Some authors in this series will address the interpretation of biblical teachings; others will focus on the history, theological integration, philosophical analysis, and application of Christian moral understanding. But all will use and apply God's moral truth in ways that convince the mind, convict the heart, and consume the soul.

In *Moral Apologetics for Contemporary Christians*, Mark Coppenger defends a biblical view of moral order against major lines of attack that are eroding standards of ethical thinking, character, and behavior in contemporary life and culture. He stands up to skeptics who dismiss Christianity on moral grounds by claiming it is either morally deficient (not the best option available) or contradictory (not reliably consistent). Coppenger insists that Christian ethics is not only reliably consistent but also better than anything else. In other words, he shows how the field of ethics is the last place skeptics of the faith should try to battle Christianity, and he does it by appealing to both hearts and minds. He demonstrates that Christian ethics not only makes good sense but is eminently desirable. The surrounding culture and even some Christians these days suppose that moral truth (thinking and believing) and moral life (desiring and doing) are separable categories, but this book argues that authentic Christian ethics is both a matter of truth and of life. It connects knowing and believing with wanting and doing. In fact, Coppenger contends there is no more effective apologetic for Christianity than arises from connecting objective moral reality with subjective moral experience. Christian ethics and apologetics are sometimes confused because people either wrongly think there is no difference, or wrongly think they are totally different. However, this book demonstrates most eloquently not only how apologetics includes defending Christian ethics, but also how Christian ethics includes defending moral truth and is not limited simply to defining, declaring, explaining, evaluating, or applying what God reveals to be morally discretionary, obligatory, or praiseworthy.

Daniel R. Heimbach
Series Editor

ACKNOWLEDGMENTS

This book is something of a destination for me, in that the track of my life has led me here. And I want to thank those who have thrown the switches shifting me from one set of rails to another.

My maternal grandfather, Allen Benjamin Crow, who was president of the Detroit Economic Club, gave our family a six-week trip around the world in 1966 (when Hong Kong still belonged to Britain, the Mount of Olives was still in Jordan, and Pan Am was still flying). Though my parents, Raymond and Agnes Coppenger, had taken us kids all over the country in connection with my dad's academic and military service (Boulder, CO; Oceanside, CA; Washington, D.C.), and visits to relatives in Michigan and Florida meant exposure to some distinct American cultures, there was nothing like this before for us.

Along the way, we visited more than a dozen countries with a wide range of faith groups, including Shinto/Buddhist Japan; Buddhist Thailand; Hindu India; Muslim Egypt; Jewish Israel; Orthodox Greece; Roman Catholic Italy; Lutheran Germany; and Anglican England. Then, in recent decades, as a pastor and denomination worker, I've enjoyed support for trips to predominantly Catholic Brazil; atheist/Orthodox Russia and Romania; Muslim Jordan, Egypt, Sudan, and Indonesia. In all this, I've been struck by the way in which belief systems impact standard of living and social tone.

So a thank you to my parents, and Grandpa Crow, and churches of the Southern Baptist Convention for running me around the world.

I'm also grateful to Vanderbilt's John Lachs for the invitation to work on a National Endowment for the Humanities project in human rights back in the mid-1970s, even though my dissertation was in epistemology. And thanks to Wheaton College for giving me major promptings and opportunities to teach and write in ethics. And to Southern Seminary for asking me to teach apologetics. And to Emmanuel and Camille Kampouris for asking me to work for *Kairos Journal*. And to Southeastern Seminary professor Daniel Heimbach for asking me to contribute to this series. And to my Apologetical Ethics seminar for helping me think through these matters.

Along this journey into ethics and apologetics, I've been nurtured and replenished by so many—above all, my wife, Sharon. And in the course of this particular writing project, the saints at Evanston Baptist Church, who prayed for me regularly. And in the editing process, Jim Baird of Broadman & Holman and Roy Zuck of Dallas Theological Seminary. And in my promiscuous reading (to use Milton's phrase) by Evanston's Amaranth Books, whose $1–3 used-book shelves provided a stream of inspiration and material. And to the estimable Evanston Public Library, in whose confines I found frequent occasion to read and write on this project.

Please don't hold the infelicities and transgressions of this book against any of these people. Much of their help was unwitting, at least as far as this project goes. But I did want to thank them as representatives of the many who have sped me down the track toward the joys of writing in this connection.

Mark Coppenger

INTRODUCTION

F OES OF THE FAITH often declare Christianity morally deficient. Christopher Hitchens for one has said that religion "poisons everything," and believers are all too familiar with attempts to hang the Crusades, the Inquisition, and even the Holocaust around their necks.[1] They have also felt the sting of being labeled "repressed, Victorian prudes," "blood-thirsty colonialists," purveyors of an ideological "opium to the masses," and insufferable "theocrats." The Bible itself has been demeaned for teaching willfully blind creationism, genocide in Canaan, homophobia, and an eternal hell.

This book is designed to push back against such criticism, arguing that Christianity is morally superior as well as true. I will engage not only the harsh critic but also the more subtly aggressive cultural relativist, with his fondness for "moral equivalency."

The book is not meant as a knockdown proof of Christianity. Indeed, no apologetic can accomplish this, and few today believe that one can. Rather, typical contemporary apologists fashion "defeater defeaters" to deflate the skeptic's claims of victory and, second, argue the greater plausibility of Christianity among its explanatory rivals. I'll try some of both.

I will note uncomfortable realities, including the misbehavior of many Christians (and false professors) but will seek to demonstrate that the moral and cultural center of mass of genuine Christianity is clearly superior to that of its competitors.

THE LITANY

In a recent book, marginal television personality Adam Carolla goes through some of his atheist moves:

1

> Every time you argue with a religious person, they pose this question: "If you were walking down a dark alley, would you rather encounter a group of Christians or a group of atheists?" Before I answer that, let me ask you a question, my religious-zealot friend. What percentage of inmates on death row are atheist or agnostic? Of course I'd rather deal with people who had their own internal moral compass rather than a group that could stab me and be absolved of their sins. And where is this alley, and what year is it? Not if the alley is in Jerusalem during the Crusades.[2]

Into this little piece of rim-shot comedy, Carolla has packed a fair amount of insulting nonsense, yet it passes for wisdom in the popular culture. He would likely get away with it, with applause and laughter, on talk shows. But look at what he's saying or strongly implying: that apologetics and evangelism are stupid zealotry; that most people on death row were genuinely religious at the time of their crimes; that atheists, like himself, have a reliable, internal moral compass; that functional atheists (as distinct from convictional atheists like himself) don't count in the calculations; that New Testament grace and Muslim jihad come to the same thing, a license to murder; that "Christian" brutality during the Crusades was unambiguous and typical.

But again, Carolla is a comedian, not accountable to the canons of academic circumspection. But fairness on these matters is hardly the rule on campus. Take, for instance, a speech recently appearing in the liberal Jewish magazine, *Tikkun*. While receiving an honorary doctorate from *Augustana Hochschule*, a Protestant seminary in Germany, Dartmouth professor Susannah Heschel quoted "Nazi Christian" Wolf Meyer-Erlach to say, "In the treatment and decision of National Socialism against Jews, Luther's intentions, after centuries, are being fulfilled."[3] Using this quote as Exhibit A, she goes on to argue that the Holocaust was an outworking of dominant Christian theology, rooted not only in the writings of this sixteenth-century Reformer but also in the work of Justin Martyr and even in the doctrine of the indwelling Holy Spirit.

She makes one reference to the Confessing Church but gives no indication it opposed Hitler perilously, and her wording is helplessly misleading:

> Even within the so-called "church struggle" between German Christians and the Confessing Church for control of the Protestant church, anti-Semitism became the glue that united the otherwise warring factions. Similarly, however much Hitler made use of images of messianism, redemption, and other Christian motifs, the most useful and consistent aspect of Christianity for the Nazi movement was its anti-Judaism, just as the single most consistent and persistent feature of Nazism was its anti-Semitism.[4]

You can easily get the false sense that "the glue that united" the Confessing Church, internally and externally, was hatred of the Jews. And there is no mention whatsoever of the Lutheran martyr Dietrich Bonhoeffer, who, for instance, defied Nazi sensibilities by writing a book emphasizing Christ's loving use of the *Hebrew* Psalms.

But believers have grown accustomed to such verbal sins of commission and omission by those who wish to defame the church.

CULTURAL APOLOGETICS

So what is one to do when the critics claim that Christianity has a baleful effect on society? Surprisingly, some first-rate apologists are wary of answering back, of arguing that Christian cultural influence is both defensible and superior.

Take, for instance, this exchange between William Lane Craig and Christopher Hitchens. It came near the end of a debate held at Biola University in 2009, one moderated by conservative radio personality Hugh Hewitt.[5] Craig had adopted a formal debater's template, foisting the burden of disproving theism upon Hitchens and then declaring Hitchens' answers inadequate. When the atheist tried to shift the discussion to moral and cultural matters and Hewitt picked up the question, Craig dismissed the matter:

HEWITT: Those who are announced atheists, those who have done evil in the world, particularly in the last . . . century, the Marxists, the Trotskyites, the Stalinists, have they done more damage in your view and more evil than the Christians?

CRAIG: Well, this is a debate, Hugh, that I don't want to get into because I think it's irrelevant. I, as a philosopher, and I mean this, am interested in the truth of these worldviews more than I'm interested in the social impact. And you cannot judge the truth of a worldview by its social impact. That's just irrelevant. Bertrand Russell in his essay, "Why I am not a Christian," understood this. Russell said that you cannot assess the truth of a worldview by seeing whether it's good for society or not. Now the irony was that when Russell wrote that back in the twenties, he was trying to refute those who said you should believe in Christianity because it's so socially beneficial to society. It was just the mirror image of Christopher Hitchens' argument, saying you shouldn't believe in it because it's socially detrimental to human culture. But I think Russell's point cuts both ways because it's a valid point. You can't assess the truth of a worldview by argument about its cultural and social impact. There are true ideas that may have had negative social impact. And, therefore, we have to deal with the truth of these, the arguments for and against them, and not get into arguments about, "Has Marxism or Chinese Communism been responsible for more deaths than theism in the 20th century."

HITCHENS: No, I completely concur with what you say there. . . . I think the concession is very well worth having that there is absolutely no proof at all that Christianity makes people behave better.

CRAIG: Wait a minute. I didn't concede that. . . . I said I wasn't going to argue that because it's irrelevant, but by no means did I concede that. . . .

One might chalk this up to Craig's effort to keep things on the track he carefully laid for the evening. Indeed, at one point he said, "We're not here tonight to debate the social impact of religion [or OT ethics or biblical inerrancy]—all interesting and important topics, no doubt, but not the subject of tonight's debate."[6] But his impatience was more than occasional. It actually reflected his settled dissatisfaction with appealing to social impact in defending orthodoxy. As he writes in *Reasonable Faith*:

> [T]he apologetic for Christianity based on the human predicament is an extremely recent phenomenon, associated primarily with Francis Schaeffer. Often it is referred to as "cultural apologetics" because of its analysis of post-Christian culture. This approach constitutes an entirely different sort of apologetics than the traditional models, since it is not concerned with epistemological issues of justification and warrant. Indeed, in a sense it does not even attempt to show in a positive sense that Christianity is true; it simply explores the disastrous consequences for human existence, society, and culture if Christianity should be false. In this respect, this approach is somewhat akin to existentialism: the precursors of this approach were also precursors of existentialism, and much of its analysis of the human predicament is drawn from the insights of 20th-century atheistic existentialism.[7]

I find much of this to be odd, and I think it helps to say why in some detail; it helps to set the course for this book:

1. If Christians claim that God is infinite in power and knowledge and that his commands are wise and good, then obedience should result in wonderful things, which should reflect well on tenets of the faith.
2. Evidence of negative social impact, if and where it occurs, is problematic for Christianity; it makes the case for a sovereign, self-revealing, benevolent God more difficult, and it demands explanation.
3. True ideas do not, in the end, have negative social impact; they bring light and life to society.
4. It is perfectly reasonable, worthwhile, and apologetically responsible to remind the critic of Christianity wearing a Che Guevara T-shirt that 20th-century Communists such as Pol Pot, Stalin, and Mao have intentionally killed, respectively, millions, tens of millions, and scores of millions of innocent people.
5. Cultural apologetics is an ancient enterprise, practiced by the likes of Augustine, who, in *City of God*, "dilates . . . on the vices of pagan society,"[8] and Thomas Aquinas, who, in *Summa contra gentiles*, derides both Islam and Muslims.[9]
6. Cultural apologetics is, of course, "concerned with epistemological issues of justification and warrant." It fits in the Teleological Argument family, along with Intelligent Design. For analogy, if a once dissolute and surly

young man returns to town a sharp, hard working, polite citizen and is asked what happened, he might reply, "I became a Marine." This is at least prima facie evidence that Marines exist and that they are good for men.

7. Cultural apologetics is as positive as it is negative. As Francis Schaeffer demonstrated, the Reformation did much to foster the arts, science, and technology.

8. Cultural apologetics is less "somewhat akin" to existentialism than it is to Francis Schaeffer's conservative Presbyterianism; and Schaeffer was hard on Kierkegaard and Sartre.

9. The "precursors" of cultural apologetics were biblical personalities, not existentialists. Whether Daniel, Nehemiah, and Esther in Mesopotamia, Joseph in Egypt, or the early Christians in Jerusalem, believers have pointed others to the Lord by their outstanding integrity, industry, courage, wisdom, beneficence, and grace.

10. To many observers, such iterations of the Design Argument are far more intuitive and persuasive than versions of the ontological and cosmological arguments, which strike many as word play or rationalistic stipulation.

Speaking of his concern that "the gospel can be heard as an intellectually viable option for thinking people," Craig remarks, "In Europe, we have seen the bitter fruit of secularization, which now threatens North America."[10] I hope to show or remind the reader that the "bitter fruit" of rejecting Christianity extends well beyond the intellectual climate to the well-being of society in general.

MORAL APOLOGETICS OR APOLOGETICAL ETHICS

It is useful, then, to consider the ways in which a Christian ethic serves and intersects with apologetics, whether we call the study "moral apologetics" or "apologetical ethics." It deals with four contrasts:

1. *Christian Ethics vs. Secular Ethics* (chaps. 1–5): When pushed, or even examined on the face, systems of right and wrong based on things other than God's rule and revelation are faulty; in contrast, the splendor of a full-orbed Christian ethic lends credence to the claim that God is its author and Lord.

2. *Christian Ethicists vs. Secular Ethicists* (chaps. 6–9): Though there are remarkable exceptions to the rule, those who lead out in Christian thought and instruction live admirable lives. In contrast, many, but not all, of those who espouse and advance non-Christian values and principles live unseemly or uninspiring lives.

3. *Christian Fruit vs. Secular Fruit* (chaps. 10–13): Allowing for the unfortunate consequences flowing from the actions of some who call themselves "Christian" and the gratifying products of non-Christian lives and cultures, we

may still demonstrate that cultures are distinctively blessed when permeated—or even touched—by Christianity.

4. *Admirable Apologetics vs. Irresponsible Apologetics* (chaps. 14–18): The discourse in and around apologetics varies greatly in its quality; some of it is praiseworthy, some not. Both Christians and non-Christians can be found producing both sorts, and we will examine some examples. This section is essentially an introduction to "virtue apologetics." (Of course, critics of this book will likely jump at the chance to turn my expressions "irresponsible apologetics" and "infelicities" back on the book itself, and that is their prerogative—if only they will give the case I outline a fair reading.)

A SAMPLER

The scarcity of material on some topics makes research a daunting task—the prayer life of Shakespeare or evangelicals working in the *film noir* genre. But the one who works at moral apologetics has the opposite problem; he drowns in useful material. It is hard to open a newspaper, walk through a library, or turn on the television without seeing fresh evidence that a Christian approach to life makes people and societies flourish and that those who turn their backs on genuine Christianity are liable to behave wickedly. Similarly, the maxims of the lost are often pathetic or distasteful; the watchwords of the regenerate are more characteristically sound and stirring.

So much could be said about the contrasting moral worth of faith and faithlessness—in terms of constitution, walk, and effects—that a book of this size can only be a sampler, a taste of this and that.

And again, I do not pretend that this will carry the day against the skeptic, whether the nonbeliever who finds the faith unsavory or the Christian who thinks my enterprise is a waste of time. But I do hope this book will help prompt a closer look at the way Christians should be grateful for their ethical heritage and more inclined to cite it in their defense of the faith.

French philosopher Blaise Pascal observed, "No one is so happy as a true Christian, or so reasonable, virtuous, and lovable."[11] He was right, and demonstrably so, though his statement strikes the modern ear as outlandish and arrogant. Unfortunately, Christians have lost much of their conviction and will to speak as Pascal did. I hope to help replenish this loss of cultural confidence. We have a great moral story to tell, and it surely points to the Author of Light and Life.

AN AFFRONT

I wish this book might be met at every turn with affirmation, but I know it will be an affront to many. First of all, it will offend the tender, and the not so tender, souls who gravitate toward cultural relativism, counting any sort of exceptionalism as arrogant and hopelessly biased. Second, at certain points it begs to differ with personalities and perspectives popular in the contemporary church, though I hope the reader will see that my concerns and positions are licit and plausible. Third, the broad scope of this book makes inevitable the complaint that I don't "do justice" to first one thing and then another. Fourth, the combination of academic and popular writing can frustrate purists in both camps.

Still, I pray the reader will see that this is a good faith effort at saying important and true things in an understandable, engaging, and decent way.

Notes

1 See, for instance, Elizabeth Anderson, "If God Is Dead, Is Everything Permitted?" *Philosophers Without Gods: Meditations on Atheism and the Secular Life* (Oxford: Oxford University Press, 2007), 222. Her list of "Christian" transgressions also includes "the Thirty Years War, the English Civil War, witch-hunts, the cultural genocide of Mayan civilization, the brutal conquest of the Aztec and the Inca, religious support for ethnic cleansing of Native Americans, slavery of Africans in the Americas, colonialist tyranny across the globe, confinement of the Jews to ghettos, and periodic pogroms against them."

2 Adam Carolla, *In Fifty Years We'll All Be Chicks . . . and Other Complaints from an Angry Middle-Aged White Guy* (New York: Crown, 2010), 150.

3 Susannah Heschel, "Strange Affinities: Biblical Scholarship and the Rise of Racism: A Speech to a Protestant Seminary in German," *Tikkun* (March/April 2009), 24. Also accessible at http://www.tikkun.org/article.php/mar09_heschel.

4 Ibid., 24.

5 William Lane Craig and Christopher Hitchens, *"Does God Exist?": A Debate* (La Mirada, CA: Biola University, 2009). DVD available at http://www.biola.edu/academics/sas/apologetics/events/#PriorEvents.

6 Ibid.

7 William Lane Craig, *Reasonable Faith: Christian Truth and Apologetics*, 3rd ed. (Wheaton: Crossway, 1984, 1994, 2008), 65.

8 Avery Cardinal Dulles, *A History of Apologetics* (San Francisco: Ignatius, 2005), 84.

9 Ibid., 119–20.

10 Craig, *Reasonable Faith: Christian Truth and Apologetics*, 17–18.

11 Peter Kreeft, *Christianity for Modern Pagans: Pascal's Pensées Edited, Outlined and Explained* (San Francisco: Ignatius, 1966), 278.

FAULTY SECULAR FOUNDATIONS
ENTHRONING THE INDIVIDUAL

IN PLATO'S DIALOGUE, *EUTHYPHRO,* Socrates asks a self-righteous young man to explain righteousness. The fellow relates it to divine approval, but then Socrates asks him whether something is righteous because the gods approve of it or if they approve of it because it is righteous. That is, which comes first, the chicken or the egg? This question confuses the fellow, tying him in knots, as it has philosophers and theologians for centuries.

Today the issue falls under "metaethics," the effort to establish the base for moral thinking. This base supports principles (such as justice and love), which are spelled out in rules (such as "Don't murder" and "Don't commit adultery"), which in turn are applied to interesting cases (such as whether artificial insemination with a donor constitutes adultery). But these case studies in "normative ethics" all lead back to the fundamental issue: What makes something right or wrong in the first place?[1]

The range of answers to that question is astonishing. Some emphasize raw duty, while others focus on happy consequences, naturalness, or virtuous character, but it is not a tidy matter. These answers often overlap or simply address different questions. It is impossible to do them much justice in a few short chapters; indeed many books have been written on single ethical theories. But a quick survey will be useful.

The apologetic point of these first three chapters is that non-Christian ethical systems stumble and reflect poorly on the worldviews that craft and cherish them. Then, in chap. 4, we'll examine religiously based ethics, finding fault with the offerings of false religions. Then, in chap. 5, we'll consider the superiority of a full-orbed Christian approach.

Here then is a selection of pretenders to the throne, beginning with secular approaches which ground morality in the individual.

AESTHETIC PLEASURE

For some the highest moral categories are cast in aesthetic terms, whether beauty, intrigue, gracefulness, or rhythm. As conservative art critic Roger Kimball notes, it turns ruinous: "At the center of that way of life is the imperative to regard all experience as an occasion for aesthetic delectation: a seemingly attractive proposition, perhaps, until one realizes that it depends upon a narcissistic self-absorption that renders every moral demand negotiable."[2]

British painter Lucien Freud is an example. "Quite a few friends were crooks and psychopaths. Freud liked homosexual gangster Ronnie Kray because 'he said interesting things, although he was, as everyone knows, a sadistic murderer.'"[3]

Walter Pater

Nineteenth-century English essayist and critic Walter Pater is case in point. In his book on the Renaissance, he claimed that experience is its own end. For "a counted number of pulses only is given to us of a variegated, dramatic life." Thus we must focus on "getting as many pulsations as possible into the given time." So we reach for "any exquisite passion, or any contribution to knowledge that seems by a lifted horizon to set the spirit free for a moment, or any stirring of the senses, strange dyes, strange colours, and curious odours, or work of the artist's hands, or the face of one's friend."[4]

The aim was total self-satisfaction: "To burn always with this hard, gem-like flame, to maintain this ecstasy, is success in life. . . . In a sense it might even be said that our failure is to form habits."[5] So to be comfortably consistent in the ways of virtue is a dead end. Better to be breaking fresh ground and getting a new rush, whatever the cost.

And though he was a fairly colorless man, his fantasies ran toward the illicit: "He was, for example, overheard to say that it would be great fun to take Holy Orders without believing a word of Christian doctrine." Fortunately a friend wrote the bishop of London about this, heading off any attempt at it.[6]

Poor Walter. He was always bemoaning the fact that he lacked "so-and-so's courage and hardihood." Were he so endowed, he once observed, with a little laugh, "I might have been a criminal."[7]

Adolph Hitler

A painter of modest skill, Adolph Hitler was frustrated by lack of acclaim in the galleries of Vienna, but he found a larger canvas on which to work. A

"Central European Romantic," he "worshipped the artist and his achievement as the embodiment of the highest social aspirations of an age," and he repeatedly "define[d] his historic mission in artistic terms."[8]

> In fact, Hitler took the practice of politics-as-an-art vastly beyond anything imagined by the Iron Chancellor [Bismarck]—to the extent, indeed, where he could, in an unguarded moment, style himself "the greatest actor in Europe." With no immodesty he might have added that he was also the greatest theatrical impresario, the most daring playwright and the cleverest stage manager on the inter-war political scene.[9]

Of course his palette included the blood of Jews, and his sound effects were the breaking of Jewish shop windows on *Kristallnacht*.

AUTONOMY

Ethical autonomists make their personal choices the highest good—freedom above all—and they count as wicked any attempt to hold them accountable to standards outside themselves. This stance comes in many flavors, but its spirit of total rebellion is recognizable throughout, as is its connection to the primordial lie of the serpent, that Adam and Eve could be like gods themselves.

Jean-Paul Sartre

The atheistic existentialist philosopher, Jean-Paul Sartre, defines his school of thought, existentialism, with the formula, "Existence precedes essence." He uses a paper cutter for contrast: "Here is an object which has been made by an artisan whose inspiration came from a concept." Its "essence—that is, the ensemble of both the production routines and the properties which enable it to be both produced and defined—precedes existence."

But according to Sartre, man is just the opposite. He argues that

> man exists, turns up, appears on the scene, and, only afterwards, defines himself. . . . There is no human nature, since there is no God to conceive it. Not only is man what he conceives himself to be, but he is also only what he wills himself to be after this thrust toward existence. Man is nothing else but what he makes of himself. Such is the first principle of existentialism.[10]

Thus answerable to nothing but himself, he makes up his own rules.

Of course the problem should be obvious. This ethic is entirely compatible with anything, including bestiality, pedophilia, and mass murder. Furthermore, as Sartre demonstrated in his own life, this view is virtually impossible to maintain, for he took stands against the involvement of the United States in Vietnam, signing manifestos that presupposed a universal morality.

Above all he loved the outlaw stance. He "felt a . . . pull towards 'low places and shady young men,' and his rejection of middle-class rules, his fascination with the thief Jean Genet, and his art all bear comparison with Dostoevsky's convict code," namely, "to live life according to one's own passions, to create one's own laws!"[11]

Anarchists

Anarchists gained celebrity status when they heaved bricks through Seattle storefront windows during the World Trade Organization meeting in 1999.[12] Here is a statement of their perspective:

> Anarchists are anti-authoritarians because they believe that no human being should dom-inate another. . . . Domination is inherently degrading and demeaning, since it submerges the will and judgment of the dominated to the will and judgement of the dominators, thus destroying the dignity and self-respect that comes only from personal autonomy. . . . So, in a nutshell, Anarchists seek a society in which people interact in ways which enhance the liberty of all rather than crush the liberty (and so potential) of the many for the benefit of a few. Anarchists do not want to give others power over themselves, the power to tell them what to do under the threat of punishment if they do not obey. Perhaps non-anarchists, rather than be puzzled why anarchists are anarchists, would be better off asking what it says about themselves that they feel this attitude needs any sort of explanation.[13]

Most would find their utter disregard for authority, whether human or divine, to be the perfect recipe for moral and social chaos.

Sheila Larson

In *Habits of the Heart,* sociologist Robert Bellah and his colleagues describe a young nurse who was "in part, trying to find a center in herself after liberating herself from an oppressively conformist early family life."[14]

> One person we interviewed has actually named her religion (she calls it her "faith") after herself. This suggests the logical possibility of over 220 million American religions, one for each of us. Sheila Larson is a young nurse who has received a good deal of therapy and who describes her faith as "Sheilaism." "I believe in God. I'm not a religious fanatic. I can't remember the last time I went to church. My faith has carried me a long way. It's Sheila-ism. Just my own little voice." Sheila's faith has some tenets beyond belief in God, though not many. In defining "my own Sheilaism," she said: "It's just trying to love yourself and be gentle with yourself. You know, I guess, take care of each other. I think He would want us to take care of each other."[15]

Of course it would be unfortunate for an Osama Bin Laden to "love and be gentle with himself" instead of falling on his face in horror and contrition for his deeds. Sheila does counsel him to take care of others, but it is not clear who the others might be? Al Qaeda? Workers in the Twin Towers? And since self-love comes first, does this trump the second duty, to care for others? Does this mean that one repents only if his self-esteem remains intact?

William Ernest Henley

The movie *Invictus* shined the spotlight on William Ernest Henley's poem of the same name. It was a source of inspiration for Nelson Mandela during his years of captivity on Robben Island off the South African coast. Unfortunately it was also the favorite poem of the Oklahoma City bomber, Timothy McVeigh. One can see how both men might appreciate its message of courage, but its arrogance is unmistakable. And one can easily imagine Adolf Hitler reciting it after surviving an assassination attempt.

> Out of the night that covers me,
> Black as the pit from pole to pole,
> I thank whatever gods may be
> For my unconquerable soul.
> In the fell clutch of circumstance
> I have not winced nor cried aloud.
> Under the bludgeonings of chance
> My head is bloody, but unbowed.
> Beyond this place of wrath and tears
> Looms but the Horror of the shade,
> And yet the menace of the years
> Finds and shall find me unafraid.
> It matters not how strait the gate,
> How charged with punishments the scroll,
> I am the master of my fate:
> I am the captain of my soul.

George Carlin

As odd as it may sound, antinomianism ("lawlessness") in one form or another presumes to pass itself off as an ethic. The transgressor glories in his moral superiority to God and to convention. He works with shock, trying to explode decorum with scatological talk and brazen transgression, all the while posing as if he is looking down on the sheep who follow conventional morality. George Carlin fits this bill.

In the tradition of Lenny Bruce, he delighted in vile and irreverent speech. Having begun as a likable comic, with innocuous observational humor, he turned to the dark side in the late seventies, most notably with his monologue "Filthy Words," a celebration of "words you could never say on television." When a father complained to the FCC that his son was hit with Carlin's obscenities coming over the car radio, the Commission responded with the finding that the words were "patently offensive," and they moved to prevent such broadcasts in the future. The U.S. Supreme Court subsequently ruled in *FCC v. Pacifica Foundation* that the Commission indeed had the right to regulate such broadcast speech.[16] But Carlin was off to the races. As he put it in the monologue, "I got my Grammy. I can let my hair hang down now." And so the real George Carlin emerged.

In subsequent work he called the teaching of the Bible "the Greatest [BS] Story Ever Told." He marveled at those who taught and believed "that there's an invisible man who lives in the sky and watches everything you do, every minute of every day. And who has a special list of ten things he does not want you to do."[17]

Then, in a mock interview with Jesus, we read, concerning the Resurrection: "I: On Easter Sunday. You rose from the dead didn't you? J: Not that I know of. I think I would remember something like that. I do remember sleeping a long time after the crucifixion."[18]

Thus Carlin stakes out a moral position superior to that of mere Christianity, but then he throws it away with vicious cynicism: "I hope reincarnation is a fact so I can come back and [have illicit sex with] teenagers again"; "Let me tell you something, if we ever have a good, useful, real-life revolution in this country, I'm gonna kill a whole lot of [people] on my list. For purposes of surprise, I'm not revealing the names at this time"; "[Away with] rational thought."[19] So lust, vengeance, and insanity pass for humor in Carlin's universe. Of course this cannot sustain an ethic; it self-implodes, self-refutes. But judging from the laughter and honors he's received, many people navigate by the light of his "wisdom."

Abbie Hoffman

Abbie Hoffman was a radical activist who made his biggest splash as one of the Chicago Seven, the team of leftists who went on trial for inciting riots in Chicago during the Democratic convention of 1968. He was also celebrated for his book, *Steal This Book*, wherein he taught the reader how to defraud the airlines with false lost-luggage claims, sneak into movies through fire exits, fashion a pipe bomb, and shoplift. To justify this, he said, "It's universally wrong to steal from your neighbor, but once you get beyond the one-to-one level . . . it becomes strictly a value judgment to decide exactly who is stealing from whom. One person's crime is another person's profit."[20]

However much he wanted to pass himself off as Robin Hood, tormenting the evil sheriff of Nottingham, his focus was selfishness and chaos. And somehow it escaped him that the local five-and-dime owner was damaged by shoplifting, even his store was part of a big, "evil" chain.

In his book *Revolution for the Hell of It*, he counsels his fellow "diggers," "Don't rely on words. . . . Rely on doing—go all the way every time. . . . Accept contradictions, that's what life is all about. Have a good time. . . . It is the duty of all revolutionists to make love. Do weird things. . . . Property is the enemy—burn it, destroy it, give it away."[21]

For such ethical insights as these, he earned high praise at his funeral, following his suicide. Former NBC star Bill Walton observed, "Abbie was not a fugitive from justice. Justice was a fugitive from him."[22] In a later written eulogy, Norman Mailer called him, "Our own holy ghost of the Left" and toasted him with "Salud!"[23]

Few serious people can join in this salute.

Hugh Hefner

In 1953 Hugh Hefner began publishing *Playboy* magazine in Chicago, and he soon became a leader in the promiscuity movement, which shook and transformed the nation beginning in the 1960s. In a June 2010 interview for the *New York Times Magazine*, he brushed aside the suggestion that he was essentially a "noble champion of First Amendment rights," a view pushed in a current documentary about his life: "I think the major thing I managed to accomplish was playing some part in changing our social and sexual values, and I take a lot of pride in that. When I was in college, middle-class kids couldn't live together before they got married."[24]

That same summer an article on Hefner appeared in *Vanity Fair*. It respectfully rehearsed his efforts on behalf of racial equality, abortion, and homosexuality, but the writer then pressed him about his treating women as "objects": "Some believe you have a prurient interest in them." To which he responded, "I certainly hope so!" adding: "I'm still around and kicking at 84. I've lived out dreams and fantasies and played some part in changing the world. It's pretty sweet."[25]

Of course he couches all this in hedonistic terms, saying he wants both men and women maximally to enjoy the pleasures of sex. But his breezy admission of prurience is telling. Here is a man, who, unlike the sensual love poet of Song of Solomon, celebrates lasciviousness for its own sake and to whatever lengths it might take consenting parties.

PERSONAL PLEASURE

Personal comfort, enjoyment, and survival are normal human goods. Virtually everyone prefers a back rub to a toothache, a lullaby to fingernails on the blackboard, an A to an F, a safe landing to a fiery crash. We stretch before we run to avoid the agony of muscle pulls while gaining the bodily peace of fitness. We shy away from foods that "angry up the blood," to quote the pitcher Satchel Paige, and seek out foods that give us energy without heartburn. All this makes sense.

The problem comes when we make this the highest good, when personal pleasure trumps everything else. This is hedonism, the ethic of the self-absorbed.

Of course the smarter hedonist calculates his pains and pleasures, making sure not to overdo either. He distances himself from the one who wastes his life crafting an extreme body in the weight room, for little return, but also from the "couch potato" who turns himself into Jabba the Hut through devotion to fatty foods and indolence.

The father of hedonism, Epicurus (341–270 BC), understood this perfectly well. Though he is often characterized as a teacher of "eat, drink, and be merry, for tomorrow we die," he would have none of that. He urged a measured, modest, quiet life on his disciples: "No pleasure is a bad thing in itself. But the things which produce certain pleasures bring troubles many times greater than the pleasures."[26]

So no, hedonists are not committed to a Caligula-like lifestyle, to one Bacchanalia after another. Rather, they more often appear as the young professional who works his *New York Times* crossword puzzle in Starbucks after a brisk Sunday morning jog. They factor a wide range of pleasures and productive pains into their lives so they can achieve an equanimous lifestyle—with perspiration in an athletic club spinning class, a familiarity with wines, late-night study to meet a deadline, an occasional massage, skill at acquiring rental-car upgrades, a nice balance of bargain-shopping and expensive indulgence, and volunteer service on a socially connected charity. A sweet life. But an utterly selfish one.

The Twenty-Something in Therapy

In his book *New Rules*, social scientist Daniel Yankelovich passes along the following anecdote from a psychologist friend. It concerns "a woman in her mid-twenties" who "complained that she had become nervous and fretful because life had grown so hectic—too many big weekends, too many discos, too many late hours, too much talk, too much wine, too much pot, too much love-making." "Why don't you stop?" asked the therapist mildly. His patient stared blankly for a moment, and then her face lit up, dazzled by illumination. "You mean I really don't have to do what I want to do?" she burst out with amazement.

Yankelovich observed,

> Ordinarily we think of norms in opposition to desires—dictating what we should do (wake up early, work hard, buckle down, use moderation), as distinct from what we would like to do. It had never occurred to her, my [psychologist] friend admitted, that norms could support desires and that people could come to feel it was their moral duty to yield to their impulses.[27]

LeBron James

Raw egotism does not pass the smell test. *Chicago Sun-Times* columnist Rick Telander writes about LeBron James's decision to sign as a free-agent with the Miami Heat, leaving his home-state Cleveland Cavaliers. After much drama the star concluded, "I needed to do what is best for LeBron James," explaining, "Winning is a huge thing for me."[28] Telander's column, entitled "That Was Nauseating," begins with the words,

> I need a bath. I need a shower. I need a dip in the vermin tank. LeBron James has made me feel dirty, foul, infested with tiny crawling things that want to creep into my ears and eat my brain. Players change teams all the time, I know that. Who doesn't? Hello! But no player has ever done it with the pomp, phoniness, pseudo-humility, and rehearsed innocence of LeBron and his ESPN bed-mates.[29]

He then adds, "Doing what is best for oneself justifies anything, including fake TV."[30] But of course it does not—which is his point.

Joaquin Phoenix

In his review of *I'm Still Here*, a documentary on the disintegration of Joaquin Phoenix, *Chicago Sun-Times* film critic Roger Ebert writes:

> It documents a train wreck. A luxury train. One carrying Phoenix, his several personal assistants, his agent, his publicist and apparently not one single friend who isn't on salary. A train that flies off the tracks and tumbles into the abyss.
>
> In this film Phoenix comes across as a narcissist interested only in himself. He is bored with acting. He was only a puppet. He can no longer stand where he's told, wear what he's given, say what is written. It's not him. He has lost contact with his inner self. He allows that true self to emerge here as a fearsomely bearded, deliberately shabby chain-smoking egotist who screams at his patient assistants, blames himself on everyone else and has deluded himself into thinking that there's a future in his dreadful hip-hop lyrics.
>
> He thinks fame and fortune are due him. He earned them in his acting career, yes, but he will no longer act. He expects rap mogul Sean Combs to want to produce his CD, although Combs has worked hard to earn the respect that Phoenix manifestly doesn't deserve. He's a little surprised that Combs remains sensible during their negotiations, expecting to be paid for his services, and oh, you know, studios, musicians, sound engineers, those kinds of things. Phoenix stands in the middle of an airport, puzzled that no limousine awaits. He flies to Obama's inauguration, not invited, and doesn't make it outside his hotel room. He is mystified that he may no longer be able to afford his Los Angeles home.[31]

Pharmaceutical Adepts—Leary, Hayden, and Ginsberg

Harvard University professor Timothy Leary declared, "The cause of social conflict is usually neurological. The cure is biochemical."[32] And many people in the sixties and seventies took "the cure." Surprisingly many continue to romanticize those days, even knowing the tragedy often stemming from those highs. Sixties radical Tom Hayden admitted that it

> was difficult to work on a daily basis with people who were tripping [out on LSD] at all hours, whether in courtrooms or in the streets. Marijuana was another matter, although I came to believe that it made no sense to be stoned when under police surveillance. Long after the sixties, I experienced ayahuasca in the Amazon jungle, which reinforced an existing bond with nature and with my son.[33]

Beatnik poet Allen Ginsberg was also a drug enthusiast:

> He became more convinced than ever that the secrets to subconscious feelings and desires could be discovered through the use of different types of drugs. Each drug offered varying sensations and produced different results; each opened a different door. Before he had tried such drugs as marijuana, Benzedrine, morphine, peyote, mescaline, laughing gas, and LSD, Allen's subconscious had been revealed essentially through dreams over which he had no control; now, with the use of certain chemical substances, he could enter otherwise-hidden regions of the mind and will.[34]

Juliette Binoche

> French actress Juliette Binoche has had many boyfriends, but has never committed to one, although she has had four marriage proposals. She has even turned down overtures from French President Francois Mitterand and a White House invitation from American President Bill Clinton. "I need relationships, but sometimes when I am in one I feel claustrophobic. It is about feeling that I still have my freedom. I like to keep moving." She argues, "Sometimes to take things further is to invite disappointment. Imagination and anticipation can be the greatest aphrodisiacs."[35]

Rockers—Lee, Ryder, and Crosby

Rolling Stone magazine is an excellent source of moral insight, if, that is, one is an egoistic hedonist. When asked about favorites cities, Tommy Lee, drummer for Motley Crue, offered these words of commendation:

> "The first time I went to Amsterdam, I was, like, 'Whoa, you mean *everything* here is legal? *Nothing* matters?' People were walking down the street opening their jackets with syringes and [expletive] heroin. And we were like little kids in a candy store, going, 'Aww yeah! Look at all this!' Like a pet shop, instead of puppies in the windows, it was women. . . . It's like we were in adult Disneyland. The word no was just not part of our vocabulary." Recalling visits to Amsterdam with Ozzy Osbourne, Van Halen and AC/DC, he said, "It was [expletive] scary, man. I don't know how our security guys and tour managers ever [expletive] dealt with us and how nobody died or nobody got left behind."[36]

Apparently it occurred to him later that "doing Amsterdam" was the sort of thing that tended to make someone uncooperative, irresponsible, or dead.

Shaun Ryder of Happy Mondays and Black Grape prefers Jajouka, Morocco:

It's up in the mountains and where Brian Jones went in the Sixties. There are no telephones. The way of life ain't changed in hundreds of years. That's where all the musicians are and all the weed. It's all they do. Sift the kif [a mixture of tobacco and ganja frequently prepared and used in Morocco] and [expletive] play tunes.[37]

One might reason that in Jajouka "the way of life ain't changed in hundreds of years," including the establishment of no universities, charitable NGOs, electronics labs, and so forth, because of "all the weed."

David Crosby of Crosby, Stills, and Nash, was particularly impressed with Tahiti:

One of the few things on earth as good as you thought it was going to be. Their music is *crazy*. Sexy, wonderful people. All they want to do is get smashed and [have sex]—that's their whole program. *Ooohhh, let's get drunk! Make schooner, baby!* [Have sex with] the white boys, get the bloodlines, mixed up! Paradise.[38]

These fellows definitely disagree with Epicurus and the refined hedonists over what does and does not work, but at least they join them in their devotion to pleasure above all.

Richard Loeb

Richard Loeb, who, in 1924, joined fellow university student Nathan Leopold in murdering Chicago schoolboy Bobby Franks, engaged in a wide variety of offenses in the months before the killing. And pleasure was Loeb's overriding passion. Though he was rich, he devised a plan to cheat at cards—"not for the sake of the money . . . but more for the thrill of the experience."[39]

Richard loved to play a dangerous game—the more dangerous the better—and he always sought to raise the stakes. It was difficult to explain, even to himself, the pleasure that his vandalism provided; he knew only that he experienced a thrill—a more rapid heartbeat, a pulse of exhilaration and well-being—whenever he planned such adventures.[40]

Buddhism

Buddhism offers one form of hedonism, based not on the careful cultivation of pleasure but in the elimination of pain by extinguishing desire. On this model a person does not pine for health, love, or wealth if he ceases to care about them. He becomes "laid back" in the most committed way. Never mind that it undermines initiative and charity. Serenity is the goal.

G. K. Chesterton had had his fill of this nonsense when he attacked the British fascination with Eastern religion in the early part of the twentieth century. He pointed to the sacred architecture of the two cultures:

No two ideals could be more opposite than a Christian saint in a Gothic cathedral and a Buddhist saint in a Chinese temple. The opposition exists at every point; but perhaps the shortest statement of it is that the Buddhist saint always has his eyes shut, while the Christian saint always has them very wide open. The Buddhist saint has a sleek and harmonious body, but his eyes are heavy and sealed with sleep. The mediaeval saint's body is wasted to its crazy bones, but his eyes are frightfully alive. . . . The Buddhist is looking with a peculiar intentness inwards. The Christian is staring with a frantic intentness outwards.[41]

POWER

In *The Republic* Plato used Socratic dialogue to discredit the claim that "might makes right." Yet worship of power persists in a variety of fascistic forms and finds a strong voice in Friedrich Nietzsche. Of course a power-based ethic is kin to an autonomy-based ethic, but it adds the perspective that it is the autonomy of the strong that counts, not the self-determination of every human being.

Friedrich Nietzsche

In *Beyond Good and Evil*, nineteenth-century German philosopher Friederich Nietzsche declared, "The great epochs of our life come when we gain the courage to rechristen our evil as what is best in us."[42] In other words, though society may criticize us, we are not answerable to conventional morality with its suffocating pieties and ridiculous rules. We must break these bonds and proclaim that what our neighbors call "bad" is really wonderful. Then we ascend the moral heights.[43]

In his work *On the Genealogy of Morals*, he explains why this is so. By his account, "the noble, powerful, high-stationed and high-minded" originally set the standards of what was "good, that is, of the first rank, in contradistinction to all the low, low-minded, common and plebeian."[44] He identifies goodness with "the man of strife, of dissention . . . the man of war."[45]

Not surprisingly the lower, weaker types cannot endure this, so they turn things upside down. They label arrogance and the "lust to rule" as dangerous and presume to look down on "knightly-aristocratic value judgments, which presuppose 'a powerful physicality, a flourishing, abundant, even overflowing healthy, together with that which serves to preserve it: war, adventure, hunting, dancing, war games, and in general all that involves vigorous, free, joyful activity.'"[46]

He lays prime blame for this ethical corruption on priests, who are "the most impotent" of people. In their impotence they turn vengeful. And no group is more guilty of this than the priest-ridden Jews.

It was the Jews who, with awe-inspiring consistence, dared to invert the aristocratic value-equation (good=noble=powerful=beautiful=happy=beloved of God) and to hang on to this inversion with their teeth, the teeth of the most abysmal hatred (the hatred of impotence), saying "the wretched alone are the good; the poor, impotent, lowly alone are the good; the suffering, deprived, sick, ugly alone are pious, alone are blessed by God, blessedness is for them alone—and you, the powerful and noble, are on the contrary the evil, the cruel, the lustful, the insatiable, the godless to all eternity; and you shall be in all eternity the unblessed, accursed, and damned!"[47]

And who can doubt the identity of the keeper of this tradition, this "revolt of the slaves": "Jesus of Nazareth, the incarnate gospel of love, this 'Redeemer' who brought blessedness and victory to the poor, the sick, and the sinners."[48]

Nathan Leopold

Hitler is the best-known admirer of Nietzsche, but the aforementioned Nathan Leopold also found inspiration there. Leopold

had a tedious obsession with the philosophy of Friedrich Nietzsche; he would talk endlessly about the mythical superman who, because he was a superman, stood outside the law, beyond any moral code that might constrain the actions of ordinary men. Even murder, Nathan claimed, was an acceptable act for the superman to commit if the deed gave him pleasure. Morality did not apply in such a case, Nathan asserted. The only consideration that mattered was whether it afforded the superman pleasure—everything else faded into insignificance.[49]

Notes

1 One school of thought, emotivism, rejects the whole enterprise. It denies the cognitive content, or meaningfulness, of all ethical claims. This was the view of British logical positivist Alfred Jules Ayer, who claimed that saying, "Adultery is wrong," is nothing more than saying, "Adultery. Boo!" And to raise questions of truth and falsity about a moral statement is like asking the baseball fan who jumps to his feet and yells "Yay!" at the sight of an exquisite double-play, "Is that true?"
   It is neither true nor false; it is just a form of venting. And so it is with all ethical and aesthetic expression—just a way of letting off steam, cheering, snarling, or cooing. And since there is nothing more substantive than this at stake, there is no real moral standard—just preferences expressed with verbal grunts, sighs, snickers, and hoorahs. This leaves right and wrong, such as it is, up to the individual and his enthusiasms, which of course can be ridiculous or vile.
2 Roger Kimball, "*Art v. Aestheticism*: The Case of Walter Pater," *Experiments against Reality: The Fate of Culture in the Postmodern Age* (Chicago: Ivan Dee, 2000), 43.
3 Maureen Mullarkey, "Sitting Pretty: What's So Good About Lucian Freud?" *The Weekly Standard* (October 4, 2010): 31.
4 Kimball, "*Art v. Aestheticism*," 38.
5 Ibid.
6 Ibid., 33.
7 Ibid., 35.

8 Frederic Spotts, *Hitler and the Power of Aesthetics* (New York: Overlook, 2002), 11.

9 Ibid., 43.

10 Jean-Paul Sartre, *Essays in Existentialism*, ed. Wade Baskin (New York: Citadel, 1993).

11 Carole Seymour-Jones, *A Dangerous Liaison: A Revelatory New Biography of Simone de Beauvoir and Jean-Paul Sartre* (New York: Overlook, 2008), 291. Concerning Dostoevsky, the Paris photographer of "bordellos and opium dens, Brassai, observed, 'Thieves, murderers, convicts—his own prison companions. These criminals, cast out by society, became his mentors, their doctrine of life . . . became his ideal'" (ibid., 291).

12 Michael Krantz, Steven Frank, and Margot Hornblower, "How Organized Anarchists Led Seattle into Chaos," *Time*, December 13, 1999; http://www.time.com/time/magazine/article/0,9171,992843,00.html (accessed December 3, 2010).

13 Iaian McKay, *An Anarchist FAQ: Version 12.0* (Edinburgh: AK, 2007), 27–28.

14 Robert N. Bellah et al., *Habits of the Heart: Individualism and Commitment in American Life* (New York: Harper & Row, 1985), 235.

15 Ibid., 221.

16 438 (U.S.) 726 (1978); http://caselaw.lp.findlaw.com/scripts/getcase.pl?court=us&vol=438&invol=726 (accessed June 11, 2010).

17 George Carlin, *Napalm & Silly Putty* (New York: Hyperion, 2001), 29.

18 Ibid., 62–66.

19 Ibid., 126–27.

20 Abbie Hoffman, *The Best of Abbie Hoffman*, ed. Danile Simon (New York: Four Walls Eight Windows, 1989), 189.

21 Ibid., 19–29.

22 Wayne King, "Mourning, and Celebrating, a Radical," *The New York Times*, April 19, 1989; http://www.nytimes.com/1989/04/20/us/mourning-and-celebrating-a-radical.html?pagewanted=1 (accessed June 11, 2010).

23 Norman Mailer, "Foreword," in Simon, *The Best of Abbie Hoffman*, viii–ix.

24 Hugh Hefner, interview by D. Solomon, "Sex and the Single Man," *The New York Times Magazine* (June 11, 2010): 13.

25 John Heilpern, "To the Mansion Born: Interview with Hugh Hefner," *Vanity Fair* (August 2010): 48.

26 Epicurus, *The Principal Doctrines*, VIII. Reprinted in *Classics of Western Philosophy*, 7th ed., ed. Steven M. Cahn (Indianapolis: Hackett, 2006), 318.

27 Daniel Yankelovich, *New Rules: Searching for Self-Fulfillment in a World Turned Upside Down* (New York: Random House, 1981), 85–86.

28 Tom Withers, "LeBron Leaves Home," AP report, published in *Lexington Herald-Leader* (July 9, 2010): B1.

29 Rick Telander, "That Was Nauseating," *Chicago Sun-Times* (July 9, 2010): 68.

30 Ibid.

31 Roger Ebert, "I'm Not All There," *Chicago Sun-Times* (September 10, 2010): movies section, 5.

32 Tom Hayden, *The Long Sixties: From 1960 to Barack Obama* (Boulder: Paradigm, 2009), 161.

33 Ibid.

34 Michael Schumacher, *Dharma Lion: A Biography of Allen Ginsberg* (New York: St. Martin's, 1992), 316.

35 "Why Binoche Always Says *Non*," *The Week* (September 24, 2010): 10.

36 Tommy Lee, cited in *Rolling Stone Raves*, comp. Anthony Bozza, ed. Shawn Dahl (New York: Rolling Stone, 1999), 144–45.

37 Shaun Ryder, cited in Dahl, *Rolling Stone Raves*, 138.

38 David Crosby, cited in Dahl, *Rolling Stone Raves*, 136.

39 Simon Baatz, *For the Thrill of It: Leopold, Loeb, and the Murder That Shocked Jazz Age Chicago* (New York: Harper Perennial, 2008), 43.

40 Ibid., 44.

41 Gilbert K. Chesterton, *Orthodoxy* (New York: Image, 1990), 130–31.

42 Friederich Nietzsche, "Epigrams and Interludes" in *Beyond Good and Evil: Basic Writings of Nietzsche*, tran. and ed. Walter Kaufmann (New York: Modern Library, 1992), 276.

43 Nietzsche's "liberating" words encourage all sorts of disparaged people, including, for instance, autogynephiles (men who are sexually aroused by the thought or image of themselves as a woman). In "Resurrected Writings About Autogynephilia," "gender therapist" Anne A. Lawrence writes, "We have grown up hearing that our sexual desires are evil and unworthy, and many of us have come to believe it. But I believe, with Nietzsche, that to live fulfilling and authentic lives as transsexual women, we must be willing to rechristen our sexual desire as that which is best and most profoundly human within us"; http://www.annelawrence.com/twr/resurrected.html (accessed October 1, 2010).

44 Friederich Nietzsche, *On the Genealogy of Morals* in Kaufmann, *Basic Writings of Nietzsche*, 461–62.

45 Ibid., 467.

46 Ibid., 468–69.

47 Ibid., 470.

48 Ibid., 471.

49 Baatz, *For the Thrill of It*, 52.

Faulty Secular Systems with External Reference: Altruism to Natural Order

M ANY ETHICAL SYSTEMS ARE "outward looking," in that they find ultimate warrant, value, and obligation in something that transcends personal desires. Though they connect with the individual's conscience, reason, well-being, and such, they appeal to standards or states of affairs to which the particular person is accountable. Here are some with sample difficulties.

ALTRUISM

Those who claim the general welfare is the highest good are typically known as utilitarians. They look to consequences, to results, particularly in terms of happiness. In its earlier manifestations under Jeremy Bentham, "pleasure" rather than happiness was the standard. According to Bentham's "hedonistic calculus," one had merely to weigh the offsetting pains and pleasures to calculate the right course to take. Unlike the "egoistic hedonism" of Epicurus, Bentham presented an "altruistic hedonism," concerned more with the general populace than with one's self.

This is a common form of human reasoning. For instance, if a 60-mph speed limit meant fewer accidents and better gas mileage than an 80-mph speed limit, with little appreciable loss in commerce and driving pleasure, then the lower limit would seem appropriate.

His countryman, John Stuart Mill, made important additions to this approach. Whereas Bentham treated pains and pleasures as basic units of calculation, Mill said that some pleasures were superior to others. Hence his famous maxim, "It is better to be a human being dissatisfied than a pig satisfied; better to be Socrates dissatisfied than a fool satisfied."[1]

Socrates often found himself in a situation of frustrating puzzlement over some essential question, such as the nature of love, courage, or friendship. Meanwhile an Athenian pig might be having the time of its life, wallowing in the mud, gorging itself on corn. But the refined intellectual quest of a Socrates, with its moments of stress and strain, are to be valued over the purely sensate projects of a pig. There is a nobility and long-term fruitfulness in the former which is lacking in the latter.

So far, so good, but problems soon surface. What if a person calculates that torturing the daughter of a terrorist could force him to turn in his cohorts? The child and the parent would have some pain, his mental and hers physical, but it could save society a lot of wear and tear and ensure many happy family moments for the citizens who might otherwise have been maimed or killed by indiscriminate attacks. But this can't be acceptable.

Then there is the difficulty of calculating outcomes, whatever the decision. Who can predict how things might turn out, how the ball might bounce? And who could shoulder such an altruistic burden? It would mean a sort of "hero's paralysis." Suppose one granted that he should maximize happiness in his actions. How might he even decide to go to a movie to watch harmless entertainment when he could be out having friendly conversations with the elderly in nursing homes? How could he ever take a pleasant walk along the shore when he could be back at home writing thank-you notes to his grade-school teachers? Or should he rather be volunteering as an unpaid guinea pig for drug testing? Where would it stop? And where would there be room for "supererogation," going above and beyond the call of duty? If one's duty is to maximize happiness, there is no above and beyond.

Peter Singer

Despite the classic utilitarian's best efforts, fixation on *human* happiness seems arbitrary. Why not extend altruism to all sentient beings? In an article called "Heavy Petting," Princeton's utilitarian philosopher Peter Singer did his best to remove the taboo against bestiality. In this heavily edited selection, skirting the more lurid passages, Singer is impatient with talk of natural law and the image of God, and he excuses behavior where the parties are enjoying themselves.

> One by one, the taboos have fallen. . . . But not every taboo has crumbled. Heard anyone chatting at parties lately about how good it is having sex with their dog? Probably not. Sex with animals is still definitely taboo. . . . But the vehemence with which this prohibition continues to be held, its persistence while other non-reproductive sexual acts have become

acceptable, suggests that there is another powerful force at work: our desire to differenti-
ate ourselves, erotically and in every other way, from animals. . . . Almost a century ago,
when Freud had just published his groundbreaking *Three Essays on Sexuality*, the Viennese
writer Otto Soyka published a fiery little volume called *Beyond the Boundary of Morals*.
Never widely known, and now entirely forgotten, it was a polemic directed against the
prohibition of "unnatural" sex like bestiality, homosexuality, fetishism, and other non-
reproductive acts. Soyka saw these prohibitions as futile and misguided attempts to limit
the inexhaustible variety of human sexual desire. Only bestiality, he argued, should be
illegal, and even then, only in so far as it shows cruelty towards an animal. . . . But sex
with animals does not always involve cruelty. . . . [The fact that we are animals ourselves]
does not make sex across the species barrier normal, or natural, whatever those much-
misused words may mean, but it does imply that it ceases to be an offence to our status
and dignity as human beings.[2]

Actually, bestiality continues to be an offense to our status and dignity as
human beings, regardless of what Peter Singer might think.

Daniel Maguire

Roman Catholic philosopher Daniel Maguire is a closet utilitarian, or perhaps a utilitarian unawares. In his ethic he places personhood and humanity at
the top, but when he comes to the matter of abortion, he shows his true colors.
He writes:

The foundational moral experience is the experience of the value of persons and their
earthly home in this universe. This profound value-experience is the distinctly human
and humanizing experience and the gateway to personhood. It is this experience and the
gateway to personhood. It is this experience that marks us as human. It is the primordial
"Wow!" from which all moral theory and all healthy law, politics, and religion derive.
This experience is the seed of civilization, the root of culture, and the badge of unique
human consciousness. Without immersion in this experience, moral language would be
senseless noise. If human activities, institutions, education, and religions do not enhance
this experience, they are negligible and indeed objectionable, for they are failing at the
essential and distinctly human talent of moral evaluation.[3]

Of course this is vague, and one may wonder if this personhood adoration
extends to Satan. Apparently it does not extend to the unborn, for Maguire calls
abortion "a sacred choice" and says, "Sometimes ending an incipient life is the
best that life offers."[4] In other words the fetus is disposable because it cannot
yet enjoy that "Wow!" experience, and its death may well mean more happy
"Wows!" for his survivors. Besides, he may be one of those fetuses whose pros-
pects for happiness seem particularly dim. So the utilitarian strikes.

It seems that Maguire's "Wow"-based ethic is integrity challenged, in that
he continues to take Roman Catholic money as a tenured theology professor at
Marquette University.[5]

Joseph Fletcher

Episcopal theologian Joseph Fletcher became famous for his "situation ethics" in the 1960s. He said it rose above the normal, "prescriptive" rule-following and applied love to particular cases. Hence, "if the emotional and spiritual welfare of both parents and children in a particular family can be served best by a divorce, wrong and cheapjack as divorce commonly is, then love requires it." This is tantamount to saying that love requires that the happiness of the parties involved must be insured, the old utilitarian formula.

Picking up on this "love ethic," Anglican Bishop John A. T. Robinson was happy to join in: "Nothing can of itself always be labeled as 'wrong.' One cannot, for instance, start from the position 'sex relations before marriage' or 'divorce' are wrong or sinful in themselves. They may be in 99 cases or even 100 cases out of 100, they are not intrinsically so, for the only intrinsic evil is lack of love."[6]

Of course the problem comes when people begin to calculate vainly the love-saturated consequences of behavior contrary to the counsel of the loving God.

CULTURE

A popular practice today is to attack one who questions the sanity or decency of another's cultural values or practices: "Who are you to judge!" The answer is simple: Anyone with discriminatory powers is fit to judge, for these moral differences are often stunning. A simple walk through history reveals any number of cultural practices that men of conscience now count abominable.

Gladiatorial Games and Foot Binding

The Roman Empire tortured convicts to death on a wooden cross, and Roman citizens gathered in arenas to watch Christians torn to shreds by wild animals and slaves forced into lethal gladiatorial "games." Pompeii served as a center for licentious behavior before it was destroyed by the volcanic Mount Vesuvius. Spartans exposed their weaker offspring to the elements, an act of infanticide. Chinese mutilated their women by binding their feet from infancy. Arabs traded in slaves captured in sub-Saharan Africa. Viking raiders terrorized and looted the towns of Western Europe. The list goes on and on.

Delhi Driving

The Indian culture of driving is chaotic and dangerous. The founder of the nation's Institute of Road Traffic Education says there are "nearly 110 million traffic violations *per day* in Delhi, and with 100,000 road deaths a year, India accounts for 10% of the world's traffic fatalities." When asked how he coped, one taxi driver responded quickly, "Good brakes, good horn, good luck."[7]

To the consistent cultural relativist, this is charming, for "who are we to question how they drive." For most, it is both a technical and behavioral problem that needs attention.

DECORUM

As editor of *SBC Life*, I wrote a monthly column, often dealing with prickly matters germane to the "conservative resurgence" in the denomination. After one particularly contentious piece appeared, a lady wrote to scold me for using sarcasm. She declared that it was never appropriate for a Christian to employ this form of speech. Never mind that Elijah used it to taunt the prophets of Baal in 1 Kgs 18:27, and Paul used it to chastise proud believers in 1 Cor 4:8. She would probably say they were out of line too. On her account one should *never* speak sarcastically. After all, the word is grounded in the Greek for "rending the flesh," and that just would not be "Christlike."

George Washington's Gentleman

George Washington was a paragon of decorum. His 110 "rules of civility" were often humorously detailed (e.g., 9. Don't warm your feet by the fire if meat is cooking thereon) and occasionally off-putting (29. Stand aside when meeting those of higher station in a tight walkway), yet often admirable (48. Don't criticize others on points where you too deserve blame). But some of them seem antibiblical in their obsession with decorum and sensitivities: How, for instance, could Paul obey 68 and still write his epistle to the Galatians: "Give not advice without being asked"? And would Washington have dismissed the apostle's report on Demas in 2 Tim 4:10, that because he loved the world so much, he had deserted Paul in his hour of need? (89. "Speak not evil of the absent for it is unjust").[8]

Lawrence Kohlberg's Stage-3ers

Harvard University professor Lawrence Kohlberg, a student of cognitive psychologist Jean Piaget, argued that there are six stages in moral development and that one progresses through them by a sort of Socratic dialogue based on case studies. Interestingly he ranks niceness or decorum rather low on the scale, at only third place. By his account the child begins at the "Preconventional Level," where he is motivated first by punishment avoidance and next by a spirit of "You scratch my back and I'll scratch yours." At the "Conventional Level," he shifts to a "Good Boy—Nice Girl" mind-set (stage 3), where he wants, above all, to be liked by others. Then at stage 4, he begins to focus on "authority, fixed rules, and the maintenance of the social order." From there he rises to the "Postconventional, Autonomous, or Principled Level," where he starts at the "Social Contract" stage, with its reliance on agreements, which may be adjusted by the consent of the governed. Finally he reaches the "Universal Ethical Principle Orientation" (stage 6), which insists on the transcendent values of justice, human rights, and the dignity of human beings.[9] Here Kohlberg placed Martin Luther King, who was willing to suffer punishment, pass up comforts, be counted as "not nice," disturb the social order, and defy even the duly enacted laws of segregation.

Of course one does not need to buy into Kohlberg's system to see a certain affinity with the prophets, who were willing to "speak truth to power," as when Nathan confronted David about his adultery. If one were stuck at the level of "niceness," then morality would collapse into mere decorum. Emily Post and negativity-shunning preachers would replace Isaiah and Jeremiah as the arbiters of our highest values.

THE ECOSYSTEM

Environmentalism is all the rage; this is the day when Al Gore's apocalyptic vision wins both an Oscar and a Nobel Prize. This is also the day when philosopher Baruch Spinoza can gather new disciples because he espoused pantheism, the view that everything is equally divine, from paramecia to pebbles to people. And an overwhelming ethic follows right along.

Arne Naess

Arne Naess, chairman of the philosophy department at the University of Oslo, championed what he called "deep ecology," as opposed to shallow or reform-minded ecology. He advanced several principles that put nonhuman life on a par with human life. He wrote, "The well-being and flourishing of human and nonhuman Life on Earth have value in themselves. . . . These values are independent of the usefulness of the non-human world for human purposes." So by extension, "Humans have no right to reduce this richness and diversity except to satisfy vital needs," and "The flourishing of non-human life *requires* a smaller human population."[10]

As for an optimum number he says, "I should think we must have no more than 100 million people if we are to have the variety of cultures we had one hundred years ago. Because we need the conservation of human cultures, just as we need the conservation of animal species." But not just any culture will do. "To maximize self-realization . . . we need maximum diversity and maximum symbiosis. . . . Diversity, then, is a fundamental norm and a common delight. As deep ecologists, we take a natural delight in diversity, as long as it does not include crude, intrusive forms, like Nazi culture, that are destructive to others."[11]

For those tenderly disposed toward the environment, it is easy to miss the import of these statements. He is not saying population control is needed to make human life more livable. He is saying that human populations are making it difficult for daisies and ferrets, who have just as much right to be here as they do. To think otherwise is to be guilty of the great sin of modern environmentalism, "anthropocentrism," as opposed to the preferred "ecocentrism."

Thus environmentalism assumes the status of religion: "Environmentalists experience a sense of religious reverence and awe in the presence of nature 'untouched by human hand,' which is a modern equivalent of devout Christians in previous centuries encountering the 'Book of Nature' as written by God at the creation."[12]

Environmental historian William Cronon describes the sweeping conceit of this new faith, noting that "certain landscapes . . . are celebrated as sacred" and "much environmental writing is openly prophetic" with warnings of impending judgment. Furthermore "environmentalism is unusual among political movements in offering practical moral guidance about virtually every aspect of daily life." It "grapples with ultimate questions at every scale of human existence, from the cosmic to the quotidian, from the apocalyptic to the mundane." This in short is what religion does.[13]

Love of nature sounds good, but it turns sour when taken as the end. G. K. Chesterton put it this way:

> A man loves Nature in the morning for her innocence and amiability, and at nightfall, if he is loving her still, it is for her darkness and her cruelty. He washes at dawn in clean water as did the Wise Men of the Stoics, yet, somehow at the dark end of the day, he is bathing in hot bull's blood, as did Julian the Apostate.[14]

The Old Religion

One outworking of environmentalism is a rebirth of paganism, whereby all sorts of unseemly behavior is now excused and even praised:

> Women's spirituality, ecospirituality, and the revival of Eastern mysticisms rapidly followed [black liberation theology]. In the face of homophobia, gay, lesbian, and transgender people fought for their spiritual identity. Spanning all these separate outbreaks was a resurgence of the Old Religion, diffusing all of creation with magic and holiness, even if often described and disparaged as paganism. There was a profound misunderstanding among critics about the pronouncement "God is dead." The 1960s were an era in rebellion against the top-down authority of institutional religion, but they were not an atheistic decade. Instead, the old gods came alive.[15]

EQUALITY

Today the popular cry for "social justice" usually means the leveling of wealth, beginning with the erasure of "vast income disparity." (It is also meant to distance the speaker from the relatively "heartless" conservatives who have focused narrowly and negatively on such things as abortion and homosexuality.)

John Rawls

Many people find great comfort in the book *A Theory of Justice* by Harvard philosopher John Rawls, which advances a concept of "fairness" that tends "to spread the wealth around." According to his scheme, people should assume an imaginary "original position" that places them behind a "veil of ignorance." They have no idea what race, religion, values, IQ, education, home life, or geographical setting they might have eventually. So by Rawls's account, people will design a social and economic system that will ensure that things work out well whatever the situation might be. This sounds nice at first hearing; certainly no one wants the disadvantaged to be ruined. But cracks soon form in his system. What if a person lacks education because he dropped out of school to hitchhike around the country? What if one of a person's core values is the nightly pursuit of anonymous sex? What if his religion requires that his wife not drive a car? In short Rawls makes too little room for just inequalities.

Antony Flew

One of the first to notice this was the then-atheist Antony Flew, who before his death acknowledged the reasonableness of belief in God.[16] In his 1981 book *The Politics of Procrustes: Contradictions of Enforced Equality*, he quoted Rawls as saying that "the first principle of justice . . . requiring equal distribution" was "so obvious that we would expect it to occur to anyone immediately."[17] Rawls does add a Difference Principle: "Inequalities are permissible when they maximise, or at least all contribute to, the long-term expectations of the least fortunate group in society."[18] But this leaves open the question of whether "the least fortunate" have enough. Actually on Rawls's model, they never have enough, for as others gain wealth, they are obliged to bring everyone along with them whether they are actually hurting or deserving. This then is equality for the sake of equality, a formula that on Flew's account automatically "doled out . . . unearned benefits to inert recipients."[19] This arrangement might satisfy risk-averse people ("nescient zombies") but not those with a genuine sense of justice.[20]

Robert Nozick

Rawls's Harvard University colleague, Robert Nozick, skewered the income-equality principle with a basketball example, tied to seven-foot one-inch NBA hall-of-famer Wilt Chamberlain:

> Now suppose that Wilt Chamberlain is greatly in demand by basketball teams, being a great gate attraction. . . . He signs the following sort of contract with a team: In each home game, twenty-five cents from the price of each ticket of admission goes to him. . . . The season starts, and people cheerfully attend his team's games; they buy their tickets, each time dropping a separate twenty-five cents of their admission price into a special

box with Chamberlain's name on it. They are excited about seeing him play; it is worth the total admission price to them. Let us suppose that in one season one million persons attend his homes games, and Wilt Chamberlain winds up with $250,000, a much larger sum than the average income and larger even than anyone else has. Is he entitled to this income? . . . If so, why?[21]

Nozick lets his reader stipulate whatever wealth distribution he pleases as a beginning point. It may even mean that everyone starts with the same amount. But then things go awry for the "equalist."

Each of these persons chose to give twenty-five cents of their money to Chamberlain. They could have spent it on going to the movies, or on candy bars, or on copies of *Dissent* magazine, or of *Monthly Review*. But they all, at least one million of them, converged on giving it to Wilt Chamberlain in exchange for watching him play basketball. If D1 [the original state of affairs] was a just distribution, and people voluntarily moved from it to D2 [the current state of affairs], transferring parts of their shares they were given under D1 (what was it for if not to do something with?), isn't D2 also just? If the people were entitled to dispose of the resources to which they were entitled (under D1), didn't this include their being entitled to give it to, or exchange it with, Wilt Chamberlain? Can anyone else complain on grounds of justice?[22]

The answer is no.

HUMAN AUTHORITY

Explicating the eighteenth-century code of the Japanese samurai, Tsunetomo Yamamoto wrote:

I have found the essence of Bushido: to die! . . . In order to master this essence, you must die anew, every morning and every night. If you continually preserve the state of death in everyday life, you will understand the essence of Bushido, and you will gain freedom in Bushido. Then you will be able to fulfill your duty to the offices of the household of the Lord without a mistake and for the rest of your life.[23]

He continued: "In order to deserve the name of samurai, you must offer your life to the service of your Lord. You must become a ghost after the completion of a frenzied death. You must always keep the Lord's affairs in mind."[24] But there is a major conceptual hitch: You must exhibit absolute fealty to one who is as human as you;[25] indeed, he may be your inferior in understanding, but if you give him too much advice, he might come to hate you. Better that you "proceed to let your Lord learn little by little."[26]

How then can this fallible master's will be the touchstone of duty? Of course, any number of soldiers and policemen have died following orders, some of which were obviously flawed. But most did so with the conviction that their sacrifice served the cause of justice, protected their countrymen, honored God's directive in Romans 13, or something otherwise noble. Few saw the master's orders as virtual ends in themselves. Yet this sort of blind obedience was attractive to many Japanese, who drew on this ethos up until and through World War II.

INTUITION

Certainly the success of criticisms in this chapter turns on the reader's sense of good and evil. One cannot mount an effective reduction-to-absurdity argument in ethics if the audience has no sense of the morally absurd. But one must resist making the conscience or moral intuition sovereign.

G. E. Moore

Twentieth-century British philosopher G. E. Moore broke radically with previous ethical theory, arguing that things were right and wrong simply in themselves. To arrive at this conclusion, he posed the "open-question test." If one could meaningfully ask "So what?" about an act, even after hearing that God demanded it, or that it would maximize human happiness, or that it conformed to the natural order, then it was clear that morality did not boil down to something other than itself. To think otherwise was to be a misguided ethical "naturalist." Much better to be an ethical "nonnaturalist" who could recognize the wrongness of murder just as clearly as he could spot the redness of a fire engine.

But cultures have radically different intuitions concerning the same practice. The fall has seen to that. So among Eskimos, it was once considered appropriate to leave dying parents behind on the ice; for Westerners, this seems horrific.

And what of differences within a culture? Harriet Beecher Stowe, author of *Uncle Tom's Cabin*, suggested that intuitions and feelings of goodness varied according to gender. She said that opposing slavery was a matter of "feeling right," that is, "to consult feeling is to discover Christian truth written upon the heart." By her account "women are more likely to 'feel right' and are, therefore, less willing than men to tolerate the legalized horrors of slavery."[27] Thus intuition is a tricky standard if half the species suffers from blunted sensitivities.

There are other problems as well. For one thing Moore's approach seems coldly detached from the most important things, the divine and the human. For another, Moore seems to lay himself open to the question, "So you presume to intuit wrongness. So what?"

Ross

W. D. Ross built on this perspective. He noticed that even when intuitions did not differ, when everyone agreed that stealing and murder were wrong, there were still conflicts. What, for instance, should one do when faced with the need to "borrow" a car to chase down someone kidnapping his wife? Surely there are circumstances when one obligation gives way to another. So Ross developed a hierarchical system whereby, for instance, the value of human life was higher than the sanctity of property.

But again this runs into difficulty. For it would seem on this model that one could rob banks to get money to send to starving people in Darfur. After all, people are more valuable than property. And since there will always be starving people somewhere, can any bank be safe, even from earnest Christians?

One's intuitions show that Ross's intuited hierarchy of obligations could promote villainy.

THE NATURAL ORDER

The natural law tradition in ethics is ancient and honorable, keying on the created order. When Paul met the Epicureans and Stoics on Mars Hill in Acts 17, he and they agreed that life is lived well only in accord with essential structures and patterns and that to act otherwise is perverse. Aristotle taught this, as did his Christian admirer, the Roman Catholic theologian, Thomas Aquinas, over a millennium later. Furthermore natural law is much appreciated among Protestants, though it has its notable detractors, such as Karl Barth.[28]

For all its virtues, natural law cannot stand alone as an ethical guide, for man is a notoriously poor reader of nature's guidebook.

Pace v. Alabama

How can one know with confidence that his or her reading of the natural order is correct? The 1967 United States Supreme Court case, *Virginia v. Loving* (388 U.S. 1), shows the problem. Until this ruling, it was illegal for a black to marry a white in Virginia, and in some other states. The 1967 case overturned the 1883 decision, *Pace v. Alabama* (106 U.S. 583), which upheld the illegality of miscegenation, literally, "mixing of the races."

In the state court precursor to the Supreme Court ruling in *Pace*, an Alabama judge wrote, concerning miscegenation, "Its result may be the amalgamation of the two races, producing a mongrel population and a degraded civilization, the prevention of which is dictated by a sound policy affecting the highest interests of society and government" (*Pace & Cox v. State*, 69 Ala 231, 233 {1882}). His firm conviction was that there was something unnatural about this practice and that it should be disallowed. The Loving court disagreed, as serious people can, over what is natural and unnatural.

Carl Bean

Though classic natural-law theory presents general rules for human flourishing, many claim that "unnatural behavior" is actually a reflection of God-given nature and that their lifestyle cannot be wrong if it gives them such fulfillment.

This is the testimony of Archbishop Carl Bean, whose book title tells it all: *I Was Born This Way: A Gay Preacher's Journey Through Gospel Music, Disco Stardom, and a Ministry in Christ.* He assures the reader, "I was born not only to love other men but also with an inherent longing to be female."[29] Thus he can say, "To the Creator, thank you for placing me in this body, this skin, this orientation, this life that you have guided every step of the way."[30]

To the homosexual who asks him, "Reverend, does God hate me because I'm gay?" he answers, "No, my son. You can only be who God created you to be."[31] So "every Sunday," he preaches:

> Look, I'm an old queen who knows something about promiscuity. I've been to the bathhouses, I've been to the parks, I've been to every cruise scene imaginable. I've done it all, and I've done it twice. And if I've survived, it's because God wants to tell you that promiscuity ain't gonna fill the hole in your soul. The bathhouse will not wash you clean. Crazy sex just makes you crazier. The fun don't last and the health risks get riskier. That party's over. But another party has begun. That party goes on forever. That party isn't about getting high on happy pills or some naked body; that party is about finding joy—real joy, sustaining joy, eternal joy. We're all invited to that party—every last one of us. That's the party we're having this morning, the party celebrating God, praising God, lifting God, giving God our burdens and, in turn, accepting God's grace.[32]

Who could fault this combination of natural and supernatural joy? Certainly not Bean's parishioners, the 25,000 members of United Fellowship of Christ Church, which he founded.[33] But natural law is not a matter of counting noses. Discerning it is much more challenging than that.

Humana Vitae

Pope Paul VI's encyclical letter, *Humanae Vitae*, was a bold statement of commitment to conservative Roman Catholic values.[34] Published in 1968, it repudiated the "Sexual Revolution" and held the line against such wrongs as promiscuity, homosexuality, and abortion. It also reiterated the Catholic opposition to birth control; it made no allowance for "sexual intercourse which is deliberately contraceptive and so intrinsically wrong," even among married people. The problem was that use of the pill and condoms fail to honor the natural order of things, "the unitive significance and the procreative significance which are both inherent to the marriage act." That is, even though married sex may be a great way for couples to come together (unitive), it nullifies the baby-making possibility (procreative). The same thing could be said for homosexual acts; whatever their unitive value, they are decidedly nonprocreative. And of course masturbation fails on both accounts.

But back to contraception: Who is to say that the procreative context is required for each act of married sex? After all, the Catholics themselves use calendar and body temperature cycles to determine times of low fertility, when the wife is less likely to conceive. Instead of counting these seasons "unnatural," they eagerly chart them for sexual opportunity without the fear of pregnancy. Should they not rather wait out these "opportune" days, which tempt them to sensuality, until they are once again in the zone of ready conception?

Of course Protestants, with their doctrine of *sola Scriptura*, are more inclined to ask what the Bible says about this. The answer is "nothing directly." Yes, Gen 1:28 commands, "Be fruitful, multiply," but Ps 100:1 says to "shout triumphantly to the LORD." These verses do not say that all sex must focus on multiplication and that all worship must be aggressively loud.

Furthermore can it be "natural" to have a dozen children when the husband and wife are having trouble clothing and feeding four? Maybe so, but the question at least makes sense. And those who want to condemn contraception by appealing to the case of Onan in Gen 38:9–10 have to put on hermeneutical blinders.

Perhaps the pope overreached by speaking for nature in making such a bold assertion on contraception in the absence of pointed Scripture on the matter. In contrast, he certainly had plenty to go on with regard to homosexuality.

Supererogation

Also what should be said about deeds "above and beyond the call of duty," like a soldier throwing himself on a grenade to save his buddies' lives? If "nature" is sovereign in ethics, might one object that it is unnatural to willingly absorb blast, fire, and shrapnel, but it is nonetheless praiseworthy.

Of course the natural-law theorist has answers for such challenges and questions, but the question remains: Can he answer them properly with only an appeal to his reading of the created order?

Notes

1 John Stuart Mill, "Utilitarianism" in *The Philosophy of John Stuart Mill: Ethical, Political, and Religious*, ed. M. Cohen (New York: Modern Library, 1961), 333.

2 Peter Singer, "Heavy Petting," *Nerve* (2001); http://www.utilitarian.net/singer/by/2001 (accessed January 3, 2011).

3 Anne Hendershott, "Another Catholic University Fails a Litmus Test," *The Wall Street Journal* (June 18, 2010): W12.

4 Daniel Maguire, *Preface to Sacred Choice: The Right to Contraception and Abortion in Ten World Religions.* Accessed August 27, 2011, at http://www.religiousconsultation.org/prefacesacredchoices.htm.

5 Ibid.

6 John A. T. Robinson, *Honest to God* (Philadelphia: Westminster, 1963), 118.

7 Tom Vanderbilt, *Traffic: Why We Drive the Way We Do (and What It Says About Us)* (New York: Knopf, 2008), 213–14.

8 Richard Brookhiser, *Rules of Civility: The 110 Precepts that Guided Our First President in War and Peace* (New York: Free, 1997), 31, 43, 57, 70, 77.

9 Lawrence Kohlberg, *The Philosophy of Moral Development: Moral Stages and the Idea of Justice* (San Francisco: Harper & Row, 1981), 17–19.

10 Arne Naess, "The Deep Ecological Movement: Some Philosophical Perspectives," in *Environmental Ethics: Divergence and Convergence*, 2nd ed., ed. Richard G. Boltzer and Susan J. Armstrong (New York: McGraw Hill, 1998), 439.

11 Arne Naess, cited in Bill Devall and George Sessions, *Deep Ecology: Living as if Nature Mattered* (Salt Lake City: Gibbs Smith, 1985), 75–76.

12 Robert H. Nelson, *The New Holy Wars: Economic Religion vs. Environmental Religion in Contemporary America* (University Park, PA: Pennsylvania State University Press, 2010), xx.

13 William Cronon, cited in ibid., 2.

14 Roger Kimball, "Art v. Aestheticism: The Case of Walter Pater," *Experiments Against Reality: The Fate of Culture in the Postmodern Age* (Chicago: Ivan Dee, 2000), 30.

15 Tom Hayden, *The Long Sixties: From 1960 to Barack Obama* (Boulder, CO: Paradigm, 2009), 160.

16 "Atheist Becomes Theist"; http://www.biola.edu/antonyflew/ (accessed September 16, 2010).

17 Antony Flew, *The Politics of Procrustes: Contradictions of Enforced Equality* (London: Temple Smith, 1981), 73.

18 Ibid., 75.

19 Ibid., 90.

20 Ibid., 78.

21 Robert Nozick, *Anarchy, State, and Utopia* (New York: Basic, 1968), 161.

22 Ibid.

23 Tsunetomo Yamamoto, *Bushido: The Way of the Samurai*, ed. Justin F. Stone (Garden City Park, New York: Square One, 2002), 13–14.

24 Ibid., 19.

25 Ibid., 32.

26 Ibid., 45.

27 Amy Schrager Lang, *Prophetic Woman: Anne Hutchinson and the Problem of Dissent in the Literature of New England* (Berkeley, CA: University of California, 1987), 193.

28 See Stephen J. Grabill, *Rediscovering the Natural Law in Reformed Theological Ethics* (Grand Rapids: Eerdmans, 2006).

29 Carl Bean, *I Was Born This Way* (New York: Simon & Schuster, 2010), 22.

30 Ibid.

31 Ibid., 259.

32 Ibid., 258–59.

33 Ibid., book jacket.

34 Paul VI, *Humanae Vitae* (Rome: Vatican, 1968); http://www.vatican.va/holy_father/paul_vi/encyclicals/documents/hf_p-vi_enc_25071968_humanae-vitae_en.html (accessed December 8, 2010).

Faulty Secular Systems with External Reference: Reason to Virtue

O F COURSE, ALL ETHICAL systems employ reason in some fashion, whether calculating the greatest payoff in personal pleasure, trying to discern the natural order of things, or sorting out one's intuitions; but we resume our consideration of "external" systems with a look at one purporting to run on reason alone. It claims that the very form or logic of ethics, apart from content, will generate duties.

REASON

The eighteenth-century German philosopher Immanuel Kant had no patience for the teleologist's calculation of consequences, which deteriorates into expediency. He loved the notion of doing one's duty, letting the chips fall where they may. And where might one discover such duty? In the very form of duty itself, expressed in what he calls the Categorical [Universal] Imperative [Obligation]. Without specifying what particular duties might be, he simply insists that it pass the universality test: "Act only on that maxim through which you can at the same time will that it should become a universal law." In other words one must ask, "What if everyone did it?" A person simply plugs in the act, whether waterboarding a prisoner, having a third child, or driving a Hummer, and then sees if the result is absurd or deplorable—or salubrious.

Kant gives four examples of his Categorical Imperative at work: (1) A man contemplating suicide must see that this cannot be for everyone since it would contradict the altruistic feeling that lies at the heart of ethics. (2) A man contemplating borrowing money with no intention to repay could not countenance this as a general policy since it would destroy the trust on which borrowing and promising depend. (3) A man contemplating a life of worthless ease must see that this is an affront to natural instinct and giftedness. (4) A man considering a life of indifference to the suffering of others could not will that this be the standard because it could backfire on him when he was in need.[1]

In some instances the illicit behavior is nonsensical; in others it is simply impossible to will, given one's self-interest. But the examples reveal the Categorical Imperative's Achilles' heel. It cannot stand alone. Rather it needs to play off other ethical systems to work. (a) Regarding suicide, who says ethics is naturally altruistic? Certainly, Nietzsche does not. (b) The fraudulent borrower might also take a Nietzschean tack, figuring that he can benefit from the standing institutions of trust personally without crippling the system that allows him to continue his con. (c) The slacker looks with puzzlement at a nag who says he and others must be stewards of their talents. (d) The coldhearted man might figure he can get away with selfishness, for there are always saps who will come to his aid.

None of the examples rises to the level of formally obvious obligation. One needs something else to make them float, whether basic conscience or the projection of disastrous consequences. But these are the concerns of intuitionism, hedonism, or utilitarianism. This is the realm of calculating personal or social misery, not the realm of pure formal duty.

To clear things up a bit, Kant offered a second version, or corollary, of the Categorial Imperative. Here he explained that there are two broad metaphysical categories on earth, things that are ends to other goods (such as hammers and ice cream cones, that are justifiably discarded when they break or go bad) and things that are ends in themselves (namely, rational nature, characteristic of humans, which one does not toss aside when they "break," as when rendered quadriplegic in an auto accident). This has its impressive charms, but it also has a glaring problem. It allows for disposal of the profoundly retarded, those radically deficient in rational nature. Furthermore since it fixes on rational nature, it would well descend into a program of eugenics, so popular in early twentieth-century America.

Beside this loophole into immorality, there is a crippling conceptual problem: How should the behavior under consideration be described? Should one ask, "Must I obey my parents?" or "Must I obey parents who are admirable?" And what if a person finds his own case so exceptional that his description gives him freedom to violate basic norms? "What if everyone who was orphaned by a serial killer decided to cheat on a single exam in junior high on the day after he was not able to study since he sat up all night comforting a friend contemplating suicide?" Universalize that, and it does not look so bad.

Clearly Kant was on to something, for he designed his system to avoid or prevent expediency. One cannot help but admire the Kantian who does everything he can to continue with house payments rather than defaulting, even when the value of the house has fallen so far as to eliminate his equity. His word is his pact, even if it means he will be in debt and penury the rest of his days.

But when one examines the foundation of this nobility, one finds only the value of reason, which is a slippery and insufficient base.

Kant was also a racist, who graded people by their level of perceived intelligence. He wrote, "The negroes of Africa have by nature no feeling that rises above the trifling," that the difference between whites and blacks "appears to be as great in regard to mental capacities as in color," and, "This fellow was quite black from head to foot, a clear proof that what he said was stupid."[2]

Once a person makes reason his god, he can quite unreasonably slide into stupid, ungodly behavior.

SURVIVAL COMPACT

Some would tie morality to a form of mutual agreement, a social contract of sorts. It posits man in something of a state of nature, with rights to everything or nothing. The only way he can function is by compacting with others to forfeit certain rights, just as his neighbors do, so that they will not trample each other. And by forfeiting such rights, they gain other rights. For instance, "I give up my right to kill you so that I might gain the right not to be killed."

Thomas Hobbes

The seventeenth-century British philosopher Thomas Hobbes said that in a state of nature, man is essentially at war. It was a situation bereft of culture and commerce; "No Knowledge of the face of the Earth; no account of Time; no Arts; no Letters; no Society; and which is worst of all, continuall feare, and danger of violent death; And the life of man, solitary, poore, nasty, brutish, and short."[3]

Facing such horrors, people reasonably agreed to surrender their rights to tyrants, or so he said.

> Self-interested individuals, craving protection for their lives, contracted to create sovereign states. Sovereigns (preferably monarchs) provided this service, but the price was unfettered power and unqualified obedience. Once sheltered under sovereignty, subjects enjoyed only the right to life. They could neither demand the return of their surrendered rights nor expect to share in the exercise of power.[4]

This leaves people in submission to all sorts of government wickedness, an unconscionable "bargain" by most accounts.

The Lottery

Shirley Jackson's short story, "The Lottery," first appeared in *The New Yorker* in June 1948. Since then, it has been read by millions of high school students as well as many more in the general populace. The book tells the story of a village, which holds a lottery each year, believing their well-being depends on it: "Lottery in June, corn be heavy soon."

The tradition is deep-seated and happily accepted, much like proceedings of "the square dances, the teenage club, the Halloween program" and other "civic activities." Jackson leads the reader on through the story, with signs of normalcy—pleasant banter and a focus on their workaday lives ("Well, now . . . guess we better get started, get this over with, so's we can go back to work.")

But the story turns darker. When someone reports "that over in the north village they're talking of giving up the lottery," Old Man Warner snorts, "Pack of crazy fools. . . . Listening to the young folks, nothing's good enough for *them*. Next thing you know, they'll be wanting to go back to living in caves, nobody work any more, live *that* way for a while." He continues, "First thing you know, we'd all be eating stewed chickweed and acorns. There's always been a lottery."

And so they continue placidly, the head of each household drawing slips of paper from a well-worn box. When the lot falls to Bill Hutchinson, he then puts five pieces of paper in the box, one for each family member. His wife Tessie claims that the drawing was not fair since her husband was rushed, but her protests fall on deaf ears. And on the last draw she gets the one with the heavy pencil mark. Then, in short order, the village people begin to stone her to death. Someone even "gave little Davy Hutchinson [her son] a few pebbles."

This is chilling, disgusting behavior but strictly according to the village's "social contract."[5]

THE TRIBE

The headline, "Tribal Ties Impede Yemen's War on al Qaeda," says volumes about the problem with "family above all" thinking. The article quotes President Ali Abdullah Saleh: "In Yemen, the tribe comes first, and once tribal blood starts to spill, the bloodshed is hard to stop."[6] Indeed. But tribalism is unfortunately operative in the West as well.

Cornell West

In an essay entitled "Black Strivings in a Twilight Civilization," Princeton University professor Cornel West distances himself from the "conservatism" of W. E. B. DuBois, who is regarded by most blacks as a progressive and admirable thinker. He also prides himself on being edgy and more threatening than Frederick Douglas, who in turn was more "dangerous" than Booker T. Washington, who was still more admirable than the "Uncle Tom," George Washington Carver.[7]

Though he has been blessed with professorial positions at Harvard and Princeton, West insists that his compatriots are in continual war with the oppressors:

> Black nationalists usually call upon black people to close ranks, to distrust most whites (since the reliable whites are few and relatively powerless in the face of white supremacy) and to promote forms of black self-love, self-defense and self-determination. It views white supremacy as the definitive systemic constraint on black cultural, political and economic development. More pointedly, black nationalists claim that American democracy is a modern form of tyranny on the part of the white majority over the black minority. For them, black sanity and freedom require that America not serve as the major framework in which to understand the future of black people. . . . And owing to its deep-seated racism, this [American] society does not warrant black allegiance or loyalty. White supremacy dictates the limits of the operation of America democracy—with black folks the indispensable sacrificial lamb vital to its sustenance.[8]

There is no denying the horrors of America's racist path, extending well beyond the Civil War. For instance one is not surprised to read that a "Tucson, Arizona, saloonkeeper recounted in his diary of the 1870s how one man was hanged for stealing a mule and how another was paid to leave town after killing a black."[9] But West injures himself morally by obsessing over what was once the plight of his tribe and by reading every modern slight as fresh grounds for insolent insularity.

Valerie Solanas

Valerie Solanas, who shot Andy Warhol in 1968, authored the virulent, obscene SCUM Manifesto the previous year. Here is one of its tamer pronouncements of hatred toward the tribe of men: "A 'male artist' is a contradiction in terms. A degenerate can only produce degenerate 'art.' The true artist is every self-confident, healthy female, and in a female society the only Art, the only Culture, will be conceited, kooky, funky females grooving on each other and on everything else in the universe."[10]

The Manifesto is simply a reduction to absurdity of radical feminist tribalism,[11] the revelation of "a tormented woman's hellish inner world."[12] Molested by her father, Solanas "hated him so much that she built an entire theoretical edifice on that loathing."[13]

Guy Burgess

In evaluating the British traitor, Guy Burgess, director of the Courtauld Institute of Art and Surveyor of the Queen's Pictures, said, "The Cambridge liberal conscience [was] at its very best, reasonable, sensible, and firm in the faith that personal relations are the highest of all values."[14] This attitude is perfectly reflected in "E. M. Forster's notorious claim that if forced to choose between betraying his friends and betraying his country, he hoped he would have the guts to betray his country."[15]

This was not a noble rejection of "my country, right or wrong." It was mere substitution of an equally absurd standard, "my friends, right or wrong."

UTOPIA

Throughout the centuries thinkers have projected ideal states of affairs, toward which they urge all to work and sacrifice. The word *utopia*, meaning "no place," was coined by sixteenth-century English Chancellor Thomas More; and the expression is ambiguous. It can mean that there is now no such situation but that it is one toward which one must work, in that it is attainable. The other notion is that it is simply a fantastical fiction, one not attainable.

The names of these utopian dreams are legion, whether Thomas Campanella's City of the Sun, Francis Bacon's New Atlantis, Etienne Cabet's Icaria, Samuel Butler's Erewhon ("nowhere" spelled backwards, more or less), Elizabeth Burgoyne Corbett's New Amazonia, or Charlotte Perkins Gilman's Herland.[16] Some are focused on limited plots of land, others on the whole world. Some are feminist, some communist, some fundamentalist.

Of course some utopian dreams can sound scary, but most think the notion of utopia itself is morally neutral or harmless. Not so, says British philosopher Sir Karl Popper, whose work, *The Open Society and Its Enemies*, suggests that utopias are intrinsically coercive. While he has no problem with what he calls "piecemeal engineering," whereby societies fine-tune justice, as with adjustments to the civil and criminal law codes, he is dead set against "Utopian engineering," an approach to politics he counts "most dangerous."[17]

Once a leader or nation decides to work to achieve the "Ideal State," then every act should be judged in light of whether it contributes to that end. This "blueprint"-based approach to public policy is "convincing and attractive," making it "only the more dangerous, and its criticism the more imperative."[18] The problem is simply that utopianism leads to totalitarianism.

Karl Popper lumps Plato (with his *Republic*) in with Karl Marx (with his "workers' paradise"), saying they exemplify the utopian practice of "aestheticism," with its desire to build a world which is not only a little better and more rational than ours, but which is free from all its ugliness: not a crazy quilt, an old garment badly patched, but an entirely new coat, a really beautiful new world."[19] Alas, "The artist-politician has first to make his canvas clean, to destroy existing institutions, to purify, to purge." This is the way of "all political radicalism, of the aestheticist's refusal to compromise," a track that "leads only too easily to violent measures."[20] This for instance, was the way of Vladimir Lenin.

Port Huron Declaration

In his book *The Long Sixties: From 1960 to Barack Obama*, Tom Hayden, founder of the radical Students for a Democratic Society (SDS), argues that, despite the bad press, the sixties had a wonderful effect on society. Along with the undeniably good "voting rights for southern black people," he lists "amnesty for fifty thousand draft evaders in Canada," the abortion-rights *Roe v. Wade* decision, and "freedom of sexual desire" as desirables (as if his crew were responsible for the civil rights movement and as if his critics would find the other examples gratifying).[21]

All are in perfect alignment with his highest value, freedom, as expressed in the Port Huron Declaration, whose first draft he authored. Therein he states, "The goal of man and society should be human independence." And through a regimen of disarmament, workers' liberation, "participatory democracy," and such, there will be a brave new world of joy. This utopian ideal is the only one worth pursuing: "The United States' principal goal should be creating a world where hunger, poverty, disease, ignorance, violence, and exploitation are replaced as central features by abundance, reason, love, and international cooperation."[22]

The problem is that "sweetness and light" turned aggressive in pursuit of its ends, for as with all utopias, ends come to justify means. Though Hayden has tried to distance himself from the radicals in SDS, who seized and sacked the president's office at Columbia University in 1968,[23] he once gloried in the invasion, which was spurred by the removal of draft deferments for graduate students during the Vietnam War.

As a proper utopian, he was ready to justify brute force to move things forward. He quoted black liberation theologian James Cone, who said that "the violence in the cities, which appears to contradict Christian love, is nothing but the black man's attempt to say Yes to his being defined by God in a world that would make his being into nonbeing."[24] And Hayden was ready to exonerate the Weather Underground, two of whose members were blown to bits preparing pipe bombs filled with nails for detonation at "a dance for military officers, their wives, and their girlfriends at nearby Fort Dix, over the river in New Jersey."[25] These terrorists "originated as one inevitable response to the Vietnam War by an alienated handful of the sixties generation." These were "young people driven mad by their comfortable privileges" who "struck back in a fury consistent with their shame."[26]

But the Port Huron dream was not all work. They knew how to unwind. As Tom Hayden put it:

> There was nothing wrong with smoking marijuana in a society of tobacco smokers and alcoholics. There was nothing wrong with sex out of marriage or monogamy, or communal living, or gay/lesbian sex for consenting partners. There was nothing wrong with obscenity. There was nothing wrong with hitchhiking or dropping out, and who in their right mind could complain about heretical poetry? The extremes of destruction do not render the behavior illegitimate."[27]

Angela Davis

During the author's days in graduate school at Vanderbilt University in the early 1970s, he and his wife drove across Nashville to Fisk University to hear the radical Marxist Angela Davis, only to discover that he and his wife were virtually the only white people in a crowd of 200 or so. The program began with music by the Fisk Jubilee Singers, with a glorious history of gospel singing. (For instance, they performed for President Grant in the White House in 1872, and in 1873 Queen Victoria commissioned a portrait of the group, which still hangs on campus.)

After their music, Angela began her rant, which culminated in the declaration that an offended, black civil servant who shot her boss to death in Atlanta was not guilty of the crime. Rather, it was society who pulled the trigger. At that point the crowd gave her a standing ovation, in which the author and his wife declined to participate. This was an awkward choice, to say the least.

It is one thing to take to the barricades, quite another to erase human responsibility for murder. Utopians do not share these scruples.

VIRTUE

In large measure because of the work of Alasdair Macintyre, contemporary ethics has given fresh attention to virtue-based ethics. His book *After Virtue*[28] shifted some of the focus from questions of the morality of war and abortion (good behavior) to questions of character. It insisted that there be good actors as well as good acts.

Aristotle's *Nicomacheaen Ethics* was a strong early statement of this perspective, one in which he located various virtues as the Golden Mean between two unfortunate excesses. For instance the virtue of courage lies midway between foolhardiness (too much courage) and cowardice (too little courage). In the popular press Bill Bennett's *The Book of Virtues*[29] has advanced appreciation of character traits such as self-discipline, compassion, and honesty. And Roman Catholic philosopher Peter Kreeft has written about the "cardinal virtues" (justice, wisdom, courage, and moderation), the "theological virtues" (faith, hope, and love), and the way in which "the Beatitudes confront the Seven Deadly Sins."[30]

Furthermore the new emphasis on virtue has spawned a variety of niche studies, such as "virtue epistemology." In this vein Wheaton College philosopher Jay Wood has urged care in the way one acquires, maintains, communicates, and applies beliefs, lifting up such desiderata in belief acquisition as "inquisitiveness, teachableness, attentiveness, persistence, [and] circumspection."[31] As for communication, he praises "insight, articulateness, precision, eloquence, [and] persuasiveness."[32] Intellectual vices, on the other hand, include "traits such as obtuseness, gullibility, superstitiousness, close-mindedness, willful naivete and superficiality of thought."[33]

The Compassionate Salesman

As admirable as these virtues may be, they cannot ensure that the right thing is done. To illustrate, let me recount a story I heard from a radio preacher in Indianapolis in the early 1990s: It was late on a snowy night as a train was making its way across the Midwest prairie. A traveling salesman was seated across from a young mother and her baby. She and the child had never passed this way before, and she was afraid that they would miss their stop. The salesman heard the conductor assure her repeatedly that he would alert her in plenty of time.

But when the time came, the conductor was nowhere to be seen. The salesman, a veteran of this particular stretch of track, waited until the last minute before jumping in to say she needed to get off here. She asked whether he was certain, and he assured her he was since he had been this way a hundred times.

She thanked him, bundled up the child, and stepped out into the night. Then, some 20 minutes later, the conductor came by and asked about the lady. The salesman, a little peeved, said he had stepped in to help her. But it had been a terrible mistake. For this night only, the train had added an extra stop, setting off some farm supplies out by a pasture, where there was no station.

The engineer stopped the train immediately and backed up to the spot. From there the crew disembarked and walked about in the blizzard with flashlights calling for the woman and her baby but to no avail. The next morning they found her and the child about a mile away, crouched and frozen beside a fence.

In this tragic case the virtue of compassion was everywhere to be found, in the mother for her child and in the salesman and conductor for the pair. Neither man was careless in his performance, for both were working with the considerable experience they had, and sometimes emergencies require snap judgments. In short, no one was really blameworthy or deficient in virtue, but the salesman made a terrible mistake.

The same can be said of the other virtues. Loyalty, courage, and persever-ance can all misfire, even when done with admirable moderation. And if one grounds his ethic in spotting and affirming virtue, he might well end up prais-ing the diligent Klansman and the self-sacrificial kamikaze pilot. It leaves open the essential question of whether they were mustering their considerable virtues in the service of the right cause.

FAULTY SECULAR FOUNDATIONS

These first three chapters have discussed a representative list of secular responses to Plato's *Euthyphro* question, "What, at base, makes things right or wrong?" In each case there are problems; no foundation is adequate to the task of supporting the weight of all morality. This chart recaps the 16 issues discussed.

BASE	PROBLEM
Autonomy	Moral anarchy
Aesthetic pleasure	Decadence
Power and authority	Cruelty and blind obedience
Survival compact	Tyranny
Culture	Absurdities and evils
Decorum	Fecklessness
Ecosystem	Paganism and inhumanity
Equality	Oppression
Altruism	Expediency or paralysis
Intuition	Subjectivity
Natural order	Epistemological confusion
Personal pleasure	Degeneracy
Reason	Callous elitism
Tribe	Pointless strife or treachery
Utopia	Totalitarianism
Virtue	Misfires

Certainly there are other candidates for the foundation. (For instance draw-ing from Søren Kierkegaard, we could consider the primacy of "inwardness" and passion.) And of course there are many and lengthy discussions of the shortcomings of each proposed base, along with replies from the partisans. (For instance this chapter could have discussed the Promulgation Argument and Hedonistic Paradox, both of which tell against egoistic hedonism.) Ethics text-books are full of such points and counterpoints.[34]

Hopefully, though, this brief survey will help set the stage for great appreciation of the Christian approach to ethics, which we will soon consider. As with Elijah on Mount Carmel, this chapter has begun to challenge rival "gods" who presume to obviate the need for Scripture.

In chap. 4, we look briefly at the ethical standards of false religions before moving on to a biblical approach in chap 5. Euthyphro told Socrates that the gods' approval was sufficient for righteousness, but that depends on what god you have in mind. And even if you are working with the right god, indeed, with the true God Himself, there is more to be said than the fact that He commanded something.

Notes

1 Immanuel Kant, *Fundamental Principles of the Metaphysic of Morals*, trans. Thomas Kingsmill Abbott (Chicago: Encyclopedia Britannica, 1952), 268–70.

2 Kant, cited in *The Cornel West Reader* (New York: Basic, 1999), 83–84. West quotes from Winthrop Jordan, *White over Black* (Chapel Hill, NC: University of North Carolina, 1968), 436–37; and Richard H. Popkin, "Hume's Racism," *Philosophical Forum*, 9 (1977–78): 213.

3 Thomas Hobbes, *Leviathan* (Mineola, NY: Dover, 2006), 70.

4 Jeffrey Collins, "Real Government Efficiency," review of Thomas Hobbes, *Leviathan*, *Wall Street Journal* (July 14, 2010): A17.

5 Shirley Jackson, "The Lottery," *The New Yorker*, June 26, 1948, 25–28.

6 Margaret Coker, "Tribal Ties Impede Yemen's War on al Qaeda," *The Wall Street Journal* (November 2, 2010): A18.

7 Cornell West, "Black Strivings in a Twilight Civilization," *The Cornel West Reader* (New York: Basic, 1999), 87.

8 Ibid., 98.

9 Claude S. Fischer, *"Made in America: A Social History of American Culture and Character* (Chicago: University of Chicago Press, 2010), 33.

10 Valerie Solanas, "The S.C.U.M. Manifesto"; http://gos.sbc.edu/s/solanas.html (accessed July 7, 2010).

11 Ibid.

12 Ibid., 374–75.

13 Ibid.

14 A. N. Wilson, *Our Times: The Age of Elizabeth II* (New York: Farrar, Strauss, and Giroux, 2008), 26.

15 Ibid., 31.

16 John Carey, ed., *The Faber Book of Utopias* (London: Faber and Faber, 1999), v–x.

17 Karl Popper, *The Open Society and Its Enemies*, vol. 1 of *The Spell of Plato* (London: Routledge and Kegan Paul, 1945), 138.

18 Ibid., 138–39.

19 Ibid., 145.

20 Ibid., 146.

21 Tom Hayden, *The Long Sixties: From 1960 to Barack Obama* (Boulder: Paradigm, 2009), 19.

22 Port Huron Statement of the Students for a Democratic Society, 1962; http://www.h-net.
    org/~hst306/documents/huron.html (accessed July 28, 2010).
23 Hayden, *The Long Sixties*, 63–64.
24 Ibid., 156.
25 Ibid., 116.
26 Ibid., 119.
27 Ibid., 46.
28 Alasdair Macintyre, *After Virtue* (Notre Dame, IN: University of Notre Dame Press, 1981).
29 William J. Bennett, ed., *The Book of Virtues: A Treasury of Great Moral Stories* (New York:
    Simon & Schuster, 1993).
30 Peter Kreeft, *Back to Virtue* (San Francisco: Ignatius, 1992).
31 Jay Wood, *Epistemology: Becoming Intellectually Virtuous* (Downers Grove, IL: InterVarsity,
    1998), 35.
32 Ibid., 39.
33 Ibid., 47.
34 E.g., Fred Feldman, *Introductory Ethics* (Englewood Cliffs, NJ: Prentice-Hall, 1978). This
    book has been a favorite of this author through the years.

FAULTY OR INADEQUATE RELIGIOUS SYSTEMS

I N THE FIRST THREE chapters, we looked at efforts to fashion a moral standard without reference to the divine. In each instance the project was seen to be flawed or incomplete. This chapter discusses ethical systems that presume to connect with the supernatural, beginning with false religions.

We'll also look at a classic Christian answer to the *Euthyphro* question, the Divine Command Theory. It simply says that something is righteous or obligatory or good because God declares it so. We will consider some modifications to this approach and also look at what false religions can teach us about the need for adjustments.

THE ETHICS OF FALSE RELIGION

When Christopher Hitchens writes that "religion poisons everything," he has a point. Though he is wrong to lump true Christianity in with other religions and argue that it shares their toxicity, he is right to note that all sorts of evil and nonsense are advanced by faiths outside the Judeo-Christian realm. Here are some problems with those other approaches.

Hinduism

Hinduism's most influential scripture, the epic *Bhagavad-Gita*, introduces a caste system wherein certain groups are destined, indeed, entitled to rule the others. Many suppose that Eastern religion is utterly benign and winsome, but at base it warrants oppression.

We will get to the Hindu caste system and the history of widow-burning, but here we will simply note the strange kinship between Hinduism and Nazism.

Himmler and the Bhagavad-Gita. Many would find it surprising that "Heinrich Himmler, head of Hitler's SS, never went anywhere without his copy" of the *Bhagavad-Gita.* But for one thing it presents a

> system of four social classes, Brahmans, characterized by calm, self-restraint, asceticism, long-suffering, uprightness, wisdom and religious faith; warriors . . . characterised by courage, ardour, endurance, unwillingness to flee in battle, generosity, noble pride; peasants and artisans who work in the field or in trade; and finally serfs who have no other duty than to serve others.[1]

He and Hitler, were, of course, Brahmans on this model.

Furthermore Himmler saw Hitler as a Krishna, who follows the pattern of rescue expressed in the text. "Whenever the law of righteousness withers and lawlessness arises, I will be born anew" (spoken by "Lord Krishna to a warrior, Arguna, before the great battle on the field of righteousness that forms the theme of the Bhagavad-Gita"). By Himmler's lights, "It had been ordained by the Karma of the Germanic peoples that he should come to save them by waging war against the east."[2]

Himmler's biographer also observes that the path to Hindu perfection "involved a man doing his caste duty in a disinterested, passionless way. . . . And here, perhaps, is the key to the picture of Himmler, by nature a squeamish man, forcing himself silently to watch an extermination at Auschwitz."

Mein Kampf and the Hollywood Hitler film. Hindus and the chief Nazi have a mutual-admiration society. Though some of it can be attributed to lingering resentment of British colonialism and corresponding appreciation for anyone who attacked the British, India's fascination with Adolf Hitler goes deeper. His autobiography, *Mein Kampf,* is a "consistent best seller," with 70,000 copies sold in the past decade. "The book is popular among management students who see it as some sort of self-help or leadership strategy manual." A Hollywood film portraying "his last days, his love life, and his supposed connection to India" is in the works, and a few years back, "a hotelier opened a café called Hitlers' [*sic*] decorated with Nazi flags and portraits of the *Fuhrer*." Part of the resonance is likely due to "a longing for strong leaders, or the appropriation of Aryan mythology and the symbol of the swastika from Hinduism."[3]

Buddhism

As noted in chap. 1, Buddhism is much taken with avoiding pain by eliminating desire. Of course this can be a good thing if the desire is illicit. But the desire for good health, prosperity, and community can drive culture forward and give its people a sense of calling and service. Unfortunately this is not a Buddhist strong suit, particularly since the focus is on one's own personal pain and peace and not on one's neighbors. So the world does not look to Buddhist cultures for advances in medicine, transportation, and philanthropy.

Hostility to dualisms. Western thought is grounded in the principle of non-contradiction (a proposition cannot be both true and false at the same time) and an appreciation of conceptual pairings. But this will not do for the Buddhist. In trying to explain the Tibetan legal system, University of Buffalo law professor Rebecca French contrasts it with her own tradition, with its "omnipresent dualisms good/bad, nature/culture, primitive/modern, religious/secular, right/left, scholastic/scientific, faith/reason, public/private." She adds that "most of our conceptual tools are based in a dualistic form of thinking, from logic to symbolic analysis, from categorization to normative evaluation" and that "we will move first to separate and categorize, and then to label as good or bad."[4] But "to understand Buddhist legal thinking it is essential to think outside the western box of dualism and to take a more holistic view of legal actors, actions, and relationships."[5]

This Buddhist approach can sound charming next to the "harsh pigeonholing" of the West. And certainly everyone can find good reason to melt down some dualisms. For instance following Martin Luther, many are impatient with the sacred/secular split when it comes to vocations. And are not people more a mixture of good and bad rather than absolutely one or another? Yes, of course, but the fact that there is twilight does not mean that there is neither night nor day. Take away the dualisms and a person descends into nonsense and mishmash.

The Bible is clearly a book of dualisms—light and dark, lost and saved, heaven and hell, obedience and disobedience. It does not shrink from declaring bestiality bad and creation good; from honoring Ruth and defaming Jezebel; from denouncing Asherah worship and insisting that Jesus is, exclusively, "the way, the truth, and the life." Dismiss the dualisms, and one's ethic is a mess.

Dissolution of critical faculties. After tracing Buddhist complicity in the Japanese war effort, including its atrocities, Christopher Hitchens offers this summary statement:

> A faith that despises the mind and the free individual, that preaches submission and resignation, and that regards life as a poor transient thing, is ill-equipped for self-criticism. Those who become bored by conventional "Bible" religions, and seek "enlightenment" by way of the dissolution of their own critical faculties into nirvana in any form, had better take a warning. They may think they are leaving the realm of despised materialism, but they are still being asked to put their reason to sleep, and to discard their minds along with their sandals.[6]

Allen Ginsberg's vow. Not surprisingly, vagueness plagues the Buddhist project. Consider, for example, the "formal Buddhist refuge vow" that beatnik poet Allen Ginsberg wrote at the Dharmadhatu meditation center in Boulder, Colorado.

> Seated in the lotus position on stage with Trungpa, Allen repeated three times the formal vows to take refuge in Buddha, in Buddhist teachings, and in the Buddhist community. He then took formal bodhisattva vows: "Sentient beings are numberless. I vow to liberate them all. Obstacles are inexhaustible. I vow to cut through them. The gates of the Dharma are countless. I vow to enter every gate. The Buddha Path is endless. I vow to follow through."[7]

This sounds nice, even inspiring, but it is not clear how he plans to "liberate" such "sentient beings" as bubonic rats and mad dogs. Unless he means to kill them, the results can hardly be good for humanity.

Late bloomers. In his book on "the eight rival religions that run the world," Stephen Prothero graciously notes that "engaged Buddhism" emerged in the twentieth century. It refers to "efforts to apply the Buddhist principle of compassion to social and economic problems such as poverty, war, injustice, discrimination, and environmental degradation." Before that, and because of its focus on withdrawal, Buddhism was "viewed by sociologists as pessimistic, apolitical, socially apathetic, and ethically inert—perhaps the most powerful evidence of Karl Marx's claim that religion is the 'opiate of the masses.'"[8]

One would think that if the cause of public justice were endemic to Buddhism, it would have shown up in the first couple of millennia of the religion's existence.

Shintoism

When the Japanese surrendered to the Allies in 1945, Douglas MacArthur became governor of the nation. One of his first acts was to press Emperor Hirohito to announce, via radio, that he was not in fact divine. This was a welcome change, for the religion had done great harm to the world.

Immanental theocracy. In the waning years of the war, the Japanese government issued "a monthly theme on which all ministers were expected to preach." Some Christian ministers resisted, but most gave in "to the principle of 'immanental theocracy,' exemplified by the throne in which both God and Caesar were rolled into one."[9] Buddhist and Confucian clergy, who were "alarmed at the penetration of 'foreign' influence," supported the Shinto program.[10] They understood that "Christianity presented the greatest problem to the government because of its transcendental reference, its claim of universality for its doctrines, and its close ties with the churches in the West."[11]

Devotion to the emperor was so sweeping that, as defeat loomed, the government employed it to advocate "the fanatic motto of *ichioku gyokusai* (one hundred million subjects together suffer an honorable defeat)."[12] This was tantamount to suicidal warfare, down to the last man, woman, and child.

Hirohito's skepticism. Soon after World War I, the crown prince Hirohito, at the tender age of 23, toured Europe. On that trip he confided in his military aide, Nara, that he did not believe "in the divinity of his father and his imperial ancestors." Nevertheless he felt that he should keep his convictions private, maintaining the status quo. "He felt he should accept the deceit that was expected of him," and "his pragmatic, voluntary subordination of his own mind to the precepts of the imperial system forecast his (and his entourage's) active acceptance of the heightened cult of emperor worship." Thus the "public actions of this prince would never be governed by his own private standards of goodness, morality, and integrity."[13]

This was the faith that undergirded the Rape of Nanking and the recruitment of kamikaze pilots. And its god did not even believe in his own divinity—or in the importance of personal integrity for that matter.

New Thought

At its 1917 annual convention in St. Louis, the International New Thought Alliance issued a Declaration of Principles, which has been tweaked through the years. This precursor of the New Age Movement, along with Theosophy, Spiritualism, Rosicrucianism, Swedenborgianism, Divine Science, Christian Science, Kabbala, Unity, and a variety of other movements, proclaims "the inseparable oneness of God and man" and man's ability to "reproduce the Divine perfection in his body, his emotions, and in all his external affairs." The problem is that there is little direction for the outworking of that perfection in external affairs. The group affirmed "the freedom of each person in matters of belief" and the duty to "love one another, and return good for evil." But the real payoff was in a beatific state in which one enjoyed "health, supply, wisdom, love, life, truth, power, peace, beauty, and joy."[14] In short, this is essentially love as niceness, as feeling.

In this model, evil is something of an illusion, a privation. Similarly "These movements revolted against a traditional Christian view that man is a sinner, standing under God's judgment and in need of repentance and forgiveness, so that the Christian doctrines of grace and atonement are generally absent."[15] In short this is a lame base for any sort of substantive ethic.

Islam

Islam provides a perfect example of how ethics can go wrong in the hands of religious leaders.

The Qur'an. In that Mohammed is God's mouthpiece and model and the Qur'an is perfect, one is led to believe that God requires that infidels be conquered and required to pay humiliating tribute to their Muslim victors (9:29), that it is permissible to have sex with captive women, even if they are already married (4:24),[16] that mutilation and murder of Islam's opponents is licit (5:33–34).[17]

Nonie Darwish, daughter of a high-ranking Egyptian intelligence officer, converted to Christianity and writes about the dreadful inadequacy of the Qur'an. For one thing, she notes that "the word *love* is never mentioned, not even once, in the Qur'an."[18]

Hadith. By far the largest source of ethics in Islam stems from the Hadith, the life and sayings of Mohammed. Counted authoritative, they prescribe the strangest things. For instance, "there are several reliable references to Muhammad instructing a woman to suckle a grown man so that he could be considered her foster son. The reason for doing this was that the man would then become someone she was allowed to be alone with, and before whom she did not have to wear the veil."[19]

Reliance of the Traveler. Speaking of breast-feeding, a leading source of Muslim law in Southeast Asia, *Reliance of the Traveler*, extends the principle, "An infant becomes the 'child' of the female who breast-feeds him" to questions of incest (if an unrelated boy and girl baby share the same wet nurse, they become "unmarriageable kin through suckling").[20] This will strike most as absurd, as will other pronouncements, such as these taken from "Ibn hajar Haytami's List of Enormities": "plucking eyebrows"; "not straightening the row of people praying"; and "selling . . . wood or the like to someone who will make a musical instrument."[21] One has to wonder how these could qualify as "enormities" in any god's rule book, but one can find such curious, overblown rhetoric throughout the Muslim world.

This is not to say that all or even most Muslim prescriptions are bizarre. Indeed many are thoughtful and track with Christian values, such as the prohibition against borrowing money "with the intention not to repay," "goading animals to fight each other," or "pimping between men and women."[22] But this same text insists that prize money must not be offered for "a race between a camel and a horse" and declares, "It is unlawful for men to wear silk or use it in any way, even to line clothing, though it is permissible to use it as padding in a cloak, pillow, or mattress."[23]

Taliban. Of course the Taliban are notorious for such absurdities as these "decrees relating to women and other cultural issues, after the capture of Kabul, 1996," all enforced by the "Religious Police": "If any music cassette [is] found in a shop, the shopkeeper should be imprisoned and the shop locked"; "After one and a half months if anyone is observed who has shaved and/or cut his beard, they should be arrested and imprisoned until their beard gets bushy"; "If women or fashion magazines are seen in the shop the tailor should be imprisoned."[24]

Shia temporary marriages. Shia Islam, which predominates in Iran, allows for "temporary marriages," which can last as little as an hour "for a specified amount of money." These are "promoted by the ayatollahs as a way financially troubled women can make money." Feminists call it "legalized prostitution," but Iranian president Ahmadinejad has sought "to make the marriages even more male-friendly, including giving men legal cover to bypass asking permission for the relationship from their first wives."[25]

This is a popular practice in Iran, and "for young couples who can't afford to marry, the loophole, [the] only way to be together, and avoid 100 lashes [for sex outside of marriage]."[26]

Summa contra Gentiles. In *Summa contra Gentiles* Thomas Aquinas summed up the inadequacy of the Muslim ethic, contrasting

> the spread of Christianity with that of Islam. Muhammad, he says, seduced the people by promises of carnal pleasure. His precepts gave free rein to our lower appetites. He taught no new and sublime truths but only what people of moderate intelligence are capable of discovering for themselves. And even this truth, in the Qur'an is mixed with fables and errors. Muhammad, moreover, performed no miracles and fulfilled no prophecies. Those voluntarily converted to his religion were brutal inhabitants of the desert, ignorant of letters and philosophy. The further expansion of Islam took place by force of arms. Thus it is clear, Thomas concludes, that those who trust Muhammad's words believe lightly.[27]

INCOMPLETE RELIGION

The Old Testament Scriptures are moral treasures for the church, God-breathed texts for prophetic preaching. But they point beyond themselves to new revelation in Christ. Left to themselves, they tend toward legalism and ritual-based religion. And insofar as many contemporary Jews do not believe in an afterlife, they have a this-worldly perspective that undermines their sense of grace and peace.

Saturday in Tel Aviv

While on a Midwestern Baptist Theological Seminary faculty trip to the Holy Land, one of the professors broke his leg when he slipped on some rocks on the Mediterranean shore. He was taken to the Yitzhak Rabin Trauma Center in Tel Aviv, where he got the care he needed for a flight back to the United States for surgery. I stayed with him while the rest of the faculty traveled back to Jerusalem.

The next day was Saturday, the Jewish Sabbath, and I was struck by two religious curiosities. When I ordered a hamburger and milkshake from the hotel's room service, the waiter delivered them on two carts. When he wheeled in the first one, with only the hamburger aboard, I told him something was missing, but he assured me all was well. He returned to the hall and then reappeared with my shake, explaining that the separation was out of respect for Deut 14:21, which reads, "You must not boil a young goat in its mother's milk." This was their way of not mixing milk products and meat.

When I finished and was ready to go to the hospital, I discovered that one of the two hotel elevators was set to stop on every floor. I was happy to take the other one since I was well up in the building. The slower elevator was designed to spare observant Jews from the "work" of pushing the button. They simply walked on and waited patiently for their arrival in the lobby.

Halakah Electric Institute

While a graduate student in the 1970s, I read a spellbinding article about the work of an electrical institute in Israel established to help Jews remain Sabbath compliant. For instance they provided electric-eye light switches so that one could simply walk by a certain spot and the switch would click; no need to use one's hands to "light a fire," namely, the lightbulb.

My favorite was a device designed to drain power from an elevator as it descended. They reasoned that, even though the devout rider punched no button, his weight contributed to the elevator's progress downward. So they were calculating how much of a power-saver each person became by force of gravity and then trying to compensate by reducing the flow of electricity to the car. Thus the rider would not be guilty of serving as a "coworker" with the elevator.[28]

Progressive Revelation

The point is simply that without the New Testament and a strong sense of progressive revelation, ethics can become stuck in legalism. Without accepting Jesus' words in Mark 2:27 ("The Sabbath was made for man and not man for the Sabbath"), the Sabbath observer embraces such curiosities as I witnessed in Israel.

A QUESTION OF ESSENCE

Of course any religionist could point to sublime manifestations of his faith—the beauty of Buddhism, Islam, and others. And one can always find horrific and tawdry connections with another faith, whatever it might be. The Hindu, stung by alleged associations with Hitler, could point to the recitation of Bible phrases at a Ku Klux Klan rally. The Muslim, offended at someone mentioning "overnight" marriages in the Shia camp, could highlight the sexploits of "televangelists."

This sort of tit for tat is meant to discourage apologetical ethics and impose a mind-set of "moral equivalency." But this is specious, for it ignores the question of essence, of what is true to the heart of a faith and what is a perversion. It is absolutely fair to ask whether philandering preachers are true to their Scriptures in the same way the Iranians engaging in "temporary marriage" are true to theirs. Similarly one must push back against comparisons between the Klan and the Taliban, between IRA and Hezbollah bombers, between the Branch Davidians of Waco and al Qaeda. Which groups truly represent the founding documents of the faith, and which have carried the tenets of their religion to a logical but unsavory conclusion?

Any group can become more attractive through careful manipulation of its resumé. But a fair assessment requires, so to speak, a credit check, a Google search, and a visit to Bartleby.com for a look at the old texts. Furthermore, noting "what most Muslims do" is not enough. Most avowed Christians are slackers, giving relatively little, never evangelizing, and risking nothing. Some observers say that 20 percent of a church does 80 percent of the work, and everyone can recognize the reference to a new believer who was so excited and engaged that he had to backslide to have fellowship with the congregation. The key matter is which believers are truer to "New Testament Christianity"—or to "Koran/Hadith Islam" and "Bhagavad Gita Hinduism."

That being said, let us move to the biblical ethic.

DIVINE COMMAND

For many Christians who are new to metaethics, the answer to the *Euthyphro* question seems obvious: "Of course, 'God commands it' is the standard, the touchstone of right and wrong. What could be higher and more morally compelling than a directive from the living God?" But the issue is a little more complicated than that. As Socrates pressed the point in *Euthyphro*, what sort of divine authority is in play here? Is God the moral authority by virtue of His executive power or by virtue of His expertise? Or to put it otherwise, does God's commanding something make it right by definition, or does He declare it right and command it by virtue of its being right on other grounds? This is a chicken-or-egg question: Which comes first? (There are other expressions of the Divine Command Theory, choosing to focus on the Divine Will and Divine Nature, but for the purposes of this chapter they are treated as one.)

It sounds odd, even blasphemous, to suggest that moral obligation might be based on more or other than a command of God. But the point is not that God is in any way Himself insufficient. It is to say that relying strictly on His role as sovereign of the universe to explain what we mean by right and wrong is to leave out some important things.

Just because a person is the all-powerful Lord of creation, that does not mean His judgments are admirable. One has only to look at how other world religions present divinities (Kali, Molech) who are morally repugnant. In a word, might does not make right. If the only moral credentials a sovereign has are based on power, his commands can be arbitrary and disgusting.

What if God commanded that a virgin be thrown into a volcano each year or that second-born children be hacked to death to the accompaniment of a hymn? Would that make it right? Not a month passes without some horrifying report from the world of religion, where, on "orders from God," someone has killed a busload of innocents or offered up some captive or child to appease the wrath of God.

Furthermore people evaluate another faith with expressions like, "My God would never ask us to do that!" And in so doing, they seem to say that even God must pass some sort of muster before He can be counted worthy of worship.

Modified Divine Command Theory

Some of those in the Divine Command camp have a fix, that is, a patch. They say that God, if properly understood, is seen as one who would command only good things. He is not only all-powerful and all-knowing, but He is, by definition, perfectly loving and just. Factor in those characteristics, and a person has nothing to fear.

Yes, but once one says that the righteousness of God's commands are rooted in His love and justice, then the questions surface, "What's so special about love and justice? Why are they to be preferred to petulance, mendacity, and treachery? If God were to model and insist on these latter three, then would that make them worthy? Can the fact that He is God make whatever He happens to be or do right?"

No, it seems that the properties people cherish in God are those that connect with human well-being. Justice, truth, mercy, and love are characteristic of blessed individuals, societies, and nations. If they were not, then people would be hard-pressed to praise them and the God who insisted on them.

If justice and love were coldly rational, such as a mathematical formula, then God's justice could grind out horrifying numbers without corresponding benefit or relief. And even if they were grounded in the mutual relationship of the persons of the Trinity, these relationships could be grotesque from a human standpoint. If, God forbid, the Trinity were sadomasochistic but human nature were not, then one would be loath to celebrate the ethic that flowed from such an arrangement. That would not bother the *Unmodified*-Divine Command terrorist. To him the fact that God prefers it is enough. But when people speak of love and justice, they do not view them as coldly distant. Rather, they have a human face; they resonate within people's hearts.

Virtually no one simply says, "God just said it, so that settles it. Even if He had no particular reason, that's good enough for me." But that is not the God whom the typical Christian worships. When he sings, "God is so good," he's not just singing, "God is so godlike." We don't celebrate the moral goodness of pure definition but rather the goodness of justice and mercy.

Notes

1 Peter Padfield, *Himmler: Reichsführer-SS* (New York: Henry Holt, 1990), 402.

2 Ibid., 402–3.

3 "India's Fascination with Hitler," *The Christian Science Monitor*, July 12, 1020, 4.

4 "Excerpt from Rebecca Redwood French, *The Golden Yoke: The Legal Cosmology of Buddhist Tibet*, in Frank S. Ravitch, *Law and Religion, A Reader: Cases, Concepts, and Theory*, 2nd ed. (St. Paul: Thomson/West, 2008), 924–25.

5 Ravitch, *Law and Religion, A Reader*, 916.

6 Christopher Hitchens, *God Is Not Great: How Religion Poisons Everything* (New York: Twelve, 2007), 204.

7 Michael Schumacher, *Dharma Lion: A Biography of Allen Ginsberg* (New York: St. Martins, 1992), 566.

8 Stephen Prothero, *God Is Not One: The Eight Rival Religions that Run the World—and Why Their Differences Matter* (New York: HarperOne/HarperCollins, 2010), 180.

9 Joseph M. Kitagawa, *Religion in Japanese History* (New York: Columbia University Press, 1966), 248.

10 Ibid., 254.

11 Ibid., 246.

12 Ibid., 269.

13 Herbert P. Box, *Hirohito and the Making of Modern Japan* (New York: HarperCollins, 2000), 119–20.

14 J. Stillson Judah, *The History and Philosophy of the Metaphysical Movements in America* (Philadelphia: Westminster, 1967), 176.

15 Ibid., 14.

16 Mark Durie, *The Third Choice: Islam, Dhimmitude and Freedom* (Melbourne, Australia: Deror, 2010), 53.

17 Ibid., 102.

18 Nonie Darwish, *Cruel and Usual Punishment: The Terrifying Global Implications of Islamic Law* (Nashville: Thomas Nelson, 2008), 196.

19 Durie, *The Third Choice*, 71.

20 Ahmad ibn Naqib al-Misri, *Reliance of the Traveler: A Classic Manual of Islam Sacred Law*, trans. and ed. Nuh Ha Mim Keller (Beltsville, MD: Amana, 1994), 575–77.

21 Ibid., 971, 977.

22 Ibid., 978, 983.

23 Ibid., 451, 199.

24 Ahmed Rashid, *Taliban: Militant Islam, Oil and Fundamentalism in Central Asia* (New Haven, CT: Yale University Press, 2001), 218–19.

25 Patricia Treble, "Let's Get Married—for an Hour," *Macleans*, September 20, 2010): 36.

26 Ibid.

27 Avery Cardinal Dulles, *A History of Apologetics* (San Francisco: Ignatius, 2005), 119–20.

28 For more on *halakah* regulations see Parshat Vayakhel "Electricity on Shabat"; http://www.chabad.org/library/article_cdo/aid/1159378/jewish/Electricity-on-Shabbat.htm (accessed December 4, 2010).

THE IRREDUCIBLE COMPLEXITY AND
SPLENDOR OF THE CHRISTIAN ETHIC

I N HIS BOOK, *DARWIN'S BLACK BOX*, microbiologist Michael Behe argues that evolution simply cannot explain the development of such intricate processes of the human body as blood clotting and the focus of an eye. Each has a number of components in play, and they all must be at work for there to be any survival advantage. One cannot arrive at these components incrementally through mutation, for the addition of one gains nothing. In other words there is an "irreducible complexity" to certain processes. This is an all-or-nothing affair.

Behe uses a mousetrap to illustrate his point. The trap has five components, each of which must be present to catch the prey.

> (1) a flat wooden platform to act as a base; (2) a metal hammer, which does the actual job of crushing the little mouse; (3) a spring with extended ends to press against the platform and the hammer when the trap is charged; (4) a sensitive catch that releases when slight pressure is applied, and (5) a metal bar that connects to the catch and holds the hammer back when the trap is charged. (There are also assorted staples to hold the system together.)[1]

If one of these appeared by chance, we would not be one-fifth of the way toward catching the mouse.

Behe asks:

> Which part could be missing and still allow you to catch a mouse? If the wooden base were gone, there would be no platform for attaching the other components. If the hammer were gone, the mouse could dance all night on the platform without becoming pinned to the wooden base. If there were no spring, the hammer and platform would

jangle loosely, and again the rodent would be unimpeded. If there were no catch or metal hold bar, then the spring would snap the hammer shut as soon as you let go of it; in order to use a trap like that you would have to chase the mouse around while holding the trap open.[2]

Once the trap is at work, it would be odd to ask which component caught the mouse. They all did. Take one away, and no mousetrap exists.

So it is with ethics. There is an irreducible complexity to it so that if one component is removed, one fails to capture what is meant by right and wrong. To demonstrate this, the criteria in chap. 1 will be discussed, to show the biblical basis for supposing that each is in play.

If there is no human well-being to one's system, he can have a sovereign God giving orders and smashing those who ignore them. But this is tyranny, not righteousness. If there is no God, then everyone does what is right in his own eyes, without wisdom or sanctions. If a person lacks a conscience, then it is cold calculation, much like paying taxes to a hated government. And so on.

The Wrong Question

Metaethicists are wired to press the point. Of course, a lot of things connect with ethics—conscience, good eventualities, divine approbation. But what is *the* touchstone? Those who locate it in the human condition are accused of impiety; those who tie it to God are called friends of tyranny. But could the one who tries to answer the question of what *the* touchstone is be asking the wrong thing, much like the two fellows in Kant's *Critique of Pure Reason*? One is trying to milk a he-goat and the other is holding a sieve.

Ethics for the Glory of God

The Westminster Shorter Catechism says, "The chief end of man is to glorify God and enjoy Him forever." (John Piper has suggested a tweak: "to glorify God by enjoying Him forever.") I suggest that "monistic" metaethics fails to bring sufficient glory to God. It either marginalizes God or makes Him a despot. The would-be ethical man is either forced to admit that God could admirably do horrible things with no reason even remotely satisfying to human well-being or that humans could theoretically run the whole moral enterprise by themselves and do quite well. But again this is to force an issue that need not be forced. One does not have to lobotomize and desensitize himself to do ethics. By God's grace and for His glory all the things we care about in the human realm are covered in His system.

Consider how comprehensively gracious and bracing the divine structure of morality is, as it answers human concerns and undergirds the best of all things. As the values considered and rejected as touchstones in chap. 1 are considered below, one will see that these desiderata are not jettisoned but are given their best expression under God.

WWJD

Not that long ago the question posed repeatedly in Charles Sheldon's book *In His Steps* (1896) resurfaced in the popular culture, in books, on bracelets, and table games: "What would Jesus do?" It was meant as a moral guide, the sort of thing a newspaper editor could use to determine which advertising to take and which stories to cover.

The question is commendable in its devotion to Christ, but it has its limitations, stemming from the fact that people today are not God incarnate on His particular mission with His particular prerogatives. For instance, if someone asks "WWJD" when trying to decide whether to marry or whether to run for office, he would have to conclude that he should not. Certainly, Jesus did not and would not do either. And then there is the question of which Jesus is one talking about, the One who walked the shores of Galilee in Roman times or the One returning in power at the end of the age to judge all men. Both are Jesus, but the circumstances are different. And besides, how can one judge whether Jesus would read a book or visit a nursing home on a given afternoon?

Sola Scriptura

People need to focus on Jesus' directives in Scripture. The question is not so much WWJD as WWJHUD, "What would Jesus have us do?" What does He commend, counsel, and command for humans?

And the emphasis must remain on Scripture. Most Christians have spoken confidently (and, I think, legitimately) of God's personal calling or leading, whether to a ministry, a school, or a spouse. But there is a significant margin of error on those matters. So we're inclined to hold our breath when we hear a sentence beginning, "God told me to . . ."

So let us stay close to the Bible in framing our ethics. Of course, there will be implications and applications. There are no specific verses on cloning, carbon vouchers, and curfews for teenagers; but we are not paralyzed when we come to such matters. We have broad biblical principles, concepts, and models available to us as we try to do the right thing.

FEATURES OF A BIBLICAL ETHIC

The secularists' ideals discussed in chap. 1 can be good things but not as final arbiters of right and wrong. The Bible does not scorn them so much as put them in harness to serve the purposes of God. Fire can do terrible damage when set loose, but under control it warms people and cooks their food. The problem of the secular ethicist is that he turns one admirable thing or another into wild-fire—even altruism and human reason. But under God, they all pull together in their assigned positions to advance the best there is for man.

The following pages discuss these features of a biblical ethic. Take one away, and there is less than what God intended. No, the secularist would not be happy with them as seen here; secularists mean something different by them, something more sweeping and sovereign. But that is precisely the problem. They want no limits on what must be limited for the sake of light and life.

Autonomy

When Friedrich Nietzsche wrote, "The great epochs of our life come when we gain the courage to rechristen evil as that which is best in us," he styled himself the great transgressor, thumbing his nose at society, shocking convention, and upending the system of received pieties. And though he was attacking Christian society, something about his spirit is compelling. It can be bracing to be a rebel, and Christianity is rebellious and countercultural.

Anyone who supposes that Christian morals are domesticated pap needs to return to the New Testament witness, where Jesus turned over the table of the money changers in the temple and declared, "For I tell you, unless your righteousness surpasses that of the scribes and Pharisees, you will never enter the kingdom of heaven" (Matt 5:20). His followers were the ones disparaged in Acts 17:6 as "men who have turned the world upside down." Far from being tame yes-men, servants of the culture, they were preachers of the crucified Christ, "a stumbling block to the Jews and foolishness to the Gentiles" (1 Cor 1:23). Indeed, Jesus warned that popularity was likely a sign of decadence: "Woe to you when all people speak well of you, for this is the way their ancestors used to treat the false prophets" (Luke 6:26).

Christians respect the autonomy of nonbelievers, seeking to "persuade" them and not coerce them. Christians are diplomats, not marauders. "Therefore, we are ambassadors for Christ, certain that God is appealing through us. We plead on Christ's behalf, 'Be reconciled to God'" (2 Cor 5:20). And when one's hearers reject the Lord's counsel, as did the "rich young ruler" in Luke 18:18–23, believers do not change the message or threaten them to get a different answer.

Aesthetic Pleasure

Those with an eye for beauty have much to appreciate in the moral law, as well as in creation. Of course the Bible warns that "charm is deceptive and beauty is fleeting" (Prov 31:30) and that, in his highest moment of sacrificial service on the cross, Jesus did not have an impressive "form or majesty that we should look at Him, no appearance that we should desire Him" (Isa 53:2). But the value of attractiveness itself, and indeed the attractiveness of God's law, is a constant theme in Scripture.

Christians "worship the LORD in the splendor of His holiness" (1 Chr 16:29) and not in the squalor of His petulance, the grotesqueness of His narcissism, or the tawdriness of His indifference. And the work of God is captured in language reflecting other senses, as when God said that restored Israel will have "fragrance, like the forest of Lebanon" (Hos 14:6) and that his ordinances are "sweeter than honey, which comes from the honeycomb" (Ps 19:10).

His creation is beautiful, whether the "heavens [that] declare the glory of God" (Ps 19:1) or the sweet voice and lovely face of one's lover in Song 2:14. The philosopher Immanuel Kant called the former "sublime," and the latter has inspired a thousand songwriters. In Helen of Troy's case, it launched a thousand ships.

And of course the most beautiful sight on earth is a redeemed soul: "He adorns the humble with salvation" (Ps 149:4). An ugly life turned wholesome is a joy to see.

Orthodox theologian David Bentley Hart speaks of yet another kind of beauty, perceivable by the redeemed. They have an infrared scope, so to speak, that allows them to penetrate the darkness.

> This is the new Christian optics, the way of seeing the other in Christ, that diverts attention from the stable representations of secular order to the suffering, to the nameless, to the captive and the outcast, even to the dead. . . . The other is seen within and by way of love, the splendor of his glory. Everything Nietzsche deplored about Christianity—its enervating compassion for life at its most debile and deformed, the Gospels' infuriating and debased aesthetic, which finds beauty precisely where a discriminating and noble eye finds only squalor and decadence—is in fact the expression of an order of vision that cannot be confined within the canons of taste prescribed by myths of power and eminence, because it orders the aesthetics of an infinite that surpasses every sinful ordering, every totality, as form, as indeed the form of peace: an order of vision that thematizes the infinite according to the gaze of recognition and delight, which finds in every other the glory of the transcendent other, and which cannot turn away from the other because it has learned to see in the other the beauty of the crucified. Because the God who goes to his death in the form of a slave breaks open hearts, every face becomes an icon: a beauty that is infinite. If the knowledge of the light of the glory of God is given in the face of Jesus (2 Cor. 4:6), it is a knowledge that allows every other face to be seen in the light of that glory.[3]

Power and Authority

An ethical system without power is anarchical, but the Bible teaches that God is there to back up His standards. The beleaguered believer cries out to God in Ps 37:17–20:

For the arms of the wicked will be broken,
but the LORD supports the righteous.
The LORD watches over the blameless all their days,
and their inheritance will last forever.
They will not be disgraced in times of adversity;
they will be satisfied in days of hunger.
But the wicked will perish;
the LORD's enemies, like the glory of the pastures,
will fade away—
they will fade away like smoke.

For many, the question of divine sanction is critical. Indeed, "The question of how and why human beings should behave morally when there is no God was one to which [the French existentialist philosopher] Jean-Paul Sartre continually returned."[4] Sartre decided that there were really no limits and said so in print. Voltaire also paraded his atheism, but he knew there would be a cost if everyone turned away from faith. He allegedly told his mistress, Marguerite, "Whatever you do, don't tell the servants there is no God or they'll steal the silver."[5]

Though both men were contemptuous of divine sanctions, they would certainly call the police if their apartments were sacked. And their sense of justice would have been affronted if the vandals and thieves were simply allowed to run free after being identified. Anarchy is nasty business in the civic world as well as the realm of ethics.

But of course God's power is not just punitive and coercive. It is also providential. Furthermore He delegates extraordinary authority to humans. In the first chapter of the Bible, verse 28 reads, "God blessed them, and God said to them, 'Be fruitful, multiply, fill the earth, and subdue it. Rule the fish of the sea, the birds of the sky, and every creature that crawls on the earth.'"

Furthermore believers will have all the power they need to live the Christian life. As Jesus promised in Acts 1:8: "You will receive power when the Holy Spirit has come upon you, and you will be My witnesses in Jerusalem, in all Judea and Samaria, and to the ends of the earth."

There would be no ethics at all if there were no universe, and so, as Creator, God is the ground of all right and wrong. But He is also the epistemic authority. As the only omniscient Being, He is in a position to evaluate everything that might come to pass. It is the height of vanity to suppose that one could outthink God. As He says in Isa 55:8–9, "'For My thoughts are not your thoughts, and your ways are not My ways.' This is the LORD's declaration. 'For as heaven is higher than earth, so My ways are higher than your ways, and My thoughts than your thoughts.'"

Again, His authority is inescapably coercive in that He can and does hold all men responsible for their actions. Without the power of enforcement, decrees are merely resolutions, opinions, or expressions of attitude, whether positive or negative. Without punishments there is no law. Speed limits, for example, would be a waste of signage.

Survival Compact

The best known verse in the New Testament, John 3:16, sets out the basic survival compact of all history: Those who believe in the Son will not perish but will have everlasting life.

Furthermore the Bible assigns believers to a community of worship, fellowship, service, and mutual watch-care. This is no ethic for lone rangers or prima donnas. Christians are part of a body, or, as Peter called them, "living stones" who "are being built into a spiritual house" and as "a holy priesthood to offer spiritual sacrifices acceptable to God through Jesus Christ" (1 Pet 2:5). Here is a corporate identity and ethic.

One is responsible to the congregation and may be expelled for misbehavior. Matthew 18:15–20 provides guidelines for discipline, resulting either in restoration or expulsion. (The latter is a real option, as in 1 Cor 5:1–5.) And, on the positive side, the church is meant to be a society of mutual care: "Now the large group of those who believed were of one heart and mind, and no one said that any of his possessions was his own, but instead they held everything in common" (Acts 4:32).

Culture

God does not work in cookie-cutter fashion. Though His moral principles are universal, there is much not dictated by His law. He loves variety, in the distribution of gifts and in His intention to save the nations, not homogenize them—a people redeemed by Christ's blood "from every tribe and language and people and nation" (Rev 5:9).

The early church was marked by ethnic, cultural, and economic diversity, as reflected in Acts 13:1: "In the church that was at Antioch there were prophets and teachers: Barnabas, Simeon who was called Niger, Lucius the Cyrenian, Manaen, a close friend of Herod the tetrarch, and Saul"—nobodies and somebodies, Jews and Gentiles, nationals and foreigners.

One way to see the cultural range of Christians is to look at church music—hymns, cantatas, anthems, spirituals, Sacred Harp, rap, country, Celtic, Integrity Hosanna, oratorios, requiems, Stamps Baxter, and others. All of it has a place in the Christian "choir."

Decorum

Christians are gentlemen and ladies, well-mannered and thoughtful. This is the spirit of Prov 15:1, which observes, "A gentle answer turns away anger, but a harsh word stirs up wrath." And as Paul said, in Col 4:6, "Your speech should always be gracious, seasoned with salt, so that you may know how you should answer each person." Then in Rom 12:18 he urged, "If possible, on your part, live at peace with everyone."

Ecosystem

The Christian is second to none in his healthy appreciation for the environment. He knows that God created it and declared it "good"—land and sea, vegetation and living creatures in the ocean, on the earth, and in the sky. And above all, he made man, giving him orders to "be fruitful, multiply, fill the earth, and subdue it. Rule the fish of the sea, the birds of the sky, and every creature that crawls on the earth" (Gen 1:28). This was a call to procreation and stewardship.

This meant not cutting down fruit-bearing trees during war (Deut 20:19–20) and protecting mother birds (22:6–7). But this did not mean the worship of nature, for as Genesis 3 makes clear, creation is fallen and flawed: "The ground is cursed" (v. 17) and full of "thorns and thistles" (v. 18). To eat, one must engage in "painful labor" (v. 17) and "eat bread by the sweat of [the] brow" (v. 19). Indeed, all of creation was "subjected to futility" in order that man might, in weakness, turn to God for help (Rom 8:20).

Nevertheless creation is still, unmistakably, God's splendid handiwork. The Lord glories in the wonderful intricacy of animal life in Job 39—of mountain goat, horse, ostrich, and eagle—and in the power of behemoth and leviathan in Job 40 and 41. (Some think these are, respectively, hippopotamus and crocodile, while others see them as species of dinosaurs.) And of course God directed that Noah preserve every kind of animal and food plant on the ark (Gen 6:19–21).

Equality

The root of human equality is the *imago Dei*: "So God created man in His own image; He created him in the image of God; He created them male and female" (Gen 1:27). And in Gal 3:28 Paul explained that full kingdom citizenship is open to all: "There is no Jew or Greek, slave or free, male or female; for you are all one in Christ Jesus." Then James rebuked those who favor the rich over the poor.

> My brothers, hold your faith without showing favoritism as you hold on to the faith in our glorious Lord Jesus Christ. For example, a man comes into your meeting wearing a gold ring, dressed in fine clothes, and a poor man dressed in dirty clothes also comes in.

If you look with favor on the man wearing the fine clothes so that you say, "Sit here in a good place," and yet you say to the poor man, "Stand over there," or, "Sit here on the floor by my footstool," haven't you discriminated among yourselves and become judges with evil thoughts? Listen, my dear brothers: Didn't God choose the poor in this world to be rich in faith and heirs of the kingdom that He has promised to those who love Him? (Jas 2:1–5).

Complementarianism. Some seek to push equality beyond and contrary to what the Bible teaches. Though, as Gal 3:28 teaches, men and women are equally honored in the church, it is an equality of worth, not identity of roles. In several passages (e.g., 1 Tim 2:12; 3:2), Paul said there are distinct roles for men in the church, and in Eph 5:22–33 he makes application to the home. Again this preserves equality of value without teaching indistinguishability of role.

Of course this is like fingernails on a chalkboard to the modern Western ear, but those who would question Paul's teaching might take a cue from the queen of England.

Countess Mountbatten of Burma, [Prince] Philip's cousin, told a story any couple can relate to, of going for a drive with Queen and consort. Elizabeth repeatedly sucked in her breath at Philip's fast driving. "If you do that once more," he snapped, "I shall put you out of the car." Shocked, Mountbatten asked the now-silent Queen why she allowed such comments. Because, she replied, "I don't want to have to walk back."[6]

Economics. Some would press the notion of equality to the radical distribution of income, perhaps working from the aforementioned report that the early believers had all things in common (not, of course, by government force but by free choice). Though the Bible teaches that the love of money is the root of all kinds of evil (1 Tim 6:10) and that it is easier for a camel to pass through the eye of a needle than for a rich man to enter the kingdom (Matt 19:24), it does not condemn riches as such. No stigma was attached to Abraham's wealth; there was no indignation over Nicodemus's having more than Peter or Andrew. Rather, the equality the Bible presses is that which recognizes the equal standing of Nicodemus and Andrew before God in Christ.

Altruism

The biblical theme of love and care for fellowmen appears on every hand. In the New Testament are the love chapter (1 Corinthians 13) and the Golden Rule (Matt 7:12), the feeding of the 5,000 (Mark 6:31–44) and the parable of the Good Samaritan (Luke 10:25–37).

In the Old Testament God commanded, "When a foreigner lives with you in your land, you must not oppress him. You must regard the foreigner who lives with you as the native-born among you. You are to love him as yourself, for you were foreigners in the land of Egypt; I am Yahweh your God" (Lev 19:33–34). Also, "When you reap the harvest in your field, and you forget a sheaf in the field, do not go back to get it. It is to be left for the foreigner, the fatherless, and the widow, so that the LORD your God may bless you in all the work of your hands" (Deut 24:19). And though Gen 9:6 reads harshly ("Whoever sheds man's blood, his blood will be shed by man, for God made man in His image"), it is a decree of loving protection, based on the principle that human life is precious.

Also important is how altruism is intensified within the church. For Jesus taught, "By this all people will know that you are My disciples, if you have love for one another" (John 13:35).

Overlap with utilitarian concerns. As stated earlier, a biblical view is not utterly alien to the secular mind. In a good deal of overlap, Christians and nonbelievers can cooperate, either in charitable enterprises or as cobelligerents in struggles for more just public policy (as when Southern Baptists joined with some atheists in opposing partial-birth abortion).

Gertrude Himmelfarb has noticed this phenomenon in late nineteenth-century Britain:

> In Victorian England, moral principles and judgments were as much a part of social discourse as of private discourse, and as much a part of public policy as of personal life. They were not only deeply ingrained in tradition; they were also embedded in two powerful strains of Victorian thought: Utilitarianism on the one hand, Evangelicalism and Methodism on the other. These may not have been philosophically compatible, but in practice they complemented and reinforced each other, the Benthamite calculus of pleasure and pain, rewards and punishments, being the secular equivalent of the virtues and vices that Evangelicalism and Methodism derived from religion.
>
> It was this alliance of a secular ethos and a religious one that determined social policy, so that every measure of poor relief or philanthropy, for example, had to justify itself by showing that it would promote the moral as well as the material well-being of the poor.[7]

Love is not God. Reading in 1 John 4:8 that "one who does not love does not know God, because God is love," some quickly conclude that "love is God." But this is a dangerous misreading. This view leads people to sanctify whatever tender passion they might have, however ungodly it might be.

Homosexual preacher Carl Bean is a case in point. When asked,

> "Reverend, does God hate me because I'm lesbian . . . or transgendered . . . or bisexual . . . or black . . . or poor . . . or sick with disease?" Bean answers, "No my children. It is not God who causes us to live as outcasts. In their quest for power and position, human beings create categories to elevate themselves and belittle others. If we accept the world's scorn, we grow weak. If we accept God's love, we grow strong. I promise this, I know this. My life is testimony to one statement and one statement only—God is love, and love is for everyone."[8]

By Bean's standard, the doctor who truly told you that you had cancer would be less loving and godly than the one who knew you had it but didn't tell you lest it hurt your feelings. But that is not biblical love.

Intuition

A moral system that struck men as counterintuitive would be onerous, but God has made sure that its principles are "written on their hearts" (Rom 2:14–15). If this were not so, it would be difficult to expect agreement in the drafting of civil law. And certainly it would make praise of the biblical ethic difficult. No matter how august a divine declaration might be, if it seems revolting or insane to humans, then they would be reluctant to call it moral. But as the psalmist expressed it, "The ordinances of the LORD are reliable and altogether righteous. They are more desirable than gold—than an abundance of pure gold; and sweeter than honey, which comes from the honeycomb" (Ps 19:9–10).

Natural Order

God could, of course, institute laws at odds with human nature. He could require naturally social individuals to be hermits. He could demand that people be promiscuous even though this behavior would trample on human feelings, stir up jealousy and strife, leave children without parents, and spread disease. But His commands are wonderfully congruent with what is best for humans.

Romans 1 teaches that there is a creation order, a divinely instituted character to nature, and that one defies that structure at his own risk. Sometimes in class, this writer takes a newspaper and attempts to tear out selected articles. When he tears one in one direction, the edge is relatively smooth and straight; when he turns it 90 degrees, the tear is jagged, ruining the article. The reason is simple: Paper has a grain. And analogously so does nature.

Of course one could tear a somewhat straight line against the grain, with many tiny rips, but the job would be forced, slow, and ragged. The same is true for an unnatural lifestyle; a person may make a go of it for awhile, but it is not a promising, peaceful, or winsome approach.

Human universals. In chap. 1 mention was made of Jean-Paul Sartre's claim that man has no natural essence, that he creates it once he arrives. But Donald E. Brown, in his book *Human Universals*, sees all sorts of instructive similarities.[9] Working against the currents of existentialism and cultural relativism, he details aspects of human behavior that are evident around the world. They track nicely with the statutes of God in two ways: they show that man is fallen, and they show what people consider licit and illicit. For instance, "Universal People" (UP):

1. Have possessives in their grammar, concerning both "inalienable" possessions (fingers; thoughts) and "alienable" possessions (an axe). [This honors biblical pronouncements against wounding and theft.]

2. "The UP are not solitary dwellers. They live part of their lives, if not the whole of them, in groups." [Not only does this track with Aristotle's claim that man is a social being. It fits the biblical injunctions to show regard for one's neighbor.]

3. "Marriage, in the sense of a 'person' having a publicly recognized right or sexual access to a woman deemed eligible for childbearing, is institutionalized among the UP." [Hence the proscription against adultery in the seventh commandment.]

4. "The UP have a pattern of socialization: children are not left to grow up on their own. Senior kin are expected to contribute substantially to socialization." [Thus the role of the family in raising up children "in the training and instruction of the Lord" (Eph 6:4).]

5. Sexual regulations "sharply delimit, if not eliminate, mating between the genetically close kin." [This fits the commands against incest.]

6. Related to sex- and age-based divisions of labor, "men and women and adults and children are seen by the UP as having different natures." Furthermore, "in the public political sphere men form the dominant element among the UP." [This covers both the demands of special care of children and the elderly, plus the issue of complementarianism, which the Bible teaches.]

7. "Reciprocity—including its negative or retaliatory forms—is an important element in the conduct of their lives." "They understand that wronged parties may seek redress." [This covers matters of justice, whether fair trade or punishment.]

8. "The UP have government, in the sense that they have public affairs and these affairs are regulated." Also "the UP have law." [This squares with Rom 13:1–7 and marginalizes anarchy.]

9. "The UP distinguish right from wrong." [And so they are moral beings, subject to biblical ordinances and sanctions.]

10. "Etiquette and hospitality are among UP ideals." [Virtues are represented in the requirements for deacons and pastors.]

11. "They have standards of sexual modesty—even though they might customarily go about naked. People, adults in particular, do not normally copulate in public, nor do they relieve themselves without some attempt to do it modestly." [So the Bible is right, that shamelessness is shameful and that certain parts should be covered.]

12. "The UP have religious or supernatural beliefs in that they believe in something beyond the visible and palpable." [So one has to work to be an atheist.][10]

The point in all this is that the Bible follows the contours of humankind. And this is not surprising since a loving God is the author of both the race and the rules.

Natural maxims. If Christian ethics were grotesque and destructive, the petulant demands of a heartless god, then it would have little overlap with the humanistic maxims of ordinary men. But, in fact, God's rules are salubrious, conducive of well-being, and all sorts of people make observations similar to those found in Proverbs and the moral teachings of Christ, the apostles, and prophets. So a believer should not be surprised when atheist businessman Warren Buffet says, "It takes 20 years to build a reputation and five minutes to ruin it. If you think about that, you'll do things differently."[11] Or when rock legend Bo Diddley says, "I would like to give a message to teenagers, the young and old: Be cool, don't do nothin' stupid. A dare is the worst thing in the world. Somebody dare you to jump off something, don't be no [expletive] fool. . . . Bo knows, okay. All right. Yeah."[12]

Personal Pleasure

The Christian ethic is saturated with happiness and delight—from the Beatitudes to Song of Solomon, where we read in 4:10–11: "How delightful your love is, my sister, my bride. Your love is much better than wine, and the fragrance of your perfume than any balsam. Your lips drip sweetness like the honeycomb, my bride. Honey and milk are under your tongue. The fragrance of your garments is like the fragrance of Lebanon."

God is no enemy of sensuality. He invented it and set the guidelines for its proper and fullest enjoyment.

Reason

Isaiah 1:18 is classically quoted in the King James Version as "Come now, and let us reason together," but more contemporary translations capture the same sense with such expressions as "Come, let us discuss this" (HCSB), "settle this" (NLT), "talk it over" (CEV), and "talk about these things" (NCV). The object of reason in this case is this: "Though your sins are like scarlet, they will be as white as snow; though they are as red as crimson, they will be like wool." In other words one would have to be dense or insane to pass this up.

The Hebrew word for "reason" here is *yākah*, whose Greek counterpart is *dialegomai*. This was the activity Paul engaged in while in Thessalonica in Acts 17:2: "As usual, Paul went to the synagogue, and on three Sabbath days *reasoned* with them from the Scriptures. (italics added)" So argumentation and dialogue have their place in presenting God's way.

Immanuel Kant was correct in noting the universality of ethical thinking. If the yardstick of human decency were flexible, changing with each person's measurement, then measurement would be meaningless.

Though Kant meant "rational nature" when he said that people are ends in themselves, he pointed to a vital truth, that humans are precious. The Bible certainly agrees with this assessment but on different grounds, namely, the image of God, which extends to the prerational unborn as well as to geniuses.

Tribe

Though most Christians are not ethnic Jews, they have been grafted into Israel (Romans 9) and as children of faith are part of the "Israel of God" (Gal 6:16). Furthermore, the New Testament church is described with the Greek word *koinonia* ("partner, sharer in common interest"[13]), and here it refers not only to the blessings and challenges they share in Christ, but also to the sense of mutual concern.

Friendship

The Bible says a lot about friendship. Proverbs 17:17 states, "A friend loves at all times, and a brother is born for a difficult time." And Prov 27:9 says, "Oil and incense bring joy to the heart, and the sweetness of a friend is better than self-counsel." But Prov 27:6 teaches that friendship is compatible with criticism and even resistance: "The wounds of a friend are trustworthy, but the kisses of an enemy are excessive."

Of course wonderful friendships are pictured in the Bible, including that of Ruth and her mother-in-law Naomi. When their husbands died, Naomi urged Ruth to return to her Moabite people as she herself went back to Israel. But in one of the loveliest passages in the Bible, Ruth said,

> Do not persuade me to leave you or go back and not follow you. For wherever you go, I will go, and wherever you live, I will live; your people will be my people, and your God will be my God. Where you die, I will die, and there I will be buried. May Yahweh punish me, and do so severely, if anything but death separates you and me (Ruth 1:16–17).

Above all, the believer is offered friendship with God Himself, as in the case of Abraham, whose faith is the believer's model: "Abraham believed God, and it was credited to him for righteousness, and he was called God's friend" (Jas 2:23).

Utopia

The heavenly vision offered in Revelation is breathtaking:

> Then he showed me the river of living water, sparkling like crystal, flowing from the throne of God and of the Lamb down the middle of the broad street of the city. The tree

of life was on both sides of the river, bearing 12 kinds of fruit, producing its fruit every month. The leaves of the tree are for healing the nations, and there will no longer be any curse. The throne of God and of the Lamb will be in the city, and His slaves will serve Him. They will see His face, and His name will be on their foreheads. Night will no longer exist, and people will not need lamplight or sunlight, because the Lord God will give them light. And they will reign forever and ever. (Rev 22:1–5)

Heaven not on earth. In his *Open Society and Its Enemies*, Karl Popper speaks of a "heavenly city" while critiquing utopian radicalism, which leads men

to jettison reason, and to replace it by a desperate hope for political miracles. This irrational attitude which springs from an intoxication with dreams of a beautiful world is what I call Romanticism. It may seek its heavenly city in the past or in the future; it may preach "back to nature" or "forward to a world of love and beauty"; but its appeal is always to our emotions rather than to reason. Even with the best intentions of realizing heaven on earth it only succeeds in realizing hell—that hell which man alone prepares for his fellows.[14]

Of course, when believers look forward to the real heaven, they are not romanticists at all. And of course they can gain a taste of heaven in the fellowship of the redeemed.

Virtue

The apostle Paul sets the believer's eyes on virtues in Phil 4:8: "Finally brothers, whatever is true, whatever is honorable, whatever is just, whatever is pure, whatever is lovely, whatever is commendable—if there is any moral excellence and if there is any praise—dwell on these things." And then, in Gal 5:19–23, he presents the sharp contrast between the character of the Spirit-filled Christian and that of the lost man:

Now the works of the flesh are obvious: sexual immorality, moral impurity, promiscuity, idolatry, sorcery, hatreds, strife, jealousy, outbursts of anger, selfish ambitions, dissensions, factions, envy, drunkenness, carousing, and anything similar. I tell you about these things in advance—as I told you before—that those who practice such things will not inherit the kingdom of God. But the fruit of the Spirit is love, joy, peace, patience, kindness, goodness, faith, gentleness, self-control. Against such things there is no law.

FULFILLMENT OF THE "LAW"

A Christian ethic is not, then, a repudiation of the ideals advanced by the secularists and other religionists. Rather it rejects the enthronement of one false king after another. Instead it incorporates all worthy interests—the environment, equality, power, and so forth—into a system where each gets its proper due. The simple chart below gives a hint of how it comes together.

Could people today do without one or a few of these items? Perhaps. Maybe they could operate as loners without friends. Or maybe they could ignore manners and be as churlish as they pleased. Maybe they could glorify irrationality and shame the mind. But in every instance they would have lost something of what makes Christian ethics wonderful.

And why talk of giving up something when it is all there for believers to enjoy and to commend to others? So let's review:

BASE	PROBLEM	BIBLICAL RESOLUTION
Autonomy	Moral anarchy	Individual responsibility to respond to persuasion
Aesthetic pleasure	Decadence	The beauty of nature and holiness
Power and authority	Cruelty and blind obedience	Protective sanctions, delegated authority, and generous equipping
Survival compact	Tyranny	Eternal life and fellowship under a new covenant
Culture	Absurdities and evils	Great diversity among the church's peoples
Decorum	Fecklessness	A norm of graciousness
Ecosystem	Paganism and inhumanity	Stewardship and conservation of creation
Equality	Oppression	The value equality (not role identity) of persons
Altruism	Expediency or paralysis	The outworking of love
Intuition	Subjectivity	Standards written on the heart
Natural order	Epistemological confusion	Creation with a grain
Personal pleasure	Degeneracy	God-created receptors and satisfiers
Reason	Callous elitism	Godly dialogue and universal standards
Tribe	Pointless strife or treachery	A gathering of "Israelites"; relationship with God and fellow believers
Utopia	Totalitarianism	Our heavenly destiny, palpable in the church
Virtue	Misfires	Refined as the fruit of the Spirit

A FINELY BALANCED, WINSOME ETHIC

Some Bible interpreters favor a "tighten up" hermeneutic, preferring the hardest, most demanding response. For instance considering divorce, they naturally say that the *porneia* exception in Matt 5:32 is meant only for the betrothal period. Whether they have this particular reading right, they are correct to note that Jesus favored the stricter Shammai party over the looser Hillel party on this issue.

But if it is proper to "tighten up" every passage, what is one to make of Jesus' telling the Pharisees to "lighten up" when they condemned the disciples for plucking grain for food on the Sabbath? There are rocks on both sides, and the serious student of the Bible must take each text on its own merits, in its own context. That is bad news for latter-day Pharisees who want to make godliness as restrictive as possible—but also for libertines who find nothing but license in the words "God is love."

Something is stirring about Immanuel Kant's call to do everything out of a sense of duty and not according to calculated payoffs. This resonates with such tough, sacrificial passages as Luke 14:26, which calls on the believer to hate his kin, or John 15:13, which praises those who lay down their lives for their friends. But just as soon as one begins to think the Christian walk is indifferent to rewards, the Lord brings them up as an incentive, as in Matt 5:12 and Luke 6:23.

In other words great balance exists in the biblical ethic. Some of it is stern, some of it playful; some of it constrictive, some of it liberating. Errant systems mimic the faulty "tighten up" and "lighten up" hermeneutics. They insist that people "pleasure up," "reason up," "equal up," "eco up"—and "up and up and up."

When, though, in contrast, believers say the Bible answers to a wide range of interests and that it provides a balanced approach, they do not mean that the moral Christian does the balancing according to his own lights, going to church most Sundays, but then taking time for Sunday-morning pleasure on the golf course every month or so; or using reason to stay within a budget but now and then splurging on artwork he cannot afford out of pure aesthetic transport. That would be chaotic.

Fortunately God has already done the balancing, explaining what is licit and what is not, providing rewards in suitable places and times, accommodating man's weaknesses while pulling them higher, revealing Himself in His created order while providing scriptural hedges against misreading what is natural or unnatural. The task then is to submit to the generous counsels and encouragements of Scripture and to the sovereignty and providence of God.

In practical terms the believer behaves as if he is something of a divine-command theorist. He knows who knows and loves best. When God directs, the believer says, "Yes, Sir." But in response to the *Euthyphro* question, he insists that God's commands are neither arbitrary nor callous. Rather they evidence the greatness of a loving and just Creator who would not think of imposing standards on man that are inimical to a fulfilling life.

The result is a life saturated with reason, pleasure, community, altruism, stewardship, virtue, friendship, power, equality, culture, autonomy, keen intuition, and a heavenly perspective—and one that commends itself to a watching, even skeptical, world.

Notes

1 Michael Behe, *Darwin's Black Box: The Biochemical Challenge to Evolution* (New York: Free, 1996), 42–43.

2 Ibid.

3 David Bentley Hart, *The Beauty of the Infinite: The Aesthetics of Christian Truth* (Grand Rapids: Eerdmans, 2006), 343–44.

4 Carole Seymour-Jones, *A Dangerous Liaison: A Revelatory New Biography of Simone de Beauvoir and Jean-Paul Sartre* (New York: Overlook, 2008), 277.

5 Voltaire, cited in R. J. Hoffman, "Good with God? Not the Problem," *The New Oxonian* December 9, 2009; http://rjosephhoffman.wordpress.com/2009/12/09/of-the-conceptual-confession-of-the-phrase-good-without-god (accessed January 3, 2010).

6 Ken MacQueen, "All in a Day's Work," *Maclean's* (July 5 and 12, 2010): 73.

7 Gertrude Himmelfarb, *The De-Moralization of Society: From Victorian Virtues to Modern Values* (New York: Knopf, 1995), 241–42.

8 Carl Bean, *I Was Born This Way* (New York: Simon & Schuster, 2010), 259.

9 Donald E. Brown, *Human Universals* (New York: McGraw Hill, 1991).

10 Donald E. Brown, *The Norton Psychology Reader*, ed. Gary Marcus (New York: Norton, 2006), 318–29.

11 Janet Lowe, *Warren Buffett Speaks: Wit and Wisdom from the World's Greatest Investor* (New York: John Wiley & Sons, 1997), 26.

12 Bo Diddley, cited in *Rolling Stone Raves*, comp. Anthony Bozza, ed. Shawn Dahl (New York: Rolling Stone, 1999), 315.

13 A. T. Robertson, *Word Pictures in the New Testament, Concise Edition* (Nashville: Holman Reference, 2000), 268–69.

14 K. R. Popper, *The Open Society and Its Enemies*, Vol. 1 of *The Spell of Plato* (London: Routledge & Kegan Paul, 1945), 147–48.

Immoral Ethicists: Ideologues, Social Scientists, and Activists

S KEPTICS LOVE TO REHEARSE and celebrate the moral failings of crusading preachers and politicians. In their view this discredits the speaker and his crusade. To some extent Christians agree, and the minister or legislator is "defrocked" in one way or another. But believers do not, then, grant that the foundational message is nullified, insofar as it was grounded in Scripture. Whatever sin might have been in the messenger's life, the message came from Scripture, which is holy.

The situation is different with non-Christians. Their foundational text is not truly holy, and their unfortunate message is an outworking of their wayward lives, whether their ethic is religious (as in the Qur'an) or secular (as in the *Communist Manifesto*). By exposing disgusting things in a secular or heterodox "prophet's" life, one raises serious questions about his sermon's soundness.

Of course the big problem with questioning the virtue of an errant teacher is that his system may be comfortable with a generous helping of what is known as sin. One may find it difficult to shame Hugh Hefner with reports of infidelity when his published philosophy praises infidelity. One may find it difficult to embarrass a Muslim with reports of wife-beating when the Qur'an allows it. One may find it difficult to call someone a hypocrite when he does not stand for anything in the first place.

Still it is appropriate for the Christian apologist to hold the moral plumb line up against the competitors' lives and declare their shocking lack of ethical credibility. As Oscar Wilde wrote, "The fact of a man being a poisoner is nothing against his prose." That is to say, terrible people can produce remarkable things.

No one can question the aesthetic giftedness of many reprobates, whether painters, actors, or novelists. Indeed their imagination and productivity may be fueled by hatred or cocaine. But when someone ventures to preach, it takes more than a clever turn of phrase, sweeping rhetorical gestures, and an uncanny sense of timing. It requires a respect for truth, grounded not only in reality but also in one's integrity.

A QUESTION OF CHARACTER

What then should one make of character in ethics and apologetics?

Argumentum ad Hominem

Students of introductory logic are regularly taught to shy away from "informal fallacies," such as *ad misericordiam* ("appeal to pity") and *ad baculum* ("appeal to force"). Logic must remain dispassionate to be perceptive. At the top of many lists is the fallacy of attacking one's character rather than his argument (*argumentum ad hominem*). For instance it will not do for the professor to retort in class, "Why should we listen to you? You don't even have a masters degree." True enough but irrelevant, "for out of the mouths of bachelors can come great wisdom." This student may be the child in "The Emperor's New Clothes," the only one who had courage of his perceptions to tell it like it was.

But one must not overreach in declaring fallacies. The use of a fallacious argument does not ensure the falsity of one's claim. It merely shows that one needs in this case more than character critique to win the day. Exposure of another's wickedness is not nothing, so it is appropriate to size up the lives of pundits who pose as moral experts. If someone proposes to instruct others in how to live, his behavior is fair game for scrutiny.

So there is a place for examining the speaker's moral credentials. Though they cannot carry the argument, they can at least adorn it or refine it.

Impeachment of Testimony

The courts make provision for the impeachment of the witness. This is a matter of character, defined by one jurist as "a generalized description of a person's disposition, or of the disposition in respect to a general trait, such as honesty, temperance, or peacefulness."[1] Though the Federal Rules of Evidence 607, 608, and 609 insist that attorneys focus on the witness's truthfulness and not his other virtues or lack thereof, the principle is set:[2] Character matters. Of course courtroom rules are not coextensive with the rules of reason; in some cases the former are too restrictive, in others too little so. But it is useful to see that common legal practice allows the judge to turn the spotlight on the life of the one speaking.

This may bring focus on a lack of competence. For example, a witness might be impeached on the basis of his reputation for being unobservant, thus tracking with ordinary life expressions, such as "I'm sure he didn't notice. He's a space cadet."[3] And in many instances demonstrating a conflict of interest or possible motive for misrepresenting things is sufficient.

Writing in the case of *Davis v. Alaska*,[4] the U.S. Supreme Court said:

> One way of discrediting the witness is to introduce evidence of a prior criminal conviction of that witness. By doing so the cross-examiner intends to afford the jury a basis to infer that the witness' character is such that he would be less likely than the very trustworthy citizen to be truthful in his testimony. The introduction of evidence of a prior crime is thus a general attack on the credibility of the witness. A more particular attack on the witness' credibility is effected by means of cross-examination directed toward revealing possible biases, prejudices or ulterior motives of the witness as they may relate directly to issues of personality in the case at hand. The partiality of a witness is subject to exploration at trial, and is "always relevant as discrediting the witness and affecting the weight of his testimony." We have recognized that the exposure of a witness' motivation in testifying is a proper and important function of the [criminal defendant's constitutional] right of cross-examination.[5]

By this same standard it would be unfair to impeach a DNA expert's findings by raising the matter of his adultery, but to mention his record of plagiarism or of doctoring the data would be fair.

The application to ethics should be clear. When the witness speaks to matters of right and wrong, it is good to know whether his life is admirable or ignoble and whether, when he sins, he repents or excuses his behavior.

Common Sense

Whatever the strictures of courtroom procedure or the canons of academic logic, the man on the street (or in the jungle) knows that rectitude counts. In his October 1, 1855, journal, the British missionary to Africa, David Livingstone, wrote:

> Much of my influence [among the Makololo] depended upon the good name given me by the Bakwains, and that I secured only through a long course of tolerably good conduct. No one ever gains much influence in this country without purity and uprightness. The acts of a stranger are keenly scrutinized by both young and old, and seldom is the judgment pronounced, even by the heathen, unfair or charitable. I have heard women speaking in admiration of a white man because he was pure, and never guilty of any secret immorality. Had he been, they would have known it, and, untutored heathen though they be, would have despised him in consequence. Secret vice becomes known through the tribe; and while one, unacquainted with the language, may imagine a peccadillo to be hidden, it is as patent to all as it would be in London had he a placard on his back.[6]

THE ADMIRABLE LOST

None of this is meant to imply that, if a person is not a Christian, he cannot manifest decency. The Bible itself speaks, in Acts 17, of the relative nobility of the Bereans, who showed more openness to hearing the gospel than did their neighbors in Thessalonica. After all Rom 2:14–15 makes clear that even lost men have the Torah written on their hearts, impinging on their consciences. And certainly many are sensitive to the counsel of natural law and sympathy/empathy, making them better men.

Roger Williams's report on his reception by the Indians is reminiscent of Paul's comment on the Bereans.

Chased out of Massachusetts Bay colony, the nonconformist Roger Williams found a warm reception in what is now Rhode Island. Not surprisingly, he spoke of his Indian friends in warm terms. He said, "There is a favor of civility and courtesy even amongst these wild Americans, both amongst themselves and towards strangers." Of their hospitality he said, "If any stranger come in, they are presently given to eat of what they have. . . . Many a time, and at all times of the night (as I have fallen in travel upon their houses) when nothing has been ready, had themselves and their wives, risen to prepare me some refreshing." In this connection he sang,

> I have known them leave their house and mat
> To lodge a friend or stranger,
> When Jews and Christians oft have sent
> Christ Jesus to the manger.

He admired the Narragansett, saying that there were fewer scandals among them than in Europe, and that one "never hear[s] of robberies, rapes, murders"; "they never shut their doors, day nor night, and 'tis rare that any hurt is done. . . . Their wars are far less bloody, and devouring than the cruel wars of Europe; and seldom 20 slain in a pitch field."

Nevertheless Williams did not think they were saved by their good works or that somehow they had escaped the effects of the fall. In writing *A Key into the Language of America*, that is, the Algonquin tongue, he expressed the desire that it would help missionaries to "spread civility and . . . Christianity" to the natives.[7]

Furthermore if Williams had come upon a chief who presumed to be a moral teacher, he would have judged him not only by the sagacity of his words but also by the rectitude of his life. Were he a brute and a philanderer, then his pronouncements would have lost much of their force.

RIVAL SAINTS

For atheists and other opponents of Christianity, it is important to demonstrate the moral equivalency or superiority of their party by listing great men who did not follow Jesus. In this vein Christopher Hitchens writes that

> the great Colonel Robert Ingersoll, who was the nation's leading advocate of unbelief until his death in 1899, maddened his opponents because he was a person of immense generosity, a loving and constant husband and father, a gallant officer, and the possessor of what Thomas Edison with pardonable exaggeration called "all the attributes of a perfect man."[8]

Thomas Edison, himself an atheist, would have happily bestowed sainthood on Ingersoll, and it is reasonable to suppose Ingersoll was an upstanding citizen. The same sort of thing can be said of the pioneer environmentalist, Aldo Leopold, who was essentially a pantheist, whose "religion came from nature."[9] He had a sound marriage, and his children became accomplished scientists.

Of course lost people can live circumspect and productive lives for any number of reasons, but there is thoroughly predictable prevalence of moral laxness among those who reject the tenets of Christianity. To put it another way, the private lives of churchgoing evangelicals are, on average, purer than the private lives of those who "preach" against evangelical faith and practice.

Mohandas Gandhi warrants attention not because his cause was anti-Christian but because he is held up as a figure of moral equivalency to Jesus and Paul. The latter two are then thought to be nothing special since non-Christian figures can be just as sublime in their example and teaching. But Gandhi rates a closer look.

In 1982 Richard Attenborough's worshipful film *Gandhi* appeared in theaters, cementing the Indian leader's sainthood. But on release of the movie, Richard Grenier, a film and culture columnist for *The Washington Times*, *The New York Times*, and *Commentary*, was moved to report that Gandhi was not particularly adept at family values.

> When Gandhi's wife lay dying of pneumonia and British doctors insisted that a shot of penicillin would save her, Gandhi refused to have this alien medicine injected in her body and simply let her die. (It must be noted that when Gandhi contracted malaria shortly afterward he accepted for himself the alien medicine quinine, and that when he had appendicitis he allowed British doctors to perform on him the alien outrage of an appendectomy.)[10]

And this act of indifference toward his wife was consistent with his general attitude toward her. He once observed:

> I simply cannot bear to look at Ba's face. The expression is often like that on the face of a meek cow and gives one the feeling, as a cow occasionally does, that in her own dumb matter she is saying something. I see, too, that there is selfishness in this suffering of hers. . . . His wife remained illiterate. Once when she was very sick, hemorrhaging badly, and seemed to be dying, he wrote to her from jail icily: My struggle is not merely political. It is

religious and therefore quite pure. It does not matter much whether one dies in it or lives. I hope and expect that you will also think likewise and not be unhappy.[11]

Unhappy to die, that is. And his children fared no better:

He denied his sons' education—to which he was bitterly hostile. . . . He disowned his oldest son, Harilal, for wishing to marry. He banished his second son for giving his struggling older brother a small sum of money. Harilal grew quite wild with rage against his father, attacked him in print, converted to Islam, took to women, drink, and died an alcoholic in 1948.[12]

Gandhi's views on sex would not have been optimum for marriage. "Gandhi was a truly fanatical opponent of sex for pleasure, and worked it out carefully that a married couple should be allowed to have sex three or four times in a lifetime, merely to have children and favored embodying this restriction in the law of the land."

His Hinduism led him to rank people by birth:

Gandhi, needless to say, was a Hindu reformer, one of many. Until well into his 50s however, he accepted the caste system in toto as the "natural order of society," promoting control and discipline and sanctioned by his religion. Later, in bursts of zeal, he favored moderating it in a number of ways. But he stuck by the basic *varna* system (the four main caste groupings plus the Untouchables) until the end of his days, insisting that a man's position and occupation should be determined essentially by birth. Gandhi favored milder treatment of Untouchables, renaming them Harijans, "children of God," but a Harijan was still a Harijan.[13]

His political meddling on the eve of World War II was bizarre. "Gandhi also wrote an open letter to the British people, passionately urging them to surrender and accept whatever fate Hitler had prepared for them. 'Let them take possession of your beautiful island with your many beautiful buildings. You will give all these, but neither your souls, nor your minds.'"[14]

And what can one say of his sleeping habits and obsession with bathroom events?

I cannot honestly say I had any reasonable expectation that the film would show scenes of Gandhi's pretty teenage girl followers fighting "hysterically" [the word was used] for the honor of sleeping naked with the Mahatma and cuddling the septuagenarian in their arms. (Gandhi was "testing" his vow of chastity in order to gain moral strength for his mighty struggle with Jinnah [the first president of Pakistan].) When told there was a man named Freud who said that, despite his declared intention, Gandhi might actually be *enjoying* the caresses of the naked girls, Gandhi continued, unperturbed. Nor, frankly, did I expect to see Gandhi giving daily enemas to all the young girls in his ashrams (his daily greeting was, "Have you had a good bowel movement this morning, sisters?"), nor see the girls giving him his daily enema. Although Gandhi seems to have written less about home rule for India than he did about enemas, and excrement, and latrine cleaning ("the bathroom is a temple. It should be so clean and inviting that anyone would enjoy eating there"), I confess such scenes might pose problems for a Western director.[15]

But could not one find "dirt" on any great figure? Not so much. The next chapter examines the lives of some representative Christian teachers, such as Jonathan Edwards, C. S. Lewis, and Billy Graham. If they were found to act as Gandhi did, they would be discredited and scorned immediately

IGNOBLE TEACHERS

E. Michael Jones and Paul Johnson deserve special attention in this vein. Their work has done much to expose the pious frauds that set the ideological table for today. Jones, a Roman Catholic priest, has argued in *Degenerate Moderns* that "modernity" is basically "rationalized sexual misbehavior" and has devoted a chapter each to nine exemplars. He tries to show that key ideologues have come up with their ungodly theories after becoming decadent and that their theories, vocabularies, and prescriptions are efforts to excuse or normalize their sins. Turning Richard Weaver's maxim, "Ideas have consequences," on its head, one might say that Jones teaches, "Consequences have ideas." In other words people make a moral mess of themselves, and then they must fabricate systems of thought to exonerate themselves. Against those who say that one's private life is irrelevant to their intellectual products, Jones argues that it makes enormous difference.

Intellectuals written by British historian Paul Johnson, is "an examination of the moral and judgmental credentials of certain leading intellectuals to give advice to humanity on how to conduct its affairs."[16] These "shapers of the modern world" have taken it on themselves to demean traditional morality and to set themselves up as the new arbiters of what is worthy. The problem is that they were moral degenerates in their own lives and scarcely qualified to tell others what is best.

Examples drawn from these two men and their signature works are discussed throughout the pages below in the personalities featured from philosophy, the arts, popular culture, religion, and activism.

As Jones has argued in *Degenerate Moderns*, sexual immorality is common among non-Christian and anti-Christian ideologues. Indeed he claims that it is the engine that drives their philosophizing. Be that as it may, in many of the examples given below, references are made to this sort of tawdriness. And while there is also talk of drunkenness, mendacity, tax evasion, and even murder, sexual issues continue to surface. This is not intended to stir the pot with salacious material. The fact is that when one's mind is deluded and his conscience seared, sexual sin is a regular concomitant.

IDEOLOGUES, SOCIAL SCIENTISTS, AND ACTIVISTS

Mao Tse-Tung

Most are familiar with masses of Chinese lifting up copies of the *Little Red Book* of the quotations of Chairman Mao, a book containing such moral guidance as "Do not hit or swear at people" and "Do not damage crops."[17] Unfortunately the author of those sayings was a monster, one who broke every one of the Ten Commandments in striking fashion, including casting himself as something of a deity, with worshipful images of himself everywhere throughout his realm.[18] Above all, he is responsible for the "peacetime" death of 70 million of his people.[19] But to complement this murderous record, he confiscated whatever property he pleased for his own residences,[20] had orgies with young girls,[21] and refused to visit his mother on her deathbed, lest he be left with an unpleasant image of her.[22] This was not surprising behavior for a man who in his youth wrote, "Of course there are people and objects in the world, but they are all there only for me. . . . People like me only have a duty to ourselves; we have no duty to other people."[23]

Margaret Mead

At the close of the 1920s Barnard- and Columbia-trained anthropologist Margaret Mead became the toast of the intellectual elites. Her book *Coming of Age in Samoa* purported to show that the "unspoiled" South Sea islanders were sexually promiscuous and comfortable with adultery. Mead was thrilled to report, "Romantic love as it occurs in our civilization, inextricably bound up with ideas of monogamy, exclusiveness, jealousy and undeviating fidelity does not occur in Samoa."[24] And she observed that for the Samoan child,

> Sex is a natural, pleasurable thing; the freedom with which it may be indulged in is limited by just one consideration, social status. Chiefs' daughters and chiefs' wives should indulge in no extra-marital experiments. . . . Every one in the community agrees about the matter, the only dissenters are the missionaries who dissent so vainly that their protests are unimportant.[25]

Those pesky missionaries. She habitually found fault with them, except for their teaching of "the brotherhood of men and the fatherhood of God."[26] Life used to be so simple before they came, when there were accepted avenues for promiscuity. Now, as one native expressed it, "We are trying hard to learn the ways of Western man, but one thing we have not learned yet, and that is how to commit adultery properly."[27]

The implication was that people who wanted to throw off the stifling strictures of sexual restraint were the most natural and that those who looked down on promiscuity were repressed and repressive. This was like catnip to secular-minded

Westerners, and the praise flowed freely. A columnist for *The Nation* wrote that "somewhere in each of us, hidden among our more obscure desires and our impulses of escape, is a palmfringed South Sea island . . . , a languorous atmosphere promising freedom and irresponsibility. . . . Thither we run . . . to find love which is free, easy and satisfying."[28] Psychologist/anthropologist Samuel D. Schmalhausen even played Mead's findings off against the teachings of Christianity, "Samoa or Calvary: happy-go-lucky felicity or tragic intensity," and he made his own choice, "Back to the South Sea Isles!—to "naturalness and simplicity and sexual joy."[29]

The problem was that her findings were bogus. Anthropologist Derek Freeman, who spent far more time than Mead in Samoa, demonstrated that pre-Christian Samoa was serious about sexual morality and that they guarded "the virginity of daughters and sisters with a vengeance."[30] It turns out that the Samoans were putting her on. But Jones suggests that she was not simply duped; rather the "findings" served her unholy purposes. He claims that "cultural relativism, as propounded by Margaret Mead, was nothing more than a clever rationalization for her own adultery. What better way to salve the conscience than to find that Samoans, the natural man, don't take adultery seriously."[31] For as a young married anthropologist, she carried on illicit sexual affairs with two other anthropologists, Edward Sapir and Ruth Benedict.[32]

Though she kept her lesbian forays as confidential as possible, she made public statements excusing such behavior. She told the Washington Press Club that "rigid heterosexuality is a perversion of nature." In *Redbook* she spoke of "the well-documented, normal human capacity to love members of both sexes"; and she once argued that "an ideal society would consist of people who were homosexual in their youth, again in old age, and heterosexual in the middle of their lives."[33]

Alfred Kinsey

Like Margaret Mead, Indiana University sex researcher Alfred Kinsey was adored by the promiscuous. Not content to report on sexual behavior, he moved on to ethics, proclaiming, "What is abomination to one may be a worthwhile part of the next individual's life," and "Our conceptions of right and wrong, normal and abnormal, are seriously challenged by the variation studies."[34] In other words, if people depart from the norm, then the norm is invalid. (As E. Michael Jones notes, this logic would lead to the statement that truth telling must be an invalid norm since so many people lie.)

Kinsey's major book, *Sexual Behavior in the Human Male*, published in 1948, sold 200,000 copies within two months of its release.

> Kinsey found a widespread violation of traditional sexual standards with regard to masturbation, petting, and premarital or extramarital sex. He delved into more controversial

subjects by introducing his famous heterosexual-homosexual continuum, suggesting that pre-marital chastity hindered sexual fulfillment, and exploring the nature of orgasms.[35]

Hugh Hefner, who published *Playboy* magazine, testified, "Kinsey had a tremendous impact on me."[36] Indeed he said that Kinsey's book on female sexual behavior was "the foundation of his 'philosophy.'"[37] By arguing that "illicit" sexual behavior was rampant, Kinsey emboldened Hefner to press for sexual liberation as normal and free from hypocrisy. Consequently Hefner gave the Kinsey Institute thousands of dollars for more sex research.[38]

Kinsey was not only a theoretician; he was also a practitioner of the *Playboy* philosophy. In his research he "was both fascinated and attracted by . . . highly responsive women and had sex with a number of them."[39] And even though he was married to the same woman for 35 years, he had a history of homosexual practice.[40]

Kinsey was fascinated with those who departed from the norm, often traveling to Chicago to gather the sexual histories of homosexuals and prostitutes, his two favorite subject pools in addition to prison inmates. His interest ran well beyond the academic to the prurient, with his devoting as much as 700 hours to one homosexual, who enjoyed Kinsey's continual "shop talk" about sex.[41]

This fixation on the deviant skewed his results, as did his "lack of an adequate sample, too broad projections from the data to a larger population"[42] and his indifference to the fact that those most willing to reveal their deepest, darkest sexual secrets were not likely the typical man on the street. Noted psychologist Abraham Maslow, along with colleague James Sakoda, noted this research flaw in a 1952 article in *The Journal of Abnormal and Social Psychology*:

> The bias introduced into a sex study by the use of volunteers is, in general, in the direction of inflating the percentage reporting unconventional or disapproved sexual behavior. . . . The more timid and retiring individuals, evidently, are apt to be privately, as well as socially, conforming. They are likely, it seems, to refrain from volunteering for sex studies in which they are asked embarrassing questions.[43]

Kinsey was untouched by such considerations, for he had an agenda, namely, erasing all boundaries of sexual propriety. As he said to his prisoner subjects in the *San Quentin News*,

> I have found that the sexual behavior of most men and women, including even their most cantankerous and socially impossible behavior, makes sense when one learns about the handicaps, the difficulties, the disappointments, the losses, and the tragedies which have led them into such behavior. I believe that most people would exercise greater Christian tolerance of all types of sexual behavior, if they understood, as I have begun to understand, why people do what they do sexually.[44]

Of course sympathy for the abused is in order, but when that sympathy turns into indulgence, one enters the moral relativism of the therapeutic society.

Phony research is bad enough, but Kinsey was guilty of darker transgressions. His detailed report on the capacities and physiological manifestations of orgasm in children demands the question, "How do you know this?" The only reasonable answer is that the children were manipulated by adults, a form of criminal sexual abuse.[45] Biographer James H. Jones says that Kinsey's source was a "predatory pedophile," Kenneth S. Green[46] (aka "Mr. X") who had had sexual contact with hundreds of preadolescent girls and boys. Fascinated with his "research," Kinsey treated him as an anonymous colleague.

"In his eagerness to combat prudery and to celebrate Eros, he found it increasingly difficult to maintain moral boundaries. . . . He even questioned society's condemnation of pedophilia."[47] His colleague Gebhard later recalled,

> Once in a while we'd run across an occasional incest thing or an occasional child-adult contact that seemed to work out favorably, and [Kinsey] would always tell us about this and let us know that pedophilia wasn't as black as it was painted, that it could be, under proper circumstances, beneficial or something like that.[48]

Jones concludes that

> Kinsey had long believed that human beings in a state of nature were basically pansexual. Absent social constraints, he conjectured, "natural man; would commence sexual activity early in life, enjoy intercourse with both sexes, eschew fidelity, indulge in a variety of behaviors, and be much more sexually active in general for life."[49]

Of course they continue to make hagiographical films, as with *Kinsey*, with Liam Neeson in the leading role. But among serious scholars, Kinsey's work and life have been widely discredited.

Karl Marx

Karl Marx, who magnified class hatred and called religion "the opiate of the masses," was also indifferent to sexual morality. When he impregnated the family servant, Helen Demuth, and she brought forth their illegitimate son, he denied paternity. He was afraid the scandal would undermine his leadership, and so he put the child in a foster home. Marx persuaded his colleague Friedrich Engels to claim the child as his own, but Engels refused to take the lie to his grave. Dying of throat cancer, he wrote on a slate, "Freddy is Marx's son."[50]

Marx's easy approach toward truth extended well into his political writings and speeches. Scholars have been analyzing his quotations of Adam Smith and key economic reports from the government and have found a host of misrepresentations. In a particularly egregious case he utterly falsified a statement from

Prime Minister Gladstone's budget speech of 1863, twisting it to say the opposite of what Gladstone actually said. Gladstone said that he would be troubled if the great gain in national wealth were concentrated in the hands of the comfortably rich, but he continued by reporting the good news that the lot of the average British laborer had improved over the last 20 years at a historic rate. Marx could not stand for this, for his entire project was to stir up labor unrest. So he quoted Gladstone to say, "This intoxicating augmentation of wealth and power is entirely confined to classes of property." It was a bald-faced lie that he repeated in his main work, *Capital*.[51]

In summarizing Marx's life, the anarchist Mikhail Bakunin said, "Marx does not believe in God but he believes much in himself and makes everyone serve himself. His heart is not full of love but of bitterness and he has very little sympathy for the human race."[52]

Clarence Darrow

Clarence Darrow was the ACLU lawyer known best for his efforts to humiliate antievolution lawyer William Jennings Bryan in the Scopes Trial and to deliver thrill-murderers Leopold and Loeb from the death penalty. He had no use for God, and it showed in his private life.

A hard-charging young lawyer, he drifted away from the wife of his small-town-Ohio youth, and after their divorce he "plunge[d] into the *demimonde* of Chicago" where "free love was regarded as a desirable social concomitant of anarchism."[53]

But his sins were not just sexual. In the course of the McNamara trial of 1911, he found that his defendants, a pair of unionists, had actually bombed the *Los Angeles Times* building with great loss of life, just as charged. He first joined in some jury bribing and then threw in the towel when it became clear they were going to be convicted. He had them plead guilty to avoid the death penalty. Though a hung jury spared him conviction on bribery charges, he was barred from practicing law in California again.

Many of his colleagues and admirers felt disgusted and betrayed. His law partner Edgar Lee Masters (author of the *Spoon River Anthology*) denounced him in a thinly veiled poem, "On a Bust," which contained the words,

> You can crawl
> Hungry and subtle over Eden's wall . . .
> A giant as we hoped, in truth a dwarf;
> A barrel of slop that shines on Lethe's wharf . . .[54]

Ayn Rand

Enormously influential theoretician/novelist Ayn Rand championed "the virtue of selfishness" and her books *Atlas Shrugged* and *Fountainhead* inspired generations of "self-made souls" to glory in their individualism, in which "making sacrifices for one's born or unborn children, one's elderly parents, or other family members becomes anathema."[55]

She was "a dedicated enemy of Christianity" and of altruistic "volunteerism." Indeed at the Ayn Rand Institute, "students have the opportunity to fulfill their school's volunteer requirement, ironically, by working to abolish volunteerism."[56]

Christian economist George Gilder, a pioneer of "supply-side economics," infuriated Rand by suggesting that capitalism was not selfish. In her last public speech she tore into Gilder. When Marvin Olasky of *World* magazine asked, "What got her goat?" Gilder replied:

> Altruism. She thought I was ascribing altruism to capitalism. Altruism in her theory is the foundation of socialism, and she thought capitalism is supported by egoism or by individual fulfillment above all. She was blinded in part by her atheism. If you read her books, her characters lead sacrificial lives in order to serve others in many instances. But her objectivist philosophy denies the existence of God, and she found my Christian orientation obnoxious. I said businesses succeed by serving others.[57]

Though conservatives appreciate her emphasis on taking responsibility for oneself and for courageous ingenuity, the conservative magazine *National Review* recently expressed their strong reservations over Rand with two headlines, "A Greatness Stunted by Hate" and "The Great Ghastly Rand."[58]

A large measure of her ghastliness was in her personal life, as in her relationship with family friend Nathanial Branden.

> They defended the rightness and rationality of a full-throttle sexual affair in a series of conversations with their spouses [Frank and Barbara] that went on for weeks. Each was the embodiment of the other's highest values, they pointed out in the language of *Atlas Shrugged*, and because neither suffered from an irrational mind-body split, they naturally felt sexual longing for each other. Surely Frank and Barbara, both of whom subscribed to Rand's value theory of sexuality, could understand and accept this new development. . . . A month before her fiftieth birthday, she and Nathaniel received their partners' permission to meet for sex twice a week.[59]

Margaret Sanger

Birth-control pioneer Margaret Sanger has been honored with a United States Postal Service first-day cover, bearing her image and a quote, "No woman can call herself free . . . until she can choose whether or not to be a mother."[60] (Of course, contraception is not the only way a woman "can choose whether or not to be a mother.") She also strongly promoted abortion, and that is why Planned Parenthood's highest award is named for her.

One can see why she would be so keen on contraception and abortion. She was largely indifferent to the welfare of her own children, leaving them in the care of other family members as she summered in New England and sojourned in Europe,[61] where her affairs were legion. Married with three children, she still managed to have sex with Walter Roberts, Lorenzo Portet, Havelock Ellis, Billy Williams, Hugh de Selincourt, Harold Child, H. G. Wells, Noah Slee, Angus McDonald, and Hobson Pittman.[62] She was keen on eugenics and a conspirator in abortion before it was legal.[63]

Notes

1 Richard O. Lempert, Samuel R. Gross, and James S. Liebman, *A Modern Approach to Evidence: Text, Problems, Transcripts and Cass*, 3rd ed. (St. Paul, MN: West, 2000), 252.
2 Http://www.law.cornell.edu/rules/fre/rules.htm (accessed August 23, 2010).
3 Lempert, Gross, and Liebman, *A Modern Approach to Evidence*, 420.
4 415 U.S. 308, 316 (1974).
5 Http://caselaw.lp.findlaw.com/cgi-bin/getcase.pl?court=us&vol=415&invol=308 (accessed January 3, 2011).
6 David Livingstone, *Missionary Travels and Researches in South Africa, Including a Sketch of Sixteen Years' Residence in the Interior of Africa* (New York: Harper & Brothers, 1858), 552.
7 Sarah Vowell, *The Wordy Shipmates* (New York: Penguin, 2008), 154–55.
8 Christopher Hitchens, *God Is Not Great: How Religion Poisons Everything* (New York: Twelve, 2007), 187.
9 Curt Meine, *Aldo Leopold: His Life and Work* (Madison, WI: University of Wisconsin Press, 1988), 506.
10 Richard Grenier, *The Gandhi Nobody Knows* (Nashville: Thomas Nelson, 1983), 34. The essay first appeared in *Commentary*, March 1983. The entire piece is accessible at http://history.eserver.org/ghandi-nobody-knows.
11 Ibid., 94–95.
12 Ibid.
13 Ibid., 87–88.
14 Ibid., 80.
15 Ibid., 43.
16 Paul Johnson, *Intellectuals* (New York: Harper & Row, 1988), ix.
17 Mao Tse-Tung, "Discipline," *Quotations from Chairman Mao Tse-Tung*, Sec. 26, 481. This cheap copy, with no publisher listed, was acquired in a shop in Hong Kong.
18 "Mao Versus the Decalogue: The Separation of God and State," *Kairos Journal*; http://www.kairosjournal.org/document.aspx?QuadrantID=2&DocumentID=8808&L=1&CategoryID=11&TopicID=27 (accessed June 22, 2010).
19 Jung Chang and Jon Halliday, *Mao: The Unknown Story* (New York: Alfred A. Knopf, 2005), 3.
20 Ibid., 193.
21 Li Zhisui, *The Private Life of Chairman Mao* (New York: Random House, 1994), 358.
22 Chang and Halliday, *Mao: The Unknown Story*, 18.
23 Ibid., 13.
24 Margaret Mead, *Coming of Age in Samoa: A Psychological Study of Primitive Youth for Western Civilisation* (1928; reprint, New York: HarperCollins, 2001), 139.
25 Ibid., 73.

26 Margaret Mead, *New Lives for Old: Cultural Transformation—Manus, 1928–1953* (New York: William Morrow, 1975), 342.
27 Ibid., 338.
28 Cited in E. Michael Jones, *Degenerate Moderns: Modernity as Rationalized Sexual Misbehavior* (San Francisco: Ignatius, 1993), 23.
29 Ibid.
30 Ibid., 26.
31 Ibid., 16.
32 Ibid., 35.
33 Hilary Lapsley, *Margaret Mead and Ruth Benedict: The Kinship of Women* (Amherst, MA: University of Massachusetts Press, 1999), 308.
34 Jones, *Degenerate Moderns*, 97.
35 Steven Watts, *Mr. Playboy: Hugh Hefner and the American Dream* (Hoboken, NJ: Wiley, 2008), 44.
36 Ibid., 47.
37 Jonathan Gathorn-Hardy, *Sex the Measure of All Things: A Life of Alfred C. Kinsey* (Bloomington, IN: University of Indiana Press, 2000), 439.
38 Watts, *Mr. Playboy*, 179.
39 Gathorn-Hardy, *Sex the Measure of All Things*, 315–16.
40 James H. Jones, *Alfred Kinsey: A Public/Private Life* (New York: Norton, 1997), 384–85.
41 Ibid., 112.
42 Cornelia V. Christenson, *Kinsey: A Biography* (Bloomington, IN: Indiana University Press, 1971), 143.
43 Jones, *Alfred Kinsey*, 103.
44 Alfred Kinsey, "What I Believe," in Christenson, *Kinsey: A Biography*, 207.
45 Jones, *Alfred Kinsey*, 106–7.
46 Gathorn-Hardy, *Sex the Measure of All Things*, 220–25.
47 Jones, *Degenerate Moderns*, 512.
48 Ibid.
49 Ibid.
50 Johnson, *Intellectuals*, 80.
51 Ibid., 66.
52 Ibid., 73.
53 Kevin Tierney, *Darrow: A Biography* (New York: Thomas Y. Crowell, 1979), 137–39.
54 Ibid., 277.
55 Donald DeMarco and Benjamin D. Wiker, *Architects of the Culture of Death* (San Francisco: Ignatius, 2004), 56–57.
56 Ibid., 58–59.
57 George Gilder, "Server System," interview with Marvin Olasky, *World*, December 4, 2010, 28.
58 Jason Lee Steorts, "The Great Ghastly Rand," *National Review*, August 30, 2010, 43–48.
59 Anne C. Heller, *Ayn Rand and the World She Made* (New York: Doubleday, 2009), 257.
60 "Sanger's Stamp of Approval"; http://www.nyu.edu/projects/sanger/secure/newsletter/articles/sangers_stamp.htm (accessed June 22, 2010).
61 Ellen Chesler, *Woman of Valor: Margaret Sanger and the Birth Control Movement in America* (New York: Simon & Schuster, 1992), 93, 133.
62 Ibid., 92, 108, 118, 173, 183–84, 186, 244, 349, 406.
63 Ibid., 216, 301, 417.

IMMORAL ETHICISTS: PHILOSOPHERS, THEOLOGIANS, AND ARTISTS

A S WE CONTINUE OUR list, we come to "professional ethicists," some of them the most prominent spokesmen for metaethical schools of thought, such as emotivism and utilitarianism.

PHILOSOPHERS AND THEOLOGIANS

In his book *Examined Lives: From Socrates to Nietzsche*, James Miller details the shortcomings of many who presumed to theorize about ethics. As the *Economist* reviewer observes:

> If one wanted to compile a charge-sheet against the great philosophers, to show that they were unfit to lead their own lives, let alone inspire others, this book could provide some useful evidence. There are Plato's disastrous dealings with Dionysius the Younger, the tyrannical ruler of Syracuse, and Seneca's hypocritical fawning over Nero. We hear of Aristotle's support for Alexander the Great's cruel imperialism, which sits uneasily with the philosopher's professed political ideas.[1]

Miller also gives prominent play to Rousseau, whom we'll now give a closer look:

Jean-Jacques Rousseau

French revolutionary terrorist Robespierre declared, "Rousseau is the one man who, through the loftiness of his souls and the grandeur of this character, showed himself worthy of the role of teacher of mankind," and when his ashes were transferred to the Pantheon, the president of the National Convention declared, "It is to Rousseau that is due the health-giving improvement that has transformed our morals, customs, laws, feelings, and habits."[2] Who would know from this that he was the father of both 1960s morality and social engineering?

Personally promiscuous and indifferent to parenting, no wonder he was eager to celebrate the "noble savage" and cast responsibility for child-raising onto the state.

In 1745 he took a 23-year-old laundress named Therese Levasserur as his mistress for 33 years. He said that "he never felt the least glimmering of love for her . . . the sensual needs I satisfied with her were purely sexual and nothing to do with her as an individual."[3] Together they had five children, all of which they abandoned, nameless—left at the *Hopital des Enfants-trouves*.[4]

Of course this sort of behavior would not endear him to the Christians, but even atheists found him repugnant; Scottish philosopher David Hume judged him "a monster who saw himself as the only important being in the universe." French philosopher Denis Diderot called him "deceitful, vain as Satan, ungrateful, cruel, hypocritical and full of malice." And Voltaire judged him "a monster of vanity and vileness."[5]

A. J. Ayer

Alfred Jules (A. J.) Ayer was a prominent Oxford University philosopher best known for advancing logical positivism, whose practitioners claimed that the only propositions that have any meaning are those that can be demonstrated scientifically. By this standard, "Magnesium oxide burns brightly" is meaningful, but "God exists" and "Adultery is wrong" are not. To make a moral or spiritual statement was simply to vent one's feelings.[6]

This take on God and morality fit his lifestyle beautifully, for he was a serial adulterer throughout the period of his four marriages. As one mistress put it, "Girls came and went, and came and stayed, progressively I became part of a trio, a quartet, a quintet, and sextet (plus Renée [his wife])."[7]

Bertrand Russell

As a young philosopher Bertrand Russell coauthored a magisterial work of logic, *Principia Mathematica*, with Alfred North Whitehead; but when he moved into general philosophy and ethics, he showed himself an immoralist of the first order. Whether dismissing God in his essay, "Why I Am Not a Christian," or promoting promiscuity in *Marriage and Morals*, he got it wrong again and again. In the latter book he observed that "love cannot grow and flourish while it is hedged about with taboos."[8] He, indeed, kept the taboo hedge well trimmed back; reflecting on his life, he noted, "I now believe that it is not in my nature to remain physically fond of any woman for more than seven or eight years."[9]

"His first wife Alys, a gentle, loving, generous-minded American Quaker, was the victim of her husband's growing libertinism."[10] This sort of behavior continued well into his seventies, contributing to the breakup of his third marriage. Even at this advanced age he was advising American philosopher Sidney Hook on the finer points of adultery: "Hook, if you ever take a girl to a hotel and the reception clerk seems suspicious when he gives you the price of the room have her complain loudly, 'It's *much* too expensive!' He's sure to assume she is your wife." Hook wrote that, from what he had heard, Russell, "despite his advanced age, was pursuing anything in skirts that crossed his path, and that he was carrying on flagrantly even with the servant girls, not behind [his wife's] back but before her eyes and those of his house guests."[11]

Jean-Paul Sartre

Jean-Paul Sartre was a darling of the left in the 1960s, a prophet of existentialism. He was also "supreme egotist" who, when taking as his mistress the feminist Simone de Beauvoir, author of *The Second Sex*, "outlined . . . his sexual philosophy. He was frank about his desire to sleep with many women. He said his credo was 'Travel, polygamy, transparency.'" In other words he insisted on a search for shameless variety in sexual partners; and she, a moralizing icon in her own right, agreed to it.[12]

"By the early 1940s, Sartre seems to have become dangerously well-known for seducing his own female students." As one critic put it, "We all know Monsieur Sartre. He is an odd philosophy teacher who has specialized in the study of his student's underwear."[13]

By decade's end he "took up the case of the homosexual thief, Jean Genet. . . . He wrote an enormous and absurd book about Genet, nearly 700 pages long, which was really a celebration of antinomianism, anarchy and sexual incoherence."[14] And he, like other modernist moralists, was impatient with truth when it got in the way of his ideological program. For instance he wrote, "After my first visit to the USSR in 1954, I lied. Actually, lie might be too strong a word: I wrote an article . . . where I said a number of friendly things about the USSR which I did not believe."[15] He explained that he did not want to offend his recent hosts, and he had not yet made up his mind on what he thought of the Soviet Union. So he went right ahead and said that Russians did not travel abroad because they hated to leave their wonderful land and that Russians had total freedom to criticize their government, more even than was found in Western Europe.[16] It seems then that "lied" was not too strong a word but precisely the right one.

Paul Tillich

When "theologian of modernity" Joseph Fletcher introduced his "situation ethics," it resonated with Bishop John A. T. Robinson and theologian Paul Tillich. By their lights, "the correct behaviour in a situation was to be determined not by some settled law but by the principle that 'compassion for persons overrides the law.'" Robinson called it a "dangerous ethic" (likely to provoke the "Pharisees"), but he was happy to say that "it is the only ethic for 'man come of age.'" This "ethic of love" meshed with Tillich's view that "ethics in a changing world must be understood as the ethics of the *kairos*—of the God-given moment, mediating the meeting with the eternal in the temporal."[17]

The problem was that "love in the *kairos*" turned easily into licentiousness and expediency. All sorts of moral slippage can be justified in the name of love. And slip Tillich did; or perhaps it was the other way around—that he needed to craft verbal cover for the slippage that was already happening.

At Union Theological Seminary in New York City, Tillich and Reinhold Niebuhr "had been the best of friends in the 1930s."

> But their relations were cooling even during the war and in the postwar years became increasingly strained. Their intellectual debate at midcentury was a serious one—his dialogue with Tillich, he told Scarlett, reflected age-old differences within the church—but it rested in part on a person conflict that Niebuhr could not mention in print. Tillich had for years been engaged in a succession of sexual escapades. He was not just unfaithful to his wife, Hannah: he was exuberantly, compulsively promiscuous. Niebuhr once sent one of his female students to see Tillich during his office hours. He welcomed her warmly, closed the door, and—according to the student—began fondling her. She reported the episode to Niebuhr, who never forgave Tillich.[18]

His sexual sin tracked with his heterodox theology. Tillich's personal religion was deeply infused by aesthetics and psychology and at times resembled a kind of nature worship; his ethics stressed not sin and responsibility but establishing wholeness, experiencing the fullness of being.[19]

He was "so absorbed in his senses that he downplayed the role of conscience that to Niebuhr lay at the heart of the moral life. He turned further and further away from the social and political interests they had earlier shared. 'Responsibility' for Tillich was coming to mean responsibility to one's own self: adjust, develop, reach for fulfillment. For Niebuhr, as he had preached 40 years before in his first sermon, 'he who seeks his own life shall lose it.'"[20]

John Stuart Mill

At a dinner party in the summer of 1830, utilitarian philosopher John Stuart Mill was smitten by the lovely Harriet Taylor, who unfortunately was married to a prosperous merchant with whom she had had two children.[21] But this did not stand in their way. As their "friendship" developed, they came to accept Robert Owen's loose account of sexual morality: "Chastity" he defined as "sexual intercourse with affection"; "Prostitution" was "sexual intercourse *without* affection." By this standard Mill and Taylor were able to remain chaste.

This put Mill in a dangerous position, for

> "facing a brilliant future as a moral philosopher, [he] was more vulnerable than others to the touch of scandal. Like [atheistical philosopher] Auguste Comte and his Clothilde de Vaux [who was married to another], he might easily be exposed to ignominy and even ridicule, and he had none of the invincible egoism which enabled Comte to rise above it." But Harriet was unfazed; she "went and told John Taylor that she wished him to understand she had found in Mill a being who reached more deeply into her heart than he could ever do, but that there was nothing guilty in it."[22]

For both Mill and Harriet, divorce was unthinkable, and Harriet's husband John managed to tolerate her infidelity. "Two men were devoted to her; both were distinguished, and one [John] was rich. . . . Both were perfectly content that the extraordinary equipoise should last indefinitely."[23] And so for 20 years Mill and Taylor were able to continue in "unmarried intimacy" until, after her husband's death from cancer, she finally became Mill's wife.[24]

This was tawdry behavior, not what one would expect from someone who presumes to explain the ground of morality to the world.

RELIGIOUS FIGURES

Muhammed

When he was 50, Muhammed, already married, wed a six- or seven-year-old girl named Aisha, and consummated the marriage when she was nine.[25] He "ordered assassinations of Jewish women and old men, and oversaw a mass decapitation and enslavement of hundreds of his Jewish neighbors."[26] He even commissioned the murder of women and old men in their sleep.[27] He was a supreme egotist, presenting him as the best of the best—an Arab from the best tribe and clan, the clan of which he was the very best specimen. As Gabriel allegedly told him, "I searched the earth from east to west but found no man superior to Muhammed."[28]

Joseph Smith

Suffice it to say that the founder of Mormonism was an unconscionable polygamist. In her classic biography of Joseph Smith, *No Man Knows My History*, Fawn Brodie lists his "first thirty-six wives," noting that "at least twelve were married women (with living husbands)," that there were five pairs of sisters and a mother-daughter pair, and that at least one was 15 years old.[29] He claimed to have the go-ahead from God, but of course, he did not.

ARTISTS, LITERATI, AND ENTERTAINERS

Artists, in the broadest sense of the word, are a moralizing lot but with a twist. When their message is praised as deep, righteous, or bold, they are willing to accept the approval. But when someone reduces their "prophecy" to absurdity, points out inconsistencies or absurdities, most are ready to play the "art card," saying they only meant to push the envelope, promote conversation, reflect what is happening in the culture, or express themselves—like saying "King's X" to excuse themselves from criticism. Be that as it may, they are, for better or worse, major contributors to the moral tone and conversation of a nation.

But what gives these artists and their followers any sense that they have the gravitas, insight, and personal integrity to make such pronouncements? Perhaps, if their lives were fruitful and admirable, they might be counted worthy of hearing. But many are both godless and antinomian; yet they continue to presume to carry some sort of moral authority.

The Beats

Though they saw themselves as the conscience of a new generation, the Beats were thoroughgoing decadents:

> Shortly after the famous San Francisco poetry reading, Ray ([Jack]Kerouac) makes his way to Japhy's ([Gary]Snyder's) little rented house in Berkeley, then shared with [Allen] Ginsberg. After many nights of talking Buddhism, drinking, and openly sharing sex with a girlfriend of Snyder's, they agree on a trek to the summit of the Matterhorn, high in the Sierras, around whose peak much of the novel [*The Dharma Bums*] unfolds.[30]

This is the Allen Ginsberg who was notable for "conveying Buddhist sensibility to a considerable audience."

These were the same fellows who had a "prophetic vision" along the following lines:

> I see a vision of *a great rucksack revolution* of thousands or even millions of young Americans wandering around with rucksacks, going up to mountains to pray, making children laugh and old men glad, making young girls happy and old girls happier, all of 'em Zen Lunatics who go about writing poems that happen to appear in their heads for no reason and also by being kind and also by strange unexpected acts keep giving visions of eternal freedom to everybody and all living creatures.[31]

Bloomsbury

England's Bloomsbury Group (or "Bloomsbury Grope," as one satirist expressed it) was a coterie of artists and ideologues who "sought to effect a moral and spiritual liberation . . . from those vestiges of Evangelicalism and Victorianism that still persisted in the early 20th century."[32]

In 2010 Krakow, Poland's International Cultural Centre, fielded an exhibition on this group. Given the exhibit cocurator's accurate description of their decadence, it is strange that they felt entitled to offer moral judgment to anyone.

> "The Bloomsberries have been chiefly famous for their less than conventional personal relationships," Tony Bradshaw continued. "By today's standards they may not have had a dazzling number of encounters—Frances Partridge has claimed that there was more love and less sex than people tend to assume—but the homosexuality, bisexuality or at least generous open-mindedness of many members of the group permitted a fascinating web of affairs and liaisons. These ranged from the devoted partnership of Lydia Lopokova and Maynard Keynes (who had once been almost exclusively homosexual), to the open marriage at Charleston of Clive and Vanessa Bell, to the ménage at Ham Spray where Lytton Strachey loved Ralph Partridge, who married Dora Carrington, who loved only Lytton (and who took her [own] life after his death to prove it). With Virginia Woolf's own suicide, and the death of Vanessa's son Julian in the Spanish Civil War, the Bloomsbury story is laced with serious drama as well as less consequential intrigues."[33]

They were proudly godless and contemptuous of those who had faith. Virginia Woolf wrote the following about the poet T. S. Eliot's conversion. He had been in the Bloomsbury circle, but that came to an end.

> "I have had a most shameful and distressing interview with poor dear Tom Eliot," wrote Woolf, "who may be called dead to us all from this day forward. He has become an Anglo-Catholic, believes in God and immortality, and goes to church. I was really shocked. A corpse would seem to me more credible than he is. I mean, there's something obscene in a living person sitting by the fire and believing in God."[34]

Francis Bacon

Though they are quick to disavow philosophical intent and to grant themselves immunity from rigorous scrutiny, artists push a worldview, with attendant moral judgment. A case in point is the twentieth-century British painter Francis Bacon (not to be confused with the sixteenth-century English philosopher by the same name). In the summer of 2009, the Metropolitan Museum of Art in New York City displayed a massive collection of his art, and on the cover of their exhibition book, they featured one of his screaming-popes works. Bacon, an atheist, took special delight in presenting twisted versions of El Greco's portrait of Pope Innocent X. This portrait puts the pontiff in very bad light.

This goes down well in New York and not because there is a huge audience of Protestants who object to the papacy. This is a slam against religion itself, and those who shun God are eager to heap praise on Bacon for his "prophetic" treatment of religion. But one may ask, From what lofty perch is Bacon making his judgments?

Actually it is not so lofty after all. His was a dissolute life, as British painter Andrew Forge observed: "[I never had the] energy Francis got from the feeling of profligate self-waste that so many of his circle gave off . . . feeling of just flushing themselves down the drain, in a way, with so much flourish and abandon, which he admired tremendously."[35]

New York magazine's coverage of the show ran under the title, "Sacred Monster," with the opening question, "On the eve of the Met's giant retrospective, a critic asks: Was Francis Bacon really the greatest painter of the twentieth century, or just a fascinating mess?"[36] As the article shows, when talking about his character, the word "monster" works better than "mess." "Those who knew the artist—some of them his friends—described him variously as 'devil,' 'whore,' 'one of the world's leading alcoholics,' 'bilious ogre,' . . . and 'a drunken, faded sodomite swaying nocturnally through the lowest dives and gambling dens of Soho.'"

Henrik Ibsen

This Danish playwright was instrumental in advancing the permissive society, where traditional inhibitions were cast aside and the concerns of society marginalized. He cast aside his own inhibitions in fathering an illegitimate child through an affair with the housemaid.

> This girl, like Lenchen [Rousseau's mistress], behaved with the greatest discretion. She went back to her parents to have the child and never sought to get anything out of the father. But under Norwegian law, and by order of the local council, Ibsen was forced to pay maintenance until Hans Jacob was fourteen. Poor already, he resented bitterly this drain on his meager salary and never forgave either the child or the mother. Like Rousseau, like Marx, he never acknowledged Hans Jacob, took any interest in him or gave him the smallest voluntary assistance, financial or otherwise. The boy became a blacksmith and lived with his mother until he was twenty-nine. She went blind, and when her parents' house was taken away from them, she went to live in a hut. The son scrawled on the rock "Syltefjell"—Starvation Hill. Elsie too died destitute, aged seventy-four, on 5 Jun 1892, and it is unlikely that Ibsen heard of her death.[37]

He was also a hypocrite and coward of the first order. Though an atheist who hated the king, he begged a pension from Carl XV, referring to his "God-given" calling.[38] And when two colleagues were arrested for some anonymous articles he had written for a radical newspaper, he remained silent. "Terrified, he lay low for many weeks. The two men were sentenced and spent seven years in jail. Ibsen was too cowardly either to come forward on their behalf or to protest against the savage punishment."[39]

Ozzy Osbourne

Rock stars are easy prey for criticism, and none more so than Ozzy Osbourne, the lead singer of Black Sabbath, a group assuming a satanist posture. He writes,

> She was a Catholic, my mum, but she wasn't religious. None of the Osbournes went to church—although for a while I went to a Church of England Sunday school, 'cos there was [expletive] else to do, and they gave you free tea and biscuits. Didn't do me much good, all those mornings spent learning Bible stories and drawing pictures of the baby Jesus. I don't think the vicar would be proud of his ex-pupil, put it that way.[40]

Not proud, indeed. First, Ozzy is vile of speech. Page after page, his autobiography is full of profanity and obscenity, including a particular weakness for use of the "F-bomb" as an adjective, as in six times on page 26.

Of course one can overdo harsh judgment: "I can honestly say that we never took the black magic stuff seriously for one second. We just liked how theatrical it was."[41] In fact the faux satanism would prove problematical for them, attracting disciples of Anton LaVey, whom they found to be "loonies," especially in the wake of the Manson murders. But they had it coming, given their marketing choices.[42]

If their satanism was a fiction, their self-destruction was not. Once in America, Ozzy writes, "It didn't take us long to start getting into drugs big time."[43]

In 1972, they called their new album *Snowblind* in honor of cocaine. He writes,

> By now, I was putting so much of the stuff up my nose that I had to smoke a bag of dope every day just to stop my heart from exploding. . . . Booze, drugs, food, groupies—everything was delivered. On a good day there'd be bowls of white power and crates of booze in every room, and all these random rock 'n' rollers and chicks in bikinis hanging around the place—in the bedrooms, on the sofas, outside on the recliners—all of them as high as we were.[44]

After near ruin, Ozzie went through rehab, but his slurred speech and goofy ways are acknowledged results of rampant drug use. He even jokes about it. In the opening of his book, he writes:

> Other people's memories of the stuff in this book might not be the same as mine. I ain't gonna argue with 'em. Over the past forty years I've been loaded on booze, coke, acid, Quaaludes, cough mixture, heroin, Rohypnol, Klonopin, Vicodin, and too many other heavy-duty substances to list in this footnote. On more than a few occasions I was on all of those at the same time. I'm not the [expletive] *Encyclopaedia Britannica*, put it that way.

> What you read here is what dribbled out of the jelly I call my brain when I asked it for my life story. Nothing more, nothing less.[45]

Nevertheless while he was turning his brain to jelly, and, incidentally suffering from the incontinence that comes from alcohol abuse,[46] he could sing of his drug use in *Snowblind*, using words of defiance, self-satisfaction, and insult:

> Don't you think I know what I'm doing
> Don't tell me that it's doing me wrong
> You're the one who's really a loser
> This is where I feel I belong.[47]

And of course he felt well qualified to pass judgment on the military (including the leadership of General Petraeus, one must suppose):

> Generals gathered in their masses
> Just like witches at black masses
> Evil minds that plot destruction
> Sorcerers of death's construction
> In the fields the bodies burning
> As the war machine keeps turning
> Death and hatred to mankind
> Poisoning their brainwashed minds, oh Lord, yeah![48]

But, when asked if "War Pigs" is antiwar, he said he thinks "war is just a part of human nature."[49] In fact he has a kind of fatalism: "I've come to believe that everything in life is worked out in advance. So whenever [expletive] happens, there ain't nothing you can do about it. You've just got to ride it out."[50]

No one knows what he thinks his "prophetic" words are meant to accomplish. As for his metaphysics,

> The bottom line is I don't believe in a bloke called God in a white suit who sits on a fluffy cloud any more than I believe in a bloke called the Devil with a three-pronged fork and a couple of horns. But I believe that there's day, there's night, there's good, there's bad, there's black, there's white. If there is a God, it's nature. If there's a Devil, it's nature.[51]

Clearly, Ozzy is an addled mess, but thousands count him an adept.

Others

Paul Johnson's list goes on and on, chapter after chapter—to Romantic poet Percy Shelley, who approved of incest;[52] leftist man of letters, E. O. Wilson, who did not bother to pay income taxes between 1946 and 1955;[53] and communist playwright Lillian Hellman, of whom Mary McCarthy said, "Every word she writes is a lie, including 'and' and 'the.'"[54]

E. Michael Jones's treatment of "degenerate moderns" also extends to Sigmund Freud, whose relationship with his sister-in-law Mina Bernays was questionable and who was enamored of cocaine;[55] and to Pablo Picasso, whose cubism Jones connects to his loathing of used-up lovers.[56]

Biographies of the lost are also instructive: Sinclair Lewis, the writer who defamed revivalism in *Elmer Gantry*, halfheartedly fought "a losing struggle with alcoholism," traversed "stormy marriages," and tended to "flirt with younger women"[57]; and "Hanoi Jane" Fonda, who derided America for its involvement in the Vietnam War, remembers fondly her morning, over-coffee conversations with prostitutes whom her husband Roger Vadim had brought in the night before for threesomes in their bed.[58]

The list is endless, and the question persists: How can these outlandish, crusading, and unrepentant sinners continue to enjoy acclaim when a whiff of the same behavior among evangelicals would mean instant and devastating defamation in the media and in the halls of academia? The disparity is worth pointing out, and the striking differences in lifestyles can be employed in the apologetic enterprise.

Notes

1 "Philosophy as Inspiration: The Consolations of Understanding," review of James Miller, *Examined Lives: From Socrates to Nietzsche*, in *The Economist* (January 27, 2001), http://www.economist.com/node/18007809 (accessed January 31, 2001).

2 Paul Johnson, *Intellectuals* (New York: Harper & Row, 1988), 2–3.

3 Ibid., 19.

4 Ibid., 21.

5 Ibid., 26.

6 A. J. Ayer, *Part of My Life* (London: Collins, 1977), 205.

7 Ben Rogers, *A. J. Ayer: A Life* (New York: Grove, 1999), 240.

8 Bertrand Russell, *Marriage and Morals* (New York: Horace Liveright, 1957), 285.

9 Andrew Brink, *Bertrand Russell: A Psychobiography of a Moralist* (Atlantic Highlands, NJ: Humanities, 1989), 101.

10 Johnson, *Intellectuals*, 212.

11 Ibid., 218.

12 Ibid., 225, 235.

13 Ibid., 238.

14 Ibid., 242.

15 Ibid., 244.

16 Ibid., 243–44.

17 Peter J. Gomes, "Honest to God and the Dangerous Ethic," in *Honest to God 40 Years On*, ed. Colin Slee (London: SCM, 2004), 76–78.

18 Richard Fox, *Reinhold Niebuhr: A Biography* (San Francisco: Harper & Row, 1985), 257.

19 Ibid.

20 Ibid., 258.

21 Michael St. John Packe, *The Life of John Stuart Mill* (New York: Macmillan, 1954), 111.

22 Ibid., 138–39.

23 Ibid., 327.

24 Ibid., 317.

25 Mark Durie, *The Third Choice: Islam, Dhimmitude and Freedom* (Melbourne, Australia: Deror, 2010), 52.

26 Ibid., 56.

27 Ibid., 110.

28 Ibid., 88.

29 Fawn M. Brodie, *No Man Knows My History: The Life of Joseph Smith* (New York: Knopf, 1971), 334–37.

30 Tom Hayden, *The Long Sixties: 1960 to Barack Obama* (Boulder, CO: Paradigm, 2009), 163.

31 Ibid., 163–64 (italics his).

32 Gertrude Himmelfarb, "From Clapham to Bloomsbury: A Genealogy of Morals," *Commentary* 79 (February 1985): 38.

33 "British Bohemia: The Bloomsbury Group of Virginia Woolf," *Krakow Post*, September 14, 2010; http://www.krakowpost.com/article/2326 (accessed September 24, 2010).

34 Virginia Woolf, "The Long Journey Home," review of Peter Hitchens's *The Rage Against God: How Atheism Led Me to Faith* in *The American Spectator*, December 2010: 85.

35 Andrew Forge, cited in *Francis Bacon*, ed. Matthew Gale and Chris Stephens (London: Tate, 2008), 261.

36 Jerry Saltz, "Sacred Monster," *New York*, May 17, 2009; http://nymag.com/arts/art/profiles/56786/ (accessed December 7, 2010).

37 Johnson, *Intellectuals*, 92.

38 Ibid., 93.

39 Ibid., 103.

40 Ozzy Osbourne with Charles Ayers, *I Am Ozzy* (New York: Grand Central, 2009), 6.

41 Ibid., 99.

42 Ibid., 120–22.

43 Ibid., 123.

44 Ibid., 129–30.

45 Ibid., introductory remarks.

46 Ibid., 302.

47 "Snowblind" lyrics; http://www.elyrics.net/read/b/black-sabbath-lyrics/snowblind-lyrics.html (accessed August 23, 2010).

48 "War Pigs"; http://www.elyrics.net/read/b/black-sabbath-lyrics/war-pigs-lyrics.html (accessed August 23, 2010).

49 Osbourne, *I Am Ozzy*, 295.

50 Ibid., 388.

51 Ibid., 294–95.

52 Johnson, *Intellectuals*, 35.

53 Ibid., 266.

54 Ibid., 302.

55 E. Michael Jones, *Degenerate Moderns: Modernity as Rationalized Sexual Misbehavior* (San Francisco: Ignatius, 1993), 189, 196.

56 Ibid., chap. 7.

57 Richard Lingeman, *Sinclair Lewis: Rebel from Main Street* (New York: Random House, 2002), 187.

58 Jane Fonda, *My Life So Far* (New York: Random House, 2005), 154–55.

The Moral Authority of Christian Teachers: Biblical Characters

J UST AS IT IS pertinent to examine the moral credentials of enemies of the faith, it is fair to ask whether those who presume to teach Christian ethics are worthy souls. Of course believers do not claim to be perfect. (Though a perfectionist strain is taught in some churches, this perspective is neither typical nor biblically sustainable.) Rather they rejoice that the righteousness of Christ has been imputed to them by virtue of their faith in his redeeming work. But they also believe that, as born-again children of God, they are undergoing sanctification. And it should definitely show.

GOD

In attacking Christianity atheists sometimes argue that the God of the Bible is unworthy of admiration, if not downright abhorrent. Bertrand Russell did this in his essay, "Why I Am Not a Christian," and Christopher Hitchens's book title, *God Is Not Great: How Religion Poisons Everything*, signals his eagerness to disparage the Almighty. So to argue the moral qualifications of Christian ethicists, one must first argue that the chief "ethicist," God himself, is moral.

The Problem of Evil

Throughout church history skeptics have argued that believers hold inconsistent beliefs, namely, the omnipotence and goodness of God. Pointing to everything from a child dying of leukemia to a fawn caught on a barbed-wire fence to the Lisbon earthquake of 1755 to the Holocaust, skeptics say that if God could have stopped or ameliorated the suffering and he did not, then he was morally lax. Or if he faltered in doing the best he could, he was less than sovereign. Either way, orthodoxy fails.

Theists have responded in a dozen more or less thoughtful ways throughout the centuries—whether through describing evil as mere privation (Augustine), casting a vision of "the best of all possible worlds" (Gottfried Leibniz), constructing a "soul-making theodicy" (John Hick), or presenting a "free-will defense" (Alvin Plantinga). The alternatives and variations are legion.[1]

The Problem of "Evil Decrees"

While some critics are silenced by the argument that Auschwitz happened because God gave Hitler and the Nazis free wills, they are still indignant that God would himself command "genocide in Canaan" and consign people to an eternal hell, with no possibility of saving reform. By their account only a monster could decree such as this.

Again useful answers are legion. Regarding hell, some point to the infinite enormity of sin (ignored or denied by sinful man) and argue that only an infinitely enormous punishment will suffice. Others suggest that man's hateful obstinance each "day" in hell earns the next day's punishment, and so ad infinitum. Others imagine the misery of the damned were they to be transported to the eternal "church service" in heaven; all that singing and fellowshipping would be a torment to them.

Of course some professed Christians simply bail out and deny the reality of eternal suffering for the lost. They become universalists or annihilationists of one sort or another, abandoning the Bible to fashion a more amiable theology. But this is neither necessary nor admirable. And the same goes for their attempts to deny that God really told Joshua and Saul to wipe out certain people, children included. These hermeneutical "spin doctors" may quiet tender hearts, but they will not advance our understanding of and love for God.

One approach to explaining the difficult decrees is to use the skeptics' own values and principles to give them pause. As seen earlier, one of the enormous problems for the utilitarian is the lack of foreknowledge; he is simply in no position to say how things will work out, so his project of maximizing happiness is groping around in the dark.

God, on the other hand, knows all that will eventuate, either by prescience or predetermination to act on a certain course. So he well knew the consequences if Israel intermingled with the Canaanites or spared their children. Perhaps "sensitive" Israelites would have made allowance for these children to choose the religion of their departed parents; perhaps the evolving wrath of these orphans toward their parents' killers would be a ticking time bomb. Who can say? But it can be said that such was possible.

And one need not cast the Lord as a "Jeremy Bentham," concerned with maximizing pleasure of all sorts. Why not imagine him closer to Mill, who recognized that quality mattered, that it was "better to be Socrates dissatisfied than a pig satisfied"? Might the refined happiness he treasures in us come from our being filled with the Spirit in sacrificial service out of love for neighbor and gratitude to Christ? Or to put it another way, might God be making diamonds instead of mushrooms, whereby the joy of the martyr in the coliseum outweighs the pleasure of the giggling spectator stuffing himself with Roman delicacies in the stands?

At any rate, we're familiar with cases where extreme, even appalling, measures make sense when you have the whole story. For instance, some perfectly healthy women have "prophylactic mastectomies" when they discover they have the BCA1 breast cancer gene. By this radical surgery, the hope to become "previvors," avoiding the fate of their grandmothers, mothers, and aunts who have succumbed to malignancy.[2] The agony of the decision is compounded by uncertainty over whether the disease would actually eventuate or whether a future cure might be available if it did.

When God effects prophylaxis in his dealings with men, he knows precisely what the eventualities would have been had he not acted. But from our human standpoint, we're often like primitives having no knowledge whatsoever of DNA, yet passing judgment on medical procedures based on genetic testing. But if we've seen the same surgeon save our life and the lives of others, we may reasonably assume that he's up to good things when we see him use a shocking new procedure. So, too, are we inclined to trust that God was honorable in his battle orders to Joshua as the Israelites entered the Promised Land.

The Problem of God's Concern with His Own Glory

The Bible is full of divinely inspired directives to glorify God, as in 1 Chr 16:29: "Ascribe to Yahweh the glory of His name; bring an offering and come before Him. Worship the LORD in the splendor of His holiness." But this seems a bit unsavory in human terms. What kind of person would seek his own glory, even commanding people to worship him?

A skeptic could ask, "Does God, who commands his believers to be humble, to be less concerned about themselves and more concerned about others, and to desire to serve him, then reveal that his own glory and his own arbitrary will are more important to him than is the welfare of his creatures?"[3]

But surely misses the point. As Millard Erickson puts it, "For us to put any finite object, whether ourselves or some other human, ahead of God would be wrong, for it would be a denial of the very structure of reality."[4] And, of course, a demand for respect is perfectly compatible with loving care, even among humans. The earthly father who insists that his young son say, "Yes, Sir" and not hail him with "Hey, Fred" is not likely on an "ego trip." He simply understands that it's good for the child to assume a posture of respect and admiration for his parents, particularly when they are respectable and admirable (as is the case with God—indeed, infinitely so).

Again, fruitful discussion of such "problems" ranges well beyond the reach of a few paragraphs in this chapter. Many believers have written far and wide and well on these issues, and God's virtue is ably defended in the literature.

Of course, God is not holding his breath to be sure he passes muster with the skeptic; and as he demonstrated in Job, he does not sit passively while unhappy men presume to put him on trial (cp., Job 38:4, "Where were you when I established the earth?"). Nevertheless he gave people wits and the heart to bring him glory, and so believers venture some answers in the face of charges that the God they claim to represent is an impossibility.

JESUS

Of course those who understand and accept the Christ of Col 1:15–20 know that charges brought against God are brought against Jesus too—and the answers are appropriately the same. But skeptics have expressed a particular admiration for Jesus.

Voltaire

In his *Treatise on Tolerance*, Voltaire upbraids Roman Catholics and Protestants for treating each other wretchedly. He began this work with the terrible story of the eighteenth-century execution of a Protestant, Jean Calas, in the city of Toulouse. Falsely accused of murdering his son to keep him from converting to Catholicism, he fell victim to religious fanaticism.

In indicting these "Christians," Voltaire devoted a chapter to the example of Christ himself, who taught nothing that could be interpreted as a license to act vindictively toward one's neighbor. And, Voltaire noted, Jesus himself was not one to attack his foes, even though he was unfairly accused. In fact, Voltaire concluded, "If you want to be like Jesus Christ, better be a martyr than a hangman."[5]

Thomas Jefferson

Though Thomas Jefferson was unhappy with Paul's writings (and, unwittingly, unhappy with Jesus' will on the matters Paul addressed through "God-breathed" Scripture), he had nothing but praise for Jesus, whose "character" he sought to place "in its true and high light, as no impostor Himself, but a great Reformer of the Hebrew code of religion."[6]

In his *Syllabus of an Estimate of the Merit of the Doctrines of Jesus, Compared with Those of Others*, he writes,

> His [Jesus'] moral doctrines, relating to kindred and friends were more pure and perfect than those of the most correct of the philosophers, and greatly more so than those of the Jews: and they went far beyond both in inculcating universal philanthropy, not only to kindred and friends, to neighbors and countrymen, to all mankind. . . . He pushed his scrutinies into the heart of man; erected his tribunal in the region of his thoughts, and purified the waters at the fountainhead.[7]

OTHER BIBLICAL PERSONS

Under God, the prophets and apostles are the prime moral teachers in Christianity, and it is fair to examine their lives. Here is a sampling of some of those personalities.

Moses

Adopted by Pharaoh's daughter, Moses enjoyed a place of great privilege in Egypt, but he walked away, an act of spiritual integrity celebrated in Heb 11:24–27:

> By faith Moses, when he had grown up, refused to be called the son of Pharaoh's daughter and chose to suffer with the people of God rather than to enjoy the short-lived pleasure of sin. For he considered reproach because of the Messiah to be greater wealth than the treasures of Egypt, since his attention was on the reward. By faith he left Egypt behind, not being afraid of the king's anger, for he persevered as one who sees Him who is invisible.

He was to be "the great lawgiver," chosen to receive the Ten Commandments on Mount Sinai. And the demonstration of his greatness began with his willingness to step outside his comfort zone. Charles Swindoll elaborates:

> Visualize this strong young man, Hebrew within but fully Egyptian without. He would easily pass for the up-and-coming Pharaoh. . . . He knew nothing but the land of the Nile. He had never been to Canaan; he knew only Egypt. But he left it. . . . He burned the bridges. He didn't look back. He did not fear the wrath of the king. He simply took off.[8]

Elijah

When believers hear the name Elijah, most think first of his "duel" with the false prophets of Mount Carmel. Here he showed his mettle, "speaking truth to power," but exhibiting more than courage. Charles Swindoll speaks of him, recalling the words of James, who said that Elijah "was a man with nature like ours"—and not "a model which no man can match":

That means he was flesh and blood, muscle and bone. As we're about to see, he got really discouraged, and he had some huge disappointments. He had faults and failures and doubts. He was just a man, with a nature like yours and mine. He may have been a man of heroism and humility, but never forget his humanity. Elijah was our kind of man!

So what kind of man was Elijah?

Well, he wasn't afraid to square off with the king of the land or take on the prophets of Baal. The guy had guts, no question. But he wasn't too powerful to pray . . . or too confident to wait . . . or too sophisticated to see rain in the tiny cloud . . . or too proud to pull up his robe and run like a spotted ape down the mountain in the rain and mud, like the roadrunner thinking, "C'mon, Ahab . . . catch me if you can!"[9]

John the Baptist

Longtime Edinburgh University professor Alexander Whyte wrote this about the man who baptized Jesus: "John thought about no one else, and spake about no one else, for all these endless years, but the Lamb of God."[10]

Charles Spurgeon added, "John sought no honor among men. He was delighted to say concerning our Lord Jesus, 'He must increase, but I must decrease' (John 3:30). . . . A man is not to be estimated according to his rank but according to his character."[11]

Furthermore, he was ascetic in his devotion: "Throughout his whole life, he was a Nazarite, drinking neither wine nor strong drink. After spending his earliest years in his father's house, he retired to the desert, where he lived on locusts and wild honey, and was occupied in meditation and prayer. His garments were of camel hair, and he wore a leather girdle."[12]

And so single-minded was he in his devotion to the Word that, at the cost of his life, he told the ruler Herod that he had sinned for stealing his brother's wife (Mark 6:17–29).

John

John's writing, whether in his Gospel or letters, is full of talk of light, life, and love. Whyte continues,

At the Last Supper, and as soon as Judas had gone out, Jesus said to the 11, "A New Commandment I give unto you, that ye love one another. As I have loved you, that ye also love one another. By this shall all men know that ye are my disciples, if ye have love one to another." Eleven thoughtful and loving hearts heard that new commandment and the comfort that accompanied it. But in no other heart did that Divine seed fall into such good ground.[13]

Stephen

The church's first martyr, Stephen, was stoned to death in Jerusalem for boldly preaching the gospel to the "stiff-necked" Sanhedrin in Acts 6–7. But instead of dying with curses on his lips, he showed an uncanny spirit of love.

Clarence Macartney reported on John's remarkable demeanor, drawing from the life of another minister:

> Joseph Parker, at one time the celebrated preacher in London's City Temple, as a young man used to debate on the town green with infidels and atheists. One day an infidel shouted at him, "What did Christ do for Stephen when he was stoned?" Parker replied, "He gave him grace to pray for those who stoned him." Stephen's prayer for those who stoned him was in reality a greater evidence of the power and presence of Christ in his life than any miracle of deliverance would have been.[14]

As bold as Stephen was, it is easy to forget that he also had the heart of a servant; he was no prima donna. When the Twelve were overwhelmed with logistical tensions within the church, Stephen was one of "seven men of good reputation, full of the Spirit and wisdom" who were chosen to look after church economics so that the preachers could focus on their preaching (Acts 6:1–7).

Candor, Self-Effacement, and Verisimilitude

Reading both the Old and New Testaments, one cannot help but be struck by the way it presents its leaders, "warts and all," as noted above in connection with Elijah. Indeed, study Bibles often summarize the characters' weaknesses right along with their strengths: Abraham's tendency to prevaricate under pressure; Jonah's sulkiness; Thomas's pessimism; and Timothy's timidity.[15]

Alan Redpath expressed it this way: "The Bible never flatters its heroes. It tells us the truth about each one of them in order that against the background of human breakdown and failure we may magnify the grace of God and recognize that it is the delight of the Spirit of God to work upon the platform of human possibilities."[16]

One cannot help but compare this approach to that of other "prophets," whether religious or secular. Where do you find similar humility and self-mortification in the Mohammed of the Koran ("may Allah exalt his mention")?[17] Read typically effusive words over the perfections of Mohammed, and then consider how absurd this sort of comprehensively glowing talk would sound in reference to Moses or Isaiah.

Apply the same standard to the writings of the Buddha, Freud, Marx, Russell, Nietzsche, and Mao. These "scriptures" cannot match the peculiar moral dignity found in the candor and humility of the Bible.

David

King David is renowned for his exalted teaching regarding God in the Psalms. But he was also a man with tragic weakness, and no one knew it better than David himself. He stole Bathsheba from Uriah, tried to cover up the sin, and then ordered a murder to facilitate the theft. But he crumbled when the prophet Nathan confronted him with his sin. Instead of retaliating, doing harm to the messenger, he wrote Psalm 51 in anguished shame. Unlike Margaret Mead and Alfred Kinsey, he made no effort to dismiss the standards in order to justify his deeds:

> Be gracious to me, God,
> according to Your faithful love;
> according to Your abundant compassion,
> blot out my rebellion.
> Wash away my guilt
> and cleanse me from my sin.
> For I am conscious of my rebellion,
> and my sin is always before me.
> Against You—You alone—I have sinned
> and done this evil in Your sight.
> So You are right when You pass sentence;
> You are blameless when You judge.
> Indeed, I was guilty when I was born;
> I was sinful when my mother conceived me.
> Surely You desire integrity in the inner self,
> and You teach me wisdom deep within.
> Purify me with hyssop, and I will be clean;
> wash me, and I will be whiter than snow.
> Let me hear joy and gladness;
> let the bones You have crushed rejoice.
> Turn Your face away from my sins
> and blot out all my guilt.
> God, create a clean heart for me
> and renew a steadfast spirit within me. (vv. 1–10)

Imagine a Rousseau, a Sanger, or a Marx speaking in this spirit? You simply can't, absent their regeneration.

Isaiah

The self-effacing humility of the prophet, who proclaimed both judgment and hope is seen in his calling. When the Lord appeared in glory to enlist him, Isaiah cried out, "Woe is me for I am ruined because I am a man of unclean lips"—not, "But of course you have chosen me" (Isa 6:5).

Matthew

"Tax collector" was a dirty expression in first-century Palestine, but Matthew, the Gospel writer who faithfully recorded the Sermon on the Mount, did not shrink from admitting that he was once a collector of taxes. In listing the disciples in the opening verses of Matthew 10, he identified himself thus in v. 3: "Philip and Bartholomew; Thomas and Matthew the tax collector; James the son of Alphaeus, and Thaddaeus."

> Now, we would never have known that but for Matthew himself. Neither Mark, nor Luke, nor John, nor Paul ever calls Matthew by that bad name. It is Matthew himself alone who in as many words says to us, "Come, all ye that fear God, and I will tell what He has done for my soul." It is Matthew himself alone who publishes and perpetuates to all time his own infamy.[18]

Paul

Working from Paul's testimony ("This saying is trustworthy and deserving of full acceptance: 'Christ Jesus came into the world to save sinners'—and I am the worst of them" [1 Tim 1:15]), Whyte tied the apostle's humility to the testimony of other greats in church history:

- Samuel Rutherford said, "When I look at my sinfulness, my salvation is to me my Saviour's greatest miracle. He has done nothing in heaven or on earth like my salvation."
- John Bunyan's autobiography's title page reads, "Grace abounding to John Bunyan, the chief of sinners. 'come and hear, all ye that fear God, and I will declare what He hath done for my soul.'"
- Martin Luther said, "When a man like me comes to know the plague of his own heart, he is not miserable only—he is absolute misery itself; he is not sinful only—he is absolute sin itself."
- Jonathan Edwards said, "It has often appeared to me that if God were to mark my heart-iniquity my bed would be in hell."[19]

Nevertheless Whyte concluded, "Paul, I suppose, is the only minister that ever lived who could have read Richard Baxter's *Reformed Pastor* without going mad with remorse, and with a fearful looking for of judgment."[20]

Peter

In assessing the temperaments of the apostles, Whyte judged that "John was intuitive, meditative, mystical. Phillip was phlegmatic, perhaps. Thomas would appear to have been melancholy and more. While Peter was sanguine and enthusiastic and extreme both for good and for evil, beyond them all." Indeed, his passion and temper could get him into trouble, but "closely connected with Peter's peculiar temperament, and, indeed, a kind of compensation for being so possessed by it, was his exquisite sense of sin."[21]

Elaborating on Peter's "exquisite sense of sin," William Barclay writes,

> Mark's gospel is nothing other than the preaching material of Peter. It must always stand to the honor of Peter that he kept nothing back. He tells of his own mistakes, of the rebukes he sometimes received from his Master, of his own terrible disloyalty. Peter concealed nothing, for he wished to show the lengths to which the forgiving love and the re-creating grace of Christ had done for him.[22]

Fair Is Fair

This appeal to the character of biblical personages may seem strange or even illegitimate to skeptics, for they would have us believe that these individuals are fictional constructs or hopelessly embellished saints. But again, the Bible is quite blunt in noting their shortcomings. Their portrayal is marked with verisimilitude, "truthlikeness." We recognize our weaknesses in them, even as we admire them for their faith.

But more than this, the Bible is a remarkable ancient text, scrutinized as no other. And if skeptics are comfortable in claiming forebears from ancient times, drawing from Greek and Roman classics, then it is legitimate to use the Bible in speaking of the character and teaching of Moses and Paul.

Notes

1 See for example the collection in Michael Peterson, *Problem of Evil: Selected Readings* (South Bend, IN: University of Notre Dame Press, 1992).

2 Amy Harmon, "Cancer Free at 33, but Weighing a Mastectomy," *The New York Times* (September 16, 2007). Accessed August 27, 2011, at http://www.nytimes.com/2007/09/16/health/16gene.html?pagewanted=1

3 Millard J. Erickson, *God the Father: A Contemporary Exploration of the Divine Attributes* (Grand Rapids: Baker, 1998), 246.

4 Ibid.

5 Voltaire, *Treatise on Tolerance, and Other Writings*, ed. Simon Harvey (Cambridge, UK: Cambridge University Press, 2000), 69.

6 Thomas Jefferson, letter to William Short, Monticello, April 13, 1820; http://www.angelfire.com/co/JeffersonBible/jeffbsyl.html (Accessed December 11, 2010).

7 Thomas Jefferson, *Syllabus of an Estimate of the Merit of the Doctrines of Jesus, Compared with Those of Others*; http://www.angelfire.com/co/JeffersonBible/jeffbsyl.html (accessed December 11, 2010).

8 Charles Swindoll, *Moses: A Man of Selfless Dedication* (Nashville: Thomas Nelson, 1999), 355–62.

9 Charles Swindoll, *Elijah: The Man of Heroism and Humility* (Nashville: Thomas Nelson, 2000), 107.

10 Alexander Whyte, *Bible Characters—People from the New Testament* (Fearn, Ross-shire, UK: Christian Focus, 2000), 30.

11 Charles Haddon Spurgeon, *The Metropolitan Tabernacle Pulpit*, quoted in Warren Wiersbe, *Bible Personalities: A Treasury of Insights for Personal Growth and Ministry* (Grand Rapids: Baker, 2005), 100.

12 John Brown, *Brown's Dictionary of Bible Characters*, ed. Geoffrey Stonier (Fearn, Ross-shire, Scotland: Christian Focus, 2007), 389.

13 Whyte, *Bible Characters*, 45–46.

14 Clarence Macartney, *The Wisest Fool*, quoted in Wiersbe, *Bible Personalities*, 184.

15 *Life Application Study Bible*, NIV (Carol Stream and Grand Rapids: Tyndale House and Zondervan, 2005), 33, 1449, 1787, 2037.

16 Alan Redpath, *The Making of a Man*, cited in Wiersbe, *Bible Personalities*, 60.

17 "Who is Prophet Mohammed (may Allah praise him)?" *Nairaland*; http://www.nairaland.com/nigeria/topic-456524.0.html (accessed January 31, 2010).

18 Whyte, *Bible Characters*, 50.

19 Ibid., 247–48.

20 Ibid., 227.

21 Ibid., 41.

22 William Barclay, *The Master's Men*, cited in Wiersbe, *Bible Personalities*, 148.

THE MORAL AUTHORITY OF CHRISTIAN TEACHERS: CHURCH HISTORY

I T IS COMMON TO hear someone derided as acting "holier than thou," and certainly the person whose demeanor communicates moral condescension has moral problems of his own. Humility is a virtue. But in a deeper sense, a Christian should be holier—more circumspect and honorable—than those who take "the broad way."

Still, there are many who claim Christ as Savior and Lord who bring dishonor to his name, and we should be candid in listing a few. But it is equally important to put them in context, just as Christ did when he said, in Matt 7:21 (NIV), "Not everyone who says to me, 'Lord, Lord,' will enter the kingdom of heaven, but only the one who does the will of my Father who is in heaven."

So we began with a few unhappy cases, before moving to a sample listing of Christian counselors who, in the words of Titus 2:10, "adorn the teaching of God our Savior."

EMBARRASSMENTS

One does not have to be around church people long to know that they are all works in progress. Sanctification is not instantaneous. Even the apostles were aching from rebuke, as was Peter in Gal 2:11–14, where he had backslidden into legalism.

So it is important to recognize that those who claim Christ as their redeemer are capable of bad behavior. Here are two examples:

King James and the Indians

In the years 1616–19, a plague decimated the Indian tribes of New England. This was just before the Pilgrims landed in 1620. "When King James learned of the epidemic he thanked 'Almighty God in his great goodness and bounty toward us' for 'this wonderful plague among the savages.'" John Winthrop made a similar observation: "God had thereby cleared our title to this place."[1]

This is not to say that God cannot use disasters as his agents, but it can be disastrous when his followers exult in them and presume to say they are party to his thinking.

Reverend Charles Colcock Jones

Reverend Jones was "the eloquent pastor of Savannah's First Presbyterian Church who became the leading proponent of formal religious training for slaves." In the 1830s he urged "Southerners to instruct their slaves in Christian principles in order to create 'a greater subordination' among them." Conversion would help them render "respect and obedience [to] all those whom God in His providence [had] placed in authority over them." This would enhance "the peace, the order, the purity, the happiness, and the prosperity of our Southern country." He also noted that "a faithful servant is more profitable than an unfaithful one."[2]

A slave owner himself, with three rice plantations in Liberty County, Georgia, Jones was often absent from his property as he taught "ecclesiastical history" at a seminary in Columbia, South Carolina, and worked at the Presbyterian Board of Domestic Missions. His popular work, *The Religious Instruction of the Negroes in the United States*,[3] shows that he genuinely cared for the salvation and moral elevation of his slaves, but he needed some moral elevation himself. He is a good example of the fact that believers can have blind spots.

Compromising Casuistry

Sometimes the tawdriness of the teacher's life undermines the authority of his teaching. In others the tawdriness of the teaching undermines the authority of the teacher. Though "casuistry," the consideration of challenging cases, can be a noble enterprise, it can be twisted to indulge all sorts of compromise. Blaise Pascal hated this sort of thing.

In his *Provincial Letters* Pascal faulted the Jesuits for using casuistry to suppress the offense of the cross and preaching "only a glorious and not a suffering Jesus Christ."

> This plan they followed in the Indies and in China, where they permitted Christians to practise idolatry itself, with the aid of the following ingenious contrivance: they made their converts conceal under their clothes an image of Jesus Christ, to which they taught them to transfer mentally those adorations which they rendered ostensibly to the idol of Cachinchoam and Keum-fucum.[4]

And he could only mock such counsel, again from the Jesuits of his day:

> If a man doubt whether he is twenty-one years old, is he obliged to fast? No. But suppose I were to be twenty-one to-night an hour after midnight, and to-morrow were the fast, would I be obliged to fast to-morrow? No; for you were at liberty to eat as much as you pleased for an hour after midnight, not being till then fully twenty-one; and therefore having a right to break the fast day, you are not obliged to keep it.[5]

The Unregenerate

One of the sad truths of church history is that many people on "church rolls" are not regenerate, not born again. Matthew 13:24–29 speaks of weeds the enemy has sown throughout the kingdom wheat field. By New Testament standards, such as those delineated in 1 John and James, they are "false professors," counterfeits, though they may themselves think they are genuinely saved.

Critics of Christianity show little or no sympathy for this distinction and are only too pleased to lump IRA terrorists and Ku Klux Klan members in with Billy Graham and William Wilberforce as part of the great Christian mass. Unfortunately the church has brought much of this on itself by admitting and retaining people who have no business there.

I'm persuaded that two major factors in this spectacle are infant baptism and a lack of church discipline. While many believe that baptizing infants is useful and even gratifying for one reason or another, or at least innocuous, I believe it does great harm by giving the illusion that something spiritually significant has happened to the children when it has not. As they get older, whether or not they have gone through some sort of group confirmation, many cling to the conviction that they are somehow covered by that original act, though it is not "the pledge of a good conscience toward God" (1 Pet 3:21) but something undergone by the as-yet-conscienceless. This is as if they have had a vaccination or inoculation against the real thing.

When that false impression is buttressed by a ritual-based religion, then one can go throughout his whole life under the banner of Christianity, without knowing Christ as one's Savior. In this condition men and women are susceptible to all sorts of misdirection and offense, even in the name of the faith, which in their case is little more than a form of sentimentalism, tribalism, or opportunism.

Then when the member behaves atrociously, the church often fails to cleanse itself according to the counsel of Jesus in Matt 18:15–20 and Paul in 1 Cor 5:1–13. And so the church is defamed for its slackness.

One might argue that this is too convenient for apologetics. When Christians behave badly, then they are said to be non-Christian. By that approach, there are no bad Christians. But the situation is not so easy as that. As already mentioned, genuine believers exhibit gaps in their moral understanding or pass through seasons of transgression.

THE MORAL COMPONENT OF CONVERSION ACCOUNTS

Of course the Christian understanding of salvation, as expressed in John 3:16, focuses on eternal life, but belief in Christ has a major social component as well. When one is "born again," there are great ethical changes, as evidenced by the following cases.

Billy Graham

As a youth, Graham would shun black barbers if there was a white one to be found. But as he later testified, "It rarely occurred to me in my childhood to think about the difficulties, problems, and oppressions of black people. In high school, I began to question some of the practices, but it was not until I'd actually committed my life to Christ that I began to think more deeply about it."[6]

Later in what he called one of his "first acts of conscience on the race question," he decided he "would never preach to another segregated audience."[7] And his voice grew stronger through the years, declaring, "Any man who has a genuine conversion experience will find his racial attitudes greatly changed," for the believer "forgets all about race when he is giving his life to Christ."[8]

Charles Colson

In *Born Again*, the account of his conversion, Charles Colson recounts how he was called President Nixon's "hatchet man" and how he once said, "I would walk over my grandmother if necessary." This fit the White House inner circle, where "machismo and toughness were equated with trust and loyalty," where "*hubris* became the mark of the Nixon man because *hubris* was the quality Nixon admired most."[9]

When the administration collapsed in the Watergate scandal, Colson found himself facing prison but also ministered to by friends and new acquaintances concerned for his soul. One read him a chapter from C. S. Lewis's *Mere Christianity*, and by Colson's account "one passage in particular seemed to sum up what had happened to all of us at the White House: 'For Pride is spiritual cancer: it eats up the very possibility of love, or contentment, or even common sense.'"[10]

He was, as the British say, gobsmacked by the realization that his whole life had been a matter of "clawing and straining for status and position." As he drove away from the meeting, he cried profusely as he realized his spiritual folly: "With my face cupped in my hands, head leaning forward against the wheel, I forgot about machismo, about pretenses, about fears of being weak. And as I did, I began to experience a wonderful feeling of being released."[11]

As he moved toward a saving faith in Christ and then began to grow as a Christian, his life took on a new cast. First as an inmate and later as a minister to inmates through his organization, Prison Fellowship, he became a channel of grace and healing.

Now he is a leading commentator on cultural matters, through books such as *How Shall We Now Live?* and through his radio program, *Breakpoint*. His life backs up his message.

Columba

Columba (c. 521–597) had a radical change in heart, which meant great blessing to Scotland. A zealous young monk in Ireland, he copied, without permission, a treasured manuscript, Jerome's version of the Psalter and the Gospels. The charge of "copyright" violation went before the "high king at Tara," who ruled against Columba, but the copyist held on to his work, and a civil war developed as northern clansmen used this as a pretext for resisting the king.

Columba's allies won a decisive victory near Sligo, but over 3,000 lives were lost that day. Appalled at the carnage, in "an act of rededication," he decided to leave his native Ireland and become a missionary, an "exile for Christ." "Determined to win to Christ at least as many souls as had been lost at Culdrevney, he was eventually to convert many times that number during the last thirty-four years of his life."[12]

Establishing a base of operation on the island of Iona, off the Scottish coast, he "lived in the greatest austerity, sleeping on a bare rock with a stone pillow." Leading a team of "sea-roving evangelists . . . his Christian devotion contributed to the generally pacifying effect that he seemed to have over the warlike Picts and Scots." Drawing from "his own personal experiences as a young hothead in Ireland before his life-changing departure . . . in 563," he "sought to settle disputes and to minimize violence wherever he could."[13]

THE WALK

While Christian moral teachers are still fallen creatures, enticed and battered by "the world, the flesh, and the devil," typically a consistent walk, a record of holiness and fruitfulness honors their teachings.

Hagiography has come to be a word of disparagement since the lives of the saints have been marked with exaggerations and other fictions. Yet they would not be saints were they not extraordinarily admirable Christians. Celebrating "Lives of the Saints" is often a Roman Catholic enterprise, but of course the genre extends to Protestants and the Orthodox as well. In some cases, particularly the ancient ones, the accounts can be fantastical in places, but there is an overwhelming moral weight to these lives, one that gives ballast to their teachings.

St. Francis of Assisi

Francis of Assisi (1181–1226) is known for founding an order dedicated to reforming the church in the direction of "gospel simplicity," including personal destitution. Those who would join him were required to enter in poverty and chastity, care for their sick brothers, refrain from quarreling, and to be habitually joyous.[14]

Morris Bishop of Cornell University surmised that Francis "felt . . . a pathological need for public confession and abasement." But there could well be an element of pride in this—pride at one's humility—and Francis was aware of this. "Once he gave a poor old woman his cloak. Then he felt a puff of vanity, self-applause, pride, rise within him, and he proclaimed his repentance."[15]

Concerned with sexual passion, "he would roll in ditches full of snow, to keep his white robe of chastity undefiled, saying: 'It is more tolerable for a spiritual man to bear intense cold than to feel the heat of carnal lust in his mind.'"[16] Once when he returned to his base near Assisi, "he saw with horror a new stone building rising among the huts and hovels. . . . Raging at this defiance of poverty, he climbed to the roof, and, sobbing, began throwing down the tiles, while calling on the brothers to aid him."[17]

Of course one can fault Francis's theology and psychoanalyze his abasements, but it is hard to gainsay the moral rigor of his walk, and his words of repentance when he stumbled.

As his ministry began,

> his work for lepers, like his manual labor, renunciation of self-indulgence and sex, and dedication to every kind of underdog, were an uncomfortable challenge to the people of Assisi, where they fought continually for position, money and power; where the records are littered with public accusations of sodomy, incest, adultery, prostitution, and rape; and where brutal punishments failed to reduce theft, fighting arson, murder and treason. But his challenge soon struck a chord among some remarkable men, who became as keen to share his crusts and water as others had his banquets and debaucheries.[18]

Called "the morning star of the Italian Renaissance" and the "patron saint for ecologists," Francis was arguably Dante's inspiration (through his "Canticle of Brother Sun") for writing *The Divine Comedy* in Italian rather than Latin. His was a life admired by nonbelievers as well; French scholar and agnostic Ernest Renan said, "After Jesus Francis of Assisi has been the only perfect Christian."[19]

Abraham Booth

Abraham Booth was a leading Baptist pastor of the eighteenth century, a slave-trade abolitionist and an earnest minister to his people.

> He worked so diligently as a shepherd of this flock, that he was known frequently to travel the streets, the whole length of London, in search of a member who had been absent from services. He was unwearied in his ministries to the poor, the rich, the saint, and the sinner. One time a woman in his congregation left him a sizeable legacy, which he quietly deposited in the Bank of England to the account of some of her poor relations whom he had discovered.[20]

This act of integrity toward a surprising gift is indicative of the spirit of many pastors.

Billy Graham

As Billy Graham has testified, sexual fidelity, and even the absence of innuendo and suspicion is no accident with him. He has taken great pains to avoid compromising situations. "I'm sure I've been tempted, especially in my younger years. But there has never been anything close to an incident. I took precautions. From the earliest days I've never had a meal alone with a woman other than Ruth, not even in a restaurant. I've never ridden in an automobile alone with a woman."[21]

The Amish Parents of Nickel Mines Schoolgirls

On October 2, 2006, Pennsylvania milk truck driver Charles Roberts drove to the Nickel Mines Amish schoolhouse and shot 10 schoolgirls. That morning he left a note, making reference to his daughter Elise who in 1997 was born prematurely and died 20 minutes later.

> It changed my life forever. I haven't been the same since it affected me in a way I never felt possible. I am filled with so much hate, hate toward myself, hate toward God, and unimaginable emptiness it seems like every time we do something fun I think about how Elise wasn't here to share it with us and I go right back to anger.[22]

When he was about to kill the girls in the schoolhouse, he said, "I'm going to make you pay for my daughter."[23] And then he began shooting, killing five and leaving five grievously wounded before taking his own life.

What followed astonished the nation. The Amish refused to express anger or judgment on Roberts or his family. Immediately following the shooting, when Charles Roberts was identified as the gunman, a few of the Amish neighbors walked over to his house to meet with his wife and parents. Despite their shock and sadness over losing so many children, they were also concerned about Marie: Was she OK? How were the children holding up? Could they do anything to help?[24]

Newscast after newscast noted that the Amish were "turning the other cheek, urging forgiveness of the killer, and quietly accepting what comes their way as God's will."[25]

A biker gang in full black leather drove over from Carlisle to provide security if needed for the funeral procession. And as the hearse and buggies passed, one of them confessed, "I have never forgiven the guy [a drunk driver] that killed my son. Never forgiven him. You know what? Maybe I should. If these folks can forgive that man that shot their little girls, maybe I should forgive the guy that killed my son."[26]

Elizabeth Elliot

Elizabeth Elliot has written extensively on the ethics of the Christian life, with particular focus on the role of women. Her words are backed up by an extraordinary life of grace and courage.

On January 8, 1956, her husband, Jim Elliot, and three missionary colleagues were speared to death by Auca natives on a riverbank in Ecuador. Their story is told most notably in Elisabeth's book, *Through Gates of Splendor*.[27] But the story does not end there. Hearing that her husband had been murdered, she prayed, "If there's anything You ever want me to do about the Aucas, I'm available."

God did, indeed, have a mission for her, and two years later she was back among these people, living in a dirt-floored house without walls and furniture, trying to learn their language and ways. From this experience came another book, *The Savage, My Kinsman*,[28] which traces the beginnings of her forgiving ministry to these truly savage people.

Of course single acts of moral splendor do not guarantee the truth or wisdom of the person's position, but individual lives do count toward a general argument that Christian moralists are "on average" moral. They "walk the walk as well as talk the talk."

Dietrich Bonhoeffer

Dietrich Bonhoeffer is justifiably well known for his writings on radical discipleship and for his sacrificial efforts to preserve the faith in Hitler's Germany. He ultimately joined in a plot to assassinate Hitler and was hanged for it, along with others. The plaque erected at his place of execution reads, "In resistance against dictatorship and terror they gave their lives for freedom, justice, and humanity."[29]

Over the years of his resistance, he showed his courage and honor in many ways—by publishing a book on praying the Psalms "along with Christ" (an affront to Nazi efforts to suppress the "Jewish" Scriptures and detach them from Christianity);[30] by conducting his courtship of Maria von Wedemeyer with holiness, urging her to join him in "thanks and boundless trust in God, who has led us to this point and now loves us";[31] by refusing to trade on his prominent family connections when in prison, rejecting larger food portions "knowing it would have been at the expense of other prisoners."[32]

He was strong in his convictions and declarations, calling abortion "nothing but murder."[33] But he was not one to heap burdens on others that he was unwilling to bear himself. This was the posture he both prescribed and accepted for himself: "If God determines where he is to be found, then it will be in a place which is not immediately pleasing to my nature and which is not at all congenial to me. This place is the Cross of Christ. And whosoever would find him must go to the foot of the Cross, as the Sermon on the Mount commands."[34]

Thomas Aquinas

Before writing his classic biography on Thomas Aquinas, whose title repeats the ironic nickname, "The Dumb Ox," G. K. Chesterton wrote a piece in *The Spectator*, which sketched out his honorable life:

> He was born in high station, related to the Imperial house, the son of a great noble of Aquino, not far from Naples, and when he expressed a wish to be a monk, it is typical of the time that everything was made smooth for him—up to a point. A great gentleman could be decorously admitted into the now ancient routine of the Benedictines; like a squire's younger son becoming a parson. But the world had just been shaken by a religious revolution, and strange feet were on all the highways. And when young Thomas insisted on becoming a Dominican—that is, a wandering and begging friar—his brothers pursued him, kidnapped him and shut him up in a gaol. It was as if the squire's son had become a gipsy or a Communist. However, he managed to become a friar; and the favourite pupil of the great Albertus Magnus at Cologne. He afterwards proceeded to Paris, and was prominent in defending the new mendicant orders at the Sorbonne and elsewhere. From this he passed to the great central controversy on Averroes and Aristotle; in effect to the great reconciliation of Christian faith and Pagan philosophy. His external life was prodigiously preoccupied with these things. He was a big, burly, baldish man, patient and good-natured, but given to blank trances of absence of mind. When dining with St. Louis, the French King, he fell into a brown study and suddenly smote the table with a mighty fist, saying: "And that will settle the Manichees!" The King, with his fine irony of innocence, sent a secretary to take down the line of argument, lest it be forgotten.[35]

Elizabeth Fry

Prison reform activist and evangelical Quaker Elizabeth Fry exhibited a personal warmth, integrity, and familial devotion one does not find in such secular "progressives" as Karl Marx, Sigmund Freud, and Bertrand Russell. Besides caring for her 11 children, she provided "an example of the scope of philanthropy among Christian ladies"—including "a shelter for destitute children in London . . . collections of improving books for isolated coastguards, and training for a small nursing order, the Protestant Sisters of Charity."[36]

This "friend of the prisoner, the bondman, the lunatic, the beggar" was courageous in her benevolence.

> Many a time, in spite of the sneers of vulgar turnkeys, and the positive assurances of respectable keepers, that her purse and even her life would be at stake if she entered the wards of the prison, she boldly went in amongst the swearing, quarreling wretches, and, with the doors bolted behind her, encountered them with dignified demeanor and kindly words, that soon produced a state of order and repose which whips and chains had vainly endeavored to enforce.[37]

The king of Prussia was such an admirer that he visited her at her home on a visit to England—fitting honor for a woman widely known for "ameliorating the Penal Code, and improving the condition of convict ships and penal colonies," along with other charitable acts.

Jonathan Edwards

Though his preaching was central to a Great Awakening in America in the 1740s, Jonathan Edwards (1703–58), of Northampton, Massachusetts, so irritated his congregation that they forced him to leave. The problem stemmed from his

> insistence that professions of faith must show evidence of being. . . . True religion, he had long held, must involve the affections. The will must be radically transformed from its natural self-love to love to God. The great divide among people was between those whose hearts were enraptured by this love and beauty and those whose self-indulgent hearts rejected it. Whatever their relatively good intentions, persons, who could not show heartfelt evidence of regeneration must be judged to be on the wrong side of this divide.[38]

This conviction led him to overturn an inherited policy at his church, one that accommodated a "half-way covenant" allowing lost people to have a sort of church membership. To him this was a matter of integrity and witness to the spiritual reality so essential to salvation.

From Northampton he went to pastor in Stockbridge, with a strong outreach to Indians. He was dismayed that "English traders typically defrauded the Indians" and was determined that they be treated with dignity and that "the girls be educated as well as boys and that they all be taught not only reading, but spelling and the basics of arithmetic."[39]

Edwards is best known for his sermon "Sinners in the Hands of an Angry God," a message in which he declared the following about those who have not accepted Christ.

> Your wickedness makes you as it were heavy as lead, and to tend downwards with great weight and pressure towards hell; and if God should let you go, you would immediately sink and swiftly descend and plunge into the bottomless gulf; and your healthy constitution, and your own care and prudence, and best contrivance, and all your righteousness, would have no more influence to uphold you and keep you out of hell, than a spider's web would have to stop a falling rock.[40]

Skeptics would love nothing better than to expose a man who talks like this as a charlatan and villain. His head would make a nice trophy on their wall. But Edwards's virtues are unassailable, and his words stand with him.

C. S. Lewis

Clive Staples Lewis (1898–1963), professor at both Oxford and Cambridge universities, was an outstanding spokesman for Christian perspectives in the twentieth century. He wrote on a wide range of issues, including capital punishment ("The Humanitarian Theory of Punishment") and animal experimentation ("Vivisection"), both collected in a book of his essays, *God in the Dock*.[41]

Long an atheist, Lewis was converted at age 32, and his life took a remarkable turn. Religiously ambivalent biographer A. N. Wilson suggests he had an illicit affair before his conversion, though many disagree. At any rate, the woman in question was unenthusiastic over his turn to Christ, and as a believer Lewis was emphatic: "There is no getting away from it: the Christian rule is 'Either marriage, with complete faithfulness to your partner, or else total abstinence.'" And, as Wilson adds, "He was not a man to say one thing and do another. He meant his Christian commitment to be total."[42]

One sign of Lewis's new life was his treatment of Joy Davidman, a divorced Jewish convert whose husband had been a womanizing drunk. She and her boys had moved to England, and her friendship with Lewis, with whom she had first corresponded at length, deepened. When her visa was expiring and it looked as though she could not stay in England, Lewis asked her to marry him.

It was awkward since the Church of England would not solemnize the union, given her divorce. But they went ahead with a civil ceremony. That same year she was diagnosed with cancer and immediately underwent treatment, which seemed to help. But early the next year, "tests showed that Joy's condition was steadily growing worse. This shattering blow only intensified Jack's feelings for Joy. 'Never have I loved her more than since she was struck down,' he told Arthur Greeves."[43]

She enjoyed a measure of recovery, and "once Joy was more or less well again, they decided they would live life to the full, enjoy the time they had left and spend as much of it together as they could."[44] As normal as this might seem to the Christian reader, it is not so typical in the world at large, where such a reversal, with possible attendant loss of physical beauty, could mean the cooling of affection. But the Lewises were walking together in the Lord, and their devotion was a testimony to the seriousness of their faith.

Before he met Joy, he resisted an admirer's suggestion that he write a book on prayer: "I think it would be rather 'cheek' on my part." But after "he had been through the fire with his grief over Joy," he was ready to write such a book, namely, *Letters to Malcolm Chiefly on Prayer*, published only after his death.[45]

John Wesley

The father of Methodism was a diligent journaler, and the record of his journeys is inspiring. John Wesley (1703–91) endured all kinds of discomfort and indignity, but his spirit, bolstered by the Holy Spirit, was resilient and loving. When, in the streets of Newcastle, where he heard "the senseless, shameless, wickedness, the ignorant profaneness" of the soldiers stationed there, he was moved to pity. Though offended by "the continual cursing and swearing, the wanton blasphemy" which "must needs be a torture to the sober ear," he was concerned about their souls.

> I would to God it were in my power, in any degree, to supply their lack of service. I am ready to do what in me lies to call these poor sinners to repentance, once or twice a day (while I remain in these parts), at any hour, or at any place. And I desire no pay at all for doing this; unless what my Lord shall give at His appearing.[46]

This is the minister's heart on display—no illusions over the reality and awfulness of sin; no hesitancy to proclaim the will of God; no deficiency of love; no preoccupation with self; no limit to service, except those imposed by circumstances and strength.

Mother Teresa

Christopher Hitchens has written harshly about Mother Teresa (1910–97), but both her moral courage and moral standing are unmistakable. At a prayer breakfast she spoke prophetically on abortion to President Clinton and the First Lady, and got away with it. In an interview for *Christianity Today*, pastor Max Lucado observed,

> Compassion is the best apologetic. There are many controversial issues in our culture. The church should take a strong stance on issues like abortion and same-sex marriage. But there's something about compassion that causes society to say, "We're going to take

this person seriously." Take Mother Teresa. She was confrontational on abortion, but she wasn't rejected by society.[47]

MINISTERIAL HANDBOOKS

Gospel ministers are solicitous of their reputations, lest they bring dishonor on Christ.

Richard Baxter

Seventeenth-century English pastor Richard Baxter (1615–91) was tireless in his ministry, circumspect in his life, and bountiful in his counsel. "Above all he was a zealous pastor and preacher, all the more zealous because he believed that his very precarious health presaged an early death."[48] His classic work, *The Reformed Pastor*, laid standards, which he himself met. "The leaders of the flock must be exemplary to the rest; and therefore in this duty as well as in any other. It is not our part only to teach them repentance, but to go before them in the exercise of it ourselves."[49] "It is a palpable error in those ministers who make such a disproportion between their preaching and their living; that they will study hard to preach exactly, and study little or not at all to live exactly."[50]

Robert Barrett

Baylor University professor Robert Barrett penned a classic in 1901. Here is a sample of his counsel:

- He should not court the favor of the wealthy and influential to the neglect of the lowly, for Christ's ambassador should be no respecter of persons.
- The very presence of a truly devout man reproves profanity in the most wicked.
- The preacher, as a servant of God, is under obligation to make the most possible of his powers. His intellect is to be educated—"drawn out"—to its fullest capacity.
- The fundamental obligation of matrimony is propagation of offspring. . . . It should be an incredible thing that a servant of God, the husband of a wife, should shirk this responsibility, and transgress this positive command.
- He should be acquainted with the local history, traditions and folklore, as well as the customs of his people. . . . The preacher who lives in a mining town and does not know all about ores and the methods of extracting them, will be despised as a "tender foot."
- The frugal, Christlike minister will shave himself, black his own shoes, and it will not hurt him nor take too much of his time, but be of a great benefit to his health, for him to cultivate his own garden and saw his wood.[51]

Of course some of this may sound quaint, but the reader should readily recognize the tone of surrender to a high calling.

SPIRITUAL DISCIPLINES

Ministers are not the only ones intent on righteous living. Throughout church history laymen have also been keen to cultivate virtuous habits so that their walk and witness would not be hindered. Here are two pastor-written resources many have found helpful, one from the eighteenth century and one from the twentieth century.

William Gurnall

In his book *The Christian in Complete Armour*, the Puritan William Gurnall discusses Eph 6:10–20, urging believers to resist the destructive tactics of the devil. "Do not think simply putting on the grace of God will frighten the enemy away. He is not impressed by a show of force. On the contrary, the very sight of God's armour upon your back is like waving a red flag at Satan. So to have it on for show is not enough; you must have it securely fastened at every point."[52]

He then gives examples of Bible characters who let down their guard, including David. ("Oh, the battering he took by removing his breastplate of righteousness in the matter of Uriah.")[53]

Fortunately many Christians who presume to offer moral counsel have taken care to wear securely their spiritual armor—the belt of truth, breastplate of righteousness, gospel sandals, shield of faith, helmet of salvation, and sword of the Spirit. And this armament has strengthened their authority as God's spokesmen.

Don Whitney

Southern Baptist Theological Seminary professor Donald Whitney has written a widely read book on the subject, *Spiritual Disciplines for the Christian Life*. Chapter by chapter, he explains and commends Bible intake, prayer, worship, evangelism, serving, stewardship, fasting, silence and solitude, journaling, and learning.

> Regarding the first discipline on this list, Bible intake, he tells the story of "a man in Kansas City who was severely injured in an explosion. He face was badly disfigured, and he lost his eyesight as well as both hands. He had just become a Christian when the accident happened, and one of his greatest disappointments was that he could no longer read the Bible. Then he heard about a lady in England who read Braille with her lips. Hoping to do the same, he sent for some books of the Bible in Braille. But he discovered that the nerve endings in his lips had been too badly damaged to distinguish the characters. One day, as he brought one of the Braille pages to his lips, his tongue happened to touch a few of the raised characters and he could feel them. Like a flash he thought, 'I can read the Bible using my tongue.'"[54]

He eventually read through the entire Bible four times—not for glory but for the sheer love of knowing the Word of God.

Notes

1 Sarah Vowell, *The Wordy Shipmates* (New York: Penguin, 2008), 31–32.
2 Robert S. Starobin, ed., *Blacks in Bondage: Letters of American Slaves* (New York: Barnes & Noble, 1974), 42.
3 Charles C. Jones, *The Religious Instruction of the Negroes in the United States* (Savannah: Thomas Purse, 1842); http://docsouth.unc.edu/church/jones/jones.html (accessed November 6, 2010).
4 Blaise Pascal, *The Provincial Letters*, vol. 33 of Great Books of the Western World (Chicago: Encyclopedia Britannica, 1952), 28–29.
5 Ibid., 31.
6 Janet Lowe, *Billy Graham Speaks: Insight from the World's Greatest Preacher* (New York: John Wiley & Sons, 1999), 120.
7 Ibid., 121.
8 Ibid., 125–26.
9 Charles Colson, *Born Again* (New York: Bantam, 1976), 75–76.
10 Ibid., 124.
11 Ibid., 128.
12 Robert Linder, "Columba: Missionary to the Scots," in *Great Leaders of the Christian Church*, ed. John D. Woodbridge (Chicago: Moody, 1988), 101.
13 Ibid., 104.
14 Morris Bishop, *Saint Francis of Assisi* (Boston: Little, Brown, 1974), 141.
15 Ibid., 58, 73–74.
16 Ibid., 56.
17 Ibid., 138.
18 Adrian House, *Francis of Assisi* (Mahwah, NJ: Paulist, 2001), 81.
19 Ibid., 9–11.
20 Raymond Arthur Coppenger, *A Messenger of Grace: A Study of the Life and Thought of Abraham Booth* (Ontario, ON: Joshua, 2009), 39.
21 Lowe, *Billy Graham Speak*, 102–3.
22 Jonas Beiler with Shawn Smucker, *Think No Evil: Inside the Story of the Amish Schoolhouse Shooting . . . and Beyond* (New York: Howard/Simon & Schuster, 2009), 41.
23 Ibid., 58.
24 Ibid., 165.
25 Ibid., 117.
26 Ibid., 149–50.
27 Elisabeth Elliot, *Through Gates of Splendor* (New York: Harper, 1957).
28 Elisabeth Elliot, *The Savage, My Kinsman* (New York: Harper, 1961).
29 Eric Metaxas, *Bonhoeffer: Pastor, Martyr, Prophet, Spy* (Nashville: Thomas Nelson, 2010), unnumbered photographic page facing 467.
30 Ibid., 368.
31 Ibid., 421.
32 Ibid., 449.
33 Ibid., 472.
34 Ibid., 137.

35 G. K. Chesterton, "St. Thomas Aquinas," The American Chesterton Society (this uncollected essay first appeared in *The Spectator*, February 27, 1932, before Hodder and Stoughton commissioned Chesterton to write his book-length study of St. Thomas Aquinas); http://www.chesterton.org/gkc/theologian/aquinas.htm (accessed October 18, 2010).

36 David Bebbington, "Elizabeth Fry," in Woodbridge *Great Leaders of the Christian Church*, 315.

37 Henry B. Stanton, *Sketches of Reforms and Reformers of Great Britain and Ireland* (New York: Baker and Scribner, 1850), 349.

38 George Marsden, *Jonathan Edwards: A Life* (New Haven, CT: Yale University Press, 2003), 352–53.

39 Ibid., 388–90.

40 Jonathan Edwards, "Sinners in the Hands of an Angry God," *The Works of Jonathan Edwards* (Carlisle, PA: Banner of Truth, 1979), 2:9.

41 C. S. Lewis, *God in the Dock*, ed. Walter Hooper (Grand Rapids: Eerdmans, 1970).

42 A. N. Wilson, *C. S. Lewis: A Biography* (New York: W.W. Norton, 1990), 128.

43 Michael White, *C. S. Lewis: A Life* (New York: Carroll & Graf, 2004), 192–95.

44 Ibid., 198.

45 Harry Lee Poe, *The Inklings of Oxford: C. S. Lewis, J. R. R. Tolkien, and Their Friends*, photographed by James Ray Veneman (Grand Rapids: Zondervan, 2009), 153.

46 John Wesley, *The Heart of John Wesley's Journal*, ed. Percy Livingston Parker (Peabody, MA: Hendrickson, 2008), 171.

47 Max Lucado, "Compassion: The Best Apologetic," interview by Sarah Pulliam Bailey, *Christianity Today*, October 8, 2010, 65.

48 Hugh Martin, "Editor's Foreword," in Richard Baxter, *The Reformed Pastor* (Richmond, VA: John Knox, 1956), 9.

49 Baxter, *The Reformed Pastor*, 15.

50 Ibid., 35.

51 Robert N. Barrett, *Ethics of the Ministry with Practical Suggestions to Pastors and Other Ministers* (Cleona, PA: G. Holzapfel, 1901), 32, 45, 66, 94, 159, 177–78.

52 William Gurnall, *The Christian in Complete Armour* (reprint, Carlisle, PA: Banner of Truth, 1986), 245–46.

53 Ibid., 246.

54 Donald S. Whitney, *Spiritual Disciplines for the Christian Life* (Colorado Springs: NavPress, 1991), 35.

The Fruit of False Systems: Islam

WHATEVER ONE MAY THINK of the separation of church and state, there is no separating church (or the absence thereof) and culture. If a boatload of Muslims, Hindus, animists, Buddhists, or atheists had landed on Pilgrim Rock, America would be a different nation, if a nation at all.

In an effort to make everyone feel appreciated, the U.S. Postal Service now produces each year a range of holiday stamps for Christmas, where there used to be only one. Now alongside one bearing a nativity scene, postal patrons can find a stamp for the Chinese New Year, keyed to superstitious belief in the Zodiac (1992), Jewish Hanukah (1996), Kwanza (1997), and Muslim Eid (2001). But America would not be America had the preponderance of settlers timed their decisions to coincide with the Year of the Dragon or had sacrificed animals annually, as is the custom in Muslim-majority countries.

The stamp world is a fascinating world of values. Much of it is good—whether featuring wildflowers, "legends of baseball," or the American flag. But when it comes to honoring individuals, things can go awry. For years Yale University has been campaigning for a Jonathan Edwards stamp,[1] but to no avail.

In making their case, they argue that American historians have long "called Jonathan Edwards and Benjamin Franklin the two greatest minds in eighteenth-century America." Proponents argue that "Franklin and the other 'secular' founders of the Republic have been honored with numerous stamps, not to mention currency. The time has come to give similar recognition to Edwards." They add, "Historian Martin Marty recounts that over a number of years he asked his audiences which four religious figures they would carve in Mt. Rushmore. The only unanimous nominee was Edwards."[2]

Perhaps the authorities think this would collapse the separation of church and state and create great controversy. But in 1985, the U.S. Postal Service issued one that honored a Roman Catholic priest, Father Junipero Serra, who was instrumental in founding the California missions of San Diego, Santa Barbara, San Luis Obispo, San Francisco, and Santa Clara, to name a few. The nation did not slide into theocracy over that, and an Edwards stamp would likely be no threat to the First Amendment either.

As for their aversion to controversy, this does not square with their honoring such outspokenly non-Christian and anti-Christian figures as Ayn Rand and James Baldwin or with stamps for such gifted but unholy figures like James Dean and Jelly Roll Morton. And when stamps honor Elvis, Bugs Bunny, and Lucille Ball, it would seem permissible to include a central figure of the Great Awakening and a president of Princeton University in the collection.

Of course the stamp issue is not critical, but the ideology behind the decision to exclude Edwards is troubling. This decision reflects a spiritual lethargy brought on by historical amnesia and relativistic multiculturalism. This chapter attempts to correct that sort of thing and "disturb the peace" to some extent.

THE UNDENIABLE CONTRIBUTION OF NONBELIEVERS

No doubt nonbelievers have done many remarkable and beneficial things. Certainly Cyrus was a great help to Israel when he granted God's people safe conduct back from captivity. And world history shows the great debt the church and society owe to "pagans." For instance Alan Turing, a critical member of the Government Code and Cipher School at Bletchley Park, England, was instrumental in designing equipment to decipher encrypted Nazi messages, thus hastening Hitler's defeat. Sadly, at age 41, this "fragile genius . . . committed suicide in 1954 by eating an apple laced with cyanide."[3]

Similarly T. H. Lawrence, a hero of World War I, enlisted nomadic Arabs to fight the Ottoman Turks, thus greatly assisting the Allies. Still he was, as one has put it, "an enigmatic, asexual, masochistic, retiring, exhibitionistic, difficult, and charming" man. He was not an evangelical by any stretch of the imagination.[4]

The list goes on. The morally challenged and spiritually chaotic actress Angelina Jolie stole Brad Pitt from his wife Jennifer Anniston, but she has helped clear land mines in Cambodia and donated $50,000 to an orphanage in Tanzania.[5] Cecile B. DeMille had extramarital affairs with Jeanie Macpherson, Julia Faye, and Gladys Rosson,[6] but he also blessed millions of Christians by producing and directing *The Ten Commandments*; he even helped design the Ten Commandments monument, which now stands in front of the Texas capitol.[7]

NEVERTHELESS: THE BAD FRUIT OF FALSE SYSTEMS

The August 24, 2010, cover of *The Christian Century* presents four sad statistics. (1) Every day 25,000 people die of hunger-related causes. (2) more than one billion people are undernourished. (3) Of the world's hungry 93 percent live in Asia, the Pacific, and Africa. (4) Seven countries account for almost two-thirds of the world's hungry (India, China, Congo, Bangladesh, Indonesia, Pakistan, Ethiopia).[8] Regarding this list of seven, it is fair to ask what they have in common, if anything. Together their populations account for about half the world's population. China and India lead the way with over a billion each. Indeed, the top five account for 98 percent of the population of the seven, with Ethiopia and Congo supplying only about 85 million together.

In his book *Germs, Guns, and Steele,* Jared Diamond argues that those problems are basically a matter of geography and climate. Others have offered racial explanations. But the matter of religion is hard to miss. Of the five largest countries mentioned here, none is Christian. Three are overwhelmingly Muslim (Bangladesh, Indonesia, Pakistan), one overwhelmingly Hindu with a large Muslim contingent (India), and one overwhelmingly irreligious or atheist, though it has a vibrant Christian minority (China). Congo and Ethiopia have Christian majorities, Roman Catholic and Ethiopian Orthodox predominating, respectively. None of the seven is predominantly Protestant. Is this a coincidence?

Emphatically not. As G. K. Chesterton said, nothing is so impactful as a person's religion or irreligion. So it is with societies.

ISLAM

The great clash of civilizations in this day is between the West and Islam. With over a billion "members," this religion is typically totalitarian when in power, and it seeks to extend its power along with its numbers in every corner of the earth. Continual violence is performed in its name, and its record of wholesome accomplishment is meager. Strangely many Westerners are quick to declare it a "great religion," a "religion of peace." This is nonsense, though perhaps diplomats may be forgiven a measure of flattery for the sake of warm relations. Academics have far less excuse for talking this way.

President Obama's Cairo Speech. Speaking to an audience at Cairo University on June 4, 2009, President Barack Obama said he had come "to seek a new beginning between the United States and Muslims around the world; one based on mutual interest and mutual respect." He was confident this could occur since the two parties shared "common principles—principles of justice and progress; tolerance and the dignity of all human beings."[9]

He rehearsed the contributions of Islam to civilization, which "carried the light of learning through so many centuries, paving the way for Europe's

Renaissance and Enlightenment," and to America, where "Islam has always been a part of [her] story." This portion of the speech has been justifiably criticized for its exaggerations.[10]

In the course of his remarks, he made two curious historical references. First, he said, "In signing the Treaty of Tripoli in 1796, our second President John Adams wrote, 'The United States has in itself no character of enmity against the laws, religion or tranquility of Muslims.'" Second, he stated, "Islam has a proud tradition of tolerance. We see it in the history of Andalusia and Cordoba during the Inquisition."[11]

With regard to the first, why was there a Treaty of Tripoli in 1796? Because, after suffering seven centuries of Muslim occupation, Spain rid herself of the invaders. In 1492, when they sent Columbus sailing west toward the New World, they cast the Moors back into their namesake homelands, today's Morocco and Mauritania. Then from their restored abode in North Africa, the Muslims began seizing commercial and military ships, demanding exorbitant sums of protection money from the maritime nations of Europe. Thus the Barbary pirates exercised a stranglehold on the Mediterranean.

For a time the United States paid the protection money, but the cost became intolerable, and the nation went to war against the pirates. In 1805 American forces won a signal victory when a unit marched overland from Egypt to defeat the foe, providing material for the Marine hymn, which notes that the "leathernecks" have fought their country's battles "to the shores of Tripoli."

Regarding the second item, what were these allegedly tolerant Muslims doing in Andalusia and Cordoba in the first place? Spain is a long way from Saudi Arabia, where Islam began. The simple answer is that this "religion of peace" had, within a hundred years of its militaristic founder's death, seized lands 1,000 miles to the east and west and 500 miles to the north and south. Mohammed died in 632, and 80 years later Muslims crossed the straits of Gibraltar into Europe. Had these Muslim forces not been stopped by Charles Martel's army at Tours, around a hundred miles from Paris, in 732, all Europe might have become Muslim. (This Muslim assault on Europe continued in the east for centuries, ending in 1683, when they were finally repelled at the outskirts of Vienna.)

So President Obama should go easy on glorying in Tripoli and Andalusia. The background stories do not serve his cause well.

Parasitism. A child of an honored family in Egypt, Nonie Darwish has now turned a critical eye on her former Muslim culture. She wrote this several years before the Obama speech in Cairo, but it speaks to his claims concerning the glories of early Islam.

Muslim societies have not contributed much to humanity, but have actually destroyed and sucked away the talent and innovation bit by bit from the nations they conquered. Contrary to conventional wisdom, it is not Arab talent that came out of the Middle East, but the talent of the great civilizations conquered by Arabs and their swords. Established great civilizations and great religions such as the Assyrians, the Egyptian Copts, and others have been practically eradicated. Just look at what happened to Egypt.

Muslim society has been a taker for a long time and not a giver. All they have given the world are memories of their old glory days when they took over Spain, Egypt, Persia, Mesopotamia, and the Ottomans and then called them "Muslim and Arab contributions to the world." The Arabian Peninsula, obsessed with preserving their way of life and exporting it to the rest of the world, must look closely to the sword on their flag and see the destruction they left behind when they forced Islam and Sharia on great civilizations, sucked the life out of their brilliance and greatness, and left them in poverty, chaos, and destruction. Just as the desert-raiding tribes of history did to each other, they did and are still doing that to the world.

If it was not for the discovery of oil—even that was discovered and developed by the West—I do not know what the Saudis would have contributed to the world other than terrorism, fanaticism, injustice, and Fascist states under the guise of religion. They hate infidels and want to kill them, but love the infidel's technology, their dollars, their air conditioners, their cars, and their many gadgets. They love it so much, they have created huge American-style indoor shopping malls with all the American stores; they have used their oil wealth to fabricate tropical islands off their coasts and create indoor Alpine-style ski slopes in the desert, snow and all. Yet they curse the infidel they love to imitate.[12]

Chile mine relief. In the fall of 2010, the eyes of the world were focused on the rescue of 33 Chilean miners from more than 2,000 feet below the surface. "To ensure success, Chile's state mining company sought out the best equipment available in the world. . . . For video equipment it looked to Japan. The rescue cable came from Germany."[13] Furthermore a "U.S. company supplied the drilling technology that broke through to the miners first. NASA donated a high-calorie liquid diet. An Austrian company made the capsule's winch-and-pulley system."[14]

The list goes on: "Food service to the miners was provided by Aramark [of Philadelphia], which developed a way to get vacuum-packed food down the small bore hole after the miners were discovered alive"; NASA also "provided advice on how the miners could cope psychologically . . . and aided in design and construction of the pod that hauled the miners to the surface"; UPS shipped mining equipment to the site; "a cell phone with its own projector came from Samsung of South Korea"; "socks made with copper fiber that eliminated bacteria, thereby reducing odor and infection, came from Cupron Inc. of Richmond"; the drill bit and rig came from two companies in Pennsylvania, Center Rock and Schramm.[15]

Not surprising in all this is the lack of technological help from a Muslim-majority country. Science and engineering do not flourish in their repressive cultures. As Chicago musical instrument dealer Najib Shaheen puts it, with a laugh, "We Arabs export two major things, oil and ouds [a forerunner to the mandolin]."[16] Or to put it more precisely, "The combined non-oil exports of Middle Eastern and North African countries is about US $40 billion per year, which is lower than that of Finland."[17] That is, one small Scandinavian nation outweighs dozens of Muslim nations in this respect.

Haiti relief. In this same vein Muslim-majority nations were absent from the list of nations rushing to bring aid to Haiti in the days immediately following the earthquake. The United States gave $100 million and sent "ships, helicopters, planes, rescue teams, a floating hospital and more than 5,000 troops." Australia committed $10 million, Japan $5 million, and both Brazil and Britain designated $10 million. Canada offered to match citizen donations up to $105 million and provided military rescue and relief. China sent 50 soldiers, who brought three sniffer dogs with them, and a rescue team, plus 20 tons of aid. France provided "two teams of firefighters with trained dogs, rescue team and relief supplies." Cuba supplied 30 doctors. And so it went, with dozens of nations pitching in. The European Commission sent $4.7 million, the Arab League nothing.[18]

To this early *Sydney Morning Herald* tally, the Associated Press added $5.3 million from Norway, $1.46 million from Italy, $2 million each from the Netherlands and the Italian bishops' conference, $4.37 million from Spain, $2.17 million from Germany, and much in the way of water purification equipment, rescue teams, tentage, surgical theaters, food, and other items from Sweden, Venezuela, Iceland, Portugal, Taiwan, Switzerland, and Israel.[19]

To be fair, subsequent reports noted $1 million pledges from Kuwait and Morocco, a mobile hospital from Turkey, a planeload of supplies from Jordan, and materiel from Qatar and Iran.[20] Then came Indonesia, with the world's largest Muslim population,[21] and finally, two weeks after the quake, the oil-rich Saudis, "after taking a beating in the media . . . agreed to pitch in $50 million to help the poor Caribbean Sea nation"[22] But there was no mistaking who was primed for charity at the moment of crisis, and who did not need a media storm to get them to do the right thing.

"Happy Arabia." With the rise of terrorism in Yemen, *The New York Times Magazine* ran a piece on this benighted land with a surprising history of pre-Muslim prosperity:

> Two thousand years ago, the area east of Sana held one of the earth's most prosperous kingdoms, a lush agricultural region of spices and fruits, fed by irrigation canals from a vast man-made dam. The Romans called Yemen "Arabia Felis," or Happy Arabia. Today, the eastern region is an arid wasteland. Most people scrape by on less than $2 a day, even though they live atop Yemen's oil and gas fields. There are few ways to make a living other

than smuggling, goat-herding and kidnapping. The region is also, chronically, a war zone. Tribal feuds have always been part of life here, but in recent years they have grown so common and so deadly that as much as a quarter of the population cannot go to school or work for fear of being killed. The feuds often devolve into battles with bands of raiders mowing down their rivals with machine-gun fire or launching mortars into a neighboring village. No one knows how many people die in these wars, but Khaled Fattah, a sociologist who has studied Yemen's tribes for years, told me that hundreds of victims a year is a conservative estimate. Every time I drive out of Sana I get an ominous sense of going backward in time to a more lawless era.[23]

Centuries of intellectual drought. Reviewing Christopher Caldwell's *Reflections on the Revolution in Europe*, Manhattan Institute fellow Theodore Dalrymple observes,

Islam has added nothing to the stock of human knowledge or intellect for hundreds of years and it is unlikely ever to do so again. Islamic polities usually stink of iniquity and corruption; Islam is incompatible with the modern world so long as it does not permit apostasy and believes in the legal inferiority of people of other religions. The problem for Islam is that an alteration of its attitudes in this regard implies error in the past; an admission of error in the past undermines all its claims to inerrancy.[24]

Dalrymple continues:

Though the British were once mighty, the collapse of the Church has meant the collapse of culture. Though the mighty British Empire once took a paternalistic approach to the poor Indians, now Hindu and Sikh immigrants to Britain have lower unemployment and imprisonment rates and better educational test scores than their native, white counterparts. Alas, the Muslims fall to the bottom of all groups. Only when Islam is mixed with other religions or watered-down as with the Indonesians in the Netherlands, new immigrants fare well.[25]

Polygamy and marriage. Islam is rough on marriage. As the aforementioned Nonie Darwish, daughter of a high-ranking Egyptian army officer, observed:

Many of the Arab/Muslim social problems stem directly from the institution of polygamy. The pre-Islamic tribal desert culture in the Arabian Peninsula practiced polygamy for centuries. When Islam came upon the scene in the seventh century, instead of abolishing the practice, it codified polygamy into Islamic law, limiting men to four wives plus any number of slave women. And so this ancient form of marriage, practiced long before Muhammed arrived, ended up becoming the law for Muslims around the world and in all cultures to this day. A complex of Islamic marriage and divorce laws, designed to protect men's "honor" and maintain their total control over women, compounds the devastating consequences of this practice. . . . How does this affect the dynamics between a husband and wife? Men do not even have to exercise their right to additional wives for the damage to be done. By allowing men to be "loyal" to up to four wives, the stage is set for women always to distrust their husbands. Nor can they trust women friends. Any other woman could shamelessly become an eligible "bachelorette" for one's husband. . . .

The end result is en environment that sets women up as adversaries against one another, causing much unnecessary distrust and caution. Competitive relationships among women also deprive them of forming support groups to stand up to the many injustices they are all suffering under. Thus relationships among women in Muslim countries become haphazard, strained, and even hostile. Few Muslim women venture to form relationships outside the family or clan, and very often husbands discourage it. Women's groups and organizations for a common cause and to influence change are almost nonexistent in the clanlike Muslim culture. . . .

And, of course, fear of polygamy makes it impossible for a wife to form a bond of trust with her husband. When a husband starts earning more money, a warning bell starts ringing in a woman's head, since he can now afford the second wife. I remember hearing conversations among Arab wives advising one another to "pluck up his feathers," meaning spend his money as fast as possible before there is extra for another wife. . . .

A Muslim wife is threatened by single women in a way that no Christian wife can imagine. It is true that Christian husbands can and do cheat on their wives, but the threat of a mistress and the threat of a legal wife in the eyes of society and God are two very different things.[26]

Car rental and restaurant seating. Writing for *Vanity Fair*, *New York Times* columnist Maureen Dowd chronicled the indignities and absurdities she encountered as a woman on a trip to Saudi Arabia:

- On this trip, at a Budget Rent a Car, the man at the counter explained to me that women could rent cars only if they paid extra for a driver. (And, to boot, it would be dishonorable for a woman to sit in the passenger seat unless a male relative were driving.)
- At various establishments I began amusing myself by seeing how long it took for a male Cerberus to dart forward and block the way to the front sections reserved for men. . . . I did manage a moment of Pyrrhic triumph in the deserted men's section in the lobby café of the Jidda Hilton, ordering a cappuccino, but then the waiter informed me that he couldn't serve it until I moved five feet back to the women's section.
- I wore a hot-pink shirt with fringe to go to an interview with the Saudi education minister. When I came down from my hotel room, the men in the lobby glared with such hostility that I thought they'd pelt me to death with their [palm] dates. My minder turned me back to the elevator. "Go get your abaya!" he yelled. "They'll kill you!" . . . This was right around the time when 15 Saudi schoolgirls had died in a fire because the *mutawa* [the religious police, formally known as the Commission for the Promotion of Virtue and Prevention of Vice] wouldn't let them escape without their headscarves and abayas, a horrifying episode that shook the Kingdom.
- Still, this time around I decided to look on the sunny side of repression. Feel guilty about not jogging? Don't even try! Tired of running off to every new exhibition? Lucky you—there aren't any art museums! Can't decide

which sybaritic treatment to select at the hotel spa? Relax—the spa's just for men. And you never have to stress about a bad-hair day.[27]

Muslims also find archaeology intimidating. "Many pious Muslims look askance at civilizations that pre-date Islam ('the time of ignorance,' as they call it), and they have reservations about archaeological digs that may turn up Christian sites."[28]

Women in flight. In the early days of aviation, women found access to the controls difficult: "At no point was their path easy. To fly was to cajole men into giving them rides, to beg to be taught, to meet a wall of masculine resistance." It was difficult for women to get good flight training, financial backing, or productive flying jobs. Nevertheless, they flew, and distinguished themselves at it, as with these pioneers: Ruth Law, who set a nonstop distance record in 1916, flying 590 miles from Chicago to Hornell, New York; acrobatic pilot Katherine Stinson, who became the first person to do a "sharp roll on top of a loop"; Belgium's Helene Dutrieu, who outflew 14 male pilots to win the Italian King's Cup in Florence in 1911; Germany's Malli Beese who "opened a flying school in Berlin and taught men pilots by the dozens"; Marie Marvingt whom France "invited . . . to organize a civilian air ambulance service in the . . . protectorate of Morocco"; and of course Amelia Earhart, who crossed the Atlantic in record time in 1932.[29]

From nation to nation, women pioneers climbed into the cockpit—Anesia Pinheiro of Brazil, Lidia Zvereva of Russia, Millicent Bryant of Australia, Ruthy Tu of China, and Tadashi Hyodo of Japan. And their wartime service delivering planes and towing aerial targets was critical in World War II, whether in Britain's Air Transport Auxiliary or America's Women's Auxiliary Ferrying Squadron (later the Women Airforce Service Pilots). Altogether, American women delivered 12,650 planes, flew 60 million miles, with 38 of the 1,074 pilots losing their lives.[30]

Muslim women are conspicuously absent from the list. Still, there was one, but it took a Muslim-resistant ruler to make it happen:

> Scarcely a decade after her country-women had been liberated from the harems of the ancient Ottoman Empire, a petite Turkish orphan named Sabiha Gokcen became her nation's first woman flier. . . . Influence helped. After her parents died in the upheavals that convulsed Turkey after World War I, Sabiha was adopted by Turkey's strong man, Kemal Ataturk, who ruled and modernized the country during the 1920s and 1930s. Finding his adopted daughter smitten by the rage to fly, Ataturk used his clout to have her admitted to a civilian flying school, then to the Turkish Army's air-cadet program.[31]

Honor killings. Honor killings are rife in the Muslim world. Syria's Bashar Assad made news when he doubled the maximum penalty to two years in prison. But in Jordan, the "Parliament has repeatedly blocked a law that would

impose harsher penalties on men who kill their female relatives for the sake of
honour; the lawmakers say it would encourage adultery." And the warrant for
such killing can be as simple as the wearing of immodest clothes—anything the
men consider to have "besmirched the family's moral standing."[32]

Sharia "utopias." Writing in *The Third Choice*, Australian scholar Mark Durie
observes what happens when Muslim law moves in.

> Four of the strictest Sharia-observant societies in modern times have been Iran, Afghani-
> stan under the Taliban, Saudi Arabia and Sudan. None of these are model states. . . .
> The Islamic revolution in Iran did not usher in a Sharia utopia, but a society plagued
> by homelessness, drug use, prostitution and suicide. As a result, many young Iranians
> are rejecting Islam. The Taliban, once hailed by the Muslim diaspora around the world
> as heroes of the global Islamic movement, turned out to be cruel tyrants. The Sudanese
> Islamic government's strategy of unleashing the Islamic jihad against its own citizens has
> fueled one of the bloodiest civil wars of the late 20th and early 21st century, causing the
> deaths of millions. Saudi Arabia is notorious for its human rights abuses, including discrimi-
> nating against women and religious minorities.[33]

Failed Islamic states. In his cry for reform, Malaysian Muslim Syed Akbar Ali
decries the state of affairs among his coreligionists. In his book *Malaysia and
the Club of Doom: The Collapse of the Islamic Countries*, he argues that "all the
Islamic countries are well qualified to become failed states." He wants "Muslim
readers to realize this and then hopefully they will start panicking immediately.
Perhaps they will then be motivated to urgently do something useful and positive to rectify the predicament they are in."[34] What he hopes for is a return to a
true reading of the Qur'an.

To build his case, he presents evidence that "all the 22 members of the Arab
League today are basket cases."[35] He quotes from a column by Dr. Farrukh
Saleem, one in which he observes, among other things, that (a) America's GDP
is five times that of the 57 Muslim countries combined; (b) only 1 percent of
Arabs have a computer; (c) 57 Muslim countries have a total of fewer than 600
universities whereas India has 8,407 and the United States has 5,758; (d) over
a 105-year period "1.4 billion Muslims have produced eight Nobel Laureates
while a mere 14 million Jews have produced 167 Nobel Laureates; and (e) 60
percent of Muslims are illiterate compared to 22 percent of "Christendom."[36]

Kemal Ataturk. The Muslim Ottoman Empire chose the wrong side in World
War I, suffering defeat along with the Central Powers. Seizing the teachable
moment, Mustafa Kemal launched "sweeping Western-style reforms. During
Ataturk's stupendous feat of modernization, when the hat replaced the fez,
women were forbidden to wear veils and the Latin alphabet supplanted the Arabic script."[37] He was determined "to exclude Islam from the public domain," and

early in his regime, "religion courts, which applied Muslim canon law in matters of personal status—marriage, divorce, inheritance—were closed down."[38]

> Kemal and his reformers wanted to model their new nation on the West, but all existing institutions were unmistakably Eastern. What was more, the Turks were conditioned to see themselves more as an *Ummah* (Muslim community) than a nation, and had long been discouraged from any involvement in politics, industry, commerce or other potential source of power that could challenge the absolute authority of the Ottomans. The government faced the almost impossible tasks of creating a national consciousness, absorbing Western civilization and reinterpreting Islam.[39]

This was a big job but a sadly necessary one. How much better it would have been had Muslim invaders left Turkey alone to take its natural place in the West, where civilization was developing under Christian influence. After all, this was the land of the seven churches of Asia, of Paul's journeys and letters to the Galatians and Ephesians, of Peter's letter to the saints in "Pontus, Galatia, Cappadocia, Asia, and Bithynia" (1 Pet 1:1), and of the early church councils in Nicea, Chalcedon, Ephesus, and Constantinople.

Notes

1 See http://www.yale.edu/wje/html/je_stamp_campaign.html.
2 Ibid.
3 Conn Iggulden and David Iggulden, *The Dangerous Book of Heroes* (New York: Harper-Collins/Morrow, 2010), 324.
4 Ibid., 225.
5 Andrew Morton, *Angelina: An Unauthorized Biography* (New York: St. Martin's, 2010), photo captions between pages 248 and 249.
6 Scott Eyman, *Empire of Dreams: The Epic Life of Cecil B. DeMille* (New York: Simon & Schuster, 2010), 508.
7 From dissenting opinion in *Van Orden v. Perry*, 545 U.S. 677 (2005), in Frank S. Ravitch, *Law and Religion, a Reader: Cases, Concepts, and Theory*, 2nd ed. (St. Paul: Thomson/West, 2008), 312.
8 *The Christian Century*, August 24, 2010, front cover.
9 "Text: Obama's Speech in Cairo," *The New York Times*, June 4, 2009; http://www.nytimes.com/2009/06/04/us/politics/04obama.text.html (accessed September 21, 2010).
10 See, e.g., Frank J. Tipler, "Obama Flunks History at Cairo U," *Pajamasmedia.com* (June 7, 2009); http://pajamasmedia.com/blog/obama-flunks-history-at-cairo-u (accessed December 16, 2010); and Vickie McClure Davison, "Obama's Cairo Speech: Revises & Rewrites Muslim History . . . AGAIN," *Frugal-Café* (June 10, 2009); http://www.frugal-cafe.com/public_html/frugal-blog/frugal-cafe-blogzone/2009/06/10/obamas-cairo-speech-revises-rewrites-muslim-history-again (accessed December 16, 2010).
11 Ibid.
12 Nonie Darwish, *Cruel and Usual Punishment: The Terrifying Global Implications of Islamic Law* (Nashville: Thomas Nelson, 2008), 172–73.
13 Alan Levin, "U.S. Firms had part in success," *USA Today*, October 14, 2010, 5A.

14 "Chile's Miner Miracle Pulls a Fractured World Together," *USA Today*, October 14, 2010, 8A.

15 Joe McKendrick, "Chile Mine Rescue Made Possible by Innovative Companies from Across the Globe," *Smart Planet*, October 14, 2010; http://www.smartplanet.com/business/blog/business-brains/chile-mine-rescue-made-possible-by-innovative-companies-from-across-the-globe/11020 (accessed October 16, 2010).

16 Nina Roberts, "He Plans Arab Music, Makes and Fixes Ouds," *The Wall Street Journal* (March 31, 2009): D7.

17 Nor Mohamed Yakcop, "The Way Forward for the Muslim Ummah," Malaysian Treasury Web site; http://www.treasury.gov.my/index.php?option=com_content&view=article&id=884%3Athe-way-forward-for-the-muslim-ummah-by-nor-mohamed-yakcop&catid=53%3Aucapan&Itemid=251&lang=my (accessed October 17, 2003).

18 "Where Haiti Aid Is Coming From," *Sydney Morning Herald*, January 15, 2010; http://www.smh.com.au/world/where-haiti-aid-is-coming-from-20100115-mar4.html (accessed October 16, 2010).

19 "International Aid to Haiti: Who's Giving?" Associated Press; http://www.cbsnews.com/stories/2010/01/14/world/main6097735.shtml (accessed October 16, 2010).

20 "Saudi Arabia: Unlike Qatar, Iran and Jordan, Kingdom Fails to Cough Up Haiti Cash," *Los Angeles Times*, January 17, 2010; http://latimesblogs.latimes.com/babylonbeyond/2010/01/saudi-arabia-unlike-qatar-iran-and-jordan-kingdom-fails-to-cough-up-haiti-cash.html (accessed October 16, 2010).

21 Ricki Yudhistira, "Indonesian Aid for Haiti Arrives in Dominican Rep," *Jakarta Post*, January 21, 2010; http://www.thejakartapost.com/news/2010/01/21/indonesian-aid-haiti-arrives-dominican-rep.html (accessed October 16, 2010).

22 "Saudi Arabia: Riyadh Commits $50 Million to Haiti Relief Efforts," *Los Angeles Times*, January 25, 2010; http://latimesblogs.latimes.com/babylonbeyond/2010/01/saudi-arabia-riyadh-commits-50-million-to-haiti-relief-efforts.html (accessed October 16, 2010).

23 Robert F. Worth, "The Desert War," *The New York Times Magazine*, July 11, 2010, 36.

24 Theodore Dalrymple, "Struggle for a Continent," review of Christopher Caldwell's *Reflections on the Revolution in Europe: Immigration, Islam, and the West* (New York: Doubleday, 2009) in *National Review*, August 10, 2009, 44.

25 Ibid.

26 Nonie Darwish, *Now They Call Me Infidel: Why I Renounced Jihad for America, Israel, and the War on Terror* (New York: Penguin, 2006), 67–71.

27 Maureen Dowd, "A Girl's Guide to Saudi Arabia," *Vanity Fair*, August 2010, 127–28.

28 Ibid., 128.

29 Valerie Moolman, *Women Aloft* (Alexandria, VA: Time-Life Books, 1981), 7, 10, 12, 17, 28–29, 30, 67.

30 Ibid., 20–21, 152.

31 Ibid., 136.

32 "The Law Changes. Will Attitudes?" *The Economist*, July 18, 2009, 45.

33 Mark Durie, *The Third Choice: Islam, Dhimmitude and Freedom* (Melbourne, Australia: Deror, 2010), 50.

34 Syed Akbar Ali, *Malaysia and the Club of Doom: The Collapse of the Islamic Countries* (Kuala Lumpur, Malaysia: Syed Akbar Ali, 2006), 7.

35 Ibid., 5.

36 Farrukh Saleem, "What Went Wrong?" cited in ibid., 13–14; http://islamicterrorism.
    wordpress.com/2008/07/01/muslims-amongst-worlds-poorest-weakest-illiterate-what-
    went-wrong (accessed June 8, 2010).
37 *Insight Guide: Turkey* (London: APA/Langenscheidt, 2008), 71.
38 Andrew Mango, *Ataturk: The Biography of the Founder of Modern Turkey* (Woodstock, NY:
    Overlook, 2000), 407.
39 *Insight Guide: Turkey*, 59.

THE FRUIT OF FALSE SYSTEMS: ANIMISM, EASTERN THOUGHT, AND IRRELIGION

T HOUGH THE THREAT AND failings of Islam are front and center in our consciousness today, the world continues to suffer from the baleful influence of other ancient and false perspectives. We pick up the survey with one which appeared prominently in the Old Testament—animism or nature worship, as exemplified by the cult devoted to the "storm god" Baal.

Animism

Some are inclined to romanticize nature worship of one sort of another. Americans have a particular weakness for the animistic pronouncements and worship practices of the Indians. But this approach to religion has a less-than-impressive track record.

Albinos and skull collections. In his journals British missionary explorer David Livingstone tells of a tribal custom:

> If a man wished to curry favor with a Batoka chief, he ascertained when a stranger was about to leave, and waylaid him at a distance from the town, and when he brought his head back to the chief, it was mounted as a trophy, the different chiefs viewing with each other as to which should mount the greatest number of skulls in his village.[1]

In a January 6, 1856, entry Livingstone also recounted the terrible fate of albinos.

> During the time I resided at Mabotsa, a woman came to the station with a fine boy, an Albino. The father had ordered her to throw him away, but she clung to her offspring for many years. He was remarkably intelligent for his age. The pupil of the eye was of a pink

color, and the eye itself was unsteady in vision. The hair, or rather wool, was yellow, and the features were those common among the Bechuanas. After I left the place the mother is said to have become tired of living apart from the father, who refused to have her while she retained the son. She took him out one day, and killed him close to the village of Mabotsa, and nothing was done to her by the authorities. From having met with no Albinos in Londa, I suspect they are there also put to death.[2]

Livingstone certainly recognized "frequent instances of genuine kindness and liberality" among the natives and "came to the conclusion that they are just such a strange mixture of good and evil as men are everywhere else," but he did notice one striking difference:

> There is not among them an approach to that constant stream of benevolence flowing from the rich to the poor which we have in England, nor yet the unostentatious attentions which have among our own poor to each other. . . . The rich show kindness to the poor in expectation of services, and a poor person who has no relatives will seldom be supplied even with water in illness, and, when dead, will be dragged out to be devoured by the hyaenas instead of being buried. Relatives along will condescend to touch a dead body.[3]

Little wonder that Livingstone was not the fan of multiculturalism so common today. Rather, he desired that the Bible—"the Magna Carta of all the rights and privileges of modern civilization"—be spread abroad in Africa. He had seen firsthand the transforming work of the gospel. In a culture where it was a "transgression" for a man to cry, Livingstone witnessed the following: "Baba, a mighty hunter [and] interpreter . . . sat listening to the Gospel in the church at Kuruman, and the gracious words of Christ, made to touch his heart, evidently by the Holy Spirit, melted him into tears; I have seen him and others sink down to the ground weeping."[4]

Female genital mutilation. Even today animism is the source of much backwardness. For instance "the Yoruba believe that the divinity of smallpox prowls about when the sun is hot," and the Nuer regard calamities such as drought, epidemics, locust invasions, wars, and floods as "God's will about which they can do nothing." Little wonder that modern medicine, insecticides, dams and such are slow in coming, if at all.[5]

To appease the powers of the spiritual world,

> the items for sacrifice include cattle, sheep, goats, chickens, dogs and even human beings. Items used for offerings include foodstuffs like fruits, maize, millet, nuts, cassava, vegetables, leaves, honey and eggs; beverages like porridge, milk, beer, wine and water; and other things of a miscellaneous nature like the dung of the hyrax, cloth, money, chalk, incense, agricultural implements, ornaments, tobacco and cowrie-shells. Blood is also offered by a number of societies. Thus, almost everything that man can get hold of and use is sacrificed or offered to God and other spiritual beings.[6]

Female genital mutilation is also an aspect of these cultures. Among the Nandi, this initiation ritual is detailed and grotesque. On the day of the "surgery," "the boys begin to vex the girls by calling them cowards and other despising names. This is intended to stimulate bravery and courage in the girls." Numbed by stinging nettles, the girls are spared some of the pain of the operation, but it is traumatic nonetheless. Those found to be virgins are seated on stools; those not are seated on the dirt.

> The spectators rush away quickly to spread the news of who among the girls have been cowards and who have been virgins, or otherwise. This is the most critical moment for the relatives and families whose girls are initiated. If a girl is reported to be a coward or not a virgin, the parents and brothers are so ashamed that they threaten to kill themselves or kill the girl concerned. Only the intervention of other people stops them from actually carrying out this threat.[7]

Hinduism

Unless a Westerner has been immersed in a Hindu culture, he has little understanding of what the religion entails or produces. His impression may be limited to the gentle Krishna follower he might encounter in an airport or to the pleasure he feels at a yoga class. But there is far more to the story.

Caste system. Though it was outlawed in 1950 when India became a republic, the caste system persists in the popular mind and influences the way Hindus treat one another. They can quickly determine one another's status merely by hearing the family name. And the prejudice is simply an outworking of the doctrine of karma, which says that untouchables are "burdened with demeaning tasks only because of their own misdeeds in past lives." Their duty is to play their humiliating roles well in hopes that they will fare better in their next reincarnation, even if this means carrying human dung on their heads.[8]

Untouchables, or dalits, once had "to place clay pots around their necks to prevent their spit from polluting the ground" and "attach brooms to their rumps to wipe out their footprints."[9] This is no longer the case, but discrimination still occurs, for it is rooted in the religion itself. They believe that God created the caste system and that the 165 million Dalits in India are justly consigned to their situation. This is the teaching of the Rig-Veda, dating to 1000 BC. Herein, the "cosmic giant, Purusha" gave up his body parts, mouth, arms, thighs, and feet—to establish the various orders—the priestly, warrior/landowner, merchant, and servant classes. The untouchables don't even rate.[10]

One might think that a Nobel laureate such as V. S. Naipaul would not be susceptible to such nonsense, but he is fastidious in maintaining the purity of his birth privilege. As one playwright and novelist noticed, V. S. Naipaul was self-consciously above menial work, such as making his own bed: "He is a

Brahmin, so he wouldn't do any physical work. We were asked to make our own beds, just to pull back the duvet, but Vidia refused."[11] Elsewhere in an interview he said, "I have never had to work for hire; I made a vow at an early age never to work, never to become involved with people in that way. That has given me a freedom from people, from entanglements, from rivalries, from competition. I have no enemies, no rivals, no masters; I fear no one."[12] When *Vogue* did a reverential profile of the author, they observed, "He has never wanted children. His life is distinguished and shaped by extreme fastidiousness. It manifests itself physically as a brahminical fear of contamination. He didn't want to borrow a shirt to be photographed in."[13]

Suttee. Richard Grenier writes the following about *suttee*, "the ritual immolation by fire of widows on their husbands' funeral pyre."

> In southern India the widow was flung into her husband's fire. In the valley of the Ganges she was placed on the pyre when it was already aflame. In western India, she supported the head of the corpse with her right hand, while, torch in her left, she was allowed the honor of setting the whole thing on fire herself. In the north, where perhaps women were more impious, the widow's body was constrained on the burning pyre by long poles pressed down by her relatives, just in case, screaming in terror and choking and burning to death, she might forget her *dharma*.[14]

Fortunately the missionary work of William Carey and the influence of British colonialism put a stop to this.

Buddhism

Buddhism is built on an impossibility, that of the personal quenching of desire. As sixties radical Tom Hayden observed of homosexual Buddhist poet Alan Ginsberg, "Somewhat ironic given his Buddhist values, he was systematic promoter and archivist of himself, his friends, and an endless Rolodex range of contacts among the high and mighty."[15]

Nevertheless Buddhism has a great public relations program, but it masks a deeper truth. The book *Buddhist Warfare* helps put the illusion to rest: "Though traditionally regarded as a peaceful religion, Buddhism has a dark side. On multiple occasions over the past fifteen centuries, Buddhist leaders have sanctioned violence, and even war. . . . Buddhist organizations have used religious images and rhetoric to support military conquest throughout history."[16]

And Buddhist violence is not strictly a matter of ancient wars; it manifests itself in aggression against Christian churches today. For instance in recent years in Sri Lanka, Buddhist monks have accompanied mobs throwing rocks at and breathing threats toward various Christian congregations at worship.[17]

Brit Hume, of Fox News television, was mercilessly condemned for his suggestion that Tiger Woods's Buddhism did not give him what he needed to find his way out of the mire of multiple adulteries, the loss of his family, and the ruin of his commercial cachet. Here is the background on the religious life of this golfer.

> Tiger was nine years old when [his mother] Kultida took him to Thailand to introduce him to her native country. She brought him to a Buddhist monk to analyze a chart she had kept on Tiger's life. Unaware of Tiger's accomplishments on the golf course, the monk told Kultida that Tiger was a special child destined for leadership. If he went into the military, she was told, he would become a four-star general.
>
> Tiger's decision to become a Buddhist was a choice he made as a child to follow the religion of his mother: Both Earl and Kultida promised not to pressure him; he could choose his own religion. But Earl wasn't devout; he didn't practice Christianity in the same way that Kultida practiced Buddhism. She felt that it gave her an inner peace, a tranquility that helped her to cope with the chaos around: It had been a stabilizing force in her life, and she was thrilled that Tiger was interested in following it as well.
>
> When Tiger was young, he and Kultida would practice their Buddhism together: "Tiger and Kultida used to meditate every night in their living room as he was growing up," explained a family friend. "Kultida used Buddhism to give him some peace after a day on the course with his father. Earl would push him hard during the day, and Kultida would help center him at night through prayer and mediation."
>
> Tiger continued his nightly meditation into adulthood, but he drifted away from some of the teachings that Kultida espoused. She believed that she could reach ultimate enlightenment through Buddhism. Tiger, however, believed that it was impossible to achieve perfection. The best he could do was strive to make himself into the best person he could possibly be.[18]

After he had been caught having had at least nine affairs, he delivered a message of apology. The Winter Olympics were preempted for his 13-minute talk, a talk that 30 million people saw on TV and 12 million heard on radio: "I want to say to each of you, simply and directly, I am deeply sorry for the irresponsible and selfish behavior I engaged in." He said, "I have a lot to atone for" and "It's now up to me to make amends, and that starts by never repeating the mistakes I've made. It's up to me to start living a life of integrity."[19]

He then tied recovery to his Buddhism:

> Part of following this path for me is Buddhism, which my mother taught me at a young age. People probably don't realize it, but I was raised a Buddhist, and I actively practiced my faith from childhood until I drifted away from it in recent years. Buddhism teaches that a craving for things outside ourselves causes an unhappy and pointless search for security. It teaches me to stop following every impulse and to learn restraint. Obviously I lost track of what I was taught.[20]

But Hume said, "The extent to which he can recover seems to me depends on his faith." He continued, "He is said to be a Buddhist. I don't think that faith offers the kind of forgiveness and redemption that is offered by the Christian faith. My message to Tiger would be, 'Tiger, turn to the Christian faith and you can make a total recovery and be a *great* example to the world.'"[21]

Unfortunately as yet Woods seems immune to God's offer of grace. "In the Buddhist religion you have to work for it yourself, internally, in order to achieve anything in life and set up the next life. It is all about what you do and you get out of it what you put into it."[22]

Shintoism

The Japanese have developed their own national religion, and it has paired easily with Buddhism. The joint record of these faiths was not gratifying in World War II.

- In 1941 the Japanese launched their notorious "Three All" offensive, explicitly named for its purpose, to "Kill All, Burn All, Destroy All." Several million Chinese died, including at least 50,000 in the Nanjing massacre in 1937.
- During Japan's war in China, the practices of conducting bayonet training on live prisoners, and of beheading them, became institutionalized.
- A British historian has observed that the Imperial Army's frequent resort to rape reflected the fact that the status of women in Japan was low, while those of subject peoples possessed no status at all.
- In northern Burma [Col Masanobu Tsuji] dined off the liver of a dead Allied pilot, castigating as cowards those who refused to share his meal: "The more we eat, the brighter will burn the first of our hatred for the enemy."
- When the war ended, it became possible to compare the fates of Allied servicemen under the Nazis and the Japanese. Just 4 percent of British and American POWs had died in German hands. Yet 27 percent—35,756 out of 132,134—of Western Allied prisoners lost their lives in Japanese captivity.
- When a cholera epidemic struck Tamil railway workers at Nieke in June 1943, a barracks containing 250 infected men, women, and children was simply torched.[23]

This is a terrible record, but the Japanese are averse to giving it full, penitent recognition: "Germany has paid almost $6 billion to 1.5 million victims of the Hitler era. Austria has paid $400 million to 132,000. By contrast, modern Japan goes to extraordinary lengths to escape any admission of responsibility, far less of liability for compensation, towards its wartime victims."[24]

Bushido. Bushido, the samurai or warrior ethic, is another Shinto hybrid, this one drawing on elements of Confucianism and Buddhism. It has a chilling affinity for brutality, one that showed itself throughout World War II, notably in the "Rape of Nanking" (the Nanjing massacre).

From a classic guidebook, here are words of admonition for those who would raise their children according to this ruthless code:

> Kichizaemon Yamamoto . . . learned under the guidance of his father how to hack dogs. He did this at the age of five. And at the age of fifteen, he learned how to hack criminals.
>
> It was requisite for samurais of old to cut off heads before they reached fourteen or fifteen years.
>
> Lord Kasushige, when very young, learned to cut under the direction of his father, Lord Naoshige. In due course, he could slaughter ten people on end. It is unwise not to have the children of the common (samurais) kill at all. In olden days, even the upper (Lord) engaged in this activity. Most of the samurais today say, "It is useless," or "It is not meritorious to cut bound men," or "It is foul and dirty." These are all excuses. In short, it would appear that their real intention is to polish their nails and to keep respectability, but the truth is that they fall short of the practice of the military profession.
>
> If we inquire into their disposition, we see that they make excuses not to kill by hiding behind a cloak of words. The reason they do this is that they expect they will feel uneasy at the deed.
>
> Because it is a thing for samurais to do, Naoshige coached his son. I, myself, some years ago, cut at the execution grounds at Kase. And I felt comfortable and enlivened. Thinking of it as uncomfortable is just a symptom of inner cowardice.[25]

The Japanese Meiji movement. In the mid-nineteenth century, Japan was a Buddhist and Shinto nation, dominated by shoguns and samurai, and obviously things were not working out. The nation was suffering internal discord and embarrassment on the world scene, enhanced by U.S. Admiral Matthew Perry's visit to her shores. He "presented the Japanese with gifts intended to demonstrate the wonders of modern industry, including a Morse telegraphic device and a quarter-size steam locomotive."[26] The Japanese had nothing to match this.

The rise of Emperor Meiji (from the expression, "Enlightened Rule") in 1868 marked the beginning of change of perspective.

> The turn to the West was facilitated by the rapid spread of Dutch Learning during the late eighteenth and early nineteenth centuries. After Perry's arrival, however, many Japanese were no longer content to learn about the West merely through books and surrendered themselves to a *zeitgeist* that one young man described as a "desire to speed to foreign shores and take up the great task of observing far-off lands." The first wave of the curious went abroad in the 1860s. A few stole off furtively. Among them was Niijima Jo, who begged passage aboard an American merchantman in 1864 and later returned as Japan's first ordained Protestant minister.[27]

On his return Niijima Jo gained permission to establish a Christian school in Kyoto, and it "quickly attracted large number of youths who subscribed to Niijima's view that Westernization, civilization, and Christianity formed an inseparable trinity necessary for future progress." He argued, "It is the spirit of liberty, the development of science, and the Christian morality that have given birth to European civilizations . . . . We cannot therefore believe that Japan can secure this civilization until education rests upon the same basis."[28]

Under the shoguns (military dictators who ran the country, relegating the emperor to figurehead status), Japan had begun to send investigative teams to America and Europe, but with Emperor Meiji's ascent, the program accelerated.

> The Floodgates to Western knowledge opened wide in 1868. Within a decade several hundred Japanese were studying in the United States and Europe, and an even great number of foreigners, many in the employ of the national and prefectural governments, lived in Japan, instructing the Japanese in the finer points of Western political administration, medical practices, legal philosophies, technological advances, and education systems. Increasingly, international expositions provided another avenue for learning about the wonders of the outside world.[29]

One delegation of 49 government officials set sail from Yokohama in 1871 and did not return from their travels until 1873, having spent 205 days in the United States, 122 in England, 23 in Prussia, and shorter periods in France, Russia, and other European nations.[30]

> Members of the mission concluded, modernity was . . . the accumulation of the West's particular historical experiences—the total sum of its cultural values, social organization, and educational practices as they evolved over time—that accounted for the present superior ranking of the United States and the countries of western Europe within the hierarchy of nations and for their ability to overwhelm the traditional cultures of Asia.[31]

They were particularly impressed with "American education, British industrialization, French jurisprudence, and German representational institutions."[32]

Of course romantic notions of Eastern religious culture proliferate in the popular culture today, with such celebrities as Tina Turner, Richard Gere, Phil Jackson, and Uma Thurman touting the virtues of Buddhism in one form or another. No doubt, charms can be found in the East, but where Eastern culture is largely unadulterated, as in Burma and Thailand today, the standard of living is relatively low. Simply put, Niijima Jo was right.

Irreligion

In his discussion of the ascent of science as the leading religion in modern culture, British social commentator A. N. Wilson, who is no friend of religious creeds, including Christianity, expressed his queasiness at the prospect that the old religion might pass from the scene:

> Ever since the Second World War . . . the human race has been trying not to live with the knowledge that if the blind determinisms of science and economics were the only

truths, there should be nothing to prevent another archipelago of Gulags, another Belsen, another Dachau, another Auschwitz. The little spark, the "irrational" little glow in the dark, the belief that each individual is of importance—it might not derive from religion, but when religion goes, it becomes very difficult to keep it alight.[33]

Of course this is far from a glad endorsement of religion or commendation of "the faith once delivered to the saints," but it is a candid observation, that without some sort of faith, the dignity of man is ephemeral. And it is an indictment of the moral pretenses of the unbeliever; atheism is ominous.

The following paragraphs examine primarily "sins of commission." As much could also be said about the skeptic's "sins of omission." In an article on "The Perils of Pure Secularism," *Kairos Journal* focuses on this problem in Europe:

> Throughout Europe, one finds the fruit of Judeo-Christian compassion—a German Lutheran hospital in Israel, a Jewish orphanage in the Netherlands, a Salvation Army rescue mission in England, Habitat for Humanity homebuilders in Romania, and Special Olympics teams across the continent. All these originated in communities of faith.
>
> But where are the great privately funded atheist hospitals, adoption services, disaster relief teams, and inner-city health clinics? Where is the skeptic's Red Cross? Can Europe possibly count on the growing community of agnostics, libertines, and careerists to found and sustain the great works of mercy characteristic of devout Catholics, Jews, and Protestants? Can London expect a Richard Dawkins Hospital to take its place alongside others named for Saints Bartholomew, Mary, and Pancras? Can Parisians look for a Voltaire Clinic or a Derrida Orphanage? And where is Germany's Nietzsche Camp for Children with Disabilities or the Schopenhauer Food Pantry? Of course, some secularists (as those in Doctors without Borders) engage in sacrificial acts of charity, but the formative principles and institutional precedents for their service are biblical.[34]

Stalin's collectivization. In his book on the fate of twentieth-century Europe "between Hitler and Stalin," Timothy Snyder demonstrates that

> Hitler's "Final Solution," the purge of European Jewry, was not a fully original idea. A decade before, Stalin had set out to annihilate the Ukrainian peasant class, whose "national" sentiments he perceived as a threat to his Soviet utopia. The collectivization of agriculture was the weapon of choice. Implemented savagely, collectivization brought famine. In the spring of 1933 people in Ukraine were dying at a rate of 10,000 per day.
>
> Stalin then turned on other target groups in the Soviet Union, starting with the kulaks—supposedly richer farmers, whom Stalin said needed to be "liquidated as a class"—and various ethnic minorities. In the late 1930s, Mr. Snyder argues, "the most persecuted" national group in Europe wasn't—as many of us would assume—Jews in Nazi German, a relatively small community of 400,000 whose numbers declined after the imposition of race laws forced many into emigration at a time when this was still possible. According to Mr. Snyder, the hardest hit at that time were the 600,000 or so Poles living within the Soviet Union.
>
> Convinced that this group represented a fifth column, Stalin ordered the NKVD, a precursor to the KGB, to "keep on digging out and cleaning out this Polish filth." Mr. Snyder writes that before World War II started, 111,091 Soviet Poles were executed. This

grim period is little known in Poland itself, but its detailed recounting here shows how a determined totalitarian machine could decimate a national group. Apologists for Stalin, in the West and elsewhere, have insisted that his Great Terror was needed to prepare the Soviets for a coming showdown with Hitler. Mr. Snyder destroys this argument.

Barbarism reached new lows after the Wehrmacht and the Red Army invaded Poland in 1939. The Ribbentrop-Molotov pacts, signed in August a week before the Blitzkrieg, had split sovereign Poland between the Nazi and Soviet allies. The invading Germans obeyed orders not to spare the civilian population. But the Soviets were more experienced then at brutality. In the spring of 1940, Stalin ordered the murder of 21,768 Polish officers in what came to be known as the Katyn massacres. Hundreds of thousands of other people from "enemy" classes and nationalities were deported to the east, where many died.[35]

Berlin wall. The flow of immigrants is a good indication of cultural desirability, and it is instructive at both ends in that refugees both leave someplace and head for another. The flow from officially atheistic East Germany to West Germany is a case in point. In the opening decade of the Cold War, citizens fled the Soviet-controlled Eastern bloc nations in droves. "By the fall of 1958, East Germany had lost two million people, with continued losses of more than ten-thousand per month, including some of its best-educated youth."[36] Hence the need for the Berlin wall.

Mao's cultural revolution. In writing about the strange hold Maoism has on certain intellectuals in the West, particularly in France, David Gress brings up the purge China endured under Mao in the decade before his death.

The Chinese Cultural Revolution that began in 1966 and lasted until Mao's death in 1976 . . . was actually Mao's bid to bolster his own dictatorial power by mobilizing hordes of ignorant and barbarous youth against all that he designated as evil and reactionary. Anyone with the faintest intellectual disposition—teachers, writers, artists, even party officials—was vulnerable to being denounced as a bourgeoise threat to China's glorious communist future. Hundreds of thousands, perhaps more, were killed, and millions more deprived of work. Cultural life was desolated, uncounted works of art destroyed. Mao used his Red Guard units of killers and torturers to reduce the country to chaos; only his iron fist, with the help of those same Red Guards, could quell the anarchy.[37]

And of course since Mao's death the Communist regime has not hesitated to be brutal toward its citizens when it senses dissent is reaching uncomfortable levels. The Tiananmen Square massacre is a case in point, as are efforts to erase its memory: David Aikman tells of the firing of three editors of a Chengdu newspaper. A young clerk took a classified ad from the "mothers of 6-4," not knowing that the numerals referred to June 4, 1989, the date of that incident.[38]

North Korea. North Korea is "the world's first hereditary Communist state with a leadership sanctioned by divine right." The current leader, Kim Jong Il, inherited his status from his father, Kim Il Sung, now described "as a god—the 'Sun of Love'—superior to Christ in love, superior to Buddha in benevolence, superior to Confucius in virtue and superior to Mohammed in justice." The North Korean calendar now begins on the date of the birth of Kim John Il 1912.[39]

These divine leaders, Kim Il Sung and Kim Jong Il, "are responsible for the deaths of over seven million Koreans—three million civilians in the Korean War, and, by some estimates, three million in the famine and at least a million deaths of political prisoners during the last 50 years."[40] Yet, "for [Kim Il Sung's] eightieth birthday his son spent over a billion dollars on a three-month 'loyalty festival,' which included mass gymnastics, dances, and parades, each one bigger than the last."[41]

These "Marxist Sun Kings" have enjoyed the pleasures of eight palaces with sprawling grounds:

> They contain golf courses, stables for his horses, garages full of motorbikes and luxury cars, shooting ranges, swimming pools, cinemas, funfair parks, water-jet bikes, and hunting grounds stocked with wild deer and duck. The grounds of his palaces are big enough to need cars to drive around and staffed by his personal entourage of some 2,000 doctors, nurses, cooks, maids, valets, gardeners, masseurs, dancing troupes, and body guards.[42]

Bloomsbury spies. Roman Catholic writer E. Michael Jones has chronicled the pathologies of the skeptics, and the skeptical Bloomsbury group gets its share of his critical attention.

> In England modernity has become synonymous with a group of writers and artists loosely known as Bloomsbury. By the 1920s, Virginia Woolf, E. M. Forster, Lytton Strachey, John Maynard Keynes, Roger Fry, Clive Bell—to name just the core of the group—had virtually reformed English taste by the time [Anthony] Blunt arrived at Cambridge.[43]

Lylton Strachey was best known for his book, *Eminent Victorians*, which systematically insulted the moral heroes of the British Empire, specifically "Chinese" Gordon and Florence Nightingale. Blunt was best known for his treason, for he was exposed as a spy for the Soviet Union.

Then Jones connects the dots: Bloomsbury embraced "a radically homosexual vision of the world and therefore of its very nature subversive; treason was its logical outcome."[44] Or to put it otherwise, "Left to fester long enough, the self-subversion that is implicit in every homosexual act will extend beyond itself to include an attack on society, first as manifested in the family but then as manifested in one's country as well."[45]

All the above-named Bloomsburies were gay, as was Blunt, and his fellow spies Donald Maclean, Guy Burgess, and Kim Philby. And the sexual linkages could be Byzantine as each worked out his pleasures. As Gertrude Himmelfarb summarized in an article, "In 1907, for example, Strachey discovered this his lover (and cousin) Duncan Grant was also having an affair with Arthur

Hobhouse, who, in turn, was having an affair with Keynes. The following year Strachey was even more distressed to learn that Grant was now having an affair with Keynes."[46]

And so on it went. And the priorities were clear. As E. M. Forster said famously, "If I had to choose between betraying my country and betraying my friend, I hope I should have the guts to betray my country."[47]

To sum up the ethos, Maynard Keynes wrote, "We repudiated entirely customary morals, conventions and traditional wisdom. We were, that is to say, in the strict sense of the term, immoralists. . . . In short, we repudiated all versions of the doctrine of original sin, of there being insane and irrational springs of wickedness in most men."[48]

Gertrude Himmelfarb then observes that massive deficit spending, such as Keynes espoused, can "put a premium on immediate and present satisfactions, and Keynesian economics, which is based entirely on the short run and precludes any long-term judgments."[49] Psychologist Joseph Schumpeter draws another connection: Keynes "was childless and his philosophy of life was essentially a short-run philosophy."[50]

The point is that a lifestyle of immediate gratification will toss everything aside that would frustrate it, whether heterosexuality, patriotism, or economic prudence.

Rachel Carson's lethal science. Few writings have had a greater impact on history than Rachel Carson's 1962 book *Silent Spring,* in which she blamed the insecticide DDT for poisoning the environment. The budding Environmental Protection Agency banned the substances, and farmers wishing to trade their agricultural goods with the United States (such as those raising tobacco in Zimbabwe) were forced to ban it as well, since customs would not allow DDT-tainted material to enter the country. This meant, in effect, a worldwide ban. It also meant millions of extra deaths from malaria, for DDT had been suppressing the mosquito population effectively before the ban.[51]

Still one might think that it was a tough trade-off, accepting one risk rather than the other. But the problems with DDT were far less than the problems raised by its absence, and the ban was based on shaky premises. First, the science was questionable; readings in those days were susceptible to "false positives," and the effects were exaggerated. Some studies suggest that heavy exposure can mean a thinning of bird egg shells, or in humans, premature birth and a shortened breast feeding period. But these risks pale in comparison to the mortality rate for malaria in the developing world.

Paul Mueller won the Nobel Prize for applying DDT to pest control in 1948, and later, when Rachel Carson indicted the chemical, a number of experiments showed that its effects on human test subjects were negligible.[52] One

British professor even regularly consumed a "substantial pinch of DDT" in his lectures and never suffered ill effects.[53] Still the foes were unmoved.

The big problem with Carson's crusade was its bad theology. Untouched by the testimony of the Bible, she believed that only man could produce carcinogenic material.[54] She romanticized nature by ignoring the fall and totally missed the fact that such naturally occurring items as the bracken fern[55] and radon gas were carcinogens. Thus she attacked the man-made chemical and gave the "natural" mosquito a pass.

Ethical projects are based on supposed facts, whether the existence of God, the impact on poverty, the structure of human nature, or in this case, the character of the environment. When one gets such things wrong, then morality goes askew, and the consequences can be disastrous.[56]

The drug culture. Excusing the drug culture of the 1960s, Tom Hayden wrote, "Because the elders had failed us, it seemed, all that was left was for us to fail them. Since politics and persuasion were hopeless, it was time to break on through 'the doors of perception' to the other side. Instead of patience, the young flew on acid, then on speed."[57]

The death toll was staggering. Beginning with Andy Warhol muse and collaborator Edie Sedgwick, "who died of numerous addictions," Hayden gave a partial list of "artists" who died of drug overdoses: Brian Epstein (1967), Frankie Lymon (1968), Brian Jones (1969), Janis Joplin (1970), Jimi Hendrix (1970), Alan "Blind Owl" Wilson (1970), Jim Morrison (1971), Billy Murcia (1972), Danny Whitten (1972), Gram Parsons (1973), Nick Drake (1974), Tim Buckley (1975), Phil Ochs (1976), and Keith Moon (1978).

To this list of musicians, he adds his "friends and coconspirators," Abbie Hoffman, who "overdosed and died on April 12, 1989," and Rennie Davis, who "went to India in 1972 at the height of the Vietnam War and came back transformed into a devout follower of a fourteen-year-old boy-god."[58] A sorry legacy of ruin.

Nevada. Las Vegas prides itself on its "Sin City" credentials, for the Convention and Visitor's Bureau headlines its Web site with the slogan, "What happens in Vegas, stays in Vegas." There visitors can do naughty things they would not be free to do back home. But the city and state's freedom is limited by its unbridled love for the dollar.

> One thing you won't see on Las Vegas billboards or in street brochures is an ad for any of Nevada's thirty-four legal brothels, three of which lie fifty miles west of the city in the town of Pahrump. It's illegal even to advertise prostitution within Clark County, for although the brothels are only an hour's drive or cab ride away, Las Vegas would rather its visitors spend their time and money in town. Yet the number-one industry in Pahrump depends for its survival on the number-one industry in Las Vegas, and the millions of tourists it attracts to southern Nevada each year.[59]

The fruit of all this venality is poisonous:

- "Nevada currently has the highest suicide rate in the country—double the national rate. This appears to be true for every age group."
- "Nevada has the highest . . . incidence of cirrhosis of the liver."
- Nevada "ranks high among American states in rates of abortions, teen pregnancies, and births to unmarried mothers."
- In 1992 Nevada's high school dropout rate was 14.9 percent, the highest in the country. "Fewer Nevada high-school graduates go on to college than those of any other state except Alaska."
- Nevada has more incidents of drunk driving than any other state.
- About 5 percent of the people are addicted to gambling; nationwide the percentage is half as high.
- Ten percent of the people go to Alcoholics Anonymous.[60]

As Las Vegas family therapist Volmar Franz puts it, "Keep in mind that this is a tough town. You're told that you can finally have all your dreams of wealth fulfilled; but in the meantime this town will eat you up. It's a mean town. Understand one thing: this town was built on one concept and one concept only: taking other people's money."[61]

The long march. New Criterion editor Roger Kimball has traced the devastating effect of the 1960s on American culture in his book *The Long March.* His analysis is tied to the ideologies and influence of such godless literati as the beatniks Allen Ginsberg and Jack Kerouac and "gurus like Norman Mailer, Timothy Leary, Susan Sontag, Eldridge Cleaver, and Charles Reich." Theirs is a record of tragic "wrong turns, dead ends, and blind alleys" whose effect the nation has not escaped.

As Kimball's cobelligerent Irving Kristol has observed, the "hallmark of the 1960s" is "the union of sexual liberation and radical politics." Unpacking the sad legacy, Kristol writes:

> Sexual liberation is always near the top of a countercultural agenda—though just what form the liberation takes can and does vary, sometimes quite wildly. Women's liberation, likewise, is another consistent feature of all counter-cultural movements—liberation from husbands, liberation from children, liberation from family. Indeed, the real object of these various sexual heterodoxies is to disestablish the family as the central institutions of human society, the citadel of orthodoxy.[62]

And so Christians find themselves beset and betrayed today.

Notes

1 David Livingstone, *Missionary Travels and Researches in South Africa, Including a Sketch of Sixteen Years' Residence in the Interior of Africa* (New York: Harper & Brothers, 1858), 569.

2 Ibid., 618–19.

3 Ibid., 559–60.

4 Ibid., 501.

5 John S. Mbiti, *African Religions and Philosophy*, 2nd ed. (Oxford: Heinemann, 1969), 44.

6 Ibid., 61.

7 Ibid., 125.

8 Narendra Jadhav, *Untouchables: My Family's Triumphant Journey Out of the Caste System in Modern India* (New York: Scribner: 2005), 4.

9 Ibid., 3.

10 Ibid., 1.

11 Patrick French, *The World Is What It Is: The Authorized Biography of V. S. Naipaul* (New York: Knopf, 2008), 324.

12 Ibid., 352.

13 Ibid., 391.

14 Richard Grenier, *The Gandhi Nobody Knows* (Nashville: Thomas Nelson, 1983), 106–7.

15 Tom Hayden, *The Long Sixties: From 1960 to Barack Obama* (Boulder, CO: Paradigm, 2009), 163.

16 Catalog description of *Buddhist Warfare* by Michael Jerryson and Mark Juergensmeyer (Oxford: Oxford University Press, 2009); http://www.oup.com/us/catalog/general/subject/ Sociology/Religion/?view=usa&ci=9780195394832 (accessed December 17, 2010).

17 Daniel Blake, "Violence Against Christians Escalates in Sri Lanka," *Christianity Today*, November 27, 2006; http://www.christianitytoday.com/article/violence.against.christians. escalates.in.sri.lanka/8509.htm (accessed December 17, 2010).

18 Steve Helling, *Tiger: The Real Story* (Cambridge, MA: DaCapo, 2010), 76–77.

19 Ibid., 227–29.

20 Ibid., 231.

21 Danny Shea, "Brit Hume to Tiger Woods: Convert to Christianity to Recover from Scandal (VIDEO)," *Huffington Post*, January 3, 2010; http://www.huffingtonpost. com/2010/01/03/brit-hume-to-tiger-woods_n_409720.html (accessed July 26, 2010).

22 Simon Evans, "Tiger Woods finds new challenges as a Dad," *Reuters*, March 27, 2008; http:// uk.reuters.com/article/idUKB64063720080327?sp=true (accessed August 26, 2010).

23 Max Hastings, *Retribution: The Battle for Japan, 1944–45* (New York: Knopf, 2008), 209, 50, 52–53, 346–47.

24 Ibid., 549.

25 Tsunetomo Yamamoto, *Bushido: The Way of the Samurai*, ed. Justin F. Stone (Garden City Park, NY: Square One, 2002), 73–74.

26 James L. McLain, *Japan: A Modern History* (New York: W.W. Norton, 2002), 138.

27 Ibid., 169.

28 Ibid., 175.

29 Ibid., 171.

30 Marius B. Jansen, *The Making of Modern Japan* (Cambridge, MA: Harvard, 2000), 358.

31 McLain, *Japan*, 173.

32 Jansen, *The Making of Modern Japan*, 360.

33 A. N. Wilson, *Our Times: The Age of Elizabeth II* (New York: Farrar, Straus, and Giroux, 2008), 407–8.

34 "The Perils of Pure Secularism: Part 2," *Kairos Journal*; http://www.kairosjournal.org/Document.aspx?QuadrantID=4&CategoryID=10&TopicID=50&DocumentID=9536&L=1 (accessed December 17, 2010).

35 Matthew Kaminski, "Savagery in the East," a review of *Bloodlands*, by Timothy Snyder, *The Wall Street Journal* (October 18, 2010): A17.

36 Fred Kaplan, *1959: The Year That Changed Everything* (New York: Wiley, 2009), 11.

37 David Gress, "Mao à la Française," review of *The Wind from the East*, by Richard Wolin (*The Wall Street Journal*): July 17–18, 2010, W8.

38 David Aikman, "Tiananmen Twenty Years Later," *The American Spectator*, June 2009, 18.

39 Jasper Becker, *Rogue Regime: Kim John Il and the Looming Threat of North Korea* (Oxford: Oxford University Press, 2005), 77.

40 Ibid., 266.

41 Ibid., 127.

42 Ibid., 130.

43 E. M. Jones, *Degenerate Moderns: Modernity as Rationalized Sexual Behavior* (San Francisco: Ignatius, 1993), 53.

44 Ibid., 55.

45 Ibid., 72.

46 Gertrude Himmelfarb, "From Clapham to Bloomsbury: A Genealogy of Morals," *Commentary* 79 (February 1985): 43.

47 Jones, *Degenerate Moderns*, 55.

48 Himmelfarb, 56.

49 Ibid., 60.

50 Ibid.

51 Tina Rosenberg, "What the World Needs Now Is DDT," *The New York Times Magazine*, April 4, 2004.

52 Gerald Serkin and Natalie Serkin, "DDT, Fraud, and Tragedy," *The American Spectator*, February 25, 2005; http://spectator.org/archives/2005/02/25/ddt-fraud-and-tragedy (accessed June 29, 2010).

53 Richard Black, "Battle over Anti-malaria Chemical," *BBC News*, March 4, 2004; http://news.bbc.co.uk/2/hi/science/nature/3532273.stm (accessed June 29, 2010).

54 Gustave K. Kohn, "Agriculture, Pesticides, and the American Chemical Industry," in *Silent Spring Revisited*, ed. Gino J. Marco et al. (Washington, DC: American Chemical Society, 1987), 169–70.

55 G. J. Marco, et al., "Many Roads and Other Worlds," in *Silent Spring Revisited*, 195.

56 For a longer summary of both the science and theology of the Carson case see "DDT and the Deadly Legacy of Rachel Carson's Bad Theology," *Kairos Journal*; http://www.kairosjournal.org/Document.aspx?QuadrantID=4&CategoryID=11&TopicID=44&DocumentID=6236&L=1 (accessed June 29, 2010).

57 Hayden, *The Long Sixties*, 46.

58 Ibid.

59 David Littlejohn, ed., *The Real Las Vegas: Life Beyond the Strip* (Oxford: Oxford University Press, 1999), 219.

60 Ibid., 6, 8, 85.

61 Ibid., 96.

62 Roger Kimball, *The Long March* (San Francisco: Encounter, 2000), 147.

The Cultural Fruit of Christianity:
Confession, Correction, and Commendation

THE EPISTLE OF JAMES teaches that "faith, if it doesn't have works, is dead by itself" (Jas 2:17), and the book provides precepts and examples to spell this out. Whether "[looking] after orphans and widows in their distress and [keeping] oneself unstained by the world" or by "controlling the tongue" and refusing to "show favoritism" to "the man wearing fine clothes," the regenerate person shows that he is truly born again.

Of course the New Testament teaches in no uncertain terms that a person is saved by grace and through faith—and that this salvation is "God's gift," which is "not from works, so that no one can boast" (Eph 2:8–9). But believers "created in Christ for good works" (v. 10) become salt and light to the world (Matt 5:13).

In the early church these transformed people were so winsome in their mutual care and continual fellowship that they enjoyed "favor with all the people" in Jerusalem (Acts 2:47). They were fulfilling Jesus' pronouncement in John 13:35 that "all people will know that you are My disciples, if you have love for one another." But this love was not limited to the body of Christ. Jesus also taught, through the parable of the Good Samaritan (Luke 10:25–37), that His followers' loving care should extend to the world at large.

So when Paul and Silas were accused by the Thessalonians of "[turning] the world upside down" (Acts 17:6), the angry citizens understood that Christianity meant more than a new way of worshipping. It even impacted ungodly businesses, as with the fortune-telling slave girl in Philippi (16:16–24) and later with the sale of "silver shrines of Artemis" in Ephesus (19:21–41).

The salubrious effect of strong Christian presence should be pervasive, unmistakable, and compelling wherever believers live, the more so as they predominate. If not, it is fair to ask whether Christianity is actually transformative, whether these people who call themselves Christian are genuinely so, and whether these believers somehow misconstrued or misapplied Christianity. If the faith is true and wonderful as the Bible says it is, then the splendor of its manifestations and outcomes should be obvious to the dispassionate observer. And therein lies an apologetic.

EMBARRASSMENTS

Would that Christians, or those claiming to be Christians, always acted Christianly, but the record of missteps is a long one. And, in each case, the Lord is dishonored, especially where the offender has been a high-visibility advocate for the faith. (I'm reminded of the story of a university priest who urged the school's basketball players not to cross themselves before attempting free throws if they were likely to miss. He reasoned that God didn't need that sort of public association with their incompetence.)

Nevertheless, we continue to "cross ourselves" before saying and doing unfortunate things.

The European Wars of Religion

In the Thirty Years War, Roman Catholics were killing Protestants in France, and Protestants were slaughtering Catholics in Germany. In Boston, they held a day of thanksgiving to celebrate the victory of Sweden's Protestant king Gustavus Adolphus over the city of Munich. Of such inter-Christian fighting, Roger Williams, the founder of Rhode Island, wrote that "the blood of so many hundred thousand souls of Protestants and papists, spilt in the wars of present and former ages, for their respective consciences, is not required nor accepted by Jesus Christ the Prince of Peace." Williams traced such a perverted notion of Christianity to Constantine, under whom "the guardians of Christ's churches turned into the wilderness of national religion, and the world (under Constantine's dominion) to the most unchristian Christendom."[1]

Cromwell at Drogheda

Oliver Cromwell, who established parliamentary rule in England, indulged in brutality in Ireland over a 40-week period in 1649–50. "The slaughter at Drogheda is the most infamous [instance], when Cromwell's army killed around three thousand Royalist troops, then rampaged through the town, butchering clergy, women, and children. Those who surrendered were executed."[2]

Albeit, "the rules of war of the time, with regard to sieges, were clear," and the "rule of no quarter once the walls were breached" was thought to reduce bloodshed by providing strong incentive to surrender early—and it "undoubtedly frightened many lesser garrisons into peaceful submission." Furthermore, "it must be emphasized that Cromwell gave no direct orders for the massacre of the civilian inhabitants."[3] Nevertheless, as biographer Antonia Fraser put it,

> The conclusion cannot be escaped that Cromwell lost his self-control at Drogheda, literally saw red—the red of his comrades' blood—after the failure of the first assaults, and was seized with one of those sudden brief and cataclysmic rages which would lead him later to dissolve Parliament by force and sweep away that historic bauble. There were good military reasons for behaving as he did, but they were not the motives which animated him at the time, during the day and night of uncalculated butchery. The slaughter itself stood quite outside his usual record of careful mercy as a soldier, and as he said himself, under other circumstances would have induced "remorse and regret."[4]

Nevertheless as Fraser observes, "And so quickly over, in the heat of the moment, in a foreign land, occurred the incident that has blacked Oliver Cromwell's name down history for over three hundred years."[5]

And one cannot simply dismiss this as the work of a Christian in name only. As Michael Haykin has demonstrated in his book on "the spirituality of Oliver Cromwell," he was committed to the true faith. As Cromwell lay dying, he said to his family, "Love not this world, I say unto you, it is not good that you should love the world. Children, live like Christians, and I leave you the Covenant [of Grace] to feed on."[6]

He was keenly aware of his need for grace, for he "did not hesitate to describe himself as a 'poor worm and weak servant,' one who was characterized by 'weaknesses, . . . inordinate passions,' and 'unskilfulness and everyway unfitness' for his calling. And on his deathbed he could confess, 'I think I am the poorest wretch that lives.'"[7]

Indeed Christians are capable of terrible things, but if they are genuinely saved, they, like Cromwell, will not be able to stand themselves for these missteps.

The Boers

Then there is Apartheid, the cruel racial segregation instituted by the Dutch in South Africa. Missionary David Livingstone was appalled at their behavior, given their profession of Christianity. He reported, "I have myself been an eye-witness of Boers coming to a village, and according to their usual custom, demanding twenty or thirty women to weed their gardens." And when pressed to justify this behavior, they said, "We make the people work for us, in consideration of allowing them to live in our country."

He also wrote that they were known "to shoot down in cold blood men and women, of a different color," some even "glorying in the bloody scenes in which they had been themselves the actors." But could they claim to be Christians?

> They are all traditionally religious, tracing their descent from some of the best men (Huguenots and Dutch) the world ever saw. Hence they claim to themselves the title of "Christians," and all the colored race are "black property" or "creatures." They being the chosen people of God, the heathen are given to them for an inheritance, and they are the rod of divine vengeance on the heathen, as were the Jews of old.[8]

These were the same Boers enraged by a German missionary's baptizing slaves in the late 1730s. This faithful minister "was impelled to leave by the ensuing outcry."[9]

Mel Gibson

Of course there are celebrity meltdowns, such as the one Mel Gibson underwent. From a troubled background, from which he entered Alcoholics Anonymous in 1991, he became a zealous Catholic—"anti-abortion, anti-birth control, anti-divorce. He even built his own church in the Malibu hills in 2003, where mass is celebrated in Latin, and women must wear head coverings."[10] From this new standpoint and with considerable derision from the secular elite, he produced the movie *The Passion of the Christ*, which grossed hundreds of millions of dollars worldwide.

Alas, he could not sustain this life. Beginning with a drunk-driving charge, complete with anti-Semitic rant, he descended into disgrace, divorcing his wife of 28 years in 2009 and cohabiting with a pop singer, a relationship that subsequently ended in vile phone recordings and charges of abuse. A very sad picture, one that does not reflect well on Christianity—or at least Gibson's grasp on it.

Rome Not Built in a Day

Such examples embolden critics to declare Christianity morally indifferent if not pernicious. This in turn has prompted University of Connecticut sociologist Bradley Wright to push back with a book entitled *Christians Are Hate-Filled Hypocrites . . . and Other Lies You've Been Told:*

> Essentially, people who associate themselves with Christianity, as compared to the religiously unaffiliated, are more likely to have faithful marriages, commit less crime, interact honestly with others, and not get into as much trouble with drugs or alcohol. What's more, the more committed Christians are to their faith, as measured by church attendance, the greater the impact the church's teachings seem so have on their lives.

> Clearly from these analyses we know that Christians are not perfect. Many of the numbers may disappoint you or perhaps even shock you. But the question of what we should

expect from Christians should be addressed. . . . Becoming a Christian doesn't make people good, it just makes them better. In other words, Christians believe that the Christian faith should, in fact, change how people live their lives, but this change isn't necessarily instantaneous. Rome wasn't built in a day, and it might take even longer to perfect a person than to build an empire.[11]

DENOMINATIONAL SHORTFALLS

In any number of historical studies, the religion question surfaces in the discussion of national fortunes and status. For instance, in Norman Stone's treatment of World War I, he observes that the French General Robert Nivelle "was a Protestant, and Protestants (usually engineers and doctors) were the backbone of the Third Republic, supplying the morality, the education, the spirit—including the Eiffel Tower."[12] So one is driven to ask, "Is this so? And if it is, where were the majority Catholics in the mix?"

Indeed, a candid treatment of the Christian impact on culture must note difficulties that seem to be peculiar to certain groups. And when discovered, these group embarrassments may undermine their sectarian apologetics and suggest that as professing Christians they may not have gotten things just right. Here then are challenges for the witness of Roman Catholics, Orthodox, and evangelicals.

South American Poverty

Spanish and English explorers landed in the New World—in South and North America, respectively—at roughly the same time, but the fortunes of these two colonial centers has been vastly different. When searching for explanations, scholars repeatedly come to the conclusion that it has something to do with religion, in that North America has been predominantly Protestant and South America, Catholic. As Harvard University professor Lawrence Harrison puts it, in the landmark book he edited with his colleague Samuel Huntington, *Culture Matters*, "I believe that there is no other satisfactory way to explain the sharply contrasting evolution of the North and the South in the [Western] Hemisphere than culture—the strikingly different values, attitudes, and institutions—that have flowed from the Anglo-Protestant and Ibero-Catholic traditions."[13]

After a follow-up study Harrison stuck with his thesis:

> Protestant countries do better than Catholic countries in creating prosperity. To be sure, the averages for the Catholic countries are depressed by Latin America's slow development, but even when one looks only at First World democratic-capitalist societies, Protestant countries do substantially better than Catholic countries with respect to prosperity, trust, and corruption.[14]

He did note some Catholic regions did better than others, particularly where the Basques predominate, whether in Spain or Chile. But his overall conclusion was that the "economic success of the Nordic societies, and Protestant societies in general, strongly suggests that . . . it is the Protestant virtues of education, achievement, work ethic, merit, frugality, honesty . . . that is the real force behind the spirit of capitalism."[15]

Disease. The problem is not just a lack of discretionary income but of survival. As El Salvador's archbishop Oscar Romero observed shortly before he was assassinated for criticizing the government in 1980, "It is sad to read that in El Salvador the two main causes of death are first diarrhea, and second murder. Therefore, right after the result of malnourishment, diarrhea, we have the result of crime, murder. These are the two epidemics that are killing off our people."[16]

Two decades later the *Encyclopedia of the Nations* reported that things were still terrible in El Salvador, a nation whose original name was "Provincia De Nuestro Señor Jesus Cristo, El Salvador Del Mundo" ("Province of Our Lord Jesus Christ, the Savior of the World"):

> The principal causes of death remain gastroenteritis, influenza, malaria, measles, pneumonia, and bronchitis, caused or complicated by malnutrition, bad sanitation, and poor housing. . . . Much of the progress [in health care] since the 1930s was undermined by the country's civil war, which overtaxed health care facilities while, in real terms, expenditures on health care declined. The National Medical School was shut down in 1980.[17]

Michael Novak's assessment. Catholic philosopher and theologian Michael Novak addresses these issues in *The Spirit of Democratic Capitalism:* "Why after 1850, then, did the journeys of North America and Latin America dramatically diverge? Why for the next one hundred years did one remain almost static, while the other steadily but ever more rapidly developed?"[18]

For one thing he dismisses claims that the South Americans are victims of exploitation by outsiders.

> Nothing prevented Brazilians from inventing the combustion engine, the radio, the airplane, penicillin and other technologies which give resources their utility. Although Brazil is apparently one of the most richly endowed of all nations in material resources, neither Brazil nor other Latin American nations have so far provided a system favorable to invention and discovery.[19]

He continues, "Among Nobel Prize winners in science, Protestants have been conspicuously prominent," and he speculates over why this might be so. Perhaps Catholics have been hampered by "lack of punctuality, in reluctance to compromise, in the failure to see worldly life as a spiritual vocation."[20] Perhaps "the 'Catholic' aristocratic ethic of Latin America places more emphasis on luck, heroism, status, and figure than the relatively 'Protestant' ethic of North America, which values diligent work, steadfast regularity, and the responsible seizure of opportunity."[21]

He blames much of this on the mercantilism of Spain and the baleful influence of "liberation theologians" and presents a persuasive case to Catholics that democratic capitalism is theologically compelling and thoroughly consistent with their faith. But one must ask why Catholicism has shown itself peculiarly susceptible to these forces and in need of a "liberation theology."

In his book *The Joy of Sports*, Novak extends the differences beyond the bounds of South America.

> These are rough approximations, of course, but differences between a Catholic culture and a Protestant culture become quite dramatic. The development of capitalism depended on the underpinnings of Protestant attitudes; Catholic countries for generations bore the reputation, in the face of industrial modernity, of being backward, lazy, hedonistic. Visualize the cultures of Southern Ireland, Spain, Italy, the Balkans, and Latin America. Contrast southern with northern Germany. Contrast, even, the sensibility of France with that of Scandinavia. The more easygoing, fleshly, less serious Catholic undercurrent is broadly distinguishable from the progressive, orderly, hardworking Protestant current of the modern age.[22]

Novak draws on the work of historian Hugh R. Trevor-Roper: "The Counter Reformation state impugned the religious value of commerce. It banned or restricted enterprise in the private sector. It licensed certain entrepreneurs to develop state monopolies; it favored state mercantilism over private mercantilism," undergirded by "a new alliance of church and state, more intolerable with each passing year."[23]

And Novak wishes church leaders had taught that "the vocation of the layman lay in producing wealth, economic self-reliance, industry, and commerce, and in being creative stewards thereof."[24]

David Livingstone's observation. Perhaps part of the problem is the relative Catholic neglect of the Bible, and the church's lack of confidence in the laity's ability to handle it. Though African missionary David Livingstone spoke well of Catholic missionaries who preceded him in one region, he wished they had completed the task.

> This district is said to contain upwards of 40,000 souls. Some ten or twelve miles to the north of the village of Ambaca there once stood the missionary station of Cahenda, and it is quite astonishing to observe the great numbers who can read and write in this district. This is the fruit of the labors of the Jesuit and Capuchin missionaries, for they taught the people of Ambaca; and ever since the expulsion of the teachers by the Marquis of Pombal, the natives have continued to teach each other. These devoted men are still held in high estimation throughout the country to this day. All speak well of them (*los padres Jesuitas*); and, now that they are gone from this lower sphere, I could not help wishing that these our Roman Catholic fellow-Christians had felt it to be their duty to give the people the Bible, to be a light to their feet when the good men themselves were gone.[25]

Priest Sexual Abuse

Another enormous Catholic problem is sexual abuse by priests. Though George Weigel argues vociferously to the contrary, the flood of paedophilic abuse in the Roman Catholic Church (thousands of priests and victims and billions of dollars in settlements) raises serious questions about its policy of priestly celibacy. He argues that sexual abuse is rampant in the world at large, and not just the church, and that most of the predators are not celibates. He concludes that "the church needs to become more Catholic, not less."[26]

What he does not discuss is the overwhelming incidence of *homosexual* abuse by priests, and when he denies that celibacy produces abuse, he may well be getting things backwards. Quite possibly the policy *attracts* rather than *generates* the problem. If a man is indifferent to sex with women, then giving up sex with women to become a priest is no problem. This could result in a higher concentration of homosexuals in the priesthood than in the general populace, with predictable results.

A basic reading of Scripture suggests that the Catholics have brought this on themselves, for they have fashioned the celibacy rule without biblical warrant. Indeed the "first pope," Peter, had a mother-in-law, and the criteria for "overseers" in Timothy made reference to wives and households.

This seems to be a good example of how bad exposition results in bad practice, and how it undermines the plausibility of the Catholic approach.

Technology

A study of the distribution of automobile manufacture reveals a striking difference between Christian and non-Christian cultures.[27] The nations that made up traditional "Christendom" produced world-market cars throughout the twentieth century—Ford, GM, and Chrysler in the United States; Rolls-Royce, MG, Triumph, and Mini in Britain; Citroen and Peugeot in France; Mercedes-Benz, Porsche, BMW, Volkswagen, and Audi in Germany; Saab and Volvo in Sweden; and Fiat, Ferrari, Lamborghini, and Maserati in Italy.

Non-Christian nations did not fare so well, whether heavily populated by animists (Togo), Hindus (India), Buddhists (Cambodia), or Muslims (Libya). The only two nations in the East to produce world-class cars in the twentieth century were Japan and Korea, both of which were heavily influenced by Western culture, primarily in the aftermath of World War II. And it seems that a combination of Western and Confucian thinking are technologically productive, at least where both are not suppressed, as they were in Mao's China. But where Eastern thought is insular, as in Nepal and Myanmar, technology is retarded. Yes, India and China are now developing inexpensive cars for their masses—such as, respectively, the Tata and the Chery. But these are latecomers to the field, heavily influenced by the globalization of technology and late-blooming prosperity, born of turns to Western economic models.

What is most interesting is the absence of a world-class Orthodox car. Though the Eastern bloc fielded the Skoda, Volga, Lada, and Yugo during the Cold War, these did not enjoy wide acclaim. Communism suppressed the church, so these cars were not pure representatives of the Orthodox religion. But what is one to think of Greece? Why was there nothing there to match the Fiat across the Adriatic in Italy?

The same could be said of other forms of technology in traditionally Christian Europe—Rolex watches in Switzerland, Nokia cell phones in Finland, Fokker aircraft in the Netherlands. But where is the Greek watch, cell phone, or aircraft? Could it be that Orthodoxy has some sort of primitivizing effect on culture?

Punditry

Protestants, particularly evangelicals, are in short supply among the American political commentators in the media, particularly those who themselves have not been politicians. In November 2010, *Newsweek* listed the "Power 50," their "First Annual Ranking of America's Highest-Paid Pundits and Politicos."[28] One is struck by the high incidence of those with Catholic and Jewish backgrounds.

The Catholics are represented by Rush Limbaugh, Sean Hannity, Bill O'Reilly, Laura Ingraham, Stephen Colbert, Chris Matthews, Jorge Ramons, and John McLaughlin. Jewish figures are also prominent: Jon Stewart, Mark Levin, and Paul Krugman. Then there is Glenn Beck, the Mormon, and Ariana Huffington, the Greek Orthodox/New Age. But where are the evangelicals?

Beyond the *Newsweek* list, the mind runs to many other Catholic commentators (e.g., Bill Bennett, Pat and Bay Buchanan, Bret Baier, Mark Shields, Juan Williams, Emmett Tyrrell, Kate O'Beirne, Cokie Roberts, John O'Sullivan) and Jewish pundits (e.g., Dennis Prager, Mona Charen, Jonah Goldberg, Mika Brzezinski, Michael Medved, Bill Kristol, Thomas Friedman). One also thinks of the atheist Bill Maher, the agnostic George Will, and the Unitarian Keith Olberman. But again where are the evangelicals?

Cal Thomas, Fred Barnes, and Mike Huckabee come to mind first. Ann Coulter calls herself a Protestant, as does Brit Hume. Both have said some wonderfully biblical things in the spotlight. But that is a disproportionately small group in America.

Surely, some discrimination is at work, but perhaps the answer lies in the evangelical's aversion to the dogged, probing dialogue one finds traditionally in the Jesuit schools and the Jewish households. Maybe evangelicals need to learn from the Catholics and Jews when it comes to public engagement.

DISCIPLINE AND REFORMATION

Fortunately the Bible teaches renewal, so that the church can reestablish its integrity and fruitfulness. Jesus showed the way in Matt 18:15–20, where He spoke of restoring a brother in sin. And the New Testament letters are full of corrective counsel, as when Paul shamed the "progressives" in Corinth for indulging a man who is living with his father's wife (1 Cor 5:1–8) and rebuked the circumcision party in Galatians. In this latter instance he even criticized the apostle Peter for caving in to their ungodly sensitivities (Gal 2:11–14).

In none of these passages is death the prescription, as is often the case in Islam. Rather the unrepentant offenders and defectors are merely to be struck from the church rolls. Of course the congregation and not the individual may be the offender. In that case it is not worthy of the faithful remnant in its midst and stands in peril of excommunication itself. Such was the Lord's blunt word to the Ephesian church in Rev 2:1–7: "I will come to you and remove your lampstand from its place—unless you repent" (v. 5).

The Christian church is then self-critical, always reforming—*ecclesia semper reformanda*—as it seeks to recapture the character and conviction of the early church, pictured notably in Jerusalem (Acts 4:32–36; 6:1–7), Antioch (11:19–26; 13:1–3), and Macedonia (2 Cor 8:1–5).

Some suggest, in contrast, that Islam's troubles stem from the fact that Muslims have not yet had a Reformation analogous to the Protestant Reformation of the sixteenth century, but this misses the point of origins. When Christianity goes back to its roots, it finds Jesus, the suffering Servant; when Islam goes back to its roots, it finds the warring Mohammed. Indeed with its current emphasis on jihad, Islam may well be in the midst of a reformation, just as Mormonism may be seeing one in the recent explosion of polygamy. Neither is an attractive sight.

Reformations

Again and again, Christians bring their brethren back to New Testament basics, and when this happens, the church experiences new life and fruitfulness—not at the point of a sword but through the salvation of souls and the spread of gospel "salt and light" throughout the culture. Here is a sampling:

- Martin Luther launched the Protestant Reformation by nailing 95 "theses" to the cathedral door in Wittenberg, Germany. Reading Rom 1:17, he had discovered "the righteous will live by faith," and not by ritual or works. Attacking the practice of selling "indulgences" (escapes from purgatory), Luther wrote, "It is vain to trust in salvation by indulgence letters, even though the indulgence commissary, or even the pope, were to offer his soul as security."[29]

- After years of struggle over the question of biblical inerrancy and its status in denominational agencies, most notably the seminaries, the Southern Baptist Convention appointed a Peace Committee to propose a way out of the conflict. The committee brought its report in June 1987, and the messengers to the annual meeting adopted it. The report recognized departures from trust in Scripture but declared that most Southern Baptists read the denomination's doctrinal statement to say concerning "truth without any mixture of error for its matter," that Adam and Eve were real persons, that the named authors wrote the attributed biblical books, that the "miracles described in Scripture did indeed occur as supernatural events in history," and that "the historical narratives given by biblical authors are indeed accurate and reliable as given by those authors." They added,

  > We call upon Southern Baptist institutions to recognize the great number of Southern Baptists who believe this interpretation of our confessional statement and, in the future, to build their professional staffs and faculties from those who clearly reflect such dominant convictions and beliefs held by Southern Baptists at large.[30]

  This "back-to-the-Bible" movement had a dramatic effect on the seminaries.
- Appalled at the encouragement of homosexuality in the European and North American churches, Anglican bishops, with leadership in the Global South, convened a Global Anglican Future Conference in Jerusalem in 2008. Their "Jerusalem Declaration" presented a high view of Scripture and then stood for biblical marriage: "We acknowledge God's creation of humankind as male and female and the unchangeable standard of Christian marriage between one man and one woman as the proper place for sexual intimacy and the basis of the family." They added, "We repent of our failures to maintain this standard and call for a renewed commitment to lifelong fidelity in marriage and abstinence for those who are not married."[31] Such stands by the Fellowship of Confessing Anglicans, the Convocation of Anglicans in North America, and the American Anglican Council are forcing the broader body toward reformation, if not schism.

TESTIMONY OF NONBELIEVERS

One fully expects the faithful to praise their fellow believers, but the praise of others has special cachet.

Melanie Phillips

In her book *Londonistan*, on the horrors of radical Islam's spread in England, Melanie Phillips, Jewish columnist for London's *Daily Mail*, writes:

Britain has become a largely post-Christian society, where traditional morality has been systematically undermined and replaced by an "anything goes" culture in which autonomous decisions about codes of behavior have become unchallengeable rights. With everyone's lifestyle now said to be of equal value, the very idea of moral norms is frowned upon as a vehicle for discrimination and prejudice. Judaism and Christianity, the creeds that formed the bedrock of Western civilization, have been pushed aside and their place filled by a plethora of paranormal activities and cults.[32]

Then in *The World Turned Upside Down: The Global Battle over God, Truth, and Power*, Phillips unpacks some of that Christian heritage.

Christianity embraced reason and logic as guides to religious truth because reason was a supreme gift from God and the means progressively to increase understanding of God and scripture. Augustine held that reason was indispensable to faith: while faith preceded reason "to purify the heart and make it fit to receive and endure the great light of reason," it was reason itself that persuaded us of this and so reason must also precede faith. Embodied in the great universities founded by the church, faith in the power of reason infused Western culture, stimulating the rise of science.[33]

Ayaan Hirsi Ali

Ayaan Hirsi Ali was born into a Muslim Somali family, where she was subjected to female genital mutilation according to the custom of that culture. Later she was assigned a husband, and she fled to Holland, where she rose to be a member of the Dutch parliament. In league with Theo Van Gogh, grand nephew of Vincent van Gogh, she made a film exposing the plight of women under Islam. When van Gogh was stabbed to death by an angry Muslim, Hirsi Ali went underground, finding her way to America. Today as an atheist and a lesbian, she is an ardent foe of Islam—but not of Christianity.

In fact, she urges a counteroffensive by the church: "I hope my friends Richard Dawkins, Sam Harris, and Christopher Hitchens—the esteemed trinity of atheist activists in Britain and the United States—will not be dismayed by the idea of a strategic alliance between secular people and Christians, including the Roman Catholic Church."[34]

She continues, "So long as we atheists and classical liberals have no effective programs of our own to defeat the spread of radical Islam, we should work with enlightened Christians who are willing to devise some."[35] And though she is careful to list her problems with Christianity, she can still say:

Given the choice, I would by far rather live in a Christian than a Muslim country. Christianity in the West today is more humane, more restrained, and more accepting of criticism and debate. The Christian concept of God today is more benign, more tolerant of dissent. But the most important difference between the two civilizations is the exit option. A person who chooses to opt out of Christianity may be excommunicated from the Church community, but he is not harmed; his destiny is left to God. Muslims, however, impose Allah's rules on each other. Apostates—people, like me, who leave the faith—are supposed to be killed.[36]

Gertrude Himmelfarb

Gertrude Himmelfarb is the wife and the mother of two prominent Jewish neoconservatives, Irving and William Kristol. Here she honors the eighteenth-century English evangelicals:

> When John Wesley preached "Gain all you can . . . Save all you can . . . Give all you can," he gave practical effect to those principles by taking up collections for the poor, setting up loan funds and work projects, and instructing his followers to pay "visitations" to the sick and to prisoners in jail. It is not surprising to find Methodists and Evangelicals prominent in the founding of orphanages, schools, hospitals, friendly societies, and charitable enterprises of every kind. By the late eighteenth century, the principle of "philanthropy" (still carrying with it its original meaning of "love of mankind") had given rise to full-time philanthropists like John Howard, who agitated for the reform of the prison system, and Jonas Hanway, who devised the "boarding out" system to remove infants from the poorhouses.[37]

Matthew Parris

In a 2008 *Times of London* column, Matthew Parris, an atheist, said that Africa needed more Christian missionaries. He had been raised in Nyasaland (today's Malawi) and had been back recently with one of the *Times* charities, Pump Aid, funded by the paper's Christmas appeal.[38]

Through the years he has been impressed with and thankful for the helpful work of the missionaries, but he did not want to admit that their faith was the crux of the matter. He wanted to believe that "what counted was the help, not the faith." Yet he had to admit: "Education and training alone will not do. In Africa Christianity changes people's hearts. It brings a spiritual transformation. The rebirth is real. The change is good."

Parris recalled the distinctive manner of the Christian converts with whom he had contact in his childhood.

> The Christians were always different. Far from having cowed or confined its converts, their faith appeared to have liberated and relaxed them. There was a liveliness, a curiosity, an engagement with the world—a directness in their dealings with others—that seemed to be missing in traditional African life. They stood tall.[39]

Then on a trip with friends in his twenties, he had this experience: "Whenever we entered a territory worked by missionaries, we had to acknowledge that something changed in the faces of the people we passed and spoke to: something in their eyes, the way they approached you direct, man-to-man, without look-ing down or away."[40]

Pushing back against the multicultural relativists, Parris disparages the suffocating tribalism and animism of Africa: "Anxiety—fear of evil spirits, of ancestors, of nature and the wild, of a tribal hierarchy, of quite everyday things—strikes deep into the whole structure of rural African thought." And to draw a sharp distinction, he goes back to a statement by Sir Edmund Hill-ary, who, with the Sherpa Tenzing Norgay, first claimed Mount Everest: When asked, "Why climb the mountain?" he answered, "Because it's there." Parris continues, "To the rural African mind, this is an explanation of why one would not climb the mountain. It's . . . well, there. Just there. Why interfere? Nothing to be done about it, or with it. Hillary's further explanation—that nobody else had climbed it—would stand as a second reason for passivity."[41]

Parris concludes, "A whole belief system must first be supplanted. And I'm afraid it has to be supplanted by another. Removing Christian evangelism from the African equation may leave the continent at the mercy of a malign fusion of Nike, the witch doctor, the mobile phone and the machete."[42]

A more eloquent statement of the point can hardly be imagined.

Bruce Sheiman

Bruce Sheiman's book, *An Atheist Defends Religion*, though sounding a similar note, focuses on history. He observed that the secularist's darling, the Enlightenment,

> occurred only in the context of Christianity. A commitment to human dignity, personal liberty, and individual equality did not previously appear in any other culture. Freedom in its myriad expression—of inquiry (science), government (democracy), and economics (capitalism)—first emerged in the West and nowhere else. And to explain their develop-ment, one must look at what distinguished the West culturally, namely, Christianity.[43]

Sheiman is particularly impatient with those who say that Christianity and science are foes. "Interestingly, while just 7 percent of elite scientists today claim to believe in God, if we could have performed a comparable survey of the great-est scientists throughout history, the figure may be closer to 75 percent."[44]

S. E. Cupp

Columnist and guest television commentator S. E. Cupp is another unbe-liever who has great respect for the faith. In her book *Losing Our Religion: The Liberal Media's Attack on Christianity*, she writes:

> I am an atheist. I have been an atheist for fifteen years. And so my approach to this book insofar as it is a defense of Christianity is not one from within the structure but from

outside of it. I'm not propping up a particular faith because it is my own, but because I believe in those five important tenets—that Judeo-Christian values, religious tolerance, an objective press, the benevolence of Christianity, and civility and decency make for a better democracy.[45]

Rabbi Edgar Magnin

Father Edward Joseph Flanagan, who is hailed as the founder of the Omaha orphanage, Boys Town, objected to rationalists quoting the Bible verse about neighbor-love, "as if it were all the doctrine anyone needs for the good life." He hastened to note that "it was only a half quotation. In hearty voice, blues eyes kindling, he would repeat the whole verse: 'And thou shalt love the Lord, thy God, with thy whole heart, and with thy whole soul, and with thy whole mind and with thy whole strength . . . and thy neighbor as thyself.'"[46]

He wanted to be sure love came in the proper order.

Though Flanagan was an Irish Catholic, Rabbi Edgar Magnin of Los Angeles sang his praises.

> Like Abraham, he sat at the door of his tent to welcome these strangers passing by, freckle-faced boys with torn trousers and dirty shirts. He reached out his arms, took them to his bosom. Some were black. There were Jews, Catholics, and a variety of Protestants, and those who called themselves by no name and knew no God because they had never been taught there was a God until they met Father Flanagan.[47]

Nonie Darwish

When she was a child, Nonie Darwish saw her father assassinated. As a top intelligence officer in Gaza, he was a national martyr, and her family was, in a sense, royalty in Egypt. Privileged though she was, she found much ground for dismay in Islam, and subsequently much ground for admiration in Christianity. Coming to America, she became enamored of Christian culture. She sent her children to a Christian school because she "wanted to give them the best education possible." She recalled her own experience at St. Clare College in Cairo, where she felt great peace around the nuns who taught her.

In southern California she was struck by the sight of Christians and Jews heading to church and synagogue as families. Having been saturated in Muslim culture, she "yearned for a religion that uplifted [her] spirits." And she found it in Christianity. One day she happened on a televised preacher whose sermon from 1 Corinthians 13 amazed her. The next week she took her husband to that church, which proved to be a life-changing experience:

> People were standing up singing along, clapping and raising their hands up high to praise God. We sat near the front row and listened to a message of compassion, love, acceptance,

tolerance, and prayer for all of humanity. That day—this made an indelible impression on me—there was some news of violence in the Middle East and the pastor prayed for everyone in the Middle East—Muslims, Jews, and Christians. It was a very different message from the prayers to "destroy the infidels" that I grew up with. My husband and I could barely hold back our tears.[48]

She concluded that she was "faced with a challenge, nothing less than the choice between love and hate."[49] This was the striking difference she perceived as a Muslim.

David Brog

In his book *In Defense of Faith: The Judeo-Christian Idea and the Struggle for Humanity*, David Brog, Jewish director of Christians United for Israel, reports, with relish, the "awakening" of *New York Times* columnist Nicholas Kristoff. By his own admission, the Pulitzer Prize-winning Kristoff, was once plagued by the liberal "blind spot about Evangelicals," a group "usually regarded by snooty, college-educated bicoastal elitists . . . as dangerous Neanderthals."[50]

But then he visited a Philippine island tormented by the Abu Sayyaf rebel group, which was targeting aid workers. "The only group still busy providing food and medicine in this war zone was the Christian Children's Fund." And so he confesses, "I've lost my cynicism about evangelical groups . . . because I've seen them at work abroad." He calls their wave of humanitarian activity "one of the most important—and welcome—trends in our foreign relations."[51]

Holocaust Survivors

Many are familiar with the courageous, merciful work of Oskar Schindler, of *Schindler's List*. He was not a believer, but many of those who rescued Jews were Christians, motivated by their faith and praised by those they delivered.

Phil Hallie. Jewish philosopher Phil Hallie, a decorated veteran of World War I, was profoundly depressed by the Holocaust, and he traveled back to Europe to sort out his perspective. Part of his recovery was the discovery that a little Presbyterian church in the French city of Chambon had put itself at great peril by harboring Jews from the Nazis.[52]

Led by their pastor, André Trocmé, the little congregation "hid them in barns and farmhouses, gave them false identity cards, brought them into the town's seven group homes, and later even accompanied them along dangerous escape routes into neutral Switzerland."[53]

Andre Couraqui. When Trocmé and his wife Magda were honored by the Israeli Holocaust society Yad Vashem as one of the "Righteous among the Nations," Jewish survivor Andre Couraqui commended them with these words:

Pastor Andre Trocmé was the living soul and the spiritual personification of the French resistance. Through his personal actions, as an example to others by his demands and by his writings, Pastor Andre Trocmé undoubtedly saved—directly and indirectly—numerous Jewish souls, and helped to strengthen the spirit of the French resistance which, at the end of the day, contributed to the downfall of the National Socialism of Hitler. Pastor Trocmé always offered me the most complete and reliable assistance. No month went by when I did not turn to him for help; to him or to his friends or to the members of his congregation who were hiding Jews in that area. During all the tragic years of our resistance, Pastor Trocmé always answered our calls for help. He answered them with enthusiasm, even though he knew his efforts on our behalf endangered his life, those of his wife and children, and those of his congregation. His church and his home were among the great centres of the French resistance.[54]

Klemak Nowicki. Protestants were not the only helpers. One convent near Brussels was "hiding, at the end of the war, ten Jewish adults, twenty-eight Jewish children, British parachutists, weapons, resistance fighters."[55] And two Roman Catholic bishops received special thanks from Klemak Nowicki:

We ran out in darkness, and went to this church that my mother heard about. She had heard about this bishop who apparently was friendly to the Jews. She placed herself at his mercy. She was at the end of her rope—exhausted. She told him exactly who she was. She figured it was a last-chance effort. She couldn't run anymore. So she confessed to him, and told him exactly who she was, and who I was, and so on. And he in fact did hide Jews. There were a couple of hundred Jews hiding in the basement of his church, which was extraordinarily brave of him, because he could have been killed for doing this. Now that's not common. It's a rarity. But there were a lot of righteous Christians. The bishop was that kind of person. He said he realized that my mother's survival was contingent upon not being with me. I was a dead giveaway. He suggested a convent outside of Warsaw.[56]

Nowicki did indeed go to this convent, where this occurred:

On one occasion they [the Gestapo] caught me. I remember the scene when they were taking me out. About three men were taking me out, and I remember that the bishop, the retired bishop who lived on the grounds, came and intervened, and he said, If you take him, you'll have to take me. I don't know why, but they let me go. They usually didn't [care]; they'd take everybody. But they left me alone. If it wasn't for the bishop's intervention, I would have been dead.[57]

Notes

1 Sarah Vowell, *The Wordy Shipmates* (New York: Penguin, 2008), 114–15.
2 Conn Iggulden and David Iggulden, *The Dangerous Book of Heroes* (New York: Harper-Collins/Morrow, 2009), 90.
3 Ibid.
4 Antonia Fraser, *Cromwell, The Lord Protector* (New York: Knopf, 1974), 335–40.
5 Ibid., 340.

6 Oliver Cromwell, cited in *"To Honour God": The Spirituality of Oliver Cromwell*, ed. Michael A. G. Haykin (Dundas, ON: Joshua, 1999), 126.

7 Ibid., 14.

8 David Livingstone, *Missionary Travels and Researches in South Africa* (New York: Harper & Brothers, 1858), 36–37.

9 Tim Neal, *Livingstone* (New York: G. P. Putnam's Sons, 1973), 30.

10 Jonathan Gatehouse, "Beyond Blunderdome," *Maclean's*, August 16, 2010, 50.

11 Bradley R. E. Wright, *Christians Are Hate-Filled Hypocrites . . . and Other Lies You've Been Told: A Sociologist Shatters Myths from the Secular and Christian Media* (Minneapolis: Bethany House, 2010), 152–54.

12 Norman Stone, *World War One: A Short History* (New York: Basic, 2009), 127.

13 Lawrence E. Harrison and Samuel P. Huntington, *Culture Matters: How Values Shape Human Progress* (New York: Basic, 2000), 190.

14 Lawrence E. Harrison, "Culture and Economic Development," Cato Institute, December 6, 2006; http://www.cato-unbound.org/2006/12/04/lawrence-e-harrison/culture-and-economic-development (accessed December 8, 2010).

15 Ibid.

16 Alma Guillermoprieto, "Death Comes for the Archbishop," review of "Asi matamos a monsenor Romero" (for *El Faro*) and "Monsenor: The Last Journey of Oscar Romero" (film), *New York Review of Books*, May 27, 2010.

17 *Encyclopedia of the Nations*; http://www.nationsencyclopedia.com/Americas/El-Salvador-HEALTH.html (accessed June 7, 2010).

18 Michael Novak, *The Spirit of Democratic Capitalism* (Lanham, MD: Madison, 1991), 301–2.

19 Ibid., 300.

20 Ibid., 299.

21 Ibid., 302.

22 Michael Novak, *The Joy of Sports: Endzones, Bases, Baskets, Balls, and the Consecration of the American Spirit*, rev. ed. (Lanham, MD: Madison, 1994), 228.

23 Michael Novak, *The Spirit of Democratic Capitalism*, 277.

24 Ibid., 279.

25 Livingstone, *Missionary Travels and Researches in South Africa*, 414.

26 George Weigel, "What Went Wrong?" *Newsweek*, April 12, 2010, 42.

27 See Mark Coppenger, "An Animist Automobile?" *Baptist Press*, March 23, 2004; http://www.bpnews.net/bpnews.asp?id=17913 (accessed December 8, 2010).

28 Matthew Miller and Andrew Romano, "Newsweek's Power 50," *Newsweek*, November 8, 2010, 32–44.

29 Martin Luther, *The 95 Theses*, no. 52; http://www.reformed.org/documents/index.html?mainframe=http://www.reformed.org/documents/95_theses.html (accessed October 28, 2010).

30 *Report of the Southern Baptist Convention Peace Committee*, June 16, 1987; http://www.baptist2baptist.net/b2barticle.asp?ID=65 (accessed October 29, 2010).

31 http://fca.net/resources/the_jerusalem_declaration (accessed October 29, 2010).

32 Melanie Phillips, *Londonistan* (New York: Encounter, 2006), xx.

33 Melanie Phillips, *The World Turned Upside Down: The Global Battle over God, Truth, and Power* (New York: Encounter, 2010), 329.

34 Ayaan Hirsi Ali, *Nomad: From Islam to America: A Personal Journey Through the Clash of Civilizations* (New York: Free, 2010), 240.

35 Ibid., 243.

36 Ibid., 243–44.

37 Gertrude Himmelfarb, *The De-Moralization of Society: From Victorian Virtues to Modern Values* (New York: Knopf, 1995), 144.

38 Matthew Parris, "As an Atheist, I Truly Believe Africa Needs God," *Times* online, December 27, 2008; http://www.timesonline.co.uk/tol/comment/columnists/matthew_parris/article5400568.ece (accessed June 4, 2010).

39 Ibid.

40 Ibid.

41 Ibid.

42 Ibid.

43 Bruce Sheiman, *An Atheist Defends Religion: Why Humanity Is Better Off with Religion Than Without It* (New York: Alpha/Penguin, 2009), 99.

44 Ibid., 103.

45 S. E. Cupp, *Losing Our Religion: The Liberal Media's Attack on Christianity* (New York: Threshold, 2010), 10.

46 Fulton Oursler and Will Oursler, *Father Flanagan of Boys Town* (Garden City, NY: Doubleday, 1949), 10.

47 Ibid., 8.

48 Nonie Darwish, *Now They Call Me Infidel: Why I Renounced Jihad for America, Israel, and the War on Terror* (New York: Penguin/Sentinel, 2006), 159.

49 Ibid.

50 David Brog, *In Defense of Faith: The Judeo-Christian Idea and the Struggle for Humanity* (New York: Encounter, 2010), 337.

51 Ibid., 336.

52 Philip P. Hallie, *Lest Innocent Blood Be Shed* (New York: Harper & Row, 1979).

53 Susan Glick, *Heroes of the Holocaust* (San Diego: Thomson/Gale, 2003), 68–69.

54 Ibid., 72–73.

55 Howard Greenfeld, *The Hidden Children* (New York: Ticknor & Fields, 1993), 35.

56 Ibid., 51–52.

57 Ibid., 89.

THE CULTURAL FRUIT OF
CHRISTIANITY: CELEBRATION

B ACK IN THE 1970S, when Volkswagen, Toyota, Sony, and a host of other
German and Japanese products were coming to dominate American mar-
kets, a wag observed that the best thing a country could do was to lose a war to
the United States. Whether through the Marshall Plan of European reconstruc-
tion, NATO's protection against Warsaw Pact aggression, or the democratiza-
tion of Japan, "defeated nations" were helped to flourish economically.

Whatever America's virtues or shortfalls, there is a far powerful, analogous
point to be made in the spiritual realm. There is nothing which blesses a nation
so much as voluntary, glad surrender to the King of kings. When Jesus becomes
Lord of a great many citizens, the cultural fruit is undeniable.

THE FRUIT OF CONVERSION

When someone is born again, he or she exhibits new appetites, passions, dis-
tastes, directions, and resolve. Family members and associates notice the difference, and the transformation contributes to the case for Christianity. Of course
other conversions result in better behavior. When a drug-dealing gang leader
joins the Nation of Islam in prison, he may well show gains in sobriety, sexual
morals, and circumspection in speech. This alone does not prove the validity of
Islam. First, there is no substitute for truth. But also one's performance must
be taken as a whole. Has he gained ground in grooming and punctuality but
lost ground in his treatment of Jews? Of course the same could be asked for any
religious group. Has the conversion of people in the group made them more of
a blessing to society? A look at Louis Farrakhan would suggest that the Black

Muslim ideal is less than ideal, and one would be more inclined to suspect than trust his followers.

That is not the case for genuine Christian converts, and accounts of their transformation provide material for the apologist.

Billy Sunday

Within a month of his birth in 1862, Billy Sunday lost his father to pneumonia, and the family struggled for survival. Finally his mother was forced to send him and his brother to orphan homes, first near Council Bluffs, Iowa, and then to Davenport, Iowa. Eventually he distinguished himself in sports and made it to professional baseball, where he signed with the Chicago White Stockings, where he had moderate success. He was an extraordinarily fast runner, becoming the first man to circle the bases in 14 seconds. But his life was empty.

> On a Sunday afternoon in 1886, after having a few beers with his baseball buddies and sitting out on the curb, Billy heard a gospel mission band playing what he described as "the gospels hymns I used to hear my mother sing back in the log cabin in Iowa." . . . He left his buddies and went into the Pacific Garden Mission in Chicago where he became a born-again Christian. Billy continued to play major league baseball for five more years but never again on Sunday. Sundays he spent working for the Young Men's Christian Association.[1]

In 1888 Billy Sunday was traded to Pittsburgh, where the papers were as impressed as much with his character as with his prowess on the field.

> The Pittsburgh Press reported that Billy and his former White Stockings teammate, Abner Dalrymple, shared a room on a quiet street in Allegheny city and that their presence in the neighborhood was likely to alter the public's perception of professional baseball players, for according to the paper, "two quieter or more gentlemanly men in any line of business it would be hard to find."[2]

The same paper reprinted an article from the *Chicago Interocean*, one that said the following:

> Chicago sends to Pittsburg[h] one of its best and most exemplary ball players, a young man of irreproachable habits and morals, by name William Sunday, who used to chase after sky-scrapping [*sic*] flies and daisy-destroying grounders for the White Stocking team and never utter a "cuss word" when the ball slipped through his fingers; who under no circumstances dallied with red liquor nor looked upon beer except with abhorrence; who knew not the taste of "the weed" in any form whatever; who played good ball on week days and attended church and Bible class on the Sabbath; who ran bases with such race-horse speed that a two-bagger usually landed him on third.[3]

A couple of weeks later *The Press* added fresh commentary of its own:

Billy Sunday's consistent walk in the straight and narrow path which leads to life everlasting has already won him a host of friends among the church-going people of the North Side. The roughest ball player on the diamond respects his scruples and will stifle an oath in his presence. If caught, unwittingly, they have been known to apologize in a shame-faced manner for their language. He usually acts as a peacemaker in factional contests, but when the war becomes too hot will quietly slip away. It is his unpretentions [sic] manner more than anything else that has won their respect. More like him would be a credit to any club in the country, even if they did not possess his ability.[4]

Then

In 1891, despite being offered $400 a month by the Philadelphia Phillies and $500 a month by the Cincinnati Reds, Billy took a job as the secretary of the religious department at the Chicago YMCA at a monthly salary of $83.33. In 1894 the Pittsburgh Pirates offered him $2,000 a month, but instead Sunday became the advance man for evangelist J. Wilbur Chapman for $40 a week.[5]

To be sure, Sunday later became wealthy, for the crowds and offerings at his revival meetings were enormous. He bought "fashionable clothes" and "stylish cars" and enjoyed "a rural retreat in the Hood River country of Oregon." But he was also charitable, donating, for instance, his entire offering from the April 1917 New York meeting ($120,500) to the "war work of the YMCA and Red Cross." Next year he "donated the entire free-will offering from the Chicago crusade, more than $54,000, to the Pacific Garden Mission." (In those days, the average worker made $14,000 a year.) He was also a tither.[6]

THE FRUIT OF REVIVAL

When the Spirit of God moves in extraordinary ways to save souls and reform the churches, the nations are beneficiaries. Evidence of this fact is seen in the impact of these great movements of God.

The British and American Awakenings of the 1740s

Canadian theologian and historian J. Wesley Bready observed:

Without revolution or bloodshed the Evangelical Revival, of which Wesley was the central and inspiriting prophet, abolished both the slave trade and slavery through all British domains—the greatest single social triumph in all modern history. By various pioneering means, this same Movement laid deeply and well the foundations of England's free and popular education. Through the devoted labors of Wesley, John Howard and Elizabeth Fry, it humanized the Anglo-Saxon prison system and penal code. . . . It raised up Lord Shaftesbury as "Emancipator of the Industrial Worker," and Dr. Bernardo as "Emancipator of the Outcast Child." Not least, it created the great and unparalleled philanthropic movement of the nineteenth century—a movement which only the cynic will ignore. Finally, it inspired a series of important world-wide organizations including the Sunday

School movement, the Young People's Society of Christian Endeavor, the Y.M.C.A., the Y.W.C.A., the British and American Bible Societies, the Salvation Army, and many more.[7]

J. Edwin Orr's Chronicles

Picking up on these phenomena, J. Edwin Orr, the great chronicler of revival, was ever ready to note the social impact, the cultural fruit, of awakenings. He penned a number of books focusing on particular revivals, beginning with the evangelical revivals of the late eighteenth and early nineteenth centuries. He writes of the crusading efforts of key evangelicals—John Wesley and William Wilberforce against slavery; John Howard and Elizabeth Fry for prison reform; Theodore Fliedner and Florence Nightingale for better medical care; Lord Shaftesbury, John Wood, and Richard Oastler for the improvement of working conditions and against the use of child labor; James Mackintosh and Arthur Broome against animal cruelty; and throughout the world, as William Carey fought "widow burning" (*suttee*) in India, the Moravians established a leper colony in South Africa, where David Livingstone also provided medical care.[8]

Thanks to Orr, the following presents a closer look at the transformative touch of two of these revivals:

The 1850s prayer revival. Prompted by the American prayer revival, initiated by Jeremiah Lanphier in a Dutch Reformed church in Manhattan in the fall of 1857, the British experienced their own outpouring of the Holy Spirit in the late 1850s. It included these manifestations:

- In Ulster a man rose to declare himself "a vile sinner," "the profligate of Broughshane," and "a servant of the devil," led by "the spirit of the barley." He admitted that he had "brought [his] wife and family to beggary" but that now he had reformed by the grace of Christ.[9]
- In Cardiff, Wales, "a remarkable work of the Spirit" was powerful in "affecting public morals and bringing hundreds to the house of prayer, so much so that a town councilor (Anglican) of long experience testified that police cases were dwindling and a detective added that Cardiff had become a different place."[10]
- In Lowestoft, Suffolk, police arrests for drunkenness had dropped from 120 to 20 nightly.[11]
- In Wellington, Somerset, "a notorious gambler gathered together his dice and cards, and told his wife that he was about to play his best game, and threw them into the fire. A number of cockfighters beheaded their birds and ate the fowls for dinner. Poachers and prize-fighters likewise repented."[12]

- In Belfast "certain prostitutes confessed that they were first made to consider an amended life by the falling off in business," and "the Rev. John Venn of Hereford quoted a Belfast policemen who saw a body of fourteen prostitutes making their way to a House of Refuge, the result of a visit to a prayer meeting."[13]
- From 1855 to 1861, there was a drop in annual criminal convictions in Ulster, from 889 to 593.[14]
- A "Revival School of Christian Philanthropists" emerged, "endeavouring to go straight to the heart of the slums with practical Samaritanism" and "numberless philanthropic institutions—homes, asylums, refuges, brigades, schools—were founded in all parts of the country."[15]

Of course there were foes and detractors.[16] When Irish Presbyterian moderator William Gibson wrote *The Year of Grace*, celebrating the revival, Rev. Isaac Nelson responded with a book of his own, *The Year of Delusion: A Review of "The Year of Grace,"* suggesting that Gibson might well have named his book *The Year of Blowing Our Trumpet*. Nelson, in turn, faced a polemic, penned by Rev. T. S. Woods, *The Delusion of the Rev. I. Nelson*, calling his critique "a bilious misrepresentation of the Revival" and "a low, vulgar libel on those who believe in it."

One critic noted that instances of public drunkenness increased in Belfast during the revival—from 2,539 cases in 1858 to 3,112 in 1859. The revivalists responded that this was due to "the 40,000 Roman Catholics who continued to drink freely" and "that none of the inebriates was a convert of the Revival." Furthermore *The British Standard* reported that in the city of Derry there were 100,000 Presbyterians, but "not one drunken person called himself a Presbyterian."

Others pointed to the continued slave-holding of some Americans involved in the revival but ignored the antislavery work of revivalist Charles Finney. And so on it went. Still, few can deny the generally salubrious effect and the striking conversion of thousands. Certainly British Prime Minister Lloyd George praised the evangelical revival, which, in his words, "improved the condition of the working classes in wages, hours of labour and otherwise." And of course the Salvation Army resulted from these works of God, as did the YMCA.[17]

The revival spread to other continents, with similar results. In Kerala, India, "it reformed the lives of drunkards, of deceivers and extortioners, and brought about a restitution of property wrongly acquired."[18] And the flood of missionaries flowing from the revival in the United States and Britain had great impact on the developing world, as in Mexico, in 1865. There Melinda Rankin founded a school in Monterrey, and in subsequent years her colleagues established schools "in rural areas, the first ray of hope for the mestizos in many a neglected district. . . . The schools produced many a leader in national life."[19]

The Welsh revival of the early twentieth century. In answer to the prayers of many, revival fell on Wales in 1904. It had happened once before, in 1859, when the influence of the New York Prayer Revival spread to Wales, generating as many as 100,000 conversions in this small country. But by century's end the spiritual fires had dimmed, and the Welsh were much in need of the Spirit's fresh touch. Stirred by the preaching of Evan Roberts and Seth Joshua, who cried out, "Bend us, Oh Lord," the nation saw 85,000 professions of faith that year. And the social impact was considerable: "The crime rate dropped, old debts were repaid, ale houses stood empty, and work improved in the mines."[20]

Always the fastidious and sympathetic chronicler, J. Edwin Orr traced its moral impact around the world, as the work of God spread out to the nations:

- "After the 1905 New Year, the Swansea [Wales] County Police Court announced to the public that there had not been a single charge for drunkenness over the holiday weekend, an all-time record."[21]
- "The register . . . at Somerset House in London showed a decrease of illegitimate births when measured against the one per cent increase of population, this being true of not only England but the other parts of the United Kingdom."[22]
- In Norway, "Old debts were settled and conscience money was paid up: misappropriated articles were restored, intoxication was abandoned by many, and a purer moral atmosphere was noted by observers of social conditions."[23]
- In Michigan a regional Methodist journal reported, "So completely have the principles of righteousness permeated the common thought and feeling that even the long tolerated forms of stock gambling and swindling rate-methods have come in for exposure and sharp censure."[24]
- In Malawi, "The brave but bloodthirsty Ngoni warriors were learning to live in peace with other tribes, also moved by Christian teaching."[25]
- At a Christian and Missionary Alliance orphanage in the Indian state of Gujarat, "Sixty rupees of conscience money were restored, as well as stolen articles from blankets to pins. The head carpenter returned ten stolen rupees."[26]
- In the West China city of Kiating, "idolatry, theft, murder, adultery, gambling, opium smoking, disobedience to parents and hatred of employers, quarrelsomeness, lying, cheating, and the like were confessed for forgiveness."[27]

THE SOCIAL IMPACT OF MISSIONARIES

As Christian missionaries have fanned out across the world, they have brought "the whole counsel of God," which includes not only the way to heaven but also the way to walk on earth. Of course multiculturalists are often upset that many of "the old ways" were supplanted, sometimes by harsh means, as with children in Indian schools. But the impact has been overwhelmingly good.

On the international scene some unbelievers tend to defame missionaries, calling them tools of colonialism, insensitive to the national cultures and so on, but any fair treatment of these courageous saints can only leave one with the impression that they have elevated the condition of those they have tried to reach.

Africa

> Missionaries established and pioneered schools everywhere, and these schools became the nurseries for change: they sowed the Gospel, they sowed Christianity and perhaps unawares and unintentionally they sowed also the new revolution. It is the young men and women in these schools who assimilated not only religion but science, politics, technology and so on. . . . Through missionaries too came European medicine and knowledge of hygiene which, however, had a slow influence at the beginning. In addition to the physical impact, the new medicine prepared people psychologically to become more receptive to western culture and education. Eventually the new form of medical care and knowledge began to reduce infant mortality and put under control diseases like smallpox, malaria and stomach ailments which had always been the main killers of African peoples.[28]

Indonesia

Early missionaries to Indonesia encountered a range of ruinous behaviors, "not only head hunting, continuous warfare between villages, slavery, and gambling, but also the custom of marrying at a young age, giving dowries, slaughtering large numbers of animals at social events such as funerals, and cock fighting."[29]

Under constant pressure from the missionaries, in 1913,

> the government took stern action against head hunting, acts of revenge, burying people alive and infanticide. In the same year Fr. Jos van de Kolk developed the idea of a model *kampung* (village) in Okaba. In 1914 Merauke also got its model kampung. The aim of their idea was to enforce a radical change in the life of the Marind-anim, in order to save them from extinction by the venereal disease granuloma.[30]

They sought to end the absurd "tradition that many male members of the husband's clan had the duty to have intercourse with the bride on the first night after the marriage. The venereal disease, distributed through this ritual, led to infertility due to a rupture of the uterus."[31]

Then the Great Awakening came in 1915 and lasted until 1930. "In the realms of family-life and worship there were important developments, like the acceptance of monogamy, greater freedom for women and children, and cultural developments like the songs of the awakening."[32]

Individual Missionaries

Any number of individual missionaries can be credited with enhancing the living conditions of those they sought to reach with the gospel. Here are a few:

St. Patrick of Ireland. Called back to Ireland, where he was once a slave, Patrick (now known as St. Patrick) became a missionary. The island was rife with warfare, with the Druid faith, which called for human sacrifice, and with pagan tribalism, where clan leaders were sometimes inaugurated with public acts of bestiality. As the Christian faith spread throughout the land, many devoted themselves to lives of sacrifice. Though they were not called to be "Red Martyrs," as were early Christians whose blood was shed in Rome, some became "Green Martyrs," who devoted their lives to copying Scripture in ascetic quarters and "White Martyrs," who took classical and biblical learning to sections of Europe which had lost it.[33]

David Wilkerson of New York. Touched by a courtroom drawing in *Life* magazine, Pennsylvania pastor David Wilkerson headed into New York City to see what he could do to bring the gospel to the city's violent youth offenders. Moving into a grungy office on Staten Island, he started a "program aimed at setting youngsters free," a program which is today called Teen Challenge. In 1959 his work saw great gain in power when a gang leader named Nicky Cruz came to Christ and led his followers to do the same. Eventually Wilkerson established Times Square Church, which continues strong to this day.[34]

Joe Church of Rwanda. When a terrible famine was tormenting Rwanda in 1928–29, Anglican missionary Joe Church wrote in his newsletter that "one cannot go far in any direction without seeing corpses lying by the roadside." He wrote an appeal that appeared as a full-page article in a newspaper published in neighboring Uganda. The British press, including *The Times*, picked up the article, as did the *Cambridge Daily News*, which ran the headline, "Cambridge Man's Lone Hand in Famine-Stricken Area."

The matter surfaced in both the English and Belgian Parliaments, and "in London a steady stream of gifts came in from *The Times* offices to the CMS [Church Missionary Society]," continuing for months. Belgium transferred doctors from their colony in the Congo and committed a large sum of money to road improvement and transport for relief.[35]

William Carey of India. William Carey, pioneer missionary to India, established the Serampore Press, which "had issued before his death 212,000 copies of the Sacred Scriptures, in forty different languages—the vernacular tongues of about 330,000,000 of immortal souls." Furthermore "His Sanskrit grammar was the very first elementary work in this language that was published."[36] But he not only paved the way for distribution of the gospel; he also applied Christ's morals to the culture as one of the first to petition the East India Company to abolish the Indian practice of widow burning. Between 1815 and 1826, there were 7,154 occurrences in Bengal alone. As horrible as it was, many a widow went to her death convinced "that by this sacrifice she expiates the crimes of her husband, raises him from misery to happiness, and thereby earns the right to dwell with him 35,000,000 of years in a state of perfect felicity."[37]

David Livingstone of Africa. British missionary David Livingstone was early on repulsed by the slave trade in Africa, disgusted both by the Arabs who bought them and the Africans who sold them. "He spent many hours explaining to chiefs that 'if they sell their fellows, they are like the man who holds the victim while the Arab performs the murder.'" In "two cool and lucid dispatches to the Foreign Secretary," he argued for stiff blockades by the British navy and a string of coastal depots for freed slaves so the ships could return to station more promptly—policies which helped lead to the shutdown of Zanzibar's slave market a month after his death.[38]

DOMESTIC CHARITIES

At the close of Matthew 25, Jesus addressed those whom he said ignored him in his time of need. They asked, "Lord, when did we see You hungry, or thirsty, or a stranger, or without clothes, or sick, or in prison, and not help You?" (v. 44). And he responded, "I assure you: Whatever you did not do for one of the least of these, you did not do for Me either" (v. 45). And the stakes could not be higher, for those who ignore the need are destined for "eternal punishment" (v. 46). (Of course the genuine disciple works more from love than fear.)

God's call to be charitable extends back into the Old Testament, but Christ brought the teaching to its fullness. And throughout church history his people have been models of grace, as in these instances.[39]

George Müller

Converted at 20 after some earlier run-ins with the law, George Müller became a remarkable trophy of God's grace. Beginning as a church planter, he was led to begin an orphan ministry in Bristol, England, in 1836, one of which grew over the years to amazing size. At his retirement over 2,000 children were under his care. Müller is most remarkable for his reliance on prayer for provision. Time and again help appeared in the nick of time, as when prayer was said over empty plates, with food arriving at the last moment. And as one journal entry expressed it, "August 23. Today I was again without one single penny, when [three shillings] was sent from Clapham, with a box of new clothes for the Orphans."[40]

The Clapham Church

Under the leadership of John Venn, England's Clapham Church was notable for its evangelical enthusiasm and piety at the turn of the nineteenth century. But it was also a center for Christian social work through the Society for Bettering the Condition of the Poor, which Venn organized in 1799. The Society directed its aid to the industrious, "deserving poor" and did so methodically, with directors and "visitors" attending to the needy in the parish's eight districts. They gave special attention to arresting the spread of disease and to the education of children.[41]

Jubilee Partners

Jubilee Partners, a Christian organization in northeast Georgia, is helping "Lost Boys of Sudan" settle in America. Orphaned by the tyrannical Islamic government in Khartoum, they fled southern Sudan for the relative safety of Ethiopia but were later forced by civil war to gather in Kenya. From there thousands have been flown to America where Christians have helped them with employment and education.[42]

USA Today Charities

In its Christmas Eve 2007 issue, *USA Today* devoted a page to promoting 25 selected charities, "representing a broad range of interests including environment, health, animals, arts, education, human services and public benefits." The page avoided explicitly Christian groups such as the Salvation Army and Samaritan's Purse. Nevertheless many of the charities had Christian founders and connections—Big Brothers, Big Sisters (Ernest Coulter, addressing Central Presbyterian Church, New York City); America's Second Harvest (John van Hengel, St. Mary's Basilica, Phoenix); Habitat for Humanity (Disciples of Christ Millard Fuller, inspired by Southern Baptist Clarence Jordan); Special Olympics (Anne Burke, St. Simon the Apostle Church, Chicago); Ducks Unlimited (Joseph Knapp, son of Phoebe Knapp, who wrote the music to "Blessed Assurance," and a member of John Street Methodist Church, New York City), Good Will Industries International (Methodist minister Edgar J. Helms, Boston); American Red Cross (Henry Dunant, from "a devout and charitable Calvinist family" in Geneva, Switzerland).

Welfare and Workfare

On the public policy front, law professor and columnist Stephen Carter has said that the church has a balanced influence, making sure that the destitute are rescued and the able are held accountable.

> A widespread religious conviction that we must aid the poor will inevitably find its way into legislation, and so the nation will crate welfare programs. A widespread religious conviction that long-term help is no substitute for hard work will inevitably find its way into legislation, and so welfare will evolve into workfare.[43]

A Threat to "Progressives"

Harold O. J. Brown, longtime professor of theology at Trinity Evangelical Divinity School and Reformed Theological Seminary, has observed that the Christian record of charity is so distinguished and pervasive that it poses a threat to those who favor a paternalistic state:

> In the so-called socialist, i.e., Communist, countries, Christian communities are rigidly prohibited from engaging in works of social welfare, because the government knows that the social ministry of the church has been one of its attractions from the dawn of Christianity and is determined that the people shall be beholden to the State alone. In the Western democracies, the welfare state has accomplished much the same thing by substitution rather than suppression. Christian social ethics appear unnecessary when, "All good things come of thee, O, State."[44]

SOBRIETY

Though there is disagreement among evangelicals over the morality and prudence of consuming beverage alcohol, there should be no dispute over the convictions that "wine is a mocker, beer is a brawler, and whoever staggers because of them is not wise" (Prov 20:1). Christian reform has often meant addressing the considerable problems associated with alcohol.

Prohibition

Though the Eighteenth Amendment of 1920 was repealed by the Twenty-first Amendment of 1933, and Prohibition suffered from a variety of problems including lax enforcement and the proliferation of organized crime, it had its salutary effects, often covered over or ignored by the media. Christians anticipated these benefits and so were prime crusaders for its institution—people such as revivalists Billy Sunday and Mordecai Ham and Christian women crusaders such as Francis Willard and Carry Nation, and organizations such as the Women's Christian Temperance Union.

According to [Billy] Sunday, in July of 1905, temperance legislation went into effect in that city [Kansas City, KS] of 100,000. At the time, there were 250 saloons, 200 gambling halls, and 60 houses of prostitution. Within less than a year after Prohibition began, the benefits of the legislation were already quite apparent. The president of one of the city's major banks found that deposits had increased $1.7 million and that 72 percent of the deposits were from men who had never saved a cent before. The pace of business accelerated, while court expenses decreased. The decrease in crime following Prohibition was so significant that the city canceled plans to expand its jail. The number of elderly committed to the poorhouse because their children squandered money that was needed to care for them decreased. The city had to employ eighteen additional teachers to instruct children between the ages of 12 and 18 who had not previously attended school because they were helping their drunken fathers take care of the family.[45]

Pentecostals

Chilean philosophy professor Arturo Fontaine Talavera is director of the Center of Public Studies. While tracking the impact of evangelical/Pentecostal revival in Santiago, he was struck especially by the converts' rejection of alcohol. The man "stops drinking, orders his life, abandons old friends, partying, and women, stops spending wildly, renews his marriage on the basis of respect and love, becomes involved with the children, and takes part in domestic chores." Talavera concludes, "The change is so complete that it is difficult to believe; the evidence is overwhelming, however."[46]

University of Southern California professor Donald E. Millar joins Talavera in appreciation for the impact of Pentecostalism, the benefits extending well beyond diminished interest in alcohol. "By avoiding alcohol, gambling, womanizing, and other such taboos, extremely poor people eventually have surplus capital that they can in turn use to get better education to their children and provide better health care for their families, and all this, in turn, may lead to upward social mobility."[47]

THE REFORMATION OF MANNERS

Though the expression "reformation of manners" traditionally refers to the full range of Christian behavior, including the use of alcohol, here we speak more narrowly of clean speech and a tone of graciousness and dignity.

The Companies of Cornwall

When three companies of British soldiers were dispatched from Plymouth to Truro in Cornwall for duty in the winter of 1756, minister Samuel Walker jumped at the opportunity to extend the gospel ministry to them. At first they were reluctant to hear him preach, but with the encouragement of Walker's parishioners, "they soon became a large number." As things developed over a three-week period, "a full hundred of them came to [Walker's] house asking what they must do [to be saved]"—and many were, with resultant change in barracks life. As Walker recounted, the new believers "and the others who never came near me in private, are plainly influenced, that a certain fear has restrained them from swearing and cursing, which, when they came hither, was universally their practice." Furthermore "military punishments are grown much less frequent among them."[48]

The Georgia and Mississippi Brigades

J. William Jones's chronicle of religion in the Confederate army, *Christ in the Camp*, details the effects of revival on the various units. For instance, when a notoriously dissolute captain in a Georgia brigade was converted, he told his troops, "Men, I have led you into many a battle, and you have followed me like men. Alas! I have led you into all manner of wickedness and vice, and you have followed me into this too. I have now resolved to change my course." Virtually everyone in the unit was saved, and "those former ringleaders in every species of vice had become a centre of powerful influence for the religious good of their regiment and brigade."[49]

Then in a Mississippi brigade the new believers "solemnly resolved to fast one day in every week in order that they might send that day's rations to the suffering poor of the city of Richmond."[50] And Christian soldiers throughout the Confederacy could be seen after the battle,

> going over the ground to hunt up and care for the wounded of the enemy—binding up their wounds as best they could, carrying them to the field-hospitals, and providing surgical attendance, sharing with them their scant rations, bringing them water, building brush shelters to protect them from the sun, and proving : "good Samaritans" indeed to men whom they had so lately met in the shock of battle.[51]

RACIAL JUSTICE

Because everyone is made in the image of God, discrimination on the basis of race is unconscionable, and the mistreatment of any people group is naturally the target of Christian reformers.

The Tappans

Arthur and Lewis Tappan were raised in Northampton, Massachusetts, where decades earlier Jonathan Edwards's preaching stirred the Great Awakening in America. Their mother was converted in that revival, and she led her sons to cherish Christ and the spiritual life he brought. As wealthy men (the founders of the nation's first credit rating agency, which became Dun & Bradstreet), the sons were active in what became known as the Second Great Awakening in America, and one strong application of their faith was establishment of the New

York Anti-Slavery Society in 1833. For their stance the brothers endured threats and vandalism, with a price on Arthur's head in several states. Nevertheless he was resolute: "You demand that I shall cease my anti-slavery labors. . . . I will be hung first." His brother Lewis, who served on the *Amistad* Committee, raising funds for the slaves' legal counsel, called slavery, "the worm at the root of the tree of Liberty. Unless killed the tree will die."[52] Though it took a Civil War to abolish slavery, the moral basis for such a fight was being laid by men like the Tappans earlier in the century.[53]

Ruby Nell Bridges

Immortalized in a Norman Rockwell painting, which shows her walking to school under the protection of federal marshals, Ruby Nell Bridges was a six-year-old black girl in the early days of court-ordered desegregation. Adults screamed obscenities at her as she passed by, and one even displayed a black doll in a coffin. One day her teacher saw her lips moving as she approached the school. She asked what Ruby was saying to the people gathered to heap scorn on her. She responded, "I wasn't talking to them. I was praying for them." She usually prayed in the car but had forgotten to do so that day. When she met the crowd, she began to petition God, "Please be with me . . . and be with those people too. Forgive them because they don't know what they are doing."[54]

Bulgarian Orthodox Church

Though Bulgaria became a passive ally of Germany in World War II and subsequently passed anti-Jewish laws, all its Jews were saved, despite orders to round them up and ship them to extermination sites. In fact Bulgaria's Jewish population increased during the War. The reason was simple: Leaders of the nation's Orthodox Church stood up against persecution. For instance Metropolitan Kyril of the city of Plovdiv, threatened to lie on the railroad tracks if Jews were loaded onto trains headed for the death camps. And Metropolitan Stefan defied the government at several points, including refusal to close the churches when the state ordered it to suppress the spread of damning information about deportation schemes.[55]

GRACE UNTO DEATH

The *Dorchester*

Midnight on February 3, 1943, a German torpedo ripped through the hull of the troop ship *Dorchester* in the North Atlantic. The ship sank in 27 minutes, and many of the soldiers on board were unprepared. Since their quarters were stuffy, they had come up on deck to sleep, leaving their life preservers below.

To save what lives they could, four chaplains—two Protestants, a Catholic, and a Jew—handed their own life preservers to desperate troops. Then they joined arms, prayed, recited Scripture, and sang as they went down with the ship. This was the Judeo-Christian ethic at work, an act honored with a commemorative stamp in 1948 and a special medal of heroism, granted by Congress in 1960.[56]

The *Oryoku Maru*

In recounting his terrible experience on the Japanese "death ship," the *Oryoku Maru*, on which 1,300 of 1,600 American POWs would die, Estel Myers remembers another chaplain who gave that others might live. "One chaplain consistently gave away his rations of food and water to the sick, telling the protesting corpsmen that he felt fine and would keep his next ration. But he would give the next one away, too, making the same promise until finally, after praying with the men on January 24, his weakened body gave out."[57]

Eric Liddell

Through the Academy Award-winning movie *Chariots of Fire*, many are familiar with the athletic skill and Christian devotion of Eric Liddell. But far fewer know that he died of a brain tumor as a missionary in a Japanese prison camp in China. Years later theologian Langdon Gilkey, a fellow prisoner of Liddell's, described the Olympic champion's grace under terrible conditions. He was often engaged with the youth in the game room, whether at chess, model boat-building, or square dancing—"absorbed, weary and interested, pouring all of himself into this effort to capture the minds and imaginations of those penned-up youths." Gilkey continued, "In camp he was . . . lithe and springy of step and, above all, overflowing with good humour and love of life."[58] When once a Canadian journalist asked Liddell whether he missed the limelight, Liddell replied, "Oh well, of course it's natural for a chap to think over all that sometimes, but I'm glad I'm at the work I'm engaged in now." He concluded, "A fellow's life counts for far more at this than the other. Not a corruptible crown, but an incorruptible, you know."[59]

Betsie ten Boom

In her account of prison life in the Nazi death camp system, Dutch Protestant Corrie ten Boom tells of the death of her sister. As they toiled in Ravensbruck, wielding shovels outside in the rainy November cold, Betsie began to cough up blood as her temperature rose. The bare room set aside for sick call was dismal, but for Betsie, "it was simply a setting in which to talk about Jesus." Everywhere she went, "Betsie spoke to those around her about His nearness and His yearning to come into their lives." Corrie observed that, "as her body grew weak, her faith seemed to grow bolder." Indeed Betsie chided her sister for her negativity, explaining that sick call was "such an important place. . . . Some of these people are at the threshold of heaven!"[60]

THE ARTS AND SCIENCES

A long list of prominent scientists were professing Christians, including Isaac Newton (physicist/founder of calculus), Nicholaus Copernicus (astronomer), Michael Faraday (founder of electromagnetics), Louis Pasteur (founder of bacteriology), and G. F. B. Riemann (founder of non-Euclidean geometry). The same could be said of inventors, such as George Washington Carver (crop rotation), Johannes Gutenberg (printing press), and Cyrus McCormick (mechanical reaper); and artists, from composers J. S. Bach and G. F. Handel to painters Leonardo DaVinci and Rembrandt van Rijn to literary figures Dante Alighieri and Flannery O'Conner.[61]

Northwestern University

One way to demonstrate the beneficial effects of Christianity is to uncover the background of something that is generally recognized by the unbelieving world as worthy or impressive. They may consider a particular institution, company, or municipality as a secular accomplishment, owing little or nothing to God; but a little research will show that the base on which things were laid was soundly and distinctively Christian.

For instance Northwestern University in Evanston, Illinois, is ranked among the top dozen "National Universities" by *U.S. News & World Report*. As the smallest school in the Big Ten, with fewer than 9,000 undergraduates where the other schools average over 30,000, it prides itself on being selective and challenging. Among its former students and faculty have been Nobel laureates in physics, economics, literature, medicine, and peace. And it is a thoroughly secular university.

But this was not always the case. The university seal provides a hint: There on the pages of an open book is written in Greek, "The Word, full of grace and truth," a description of Jesus taken from John 1:14. In a ring circling the book are the Latin words for "Whatsoever things are true," drawn from Phil 4:8. (This had been a university norm for centuries, as with Harvard, whose 1650 college seal bore the words, *In Christi Gloriam*.)[62]

Driving around the town of Evanston, where Northwestern is located, one sees street signs with names such as Wesley and Asbury. Even a casual student of church history will recognize the honorees as Methodist divines, and a little research will show that there are more than a dozen such street titles.

Evanston Baptist Church (SBC) has developed a list of these street names and paired them with gospel statements from their namesakes. Many of them were associated with Northwestern University, which was founded and nurtured for over a century by Christians. From time to time the church runs an ad in *The Daily Northwestern* to acquaint students with this heritage and to present the gospel by association.[63] For instance, they read, among the thirteen statements:

> We want prophets of the [prayer] closet as well as study; men whose hearts glow while their intellects shine: who feel deeply, as well as think profoundly; who experience as well as theorize: consecrated, as well as ordained: men, who walk with God and who are intrusted with his secrets: who go before the Church, and say, "Follow us as we follow Christ" (Randolph S. Foster, Northwestern University president, 1856–1860). . . .
> We thank Thee for the revelation of Thyself in Thy Son to take away all sin, in Thy Spirit to quicken every virtue, in Thy Word to dispel every superstition, in Thy Providence to protect from every peril (Charles H. Fowler, Northwestern University president, 1872–1876).

A SAMPLER

This is a particularly frustrating chapter to write since the available material is overwhelming. Book after book has been published on the cultural effects of Christianity. Some, such as Alvin Schmidt's *How Christianity Changed the World,*[64] trace the actual lines of influence (his chap. 4, for instance, shows how Christianity has elevated the status of women); others, like Robert Cowley's *What If*[65] speculate over what might have happened if Christ had not risen from the grave or Luther had been executed as a heretic. Some, like Leland Ryken's *Worldly Saints*[66] (about the Puritans) deal with the influence of a particular group of Christians; others, like D. James Kennedy and Jerry Newcombe's *What If Jesus Had Never Been Born?*[67] address the sweep of history.

Kennedy and Newcombe also team up on a book entitled *What If the Bible Had Never Been Written?* where they connect Scripture to (a) society (greater health, marriage stability, respect for law, and productivity among regular churchgoers); (b) law (the Magna Carta, Blackstone's commentaries); (c) politics (separation of powers, abolitionism), (d) science (Johannes Kepler, Carl von Linnaeus, and George Washington Carver); (e) literature (Dante, Milton, and Dostoevsky); (f) missions (the Moravians to Pennsylvania and Hudson Taylor to China); (g) exploration (Leif Erickson and Christopher Columbus); and (h) everyday things (pretzels, the calendar, expressions such as "scapegoat" and "wolves in sheep's clothing," and "blind leading the blind"; place-names such as Corpus Christi and San Francisco; flags, such as those of Norway, Switzerland, and the United Kingdom).[68]

One of the most intriguing books is Brook Larmer's *Operation Yao Ming*,[69] which traces China's basketball program back to the YMCA's missionary training school in Springfield, Massachusetts. It was there that James Naismith invented the game as a winter fitness program and the trainees took it around the world. The Chinese loved it, but most were too short of stature to compete on the international stage. Thus began a national program of matching tall men and women in hopes that their offspring could stand out on the court. Hence the emergence of Yao Ming.

Who knew? But such is the unintended reach of Christians determined to honor Christ's Great Commission.

Christopher Hitchens claims that "religion poisons everything." Actually the religion of Jesus Christ transforms everything for the better, from the seemingly trivial to the obviously grand.

Notes

1 Janice Beck Stock, *Amazing Iowa* (Nashville: Rutledge Hill/Nelson, 2003), 132.
2 Robert F. Martin, *Hero of the Heartland: Billy Sunday and the Transformation of American Society, 1862–1935* (Bloomington, IN: Indiana University Press, 2002), 40.
3 Ibid., 40.
4 Ibid.
5 Stock, *Amazing Iowa*, 132.
6 Martin, *Hero of the Heartland*, 60.
7 See J. Wesley Bready, *Faith and Freedom: The Roots of Democracy* (New York: American Tract Society, 1946).
8 J. Edwin Orr, *The Eager Feet: Evangelical Awakenings, 1790–1830*, chap. 25, "Social Outcome of Revival" (Chicago: Moody, 1975), 79–190.
9 J. Edwin Orr, *The Second Evangelical Awakening in Britain* (London: Marshall, Morgan & Scott, 1949), 42.
10 Ibid., 91–92.
11 Ibid., 121.
12 Ibid., 132.
13 Ibid., 181.
14 Ibid., 179.
15 Ibid., 210.
16 See chap. 8, "Opposition to Revival" in Orr, *The Second Evangelical Awakening*, 172–83.
17 J. Edwin Orr, *The Flaming Tongue: The Impact of Twentieth Century Revivals* (Chicago: Moody, 1973), xi–xiii.
18 J. Edwin Orr, *The Fervent Prayer: The Worldwide Impact of the Great Awakening of 1858* (Chicago: Moody, 1974), 107.
19 Ibid., 190.
20 See Kevin Adams and Emyr Jones, *A Pictorial History of Revival: The Outbreak of the 1904 Welsh Awakening* (Nashville: B&H, 2004).
21 Orr, *The Flaming Tongue*, 17.
22 Ibid., 49.
23 Ibid., 53.

24 Ibid., 98.

25 Ibid., 124.

26 Ibid., 152.

27 Ibid., 163.

28 John S. Mbiti, *African Religions and Philosophy*, 2nd ed. (Oxford: Heinemann, 1989), 213.

29 Jan Sihar Aritonang and Karel Steenbrink, eds., *A History of Christianity in Indonesia* (Boston: Brill, 2008), 146.

30 Ibid.

31 Ibid., 356.

32 Ibid., 608.

33 See Thomas Cahill, *How the Irish Saved Civilization: The Untold Story of Ireland's Heroic Role from the Fall of Rome to the Rise of Medieval Europe* (New York: Doubleday, 1995).

34 See David Wilkerson with John and Elizabeth Sherrill, *The Cross and the Switchblade* (New York: Random House, 1963).

35 Katharine Makower, *The Coming of the Rain: The Life of Dr. Joe Church, a Personal Account of Revival in Rwanda* (Carlisle, UK: Paternoster, 1999), 75–80.

36 G. Winfred Hervey, *The Story of Baptist Missions in Foreign Lands* (St. Louis: Chancy R. Barns, 1884), 41.

37 Ibid., 94–95.

38 Tim Jeal, *Livingstone* (New York: G. P. Putnam's Sons, 1973), 303–5.

39 See www.kairosjournal.org. A number of stories featured are drawn from *Kairos Journal*, an online resource for pastors.

40 See Roger Steer, *George Müller: Delighted in God* (London: Hodder and Stoughton, 1975). See also George Müller, *A Narrative of Some of the Lord's Dealings with George Müller* (Muskegon, MI: Dust and Ashes, 2003).

41 See Michael Hennell, *John Venn and the Clapham Sect* (London: Lutterworth, 1958).

42 See Abraham Nhial and DiAnn Mills, *Lost Boy No More: A True Story of Survival and Salvation* (Nashville: Broadman & Holman, 2004).

43 Mary E. Williams, ed., *Culture Wars: Opposing Viewpoints* (San Diego: Greenhaven/Thomson-Gale, 2003), 196.

44 Harold O. J. Brown, "Evangelicals and Social Ethics," in *Evangelical Affirmations*, ed. Carl F. H. Henry and Kenneth Kantzer (Grand Rapids: Academie, 1990), 268.

45 Martin, *Hero of the Heartland*, 113.

46 Arturo Fontaine Talavera, "Trends Toward Globalization in Chile," in *Many Globalizations: Cultural Diversity in the Contemporary World*, ed. Peter L. Berger and Samuel P. Huntington (New York: Oxford University Press, 2002), 252, 265–66, 271.

47 "The S Factor: A Conversation with Donald E. Miller," interview by Timothy Sato, *Books & Culture*, July/August, 2009, 11.

48 Tim Shenton, *A Cornish Revival: The Life and Times of Samuel Walker of Truro* (Faverdale, UK: Evangelical, 2003), 225.

49 Rev. J. William Jones, *Christ in the Camp or Religion in the Confederate Army* (Harrisonburg, VA: Sprinkle, 1887, 1986), 397–98.

50 Ibid., 398–99.

51 Ibid., 399.

52 Howard Jones, *Mutiny on the Amistad*, rev. ed. (New York: Oxford, 1987), 39.

53 See Rebecca J. Winter, *The Night Cometh: Two Wealthy Evangelicals Face the Nation* (South Pasadena, CA: William Carey Library, 1977).

54 See Ruby Bridges, Ruby Bridges Foundation Web site; www.rubybridges.org/story.htm (accessed August 16, 2010).

55 See Michael Bar-Zohar, *Beyond Hitler's Grasp: The Heroic Rescue of Bulgaria's Jews* (Holbrook, MA: Adams Media, 1998).

56 See the Web sites, http://www.fourchaplains.org/story.html and https:///www.homeof heroes.com/brotherhood/chaplains.html.

57 Judith L. Pearson, *Belly of the Beast: A POW's Inspiriting True Story of Faith, Courage, and Survival Aboard the Infamous WWII Japanese Hell Ship* Oryoku Maru (New York: New American Library, 2001), 213.

58 Langdon Gilkey, *Shantung Compound: The Story of Men and Women Under Pressure* (New York: Harper & Row, 1966), 192–93.

59 Sally Magnusson, *The Flying Scotsman* (New York: Quartet, 1981), 168–70.

60 Corrie ten Boom, *The Hiding Place* (Old Tappan, NJ: Fleming H. Revell, 1971), 205.

61 See D. James Kennedy and Jerry Newcombe, *What If Jesus Had Never Been Born?: The Positive Impact of Christianity in History* (Nashville: Thomas Nelson, 1994); Alvin Schmidt, *Under the Influence: How Christianity Transformed Civilization* (Grand Rapids: Zondervan, 2001); John Woodbridge, ed., *More than Conquerors: Portraits of Believers from All Walks of Life* (Chicago: Moody, 1992); Dan Graves, *Scientists of Faith: Forty-Eight Biographies of Historic Scientists and Their Christian Faith* (Grand Rapids: Kregel, 1996).

62 Samuel Eliot Morison, *The Founding of Harvard College* (Cambridge: Harvard University Press, 1935), 250.

63 "Evanston's Gospel Heritage," *The Daily Northwestern*, September 23, 2010, 9.

64 Alvin J. Schmidt, *How Christianity Changed the World* (Grand Rapids: Zondervan, 2004).

65 Robert Cowley, ed., *What If? Eminent Historians Imagine What Might Have Been* (New York: Putnam's/Penguin, 1998).

66 Leland Ryken, *Worldly Saints: The Puritans As They Really Were* (Grand Rapids: Zondervan, 1986).

67 D. James Kennedy and Jerry Newcombe, *What If Jesus Had Never Been Born?* (Nashville: Thomas Nelson, 2001).

68 D. James Kennedy and Jerry Newcombe, *What If the Bible Had Never Been Written?* (Nashville: Nelson, 1998).

69 Brook Larmer, *Operation Yao Ming: The Chinese Sports Empire, American Big Business, and the Making of an NBA Superstar* (New York: Gotham, 2005).

IRRESPONSIBLE OR INFELICITOUS
ARGUMENT: THE CHURCH

SOME OF THE ARGUMENTATION that bounces back and forth among the parties to religious dispute is irresponsible whether the conclusions they champion are right or wrong. Attacks and defenses can be cheap and even shameful. Unfortunately Christians as well as unbelievers can be the culprits.

Of course, those engaged in the battle often count their opponents' arguments reproachably weak, suffering from gaps, misdirection, or misconstruals. That's part of the give-and-take of apologetics. But it is not our concern to weigh the relative merits of this or that version of the cosmological argument or whether it's better to solve the problem of evil with a soul-making theodicy or free-will defense. We leave that to standard books in the philosophy of religion. Rather, we will look at moves that stand outside the borders of thoughtful discourse.

We will also look at a few infelicities, well-meaning shortcomings in style. Though they don't bring dishonor on the employer, they warrant a word of caution.

These two chapters consider the cause of "virtue apologetics," tracking with fresh interest in "virtue epistemology," now popular in the literature.

PROBLEMATICAL APOLOGETICS

Writing for the creationist magazine *Answers*, Ken Ham and Bodie Hodge take issue with believers who engage in "problematical apologetics."[1] For instance they object to using the shroud of Turin to prove the resurrection, for it ignores details of Jesus' burial in the Gospel of John. They say that fresh wrappings and pounds of spices would have obscured the image.

They also fault those who use Gen 10:25 ("Eber had two sons. One was named Peleg, for during his days the earth was divided") to refer to the shift of continental plates. They say the verse refers to the division of peoples and not geology. Furthermore if the geological upheaval had not happened until Peleg's day, Noah's ark would have lacked a mountainous landing zone. As for looking for the ark on today's Mount Ararat, they view this as an exercise in futility. For the Bible names a region not a mountain, and it is highly unlikely that a wooden construction would endure thousands of years of exposure to the elements and human activity. Their point is simply this: not everything is acceptable when arguing for the truth of the Bible. However much believers might like the outcome, they cannot arrive at it just any old way.

EMBARRASSING SUPPORTERS

C. S. Lewis speaks of the "embarrassing supporter," whose arguments are less than impressive. "It is brutal (and dangerous) to repel him; it is often dishonest to agree with what he says. I usually try to avoid saying anything about the validity of his argument in itself and reply 'Yes. That may do for you and me. But I'm afraid if we take that line our friend here on my left might say etc. etc.'"[2]

Of course, perfectly reasonable Christians can disagree over what constitutes an impressive argument, but some "proofs" are generally lame and obvious to all.

With that in mind, the following pages examine some ways in which argumentation can embarrass the cause it is meant to serve.

APPEASEMENT

The church has seen countless attempts to disarm the critics by surrendering aspects of the "full counsel of God" or by "throwing under the bus" certain notions and saints whose awkwardness makes the work of the gospel's public relations agents more challenging.

Of course public relations has a place in the church. Early leaders needed to assure the critics that they were not engaged in cannibalism when they "ate the body of Christ" in the Lord's Supper. But when the explanations undermine the biblical account, the enterprise hits the rocks.

Here then are some words concerning what we may call the "sons of Schleiermacher," whose *On Religion: Speeches to Its Cultured Despisers* is a classic case of appeasement, meant not only to reassure the critics but also himself.

C. S. Lewis to the Anglicans

In his paper on Christian apologetics, read originally to a gathering of Welsh Anglicans in 1945, C. S. Lewis takes compromisers to task. He warns against those who continually move the boundary lines of doctrine until they are no longer defending orthodoxy.

> Insist that wherever you draw the lines, bounding lines must exist, beyond which your doctrine will cease either to be Anglican or to be Christian: and I suggest also that the lines come a great deal sooner than many modern priests think. I think it is your duty to fix the lines clearly in your own minds: and if you wish to go beyond them you must change your profession. This is your duty not specially as Christians or as priests but as honest men.[3]

Lewis dismisses as "stagnant" a "'liberal' Christianity which considers itself free to alter the Faith whenever the Faith looks perplexing or repellent."[4] Yet,

> our upbringing and the whole atmosphere of the world we live in make it certain that our main temptation will be that of yielding to winds of doctrine not that of ignoring them. We are not at all likely to be hidebound: we are very likely indeed to be the slaves of fashion. . . . The standard of permanent Christianity must be kept clear in our minds and it is against that standard that we must test all contemporary thought. In fact, we must at all costs not move with the times. We serve One who said "heaven and Earth shall move with the times, but my words shall not move with the times."[5]

In sum, "Do not attempt to water Christianity down."[6]

This then is the tendency to defend too little. But there is a corresponding temptation to defend too much.

> We are to defend Christianity itself—the faith preached by the Apostles, attested by the Martyrs, embodied in the Creeds, expounded by the Fathers. This must be clearly distinguished from the whole of what any one of us may think about God and Man. Each of us has his individual emphasis: each holds, in addition to the Faith, many opinions which seem to him to be consistent with it and true and important. And so perhaps they are. But as apologists it is not our business to defend them. We are defending Christianity; not "my religion." When we mention our personal opinions we must always make quite clear the difference between them and the Faith itself. St Paul has given us the model in I Corinthians vii. 25: on a certain point he has "no commandment of the Lord" but gives "his judgment." No one is left in doubt as to the difference in status implied.[7]

So if one mixes in King-James-only arguments with arguments for the deity of Christ, he serves his listener poorly. Of course there is a twilight region, wherein serious believers wonder whether they have moved from essentials to nonessentials, but night and day are still identifiable to those who care to notice.

Paul Tillich

University of Chicago Divinity School dean Jerald Brauer, observed,

> Above all, Paul Tillich made it possible for countless modern men to become or remain Christian without ceasing to be modern men. He demonstrated what it meant to love God with the mind as well as with the heart and soul. He affirmed the doubts and insecurities of modern man, for he shared these fully, and only in this way could he point beyond them to the ground of hope. His life and his theology were a unity in joyfully embracing the world.[8]

This is the Tillich who said, "My whole theological work has been directed to the interpretation of religious symbols in such a way that the secular man—and we are all secular—can understand and be moved by them."[9] To accomplish this feat he ventured to claim, "It is hardly necessary . . . to refer to the symbols 'heaven' and 'hell.' First of all, they are symbols and not descriptions of localities."[10]

Harry Emerson Fosdick

In a sermon, "Despise Ye the Church of God," Harry Emerson Fosdick sympathized with men like the poet Swinburne, who "express admiration for the Nazarene while they condemn his 'leprous' bride,' the church," and with a young man considering ministry but who agrees with none of the denominations. Instead, this fellow feels that "their dividing lines do not correspond with a single real interest in modern life" and that "their creeds and rituals, rigidly insisted on for membership and ordination, are like Procrustean beds on which the modern mind, when laid, is impossibly stretched out or incontinently sawed off." The poor man is driven to exclaim, "I believe in Christ, but these churches!"[11]

Far from discouraging this fellow, Fosdick insisted that he is precisely the sort needed in the ministry. He is the sort to help the church move forward as it completes its journey "from persecution to controversy, from controversy to toleration, from toleration to co-operation, from co-operation to unity."[12]

Fosdick urged the church's critics to be understanding and patient, explaining (a) that denominations were once important in expressing liberation from Catholic tyranny at the Reformation; (b) that one does not jettison the court system because there are miscarriages of justice; (c) that all areas of human life suffer from sectarianism, including medicine—"allopathy, homeopathy, osteopathy, chiropractic"; (d) that one needs to know the Bible to understand English literature; (e) that like a twig removed from a bonfire that burns for only a short while, the person who spurns Christian fellowship loses his spiritual warmth. For these and other reasons he urges the hearer to stay with it.

He agrees that denominations are "lamentable." "The differences between them no more appertain to modern life than the boundaries of ancient Indian tribes do to the United Nations."[13] But he is staying with the church, counseling a new reformation of indifference to differences.

Interestingly Fosdick shrinks from saying, "Do not despise the church because Christ died for it, because it is His bride, because her ministers 'preach the Word' in a world impatient with 'sound doctrine.'" Elsewhere he is forced to admit that some doctrine is essential—"The existence of God, the fact of a moral order, the dependence of man on a power greater than himself, the supreme revelation of the divine character and purpose in Christ, the profound need of men to be inwardly transformed by the renewing of their minds"—,[14] but this amounts to little more than the first step in Alcoholics Anonymous.

If the whole point of the church is to unite people in charity and impress the world with displays of mutual accommodation, the denominations are a scandal. If truth matters, it would seem important to decide whether to baptize babies, pray for the dead in purgatory, or forswear military service.

Of course this book argues for the cultural advantages of the Christian faith, but to reduce religion to cultural advantage is to miss the point of its saving truth and its pointedness, for the Word of God is like a two-edged sword, not a nerf bat. All of it, and not just the warm parts, are vital: "All Scripture is inspired by God and is profitable for teaching, for rebuking, for correcting, for training in righteousness, so that the man of God may be complete, equipped for every good work" (2 Tim 3:16–17).

Blue like Jazz

Impatient with the backwardness, judgmentalism, and basic negativity of traditional Evangelicalism, Donald Miller has reached college students who have no interest in chastity and sobriety. His reverse confession booth has struck a chord in the youth culture, but yet one can question the chord he has struck.

> Each year at Reed they have a festival called Ren Fayre. They shut down the campus so students can party. Security keeps the authorities away, and everybody gets pretty drunk and high, and some people get naked. Friday night is mostly about getting drunk, and Saturday night is about getting high. The school brings in White Bird, a medical unit that specializes in treating bad drug trips. The students create special lounges with black lights and television screens to enhance kids' mushroom trips.[15]

Discussing ways in which the "few Christians on campus" could make their presence known and appreciated, Miller's group latched on to a suggestion by "Tony the Beat Poet," that they have a special kind of confession booth:

Okay, you guys, Tony gathered everybody's attention. "Here's the catch." He leaned in a little and collected his thoughts. "We are not actually going to accept confessions." We all looked at him in confusion. He continued, "We are going to confess to them. We are going to confess that, as followers of Jesus, we have not been very loving; we have been bitter, and for that we are sorry. We will apologize for the Crusades, we will apologize for televangelists, we will apologize for neglecting the poor and lonely, we will ask them to forgive us, and we will tell them that in our selfishness, we have misrepresented Jesus on this campus. We will tell people who come into the booth that Jesus loves them."[16]

The group loved the idea, and Miller became excited over the prospect of rehearsing the church's sins.

It would feel so good to apologize, to apologize for the Crusades, for Columbus and the genocide he committed in the Bahamas in the name of God, apologize for the missionaries who landed in Mexico and came up through the West slaughtering Indians in the name of Christ. I want so desperately to say that none of this was Jesus, and I wanted so desperately to apologize for the many ways I had misrepresented the Lord. I could feel that I had betrayed the Lord by judging, by not being willing to love the people He had loved and only giving lip service to issues of human rights.

For so much of my life I had been defending Christianity because I thought to admit that we had done any wrong was to discredit the religious system as a whole, but it isn't a religious system, it is people following Christ; and the important thing to do, the right thing to do, was to apologize for getting in the way of Jesus.[17]

Miller was still stinging from the snide remark of a Reed professor who had compared him to the arrogant and ill-fated Captain Cook, who had tried to civilize the natives of Hawaii. But he resolved to set his indignation aside and come clean.

It must have been cathartic for Miller, and by his account at least some of the decadent students who dropped in were impressed as well as surprised. No repentance on their part is recorded. Perhaps they would have expressed it had they been given a chance to confess their own sins. But never mind, the point was the beauty of Christian prostration before a world it had wronged.

From Miller's perspective, as is evident from his other writings, "getting in the way of Jesus" includes discrediting abortion and homosexuality, which would imply that Psalm 139 and Romans 1 are millstones around the church's neck. And he seems to have concentrated his studies in the Howard Zinn school of history, where European, American, and Christian behavior is typically noxious. No mention of Francisco de Vitoria's signal work in just-war theory on behalf of the indigenous peoples of the New World. No qualifiers concerning Columbus and Richard the Lionhearted. This is just as though he is reading a script prepared by Christopher Hitchens or Bertrand Russell. No distinctions are drawn between the behavior of the regenerate and the nominal. In short the contents of this confession are a mess.

Apologies are good, even necessary, but they need to be grounded in reality and true responsibility. Christian self-flagellation makes for a gratifying spectacle to those who count the faith empty or menacing. But it never occurred to Paul to beguile the Corinthians with this technique.

John A. T. Robinson

As Anglican bishop of Woolrich, John A. T. Robinson penned a call to theological liberalism in 1963, *Honest to God*. In this selection he capitulated to Darwin.

> In the last century a painful but decisive step forward was taken in the recognition that the Bible does contain "myth," and that this is an important form of religious truth. It was gradually acknowledged, by all except extreme fundamentalists, that the Genesis stories of the Creation and Fall were representations of the deepest truths about man and the universe in the form of myth rather than history, and were none the less valid for that. Indeed, it was essential to the defense of Christian truth to recognize and assert that these stories were not history, and not therefore in competition with the alternative accounts of anthropology or cosmology. Those who did not make this distinction were, we can now see, playing straight into the hands of Thomas Huxley and his friends.[18]

By this he means that the agnostic and antichurch Huxley (known as "Darwin's Bulldog") could make fools of creationists and bring ridicule on the people of God. Nevertheless Robinson is the one who tried to lead the church to just where Huxley wanted it to be—a place of obeisance and inconsequence.

UNDERSERVING

Sometimes the apologist leaves the unbeliever wanting more—or rather leaves him in the lurch.

Credentials

Often the simplest argument is the best, and from the mouths of laymen come deep truths, whether original or aptly recognized and repeated. But the apologetics outsider needs to be careful about working out of his depth. The lay reader may appreciate his observations, but that same reader may be embarrassed when he carries quotes forward to the university.

A simple case in point comes from Lee Strobel's *The Case for Faith*. To be sure, Strobel provides invaluable and winsome service to the church, and his apologetics are typically first rate, as I will note in the next chapter. But one passage warrants comment in this chapter. It amounts to only an infelicity, but these slips can count.[19]

In response to skeptics inclined to dismiss evangelicals as know-nothings and rubes, Strobel lifts up the work of Talbot School of Theology professor

William Lane Craig. In listing his credentials, he goes on a bit defensively long but also leaves out some important things. In the former case he does not need to list his membership in the American Philosophical Association, for anyone with a doctorate in philosophy may join, and those at Birmingham and Munich are already listed. (If Strobel has read papers at the APA, that could warrant mention.)

Then when he lists Craig's books, he does not include the publishers. A string of books says little in itself, for they may be self-published. Here it would be good to know that Craig has in fact written or edited books for Macmillan, Oxford, Brill, Routledge, Blackwell, and Rutgers. And for those interested in his evangelical credentials, it is useful to know that he has published with Baker, Broadman & Holman, Crossway, InterVarsity, Moody, and Zondervan.

These things are important for a student to know if he plans to put this book in the hands of skeptics.

Henrietta Mears

In commenting on the decline and division of Israel in 1 Kings, Henrietta Mears, long-time Christian education director at First Presbyterian Church in Hollywood and founder of Gospel Light Publishing, said the following: "Religious apostasy had been gnawing like a deadly worm at the root of Israel's life. One day the tree fell. Nothing destroys a nation like religious decline. Take the sun out of the sky and there will be no grass or flowers or orchards. Take God out of our nation and there will be no homes or schools or social life."[20]

Of course this comes in a Bible handbook, not an academic treatise, and there is a general point to what she says; but her imprecision, indeed, exaggeration, begs rebuke. If she had said that one would harm the homes, schools, and social life by pushing God aside, she would have been on the mark. But one has only to look at a range of "godless nations," such as the Soviet Union, which was the special concern in her day, to see that they had homes, schools, and a social life, however dreary or attenuated.

One can certainly take her statement with a grain of salt, but a budding, lay apologist might not do so. And if he or she quoted this in a skeptical circle, they would be pounded with counterexamples. So Christian teachers should take care not to equip their students with statements that will bring their followers only warranted grief in the marketplace.

SHOOTING ONESELF IN THE FOOT

The Hippocratic Oath stipulates, "First, do no harm." Unfortunately this principle is sometimes ignored in apologetics as well as medicine. For there are those who hurt their own cause pointlessly.

Joel Baclit

Sometimes a person makes matters worse by his answer. Joel Baclit is a case in point.[21] As a member of the Filipino Catholic apologetics group *Pinoy Defensores Fidei* and apologetics director of the Catholic Fellowship of Young Filipino Professionals, Baclit takes exception to "former Catholics who say that they'd never read a Bible until they were 'born again.'" He calls this "baloney," adding, "One could not have been Catholic and not once have had Scripture as part of their lives. The best example of this is the Catholic Mass. . . . The Mass is steeped in Scripture; it's loaded with it. There isn't a single part of it that can't be supported by the Bible and cannot be found in the Old and New Testaments."[22]

He then ties phrases in the mass to 18 Scripture verses (18 out of 31,173), but the links are tenuous and with no citation in the actual mass. For instance he ties a congregational "Amen" to 1 Chr 16:36[b], ("Then all the people said, 'Amen.'") and the expression, "Before he was given up to death" to Phil 2:8 ("He humbled Himself by becoming obedient to the point of death—even to death on a cross"). Some of the expressions are, indeed, familiar to those who know their Bibles, e.g., 2 Cor 13:13 (Priest: "The grace of our Lord Jesus Christ and the love of God and the fellowship of the Holy Spirit be with you all.") But how would a Catholic know this?

At this point Baclit interjects, "If I was following along with my Bible in the mass my head would already be spinning with the amount of Scripture I was being fed. We haven't even hit the Liturgy of the Eucharist yet, and that's really deep in Scripture."[23] He then provides a few examples of the same sort, with 2 Macc 14:36 thrown in.

Baclit hurts his cause by the lameness of his case. If a tiny number of marginal links, which the Catholic congregants would not recognize anyway, makes his head spin, then he is ill equipped to persuade skeptics of anything.

Debating Guile

In college a friend and I signed up for the debate team, thinking it would sharpen our thinking and persuasive powers. As a philosophy major I was steeped in the dialogical tradition, and I thought I might become a better Socrates. I (naively) had no idea what I was getting into.

The topic that year was the "negative income tax," and I thought I should study it assiduously in order to frame a responsible position, which I would then argue. I was surprised, then, to discover that at debate tournaments, my partner and I would each argue one side of the issue one hour and the other side the next. This called for a lot of masked insincerity, in that I would be arguing half the time for something I did not believe in.

Then, to make matters worse, the debate itself was subject to manipulation. The most egregious was the technique involved throwing out a lot of bad arguments in one's first presentation and then waiting for the opponent to answer them in his limited time. Even if we destroyed eight of ten arguments, they would rise at their closing and observe that we had not addressed two of their claims and so their case stood. (And of course they granted no points scored against the first eight.) This struck me as slick and cynical, a matter of posing and bullying rather than real discourse. But for them it worked.

But what was I thinking? The debate team was sponsored by the speech department, not a department dealing with the merits of tax systems, such as economics, philosophy, history, or even theology.

Of course there is a place for formal set pieces in debate, just as there is a place for parliamentary rules in public meetings. But when the techniques of rhetoric and forensics, the guile of tabling and question-calling supplant the determination of truth and worth, then discourse falls into the fever swamp of cynicism. A debater may have "won," but truth and right were losers.

ZINGERS

An apologetic claim or counterclaim can be distilled to a sentence or two. For example, "If there is a moral law, there is a moral lawgiver" or "The existence of pointless evil means that, if there is a God, He cannot be both all-powerful and good." But when these claims are packaged as snappy "gotchas," they derail serious conversation. One could call it "argument by laughter," a technique that can squelch conversation prematurely. The following is a classic:

> A college student was in a philosophy class, which had a discussion about God's existence.
> The professor presented the following logic:
> "Has anyone in this class ever heard God?" No one spoke.
> "Has anyone in this class ever touched God?" Again, no one spoke.
> "Has anyone in the class ever seen God?"
> When, for the third time, no one answered, he declared to the class, "Then there is no god."
> One student thought about this for a minute and then raised his hand to ask a question.
> The teacher called on him, and he stood and asked his classmates:
> "Has anyone in this class heard our professor's brain?" Silence.
> "Has anyone in this class every touched the professor's brain?" Absolute silence.
> "Has anyone in this class ever seen the professor's brain?"
> The class remained silent. After a few moments the student announced to everyone,
> "Then, according to the professor's own logic, it must be true that he has no brain."[24]

Of course this particular fictional professor had it coming. But real professors do not talk this way. They know the class members have not seen the center of the earth but that it still exists. No doubt, he is meant to represent the positivist, but he does so poorly, and he becomes a straw man, good for laughs but not much else.

Christian philosopher Alvin Plantinga has argued in *God and Other Minds* that one's belief in other souls, which cannot be perceived directly, gives some warrant to believe in a divine person. And in doing so, he wrestled with real professors, not the silly one mentioned above.

Jack Chick

Jack Chick is famous, and infamous, for his publications. Some of his tracts are rather good. But he gets sloppy in his zeal.

In *The Death Cookie* he offers a scathing criticism of the wafer or host in the Roman Catholic mass. Much of what he says reflects solid Protestant criticism of the sacerdotal system. But when he insists on tying the mass to Osiris worship in ancient Egypt, he goes off the rails. The Egyptian priests offered the people "round, sunshaped wafers made of unleavened bread" and told them that, through a miracle, they had become Osiris's flesh.[25]

Later the tract states, "IHS stands for Isis, Horeb, and Seb, the gods of Egypt." But wait, were they not worshipping Osiris? Why isn't there an "O" on the wafer? And is there nothing to the explanation that this is an abbreviation of the Greek, *Iesous Christos*, with the Greek long "e" (*eta*) written as a capital "H"? Why not think it at least as likely that this is something of a monogram on the order of the *Chi Rho*, for *Christos*?[26]

Chick needs to do a lot more to back up this connection to keep his claim from being outlandish. If he had restrained himself, he would have done much better.

MENACE

In writing about one of his converts, a chief of the Bakuena people named Sechele, missionary David Livingstone reported on his preferred method of argumentation for the faith:

> Seeing me anxious that his people should believe the words of Christ, he once said, "Do you imagine these people will ever believe by your merely talking to them? I can make them do nothing except by thrashing them; and if you like, I shall call my head men, and with our litupa (whips of rhinoceros hide) we soon make them all believe together." The idea of using entreaty and persuasion to subjects to become Christians—whose opinion on no other matter would he condescend to ask—was especially surprising to him. He considered that they ought only to be too happy to embrace Christianity at his command.[27]

This is a classic instance of *argumentum ad baculum*, "appeal to force." It can be effective, as the mobster who makes his case for protection money knows—not to mention the parent seeking to "persuade" his child not to walk out in traffic—but in adult moral discourse, it falls short.

PHOTOSHOP

Obviously apologists should not lie, but in their zeal to defend and advance the faith, some cut moral corners. Lies used to be limited to words spoken or written, but new technologies give fresh means to the mendacious. For instance photos purporting to show the bones of Nephilim are circulating on the web.[28]

Notes

1 Ken Ham and Bodie Hodge, "Problematic Apologetics," *Answers*, April-June 2009, 70–73.

2 C. S. Lewis, *God in the Dock: Essays on Theology and Ethics*, ed. Walter Hooper (Grand Rapids: Eerdmans, 1970), 100.

3 Ibid., 89–90.

4 Ibid., 91.

5 Ibid., 91–92.

6 Ibid., 99.

7 Ibid., 91.

8 Jerald C. Brauer, "Paul Tillich's Impact on America," in Paul Tillich, *The Future of Religions* (New York: Harper & Row, 1966), 21.

9 Paul Tillich, *Ultimate Concern*, ed. D. M. Brown (New York: Harper & Row, 1965).

10 Paul Tillich, *Systematic Theology: Three Volumes in One* (Chicago: University of Chicago Press, 1967), iii–419.

11 Harry Emerson Fosdick, "Despise Ye the Church of God?" *What Is Vital in Religion: Sermons on Contemporary Christian Problems* (New York: Harper & Brothers, 1955), 123–24.

12 Ibid., 130.

13 Ibid., 128.

14 Fosdick, "A Religion that Really Gets Us," 59.

15 Donald Miller, *Blue like Jazz: Nonreligious Thoughts on Christian Spirituality* (Nashville: Thomas Nelson, 2003), 116.

16 Ibid., 118.

17 Ibid.

18 John A. T. Robinson, *Honest to God* (Philadelphia: Westminster, 1963), 33.

19 Lee Strobel, *The Case for Faith: A Journalist Investigates the Toughest Objections to Christianity* (Grand Rapids: Zondervan, 2000), 80–81.

20 Henrietta Mears, *What the Bible Is All About: Bible Handbook, New International Version* (Ventura, CA: Regal, 1973), 150.

21 Joel Baclit, "Scripture in the Mass," *Filipino Express*, May 17, 2010; http://www.filipino express.com/index.php?option=com_content&view=article&id=403:scripture-in-the-mass &catid=17:columnists&Itemid=157 (accessed June 10, 2010).

22 Ibid.

23 Ibid.

24 Patrick Madrid and Kenneth Hensley, *The Godless Delusion: A Catholic Challenge to Modern Atheism* (Huntington, IN: Our Sunday Visitor, 2010), 216–17.

25 Jack Chick, *The Death Cookie* (Ontario, CA: Chick Publications, 1988); http://www.chick.com/reading/tracts/0074/0074_01.asp (accessed December 23, 2010).

26 "IHS," *The Catholic Encyclopedia*; http://www.newadvent.org/cathen/07649a.htm (accessed December 23, 2010).

27 David Livingstone, *Missionary Travels and Researches in South Africa* (New York: Harper & Brothers, 1858), 19.

28 C. Michael Patton, "'The Nephilim Have Been Found' or Yet Another Example of Really Bad Apologetics," *Parchment & Pen Blog*, Credo Ministries (April 4, 2010); http://www.reclaimingthemind.org/blog/2010/04/yet-another-example-of-really-bad-apologetics (accessed December 23, 2010).

Irresponsible or Infelicitous Argument:
The Culture (Ad Hominem to
Mackerels in Moonlight)

APOLOGETICAL CONTESTS ARE OFTEN not pretty. Cheap shots and lame claims are commonplace, and weasels are running around everywhere.

We've looked at some of this in the church. Now we'll shift our focus to non-Christian voices in the culture. Our first example concerns an "archbishop," but he has no standing to count himself a church spokesman. Rather, he more truly represents the secular gay agenda to the church instead of presenting God's revelation to the world.

AD HOMINEM

Gay minister Archbishop Carl Bean is typical of those who dismiss biblical mandates with *argumentum ad hominem* and unsubstantiated *ad hominem* at that.

> When I attended those storefront churches at night, I heard my first antigay sermons. Preachers were saying, "Sex between two men is a sin. Sex between two women is a sin. That kind of sex doesn't please God. That kind of sex is wrong. These people were an abomination." . . . Yet many of those preachers, winking and blinking, were hitting on the gay boys in the choir. The hypocrisy was blatant. I was excited by the music but confused by the church culture that endorsed the music.[1]

So that is that. They were just hypocrites, so their message was invalid. Bean says there were "many" such preachers, but even if there were, how does that invalidate the message?

GROUNDLESS INSULT

As any student of the Bible understands, there is a place for insult. Otherwise, Jesus, the apostles, and the prophets would be poor models. But their stern pronouncements were based in reality.

Michael Weisskopf

On its twentieth anniversary the conservative Media Research Center compiled a list of "outrageous quotes from the liberal media," and Christians were the butt of several. For instance, in a February 1, 1993, *Washington Post* newsstory, reporter Michael Weisskopf said that followers of Jerry Falwell and Pat Robertson were "largely poor, uneducated and easy to command."[2]

What is not clear is which data Weisskopf is using, if any. Perhaps he just intuits his view or is advancing a tautology, that one is, by definition "poor, uneducated and easy to command" if one follows these two ministers. One can imagine what would have happened if he made the same comment about the followers of Jesse Jackson and Al Sharpton. Of course he would not do this because it would take him out of the safe, free-fire zone, of abusing conservative evangelicals.

Mike Hendricks

It is especially helpful when a nonbeliever cries, "Foul!" on behalf of Christians. For instance, James Kirchick, an openly gay supporter of abortion rights, strongly objects to linking the pro-life movement to the murder of abortion doctor George Tiller. In a column for *The Wall Street Journal*, he takes issue with *The Kansas City Star*'s Mike Hendricks, who said that anyone who had called Tiller a murderer was an accomplice in his death.

Kirchick says Hendricks is like those who lump all "fundamentalists" together, whether Christian, Jewish, or Muslim. He names Chris Hedges of *The New York Times*, Christiane Amanpour of CNN, and HBO's Bill Maher as equally guilty. He retorts, "If 'Christianists' were anything like actual religious fascists, they would applaud the . . . murder as a 'heroic martyrdom operation' and suborn further mayhem." But their reaction has been just the opposite. While "radical Islamists revel in death," the crusading antiabortion group, Operation Rescue, said, "We denounce vigilantism and the cowardly act that took place this morning."[3]

As any thoughtful person understands, one cannot control the actions of every individual in a group. There are seriously disturbed fanatics, and people whose zeal is matched only by their moral confusion and/or insanity. The real issue is how the group reacts to the act in question.

Christopher Hitchens

Christopher Hitchens begins his book *God Is Not Great* with a condescending recollection of a childhood friend of his, Mrs. Jean Watts. He remembers her fondly as "a good, sincere, simple woman, of stable decent faith" and as "an affectionate and childless widow who had a friendly old sheepdog who really was named Rover." But in her role as schoolteacher, she said something that "frankly appalled" the young Hitchens, making his "little ankle-strap sandals [curl] with embarrassment." As part of a brief Scripture lesson keyed to material sent from the authorities, she concluded, "So you see, children, how powerful and generous God is. He has made all the trees and grass to be green, which is exactly the color that is most restful to our eyes. Imagine if instead, the vegetation was all purple, or orange, how awful that would be."

This observation by a "pious old trout" was too much for the little Hitchens to bear. He simply knew that "the eyes were adjusted to nature, and not the other way around."[4] But this is surely an act of premature condescension. People who design hospitals know that wall coloring makes a difference to the patients' psyches, and the administrators paint them accordingly. So why cannot Miss Watts say that God made the ambient colors pleasing? Hitchens thinks he has an easy, superior, evolutionary alternative through natural selection. But when did aesthetic distress become lethal? Why did all those preferring purple or orange vegetation die off, leaving green-vegetation fans to enjoy their preferred color?

He has some explaining to do, for he let his default contempt blind him to the merits of Miss Watts's claim. One can be just as fair in calling him an "arrogant fingerling" who grew into an "impious old carp."

H. L. Mencken

Baltimore newspaperman and curmudgeon H. L. Mencken made contempt for "rubes" in the heartland his stock in trade. He was particularly harsh toward people of faith, and each issue of his magazine, *The American Mercury*, found ready targets for derision. For instance an article in the January 1929 issue marvels at Moody Bible Institute's wealthy donor base, correcting the readership's normal impression that "fundamentalism is a craze financed by the greasy nickels and dimes of yokels and confined in influence to rural adenoidiacs who believe that the Pope has cloven hooves."[5]

In the same article William Cobb calls Dwight L. Moody a "devil-chaser" and the students "inmates." Regarding alumni, he focuses on evangelist Vom Bruch's crusade against social dancing. According to Bruch, "God pity the church member or pastor whose conception of Christ rises no higher than the bunny hug, turkey-trot, hesitation, tango, texas tommy, hug-me-tight, fox-trot, shimmy-dance, sea-gull swoop and skunk-waltz!"[6]

As for women's scanty clothing on the dance floor, "We get our styles from New York, New York from Paris, and Paris from Hell." Add to this "close bodily contact and whirling around in another's arms, breathing in their hot, passionate breath." No wonder that "many a girl tonight who has gone the full length of the dance sits with not only an illegitimate child but a broken heart."

Pointing out that "fundamentalists" are hopeless fools, Mencken serves up, without commentary, a buffet of quotes he takes to be embarrassing in his "Americana" section. This month's sampling includes a declaration in the Fayetteville *Democrat* that "'the King of Kings' is the acme of excellence in the things of the cinema"; a *Baptist Commoner* statement that "Romanism" is the beast of Rev 13:7; the account of a California pastor who during a sermon "took off his coat and vest, and put on a cook's apron and cap" to make "flap-jacks" in order to illustrate Hos 7:8; a quote from a Baltimore pastor—"Unless men and women keep the Prohibition Amendment they should not be permitted to sing 'The Star-Spangled Banner'"; and a layman's letter to the *Primitive Baptist*, asking for help in interpreting a dream about a snake.[7]

Of course Cobb could just as easily have focused on a Moody Bible Institute graduate risking his life to bring civilizing words to a tribe of headhunters, and the "Americana" section could have included quotes from deacons delivering Christmas baskets to the poor and sermons urging fellowship across racial boundaries, but those points would not fit the skeptic's template.

Besides, bad things do happen on the dance floor; Cecile B. DeMille's 1927 film *King of Kings* is a classic; "Romanism" has its problems (*pace* Martin Luther); Ezekiel and Jesus used object lessons in some of their messages; singing patriotic songs while flouting the nation's laws is hyprocrisy; even secularists think dreams are significant (*pace* Freud).

Believers may be half-baked in their thinking and clumsy in their expression, but less so than those who smile at promiscuity, reject the actual "King of kings" and his doctrines, eschew sermons, frequent speakeasies, and laugh at efforts to bring biblical perspectives to bear on all aspects of life. Of course Christians can answer Mencken and his ilk by monitoring their statements and deeds and then publishing their missteps. A little of this "get off your high horse" work can help. But these recalcitrants can retort that Christians, and not they, are the ones who claim to be especially righteous. This is their "escape clause." So it can be helpful to match this with follow-up questions to defang their scorn. For example, "So when do we sound the alarm over lewdness, excessive intimacy, and lawlessness?" "How would you communicate sound doctrine effectively?"

Richard Dawkins

Richard Dawkins's invective is offensive to even his allies. Concerning Dawkins's book *The God Delusion*, Christian philosopher Alvin Plantinga says that "one shouldn't look to this book for even-handed and thoughtful commentary. In fact, the proportion of insult, ridicule, mockery, and spleen, and vitriol is astounding." But Dawkins should take notice when fellow skeptic Michael Ruse says, "*The God Delusion* makes me embarrassed to be an atheist."[8]

"HUMOR"

A. N. Wilson observes that the Monty Python crew, Terry Jones, Michael Palin, Graham Chapman, Eric Idle, and John Cleese, "captured the mood of their generation by their expressed hatred of religion." He makes this comparison: "Earlier generations had been prepared to leave alone the shattered shell of the Christian religion, but the Python team lived in an era when the Church was on the run, and Christianity itself seemed to many people to be fraudulent, even dangerous." These were the men who produced "a spoof version of the life of Jesus," which was "an assault upon the Christian religion," one that "ends with a parody of the Crucifixion." Wilson concludes, "In a cowardly way, they covered themselves by asserting, in the first five minutes of the film, that Brian Cohen was a contemporary of Jesus, but in all the scenes which follow it is clear that Jesus himself was the object of their abuse."[9]

Of course satire has its place. One could have a legitimate field day with Hugh Hefner, the Viagra-besotted dean of debauchery. But what exactly is ludicrous about Jesus? Fortunately the Bible is an anvil that wears out many hammers.

"JOURNALISM"

Journalists style themselves watchdogs of truth and justice, "afflicting the comfortable and comforting the afflicted." Unfortunately journalists often become partisans in the war against Christian orthodoxy.

Pandering to Political Correctness

Matthew 7:14 reads, "How narrow is the gate and difficult the road that leads to life, and few find it." Accordingly genuine Christians are in the minority in most places in most ages. So it is not surprising that many readers would delight in embarrassments to the church and that journalists would be tempted to tickle the fancies of these unregenerate readers.

In this connection University of Connecticut sociologist Bradley R. E. Wright writes about the way in which "bad news about Christians spreads faster and farther than good news." It seems that "Christians acting like Christians just isn't as interesting as 'Christians gone wild.'"

To demonstrate this, he picked up on a mistaken report out of George Barna's research, which was headlined, "Atheist divorce rate is lower than Christian." Confident that he had contrary data, particularly when church attendance was factored in, Wright posted that same morning an opposing story on the Web site Digg.com, where readers rate the stories. His title was "Christian Divorce Rates Are Lower than Atheist." The negative Barna story received over 3,500 votes; Wright's story garnered fewer than a dozen.[10]

Chicago Tribune on the 9/11 Anniversary

The editors of the *Chicago Tribune* would never consider publishing the following statement of conviction on its editorial page: "We believe that Christianity has no claim to superiority and that anyone who disagrees with that is a fool and a threat to society." Nevertheless the advancement of this perspective is much at play in their pages. The September 11, 2010, issue, on the ninth anniversary of the 9/11 attack on America, is a case in point.

One might think the stories above the fold on page 1 would show the towers ablaze or a widow and orphan of that attack getting on with their lives or praying for God's help in doing so. Instead, the headline speaks of "calls for tolerance," with a photo of President Obama, quoted to say, "We are not at war against Islam." Just below him are three smiling Muslims in a Naperville, Illinois, kitchen, a mother and her two daughters. The caption explains that the teenaged daughter Dina "felt the hatred toward Muslims" in the wake of the slaughter. She "tried to laugh when her friends poke fun, asking if she's a terrorist plotting an attack" on her high school. As for the terrorists, she says, "I hate them. They ruined so much. They destroyed the name of Muslims everywhere."[11]

The article continues for over two feet of column, celebrating her winsomeness, registering her woundedness at the "vitriol" and the "tone of [a classmate's] voice that burned," "verbal attacks on their faith," "bullying and blame." On 9/11 her father came home early from work, and her mother would not leave the home; another Muslim girl sought "the safety of a [Muslim] parochial environment" to "avoid explaining herself every day" in public school; and a Muslim high school student was hurt that "strangers glared at his family in public, especially when his mother wore a headscarf."

So these would be the real victims of 9/11. And lest one miss the point that the Muslim presence is wonderful, four more pictures on page 6 show attractive Muslim students at prayer, running cross country, playing basketball, and serving as an intern in a state senator's office. Then the facing page features an article covering the President's September 10 speech, in which he explained, "If there is an increase in suspicion and resentment of Islam in this country . . . it arises during trying times when the country is feeling a sense of general anxiety."[12] He makes no allowance for those whose "suspicion and resentment" is based not only on 9/11 but on subsequent Muslim attempts to blow up Americans—as at Fort Dix, with a shoe bomb, and with plastique-laden underwear.

On that same page is a story about a dangerous religious zealot, Reverend Terry Jones of Florida, who had threatened to burn a Qur'an on the anniversary of 9/11. His plan "sparked protests Friday in Afghanistan, where at least 11 people were injured."[13] So he is the villain in the *Tribune's* narrative.

The only trace of negativity toward Islam in any of the articles is a sentence in the first one: "Earlier this summer, a group called Stop the Islamization of America placed ads on Chicago taxis implying that women who want to leave Islam faced violence from their families." But the statement, paired with reference to the Florida pastor intent on burning the Qur'an, simply provides an example of the sort of "rhetoric" American Muslims must endure.

The *Tribune* did find some Christian ministers it could honor. In a page 2 article, it covers "more than a dozen leaders of all faiths" who "spoke at a news conference at Bridgeview's Toyota Park after a prayer service attended by some 12,000 local Muslims for Edi-al-Fitr, the three-day celebration that marks the end of the Ramadan fast." The Reverend Gregory Livingston, general secretary of the Rainbow/PUSH Coalition counseled, "Instead of burning Quarans [*sic*], read the Bible and the Quaran [*sic*]. (Because) God doesn't make junk." The Reverend Paul Rugers of the Council of Religious Leaders of Metropolitan Chicago said, "Any offense against any religious community in our area is an offense against all of us."[14]

One article mentions the placement of memorial flags on a village green and a parade of preschoolers to a firehouse in honor of firemen who died on 9/11. But one searches this issue in vain for anything like, "Of course, honor killing is a problem in much of the Muslim world,"[15] or "Of course, in Muslim-majority countries, Christians do not begin to enjoy the rights that Muslims enjoy in Christian-majority countries, and none of these immigrants, while back in their homelands, objected to their native country's oppression of other faiths." Such talk would not fit the paper's template.

Everything these reporters said was at least arguably true: Muslims have had their feelings hurt; President Obama really did say those things; a few local ministers did indeed have a press conference at the soccer field. But that is not the point. Just as photographers point their cameras at what they wish, and leave much outside their frames, so too do journalists exercise great selectivity in their writing.

Of course they have to be selective. They cannot fill their pages with stories of dogs who did not bite anyone the previous day or the ramblings of a drug-damaged homeless person. They cannot feign neutrality when covering a serial murderer. But when important facts and perspectives are given no notice at all, lest they muddy the water, then the journalists have behaved badly.

To the *Tribune*'s credit, the lead editorial speaks of the "evolving threat" posed by "the virus of al-Qaida and all the other terror groups that metastasize around the world, feeding on ignorance and hate." And it wonders whether "the goofy grandstanding of a guy with a 50-member Florida church really deserved the attention of President Obama, Gen. David Petraeus and the world media." Of course it did not. But that Florida preacher was the perfect foil for pluralistic grandstanding, as in the *Tribune*'s own news pages. And how these groups "feed on ignorance and hate" without feeding on the Qur'an and its commentaries is not explained.

As for healthy religion *Tribune* reporter Jennifer Weigel offers some advice. On page 14, she shares "5 ways to stay spiritual," lessons she has implemented after consulting "gurus" for her book *I'm Spiritual, Dammit*. She wants her readers to understand that they need to take care of themselves first, "talk to dead people" (enlisting departed "loved ones with specific tasks"), "look for signs" (such as when her "dad shows up as a cardinal whenever [she needs] a boost"), "trust that you are where you're supposed to be at every moment," and go with your first impressions. With these maxims in hand, she likes to say, "I'm climbing the mountain of enlightenment with a martini in one hand and my pumps in the other."[16]

One has to wonder whether she would be an honest broker in her coverage of evangelical Christianity. And one has to wonder whether a newspaper that runs horoscopes without irony should be trusted with conveying truth at all ("Pisces . . . Responsibilities may take you across a body of water: It could be as simple as grocery shopping on the other side of the bridge. But it seems big.")[17]

Why not run a story on Augustine's ridicule of horoscopes, where he noted that twins have different fates? Why not one on the absurdity of "trusting that you are where you're supposed to be at every moment" when you're at a Klan rally?

U.S. newspapers are in trouble, and the *Tribune* is one of them, with rapidly declining sales and profits. On the basis of this issue, one has difficulty weeping at its passing.

Cecil Sherman's Obituary

When Douglas Martin of *The New York Times* wrote the obituary for Cecil Sherman, who helped found and lead the Cooperative Baptist Fellowship, he called him a moderate, opposed to conservatives. This was good, for the press used to speak of a conflict between "moderates" and "fundamentalists," using the kind word for the former and the harsh word for the latter. When I was vice president for convention relations for the Southern Baptist Convention Executive Committee, I complained about this to the Associated Press.[18] To his credit, the chief AP religion writer George Cornell agreed and changed his practice to pairing "moderate" with "conservative." This simply brought AP practice in line with its own stylebook, which noted that "fundamentalist has to a large extent taken on pejorative connotations" and stipulated, "In general, do not use 'fundamentalist' unless a group applies the word to itself."[19]

Nevertheless in Sherman's obituary, Douglas Martin managed to muddle things, making inerrantists look unjustly ridiculous. He writes that conservatives "believed that every word in the Bible came directly from God and was not open to interpretation."[20] This would seem to suggest that conservatives believe in the mechanical dictation theory and that courses in biblical interpretation at inerrantist seminaries are devoted strictly to castigating scholarship. Then Martin distinguishes Sherman from conservatives by saying he "believed that the Bible was written by errant humans with divine guidance."[21] Actually that is what conservatives believe. They do not think the writers were perfect men; they simply believe that under divine guidance they did not err in the writing of Scripture.

This is not to say that Martin is malicious; but he could have done due diligence by calling an actual conservative to see what he thought about his construals.

Incidentally the *AP Stylebook* says, "Do not use the term *Bible-believing* to distinguish one faction from another, because all Christians believe the Bible. The differences are over interpretations."[22] That's a stretch but one of the sort believers have come to expect in the press.

"KING'S X"

When kids are playing chase, sometimes one calls out, "King's X," to take a break, maybe to tie a shoe. (The expression goes back centuries to when people sought sanctuary from danger in a court or church.) Today this is just part of a game, but the point is the same—an arbitrary grab for safety just as one is about to get caught. Here are two examples:

Muslim Spin Doctors

When Muslims are caught saying terrible, embarrassing things, they are loathe to own up to it.

> An Islamic leader is quoted in the media as having incited contempt for gays, Jews, Christians, women or democracy. The media report is then condemned by Muslim groups, who dismiss it as defamatory: the material was selectively taken out of context; the directors of the mosque were not aware that these views were being promoted; the group in question were only renting the facilities; the Arabic was mistranslated; the report is an attempt to demonize Muslims and exemplifies Islamophobia and racism in the media; other faiths hold similar views but only Muslims are targets by the media; the report must be false because Islam requires Muslims to deal positively with others; and so forth. Whatever the particularities, the essence of the dissimulation is the implication that the report was defamatory—that is to say, it was false—so the Muslims involved have nothing to answer for.[23]

Walter Sinnott-Armstrong

Working in the religion-poisons-everything genre, Dartmouth philosophy professor Walter Sinnott-Armstrong brings up wars in "the Middle East, Ireland, and so on," and adds, "It is no coincidence that terrorists are so often motivated by religion, since it is harder to get non-religious people to volunteer as suicide bombers." That is a snappy line but of negligible worth; for besides lumping all religious people together (as if the problem were not Muslim), it ignores the fact that there are any number of "non-religious people" who have distinguished themselves as homicide bombers, serial killers, and disgruntled employees who have "gone postal."[24]

Be that as it may, he then executes a perfect intellectual backflip while shouting "King's X" in midair (this man is a highly trained professional; don't try this at home):

> On a more personal level, I was not prepared for the death of Matthew Shepard. When bigots kill defenseless homosexuals, they do not always cite religion as their reasons. Christianity still fuels their bigotry. If Christians did not broadcast their condemnation of homosexuals, then the bigots would be less likely to kill. Christianity is at least part of the cause. I came to see why Christianity should be held responsible for these deaths. The dangers of religion are even more evident when abortion doctors are killed by openly religious groups.[25]

First, this is a little odd that a scholar would still be treating the Matthew Shepard case as essentially a matter of bigotry instead of robbery by drug users.[26] But this reading does fit the ideological template, at least to some extent. The problem is that the killers, Aaron McKinney and Russell Henderson, were not practicing Christians. But never mind that, for whatever bigotry they might have had was "fueled" by Christianity. (One has to wonder whether he would say that nonbelievers are fueled by the atmosphere of Christian benevolence when they volunteer for hospital work.)

Now for the flip: "Of course, atheists kill, too. Russian and Chinese communist governments are famous examples. However, these atheists killed in the name of communism, not atheism. There are other ideologies besides religions that produce killers."[27]

Perfect. Atheism is insulated from blame unless atheists shout, "Glory to Skepticism" or something like that when they kill tens of millions in a short period of time. (For instance, Frank Dikotter's recent book, *Mao's Great Famine*, uses "Chinese provincial archives" to "prove that [the leader] was responsible for the starvation of between 45 and 55 million people in the years 1957–1962, under a policy called the Great Leap Forward.")[28] Unless one can imagine aging but violent Mensa members running out of Starbucks on Sunday morning with *The New York Times* (crossword puzzles half completed) folded under their arms, then we have no social case against atheism.

Actually atheism is not so much a cause as a form of vulnerability—like an unlocked car with the keys left in the ignition. Unaccountable to God (at least in their own minds), atheists sit ready to be driven around by all sorts of toxic programs—Bolshevism, hedonism, anarchism, narcissism, totalitarianism, consumerism, Baathism, jingoism, secular feminism, fascism, and so forth. And when they do their worst, they do not typically do it in the name of atheism, though their atheism cleared the way for it.

LITERARY CARICATURE

The wildly popular drama *Inherit the Wind* is cartoonish in its treatment of the Scopes Trial. And the leading antievolution character in the play is an ogre. At a rally, he prays concerning the biology teacher, "For all eternity, let his soul writhe in anguish and damnation."[29] This was the same preacher who, preaching the funeral of an 11-year-old boy who drowned, said, "Tommy didn't die in a state of grace, because his folks had never had him baptized," and "Tommy's soul was damned, writhing in hellfire!"[30]

So the playwright has cast ministers who differ with Darwin in the style of Fred Phelps, the "God hates fags" preacher from Topeka.

Then when he wants to make a fool of the William Jennings Bryan character, Matthew Brady, he has him saying ridiculous things in court. When Henry Drummond asks him, "What's the biblical evaluation of sex?" Brady answers, "It is considered 'Original Sin.'"[31] So much then for the stupidity of antievolutionists. Never mind that this is not the doctrine of original sin and that before the fall God commanded Adam and Eve to be fruitful and multiply.

As paleontologist Kurt Wise once observed, *Inherit the Wind* is indeed a historical travesty. Still, it has enormous popular impact, taken by some as a sort of proof. Thus distinguished British writer A. N. Wilson commented on the current debates between "debunking materialists on one hand" and, on the other, "'fundamentalists' or their subtler copartners the 'creationists.'" Wilson observed that these were "matters which some observers might have been thought settled for good and all by Stanley Kramer's film *Inherit the Wind* of 1960."[32] Maybe Wilson is merely saying that, like it or not, films do in fact settle things in the popular mind, but it is probably something stronger—that this film should have ended the dispute. Either way, how odd to suppose that Hollywood is the decisive witness on this issue.

This play is caricature at its worst, and any Christian who watches *Inherit the Wind* is properly indignant. The application should be clear: believers must not do to nonbelievers what playwrights Jerome Lawrence and Robert E. Lee did to believers, even if it has great effect in the marketplace.

MACKERELS IN THE MOONLIGHT

Senator John Randolph of Virginia once compared his fellow senator Henry Clay to "a rotten mackerel by moonlight"—"so brilliant yet so corrupt," he "shined and stunk." Christians have to contend with a lot of shiny mackerels, opponents who are so well packaged and slick that they can insinuate enormous error to many in a short time.

Sad to say, people are so impressed by style, bearing, eloquence, and such, that they are enthralled by the mood the defamer creates.

Tariq Ramadan

On October 8, 2010, Oxford University professor and Muslim apologist Tariq Ramadan spoke on "What I Believe" at Northwestern University. His visit was sponsored by Roberta Buffett Center for International Comparative Students at Northwestern, with strong support from the on-campus Muslim group. I was able to attend and to join in the question-and-answer session at the end of the presentation.

In two senses it was masterful; first, he both counseled and exemplified public relations skills, meant to normalize Islam and defuse any concerns Westerners might have; it was a tour de force in deception. Here are a dozen of his moves, all of which gratified his audience. Yet none really addresses the question of whether Islam is flawed and dangerous, a genuine cause of concern for those who love truth and liberty.

1. He psychologized mistrust of Islam, saying that it was largely due to globalization, which has unsettled people of the West.

2. He psychologized immigration, saying we were queasy like the citizens of Qatar, who have found themselves in the minority as they have hired a host of foreign workers.

3. He played the race card repeatedly, suggesting that the West has a problem with the skin color of Arabs and other Muslim-majority people groups. He quoted Martin Luther King Jr. as a friend of all who struggled for greater status, even though race is genetic and Islam is doxastic.

4. He typified those who would enlist public policy to resist Islam as guilty of the "instrumentalization of fear."

5. He marveled at the hubris of the EU in questioning Muslim European credentials and dismissed as a mere power play the pope's claim that Western civilization was built on Greek, Roman, and Christian foundations. (No mention was made of how Europe might have turned out like Turkey and Egypt had Charles Martel and Jan Sobieski not been victorious over Muslim invaders at Tours, France, and Vienna, Austria, respectively.)

6. He deflected substantive objections to Islam, claiming it was as complex as Christianity and that ignorance of Islam was pandemic. This gave him the ability to dismiss specific criticisms as beside the point, and it ignored both the center of mass of the two faiths and the cumulative effect.

7. He characterized Islam's critics as trap layers, always trying to trick Muslims into a faux pas, like overreacting to cartoons. Instead of admitting that serious complaints exposed fault lines in Islam, he treated everything as a public relations game.

8. He faulted the press for looking at awkward newcomers to America instead of generations-long citizen families in America, failing to note that the newcomers were more closely aligned to heartland Islam.

9. He blamed political forces for "religionizing" discussion, thus discouraging any reference to Islam's peculiarities in the public square, whether the imposition of Sharia law, loyalty to the umma, insistence on the burka for driver's license photos, outlandish requests that welfare money be used to support multiple wives in a culture where polygamy is illegal, and so forth.

10. When pressed on the need for reciprocity in religious liberty, he retorted that freedoms and respect were not things to be traded but that the West should do the right thing even when others do not. This totally ignored the point that the West has already granted vast freedoms and is in no way waiting for the Muslim-majority lands.

11. He raised the case of the Ground-Zero mosque ("community center") and mentioned a couple of dozen other instances where there was community resistance to mosque building permits, ignoring the fact that many churches

have been denied building permits and steeple clearances by zoning laws, neighbor groups, and others.

12. He argued that the terrorists were equal-opportunity abusers, citing the bombing in Amman, Jordan, and in Indonesia (Bali), ignoring the point that, just because they kill one another, that does not mean they will not kill all the more; and the fact that many of their own whom they kill are killed for the very reason that they are cooperative with the West.

All smooth, but all beside the central point—that Islam is a menacing disaster.

To see this, imagine his form of argument as a defense of apartheid in South Africa. By this standard he could charge the objectors with racism against whites and with nervously clinging to ancient tribal governance patterns. He could complain of black slurs against white employers, argue that white employees are also mistreated at times, explain that apartheid was an incredibly complex phenomenon, and charge that blacks were constantly laying public relations traps for whites to stumble into. He could link arms, so to speak, with David Livingstone and other great, white friends of Africa and argue that whites had to lock their doors at night for fear that the black majority would do them harm. He could give an example of a white youth who had trouble getting a job and use expressions like "white man's burden" and "city on a hill" to characterize the motives and program of segregation.

Who would stand for this sort of subterfuge, this studied avoidance of the central question, Is apartheid wrong? Yet that is precisely what those in attendance at Northwestern were asked to do, and the vast majority complied.

Indian Ad

The June 27, 2010, issue of *The New York Times Magazine* features two full-page ads from the American Indian College Fund. Both lead with the words, "Think Indian." One adds, "To think Indian is to make eco-buildings with spruce root or rebar." The other, "To think Indian is to save a plant that can save a people"—with the addition that Allyson Two Bears is "learning about echinacea habitat from her grandmother and her ethnobiology class" at Sitting Bull College in North Dakota. At the bottom of the page, the reader is urged, "Help Tribal College Students Preserve Their Way of Thinking," a slogan reflected in their Web site, thinkindian.org.[33]

Well, yes, there are instances of pharmaceutical wisdom in native practice, but one is hard pressed to imagine that the offspring of an unreached Sitting Bull would have come up with the cancer protocols at M. D. Anderson Hospital or the Mayo Clinic. And can *The New York Times* building really be built with spruce root? And is the coated paper on which these glossy ads are printed eco-friendly? And is the Internet on which their Web site appears the product of animism?

What exactly is the "Indian way of thinking"? In this context it means animism. And when the site says, "American Indian tribal leaders realized they would have to take control of education to reverse centuries of misguided and failed federal education policies," they repudiate the Christian training that was part of those policies.[34]

If Allyson Two Bears really wants this revival of her culture, she should move beyond echinacea cultivation and spruce rebar to the full-blown paganism of her ancestors. Her college honors Sitting Bull, but where was Indian higher education in his day six centuries after the founding of Oxford and Cambridge universities? Maybe those Christians had something the Indians needed.

Notes

1 Carl Bean, *I Was Born This Way: A Gay Preacher's Journey Through Gospel Music, Disco Stardom, and a Ministry in Christ* (New York: Simon & Schuster, 2010), 51.

2 "Top 10 Most Outrageous Liberal Media Quotes from the Last 20 Years," *Human Events*, November 6, 2011; http://www.humanevents.com/article.php?id=23251 (accessed September 30, 2010).

3 James Kirchick, "The Religious Right Didn't Kill George Tiller," *The Wall Street Journal* (June 2, 2009): A17.

4 Christopher Hitchens, *God Is Not Great: How Religion Poisons Everything* (New York: Twelve, 2007), 1–3.

5 William Cobb, "The West Point of Fundamentalism," *The American Mercury* (January 1929), 104.

6 Ibid., 111.

7 "Americana," *The American Mercury*, January 1929, 33–37.

8 Scott Hahn and Benjamin Wiker, *Answering the New Atheism: Dismantling Dawkins' Case Against God* (Steubenville, OH: Emmaus Road, 2008), 3–4.

9 A. N. Wilson, *Our Times: The Age of Elizabeth II* (New York: Farrar, Straus and Giroux, 2008), 262.

10 Bradley R. E. Wright, *Christians Are Hate-Filled Hypocrites . . . and Other Lies You've Been Told: A Sociologist Shatters Myths from the Secular and Christian Media* (Minneapolis: Bethany House, 2010), 135.

11 Manya A. Brachear, "Muslim Teens Shaped by Effects of 9/11: Children Too Young to Remember Bear Burden of That Haunting Day," *Chicago Tribune*, September 11, 2010, 1.

12 Christi Parsons, "Obama: Faith Shouldn't Divide," *Chicago Tribune*, September 11, 2010, 7.

13 Stephen Hudak, "Evangelist: No Quran Burning: He Says Plan Canceled; Florida Pastor, in N.Y., Has No Comment," *Chicago Tribune*, September 11, 2010, 7.

14 Andy Grimm, "Show of Support for Muslims: Religious Leaders Call for Tolerance amid Tensions," *Chicago Tribune*, September 11, 2010, 2.

15 When the present writer was visiting Amman in the late 1990s, *The Jordan Times* ran a story on the Jordanian queen's special project, the elimination of honor killings. Jordanian jails were full of young women in protective custody. This compares unfavorably with the

special projects of American first ladies—Ladybird Johnson and highway beautification; Nancy Reagan on drug abuse; Laura Bush on reading; Michelle Obama on fitness.

16 Jennifer Weigel, "5 Ways to Stay Spiritual," *Chicago Tribune*, September 11, 2010, 14.

17 Nancy Black and Stephanie Clement, "Horoscopes," *Chicago Tribune*, September 11, 2010, 20.

18 "When Journalists Take Sides" (pamphlet).

19 *The Associated Press Stylebook and Libel Manual: Fully Updated and Revised*, ed. Norm Goldstein (Reading, MA: Perseus, 1998), 176.

20 Douglas Martin, "Cecil Sherman, 82, Who Led a Faction of Moderate Baptists," *New York Times*, May 2, 2010, 30.

21 Ibid.

22 *Stylebook* (New York: Associated Press, 2010), 176–77.

23 Mark Durie, *The Third Choice: Islam, Dhimmitude and Freedom* (Melbourne, Australia: Deror, 2010), 68.

24 Walter Sinnott-Armstrong, "Overcoming Christianity," in *Philosophers Without Gods: Meditations on Atheism and the Secular Life*, ed. Louis M. Anthony (New York: Oxford, 2007), 76.

25 Ibid.

26 "New Details Emerge in Matthew Shepard Murder, Killers Talk About Crime That Shocked the Nation," *ABC News/20/20*, November 26, 2004; http://abcnews.go.com/2020/story?id=277685&page=1 (accessed January 4, 2011).

27 Sinnott-Armstrong, "Overcoming Christianity," 76.

28 Michael Burleigh, review of *Mao's Great Famine: The History of China's Most Devastating Catastrophe, 1958–1962, BBC History Magazine*, Christmas 2010, 64.

29 Jerome Lawrence and Robert E. Lee, *Inherit the Wind* (New York: Random House, 1955), 59.

30 Ibid., 68.

31 Ibid., 82.

32 Wilson, *Our Times: The Age of Elizabeth II*, 400.

33 *The New York Times Magazine*, June 27, 2010.

34 "About Us," American Indian College Fund; http://www.collegefund.org/about/history.html (accessed June 30, 2010).

IRRESPONSIBLE OR INFELICITOUS ARGUMENT: THE CULTURE ("MORAL EQUIVALENCE" TO WISHFUL THINKING)

S OME ILLEGITIMATE MANEUVERS ARE so prevalent in society that we scarcely notice their absurdity. To use another image, they're like the air we breathe. We resume our summary with a brief look at one of the worst conceits.

"MORAL EQUIVALENCE"

One of the favorite and lamest strategies of skeptics is the argument for moral equivalency. Actually it is more typically the declaration of moral equivalency, which allows little room for argument. Where one is attempted, it often consists of providing a case or two meant to trump the generality. For instance to counter the claim that the sex-drugs-rock 'n' roll 60s were bad for the country, the "moral equivalator" will point to Jim Bakker and Jimmy Swaggart as proof that the church is in no position to "throw stones." Check and mate.

It should be embarrassing to argue in this fashion, but people do it all the time.

Rosie O'Donnell

In commenting on civilian casualties in the Afghan and Iraq wars following 9/11, Rosie O'Donnell on *The View* on September 12, 2006, observed, "Radical Christianity is just as threatening as radical Islam in a country like America."[1] Who knows what she had in mind, but it really does not matter. What matters is what she has in *will*—namely, to level Christianity, which has demeaned her lesbianism, or to disparage the "war on terror," which does not fit her politics.

How else does one explain her irrationality? Of course when she said this, authorities had not yet broken up the attempt on Fort Dix, and Major Hasan had not yet shot 13 to death at Fort Hood. But 16, post-9/11 Islamic plots on American had been foiled, including those of Jose Padilla, the Lackawanna Six, and the Virginia Jihad Network.[2]

Yes, Topeka's Pastor Fred Phelps is creepy, as is Chicago's Pastor Jeremiah Wright, but they are not violent. So who are the dangerous "radicals"? Alabama Pastor David Platt has written a book entitled *Radical: Taking Back Your Faith from the American Dream*, but he is talking about a simpler lifestyle to free up more money for nonviolent missions.

Tavis Smiley

In an interview with former Muslim Ayaan Hirsi Ali, PBS's Tavis Smiley defended Islam by demeaning Christianity.[3] Hirsi Ali was on his show to discuss her book *Infidel* about the threat of global jihad. Smiley was skeptical and particularly puzzled by her admiration for Christianity, given that she was now an atheist. She responded that Christians were self-critical, able to moderate their views.

She brought up Fort Hood's Major Hasan and Faisal Shahzad, who tried to detonate a van full of explosives in Times Square. "Somehow, the idea got into their minds that to kill other people is a great thing to do and that they would be rewarded in the hereafter."

SMILEY: But Christians do that every single day in this country.

ALI: Do they blow people up [unintelligible]?

SMILEY: Yes. Oh, Christians, every day, people walk into post offices, they walk into schools, that's what Columbine is—I could do this all day long. There are so many more examples of Christians—and I happen to be a Christian. That's back to this notion of your idealizing Christianity in my mind, to my read. There are so many more examples, Ayaan, of Christians who do that than you could ever give me examples of Muslims who have done that inside this country, where you live and work.

ALI: Well, I think you and I disagree, not so much on is there extremism in Christianity—I fully acknowledge that. There are people who want to take the bible and use passages from the bible as justification for violent behavior. I'm not denying that in the least. But mainstream Christians in the twenty-first century are more like you.

I'm an atheist, I'm not a Christian, but they are more like you—accepting of other religions and tolerant. The latest example, "South Park," where Jesus Christ was made fun of, watching pornography, people, Christians, maybe have been annoyed by it but the producers of "South Park" were not threatened by Christians.

They were not threatened by Buddhists. They showed Buddha snorting cocaine. Muhammad, whose picture wasn't shown—there was a line saying "censored" and he was imagined to be in a teddy bear—some of the followers of Muhammad got very angry. A few of them posted threats about the producers, and this is very mild.

> There are today—I don't want to say, and it's been established, not all Muslims are terrorists, we must emphasize that, but almost all terrorist activities that take place today in our time are done and justified in the name of Islam.

One has to wonder how Smiley can claim to be a Christian when he counts Eric Harris and Dylan Klebold as members of the body of Christ. Does he fail to understand regeneration? And no Christians shouted the Christian version of *Allahu Akbar!* as they murdered 12 fellow students and one teacher at Columbine High School. Yet Smiley qualifies as a public intellectual in America.

The Bible and the Qur'an

On typical Muslim lay Web sites like mostmerciful.com, the counterattacks there are so weak that they make the reader wince in sympathy. For instance, regarding the status of women, a definite sore point for Muslims, one apologist means to even things by quoting from Paul's complementarian directives, a word about contentious women in Proverbs, and the verse about pain in childbearing in Genesis 3.

But, none of this can match the Muslim man's liberty to beat his wife (Qur'an, Sura 4). And it totally ignores such towering texts as Proverbs 31, the example of Aquila and Priscilla who instructed Apollos (Acts 18), and Paul's command for husbands to love their wives as Christ loved the church (Ephesians 5). The Qur'an has no Gal 3:28, no woman at the well, no widow's mite, no parable of the Importunate Widow.

When this Muslim apologist turns to the matter of holy wars, he quotes only from the Old Testament, specifically concerning the invasion of Canaan and some language from the imprecatory psalms. There is no apparent recognition (or admission) of the principle of progressive revelation. While Muslims use the principle of abrogation to trump earlier passages with later ones, they grant none of that to the Christian. And the simple truth is that the Qur'an and the Bible are opposites in this connection. As Mohammed's revelation developed, it became more violent; as the Bible developed, it became less so.

Of course the warning to Christians should be clear. If they presume to criticize the Qur'an, they should be familiar with it and do it justice.

OBSCENITY

Upset that Senator Jesse Helms of North Carolina had introduced an amendment "to prohibit alleged obscenity in publicly funded art" (such as Serrano's immersion of a crucifix in urine), various artists struck back in their genre. One group with an obscene name, "positioned an unflattering statue of the Senator on the Capitol steps: paunchy, naked and anatomically complete (albeit under-endowed). They smashed the effigy before the demonstration ended." One artist displayed "a photograph of the Senator submerged in amber liquid (beer, not urine)"; yet another group pictured a "forlorn, crucified Helms, naked except for a necktie emblazoned with a swastika."[4]

Well, that certainly helped their cause!

Psychologizing

Roman Catholic professor Paul Vitz has written a fascinating book relating the irreligion of famous skeptics to their lack of a proper father figure in their lives. The book provides an argument for godly fatherhood and even offers a cause for sympathy toward atheists. But one must not think that this settles the matter—that atheism is false because it is tied to deep unhappiness. A position cannot be dismissed simply because one thinks he knows that it came from a place not bathed in rationality. Regrettably this is a popular move today.

Freudian Condescension

Sigmund Freud is the best-known proponent of the view that the idea of God is merely a human projection based on man's insecurities. People, he says, need a cosmic father to comfort them and give them meaning.

In an interview with *Maclean's*, the Canadian newsmagazine, Christopher Hitchens, picks up the familiar strain.

> Clearly such thinking does not come from nowhere, it comes from people lying awake and having perhaps strange thoughts they cannot deal with, or emotional experiences they hadn't been able to predict, or moments where you feel that there's something larger than yourself. . . . We aren't a particularly rational species, we look for patterns and we find them much too easily. It's good that we look but we're very afraid, easily scared, terrified of death, and often we are very stiffed without quite knowing why.[5]

The photos accompanying the interview show Hitchens hairless, the result of his cancer treatment. For him this is not an academic question but one of looming destiny. He is determined not to cave in to Christianity in his moment of mortal peril. Still he should go easy on his psychological condescension, for it is a double-edged sword. One could just as well appeal to his recent biography, *Hitch-22*, to explain his pitiful resistance toward the Creator of the universe.

Recalling his Oxford days and his minimal connections with William Jefferson Clinton, then a Rhodes Scholar, he writes:

> He and I both became peripherally involved (at different times, I hasten to add) with a pair of Leckford Road girls who, principally Sapphic in their interests, would arrange for sessions of group frolic. The men who flattered themselves that they were the desired objective would later discover that they were merely the goats tethered in the clearing, the better to magnetize more women into the trap. I have always thought that to be a deft and sinuous scheme and wish that I had understood its dynamics better at the time.

> But this is very much like the rest of life, where, as Kierkegaard so shrewdly observes, one is condemned to live it forward and review it backward. If you are going to sleep with Thatcher's future ministers and toy with a future president's lesbian girlfriend, in other words, you will not be able to savor it fully at the time and will have to content yourself with recollecting it in some kind of tranquility.[6]

Whether one can fault the accuracy of this account, its spirit is unmistakable. Hitchens relishes this story and is not the least repentant for his promiscuity. And one could reasonably suggest that Hitchens does not want to accept God because he does not want the accountability, the transcendent judgment that some of his cherished choices have been wicked. For all his intellectual huff and puff, he rages against Christianity because he does not want a divine boss. This is a matter of will from start to finish.

That may be so, but it still does not remove the responsibility to weigh his arguments on their own merit. But if he ventures to psychologize, fair is fair. He can be put on the couch as well.

One other thing: Just because God answers to man's insecurities, that does not mean he does not exist. As the old maxim goes, "Just because you are paranoid, that does not mean they are not trying to get you."

The Phobia Ploy

The homosexual community has been particularly adept at altering the language through the word *homophobia*, an expression that tars those who declare the practice illicit as irrationally fearful, even pathetic. The Muslims have picked up the theme, insisting that opposition to Islam is something of a malady and not a reasoned position.

The Council on American-Islamic Relations (CAIR) provides this list of "misconceptions" constituting Islamophobia, which has come to enjoy "general and unquestioned acceptance": (a) Islam is monolithic and cannot adapt to new realities. (b) Islam does not share common values with other major faiths. (c) Islam as a religion is inferior to the West. It is archaic, barbaric, and irrational. (d) Islam is a religion of violence and supports terrorism. (e) Islam is a violent political ideology.[7]

If this sort of thing is allowed to spread, then horrible things will happen:

> Islamophobia refers to unfounded fear of and hostility towards Islam. Such fear and hostility leads to discriminations against Muslims, exclusion of Muslims from mainstream political or social process, stereotyping, the presumption of guilt by association, and finally hate crimes. In twenty-first-century America, all of these evils are present and in some quarters tolerated. While America has made major progress in racial harmony, there is still a long road ahead of us to reach our destination when all people are judged on the content of their character and neither on the color of their skin or their faith.[8]

Of course this is weasel talk, par excellence. No human enterprise is "monolithic" and utterly immune to the slightest change. Every belief system shares something with every other belief system. And just one instance each can make a transgression "present" and "tolerated." And is judging one according to "the content of . . . their faith," wrong per se? What if that faith is in Moloch? In Hale Bopp? Is that really the same thing as judging one's skin color?

As for the fear, how can it be irrational when men shouting, "Allahu Akbar," have blown up people in most nations on earth in recent years—from the World Trade Center (U.S.), to the Bali nightclub (Indonesia), to the Bosnian school (North Ossetia), to a wedding reception in Amman (Jordan). And what is it but "Islamophobia" driving the TSA pat downs? Are not they an arguably reasonable response to the actions of such Muslims as Umar Farouk Abdulmutallab (the Nigerian "underwear bomber"), Richard Covin Reid (the British "shoe bomber"), and Abdulla Ahmed Ali (the British "liquid bomber")—not to mention the "box-cutter-hijackers" of 9/11?

To charge all who have fears with "Islamophobia" is like the Catholic Church dismissing concerns over paedophilia with "priestophobia."

QUESTIONABLE STATISTICS

Statistics are notoriously misleading and misused. They can be manipulated to "demonstrate" all sorts of things. ("For example 100 percent of heroin addicts began on milk.") So they always call for careful scrutiny.

University of Connecticut sociologist Brad Taylor is skeptical of one of the Barna Group's surveys (of 270 non-Christians), one which showed that only 22 percent of Americans had a favorable impression of evangelicals. The contrasting unfavorables ran 23 percent and the in-betweens, 33 percent. Barna concluded, "One reason why evangelical churches across the nation are not growing is due to the image that non-Christian adults have of evangelical individuals." But Taylor noticed that the "don't knows" who answered the question about evangelicals (22 percent) were twice as high as for any other question, whether the respondents were sizing up "born-again Christians" (10 percent), real estate agents (8 percent), or prostitutes (11 percent). Taylor concluded that there was probably some confusion over what evangelicals were in the first place: "Perhaps some respondents thought the survey was asking about evangelists—the people who knock at your door when you're just sitting down for dinner."[9]

Such obvious problems did not prevent magazines such as *The Atlantic* and books such as *The Fall of the Evangelical Nation* and Web sites such as offthemap.com from concluding that evangelicals ranked little higher than prostitutes in reputation.[10]

RIP VAN WINKLE

In a guest commentary for *USA Today*, University of Chicago professor of ecology and evolution Jerry A. Coyne declares, "Science and faith are fundamentally *incompatible*, and for precisely the same reason that irrationality and rationality are incompatible." He adds, "In religion faith is a virtue; in science it's a vice."[11]

So much is wrong with the article that it could provide an outline for a full course in apologetics. His attack is far ranging and predictable—from the problem of evil to questions of falsifiability to wicked deeds done in the name of religion. But he insists on talking as though nothing had been published in the philosophy, history, and sociology of science since 1960.

Of course religionists can be boneheaded, mendacious, and treacherous. So can scientists, as they demonstrate repeatedly, as in the global warming debate. Surely Coyne has read Thomas Kuhn's seminal work, *The Structure of Scientific Revolutions*, which shows how scientists can be captives of, willful partisans for, and nonobjective beneficiaries of theoretical "paradigms." He speaks glowingly of the scientific community's acceptance of continental drift, but he fails to note the way scientists cling to outmoded theories unto death, a phenomenon strikingly noted by Nobel physicist and quantum theory founder Max Planck: "A new scientific truth does not triumph by convincing its opponents and making them see the light, but rather because its opponents eventually die, and a new generation grows up that is familiar with it."[12]

Coyne gives no evidence whatsoever of having read Oxford's Michael Polanyi and Berkeley's Paul Feyerabend,[13] who have underscored the relativistic aspects of the scientific enterprise. He seems oblivious to the herd mentality of science, the sort of mass delusion science writer Michael Crichton mocked in *State of Fear*, concerning global warming. Though this was a work of fiction, at the end of the novel, he appends a nonfiction account of "scientific irrationality," which captivated Alexander Graham Bell, the Carnegie and Rockefeller foundations; universities such as Harvard, Johns Hopkins, and Stanford; and a collection of Nobel laureates. The cause was eugenics, which lost its cachet only when Hitler became its leading enthusiast and practitioner.[14]

He seems oblivious to the psychology of scientists, with their temptations, including the "aggressive pursuit of economic self-interest" and "a concern for credit and reputation"; their reliance on questionable "auxiliary assumptions"; and their "belief-perseverance" ("when people work very hard on something over a long period of time, they tend to become committed or attached to it; they strongly want it to be correct and find it increasingly difficult to envision the possibility that it might be false").[15]

Of course Coyne is perfectly free to argue the purity of science as opposed to the corruption of religion, but he is not so free to act as if no one has ever questioned the purity of science. To do so is to appear as if one has awakened from a half-century sleep.

SELECTIVE MEMORY

In his book *A Devil's Chaplain*, Richard Dawkins praises the headmaster of Oundle School, Frederick William Sanderson, who taught him science. Dawkins loves the way Sanderson encouraged their creativity and pursuit of truth, keeping the labs unlocked so they could pursue their experiments whenever they pleased. And Dawkins remembers Sanderson's chapel sermons, in one of which he spoke of "mighty men of science and mighty deeds. A Newton who binds the universe together in uniform law; Lagrange, Laplace, Leibniz in their wondrous mathematical harmonies."[16]

The problem is, as non-Christian biographer A. N. Wilson notes, Dawkins edits the sermon to leave out Sanderson's observation concerning these as well as other scientists such as Faraday, Ohm, Ampere, Joule, Maxwell, Hertz, and Rontgen, that all are "we may be sure, living daily in the presence of God, bending like the reed before His will."[17] This is the same Sanderson who told the students, "We perish if we cease from prayer," and who exulted, "Thou, O God, dost reveal thyself in all the multitude of Thy works," and who said that man's purpose is "above all to reveal the spirit of God in all the works of God."[18]

Wilson comments,

> Some would consider it dishonest of Dawkins to have omitted these sayings in the account of his hero. Obviously, what Dawkins admired in Sanderson (the communicated enthusiasm for science) would have been admirable whether or not he himself shared the religious beliefs. But no one would guess from the account in *A Devil's Chaplain* that religious belief underlay all Sanderson's wonder at scientific discovery and all his faith in the curiosity, resourcefulness and healing creativity of human beings.[19]

Of course Dawkins does not need to agree with Sanderson's worldview, but candor should have led him to acknowledge it, if only to discount it or to distance himself from it. As it stands, Dawkins's treatment of Sanderson is indeed dishonest but understandable, for even passing acknowledgment of Sanderson's faith would undermine his general thesis that Christians are dolts.

SHEER CONTRADICTION

A famous *Monty Python* skit features a man who comes into an office offering arguments for sale. He opts for the five-minute version costing a pound instead of going for the discounted offer of eight pounds for a course of ten.

As the man makes his way down the hall, he turns into one room where he is met with "Your type makes me puke! You vacuous toffee-nosed malodorous pervert!"—only to discover this one offers abuse, not argument. He is redirected to room 12, where the conversation starts immediately:

> Is this the right room for an argument?
> I've told you once.
> No, you haven't.
> Yes, I have.
> When?
> Just now!
> No, you didn't.
> Yes, I did!
> Didn't . . .
> This goes on for a while, when the client finally says,
> Look, this isn't an argument.
> Yes, it is.
> No, it isn't, it's just contradiction.
> No, it isn't.
> Yes, it is.[20]

Reading some skeptics is about as frustrating as this visit to room 12.

Gary Greenberg's *101 Myths of the Bible* is a case in point. His modus operandi is to repeat a plain teaching of the Bible and then deny it without nuance, qualification, or caution—saying it all came from somewhere else:

> Myth # 2: God initiated Creation with a spoken word . . .
> Reality: The initiation of Creation by spoken word comes from the Egyptian Creation myths . . .
> Myth # 90: Joshua led Israel after the death of Moses . . .
> Reality: Joshua's name indicates that he was a mythological figure named after two Egyptian creation deities.[21]

He seems to think that if he can find someone in the ancient world who said or did anything remotely like the statement or action in question, then the biblical account is derivative and false. By this strange assumption one could call Gary Greenberg and his judgments myths simply because there was another skeptic, this one named Henri, who lived in France and who believed that Joshua *was* historical but that Caleb was not.

The reader quickly looks for the exit and returns to the room, offering mere abuse rather than hair-trigger denials.

SIX DEGREES OF KEVIN BACON

Actor Kevin Bacon has appeared in many movies, and a trivia game has grown up around this fact—"Bacon appeared with x, who appeared with y in another film, who appeared with z in yet another film." The premise is that through no more than six links ("six degrees of separation"), Bacon can be tied to any actor in the business.

Nonbelievers who seek to discredit Christianity are masters at making connections between godly people and ungodly people, phenomena, or statements. If they are determined enough, they can even link Joni Eareckson Tada to Jack the Ripper.

The Reformer Martin Luther is arguably the skeptic's favorite Kevin Bacon. Here is a typical rendering from Lucy Dawidowicz:

> A line of anti-Semitic descent from Martin Luther to Adolph Hitler is easy to draw. Both Luther and Hitler were obsessed by a demonologized universe inhabited by Jews. "Know, Christian," wrote Luther, "that next to the devil thou hast no enemy more cruel, more venomous, and violent than a true Jew." Hitler himself, in that early dialogue with Dietrick Eckhart, asserted that the later Luther—this is, the violently anti-Semitic Luther—was the genuine Luther. Luther's protective authority was invoked by the Nazis when they came to power, and his anti-Semitic writings enjoyed a revival of popularity. To be sure, the similarities of Luther's anti-Jewish exhortations with modern racial anti-Semitism and even with Hitler's racial policies are not merely coincidental. They all derive from a common historic tradition of Jew-hatred, whose provenance can be traced back to Haman's advice to Ahasuerus. But modern German anti-Semitism had more recent roots than Luther and grew out of a different soil—not that German anti-Semitism was new; it drew part of its sustenance from Christian anti-Semitism, whose foundation had been laid by the Catholic Church and upon which Luther built. It was equally a product of German nationalism. Modern German anti-Semitism was the bastard child of the union of Christian anti-Semitism with German nationalism.[22]

Dawidowicz made absolutely no reference to the Lutheran opposition to Hitler, whether through the Barmen Declaration of the Confessing Church or the martyrdom of Dietrich Bonhoeffer. And she shows no interest in a more nuanced treatment of Luther on the question of the Jews, such as can be found in Eric Metaxas's recent Bonhoeffer biography. Metaxas shows the tragic deterioration of Luther's rhetoric, matching the disintegration of his health. The early Luther "was sickened at how Christians had treated Jews," and in "1519 he asked why Jews would ever want to become converted to Christianity given the cruelty and enmity we wreak on them—that in our behavior towards them we less resemble Christians than beasts."[23]

Later, Luther wrote in an essay entitled "That Jesus Christ Was Born a Jew," "If I had been a Jew and had seen such dolts and blockheads govern and teach the Christian faith, I would sooner have become a hog than a Christian. They have dealt with the Jews as if they were dogs rather than human beings; they have done little else than deride them and seize their property."[24]

In her contempt for Luther, Dawidowicz avoids or misses a range of mitigating factors. For one thing, many have argued that the German church had been corrupted by higher criticism, making it susceptible to all sorts of doctrinal pathologies. The culprit would have been David F. Strauss or Adolf von Harnack rather than Luther. Also her sweeping smear of Christianity ignores the hearty opposition of genuine Christians to the corruptions of the so-called German Christian Movement.

Metaxas continues, recounting the sorry record of the so-called German Christians who struggled with Bonhoeffer and his compatriots for the soul of the church. These bogus "German Christians" were keen to eliminate the Old Testament as "too Jewish" and twist New Testament passages toward their anti-Semitic purposes ("the phrase ['den of thieves'] in the temple-moneychanger passage") "was replaced with the German *Kaufhaus* (department store), most of which were then owned by Jews."[25] They also dismissed grace as "un-German," construed communion wine as "the blood of the earth," and scrubbed "Israelite elements" from traditional hymns ("one author proposed changing Jerusalem to heavenly abode—and cedars of Lebanon to firs of the German forest").[26]

Dawidowicz also missed the point that anti-Semitism was not a distinctly "Christian" phenomenon, for those who did what they could to demean the faith were just as liable to exemplify it. For instance the skeptic Voltaire called Jews "vagrants, robbers, slaves, or seditious."[27]

STIPULATING MASKED MOTIVES

In his attack on conservativism, charmingly entitled *Idiot America: How Stupidity Became a Virtue in the Land of the Free*, longtime staff writer for the *Boston Globe Magazine* Charles P. Pierce defames Intelligent Design (ID). (One could hardly find a clearer paradigm of the "Main Stream Media," for his work has appeared in *Esquire, American Prospect, Slate, The New York Times Magazine*, the *Los Angeles Times Magazine, The Nation, The Atlantic*, and the *Chicago Tribune*. He is also a regular on National Public Radio.)

By his account, "In *Edwards v. Aguillard*, the court determined that 'creation science' was religion in sheep's clothing and, hence, violated the establishment clause of the First Amendment." He continues, "This put a considerable crimp in [the] Christian right's marketing strategy and, almost immediately, another attempt at rebranding was under way."[28] He says the new brand name, Intelligent Design, was "brilliant." But he and others were on to them.

The "smoking gun" was the Discovery Institute's "Wedge Document," which said believers would now lead with ID. And the judge in *Kitzmiller v. Dover Area School Board* could see right through it. "In Jones's view the members of the Dover school board had volunteered their town as a test market for those who wanted to sell ID nationwide."[29]

In a strident, 139-page decision, Judge Jones

> found ID ludicrous as science and preposterous as law. He saw the attempts to foist it on high school students as the worst kind of bunco scheme, dealing harshly with the notion of "teaching the controversy"—a "canard," he wrote, designed merely as the next form of camouflage by which creationism hoped to insinuate itself into the public schools.[30]

Together Pierce and Jones make a great pair of defamers, with "bunco" and "canard" meaning "swindle" and "hoax," respectively. A few pages later Pierce calls Ben Stein's pro-ID film, *Expelled*, "a vanity project."[31] How Pierce knows it to be vanity is not clear since Stein took an incredible beating in the media and academy for identifying with ID. What is clear is the fact that Jones and Pierce are keen to suggest dark motives as disqualifiers.

Well, certainly, there are dark motives in the world, and it can be helpful to expose them. But first, one man's dark motive is another's luminescent motive (advancing the notion that God and not blind matter is the source of human life); second, true motives can be tough to discover; third, motives are irrelevant to the truth or reasonableness of the claim; fourth, lawsuits are the product of all sorts of ulterior motives. If Jones and Pierce are turned off by the spectacle of "outsiders" using locals to advance a national agenda, he should dismiss the work of the ACLU in the Scopes Trial and *Roe v. Wade*, not to mention their work against the Dover School Board in his own courtroom.

This book is a cautionary item, showing how ugly and silly a person can get if he judges his opponents largely by their motives, with insufficient attention to the content of their claims.

SUPPRESSION OF EVIDENCE

No church or denomination would open all its files to the public, nor should it. Delicate personnel and financial matters are appropriately off limits to the public, just as with any institution, company, or family. But when matters both surprising and central to the performance of the church are at hand, secrecy becomes mendacity in that it leaves a seriously false impression.

The Mormon Church has an unfortunate record in this connection, and this has made them vulnerable to fraud. The problem is that its founders, Joseph Smith and Brigham Young, could be right embarrassing, and there were incidents in Mormon history that the Mormon Church would rather be forgotten. So the leaders are interested in acquiring problematic documents and stashing them in The Vault, "the final resting place of all the uncomfortable truths."[32]

Onto the scene came master forger, Mark Hofmann, who had fabricated a letter from Joseph Smith's associate, Martin Harris. It basically said that Smith did not get the gold tablets from the Angel Moroni: "Instead of a benevolent angel, [it was] a cantankerous and tricky 'old spirit' who transforms himself into a *white salamander!*"[33] It pictured Smith as dabbling in the occult and misrepresenting the basic revelatory encounter.

Hofmann was able to get $20,000 worth of benign Mormon historical treasures for the letter, and he was encouraged to try for more with other forgeries. Eventually his deceit unraveled, and he turned to murder in an attempt to cover his tracks.

The most interesting thing is the Mormon hierarchy's interest in cloaking the behavior of its patriarchs. Imagine the Southern Baptist Convention's trying to purchase the only copy of a "lost gospel" or some ossuary purportedly holding the bones of Jesus, all in fear that if they got into circulation, they would undermine respect for Christianity. This sounds as absurd as *The DaVinci Code.* But there are currents of this in the Mormon Church, which undermines its own case by an apologetics of suppression.

THREE CARD MONTE

Through movies we're all familiar with the "hand is quicker than the eye" card tricks, whereby rustics are separated from their money in the big city or at the traveling fair. Here's one:

Hitchens's Challenge

When apologists claim that skeptics have groundless morals, nonbelievers respond that they have all they need for every good work. Christopher Hitchens picks up this retort, asking for a counterexample. "Show me what there is, ethically, in any religion that can't be duplicated by humanism. In other words, can you name me a single moral action performed or moral statement uttered by a person of faith that couldn't be just as well pronounced or undertaken by a civilian?"[34]

Some apologists gamely offer suggestions such as tithing or intercessory prayer. But this is a losing game. For one thing, God's laws are salutary, and humanists who appeal to human well-being for their ethic will find resonance with the ethics of Christianity. For instance both can oppose incest and thievery. So when skeptics are giving "humane" justifications, they are just tracking with God-designed patterns of blessedness.

But the main problem is that Hitchens has challenged his opponent to deny a truism or provide a counterexample to a trivial truth—namely, that people can perversely use anything to justify anything, and then declare their justification to be "just as well" executed as the next person's.

John Humphrey Noyes is a case in point. Thrown out of Yale University for heresy in the 1830s, he founded a "perfectionist" community whose members entered in to degenerate "complex marriage." Arguing that, since Jesus came to "take away the sins of the world," men could become sin free. He then crafted a "biblical" regimen for deliverance, wherein Matt 22:30 ("in the resurrection they neither marry nor are given in marriage") was used to justify multiple adulteries. His followers at Putney, Vermont, and later at Oneida, New York, did not marry, so they could not be unfaithful to their spouses. By his light, "the marriage supper of the Lamb is a feast at which every dish is free to every guest." Still, he made sure that breeding fit with a eugenics program, which they also based on the Bible, with justifying charts rehearsing the procreative activities of Abram, Nahor, Laban, and others.[35]

So one might well challenge Hitchens, "Name one evil deed performed by a humanist that a professing believer cannot himself perform, appealing to Scripture." For that matter, can he name any evil deed on earth that a humanist could not justify and perform? Or can he name any virtuous act that a person of faith could not justify or perform?

The real issue is not whether one can base his ethic on this or that but whether he can do it well. And the Christian claim still stands: The naturalist/humanist behaving morally is like a dog walking on his hind legs; it's doable but forced.

WISHFUL THINKING

Back in the 1980s, when the Iron Curtain still hung from its Soviet frame, columnist John Leo had fun with the Russian claim that they had invented baseball, that it was actually derived from a game called Lapta.[36] There is great cachet in being the home-people of a pioneer or founder. Greeks take pride in Euclid and the French in the Curies. But there is strong temptation to go beyond reality to fantasy, claiming more than one ought. And this project is aided by a lack of clearcut standards; how can one say what qualifies someone to be "the father of something" when any number of streams can flow into the river of a discipline?

Perhaps that is why British Muslim physicist Jim Al-Khalili can speak so expansively of Al-Biruni (973–1048), describing him as "a Persian-Muslim polymath," as "the father of geology" and "the father of anthropology," as well as one who "developed trigonometry" and "a lot of areas of mathematics." Unfortunately "a lot of his work didn't get translated into Latin" and "he doesn't get the credit in the history of science that he deserves."[37]

Al-Biruni was no doubt a remarkable man, but Al-Khalili grasps at straws to connect him to Islam. Though "some historians have said that Biruni was agnostic in his religious views," Al-Khalili finds some hope in Biruni's rebuke of another scientist of his day. This is a stretch, as is the claim that he was the "father" of anything. But this fits in with a major Muslim face-saving program, to show that the religion has not been a social disaster, despite what one sees today.

The most common father-names for geology and anthropology are respectively James Hutton and Franz Boas or in ancient terms Aristotle and Marco Polo. A lot of famous scholars studied rocks and people groups. And yes, Biruni was one of them.

Still, academic circumspection can give way to apologetic zeal, whether one is a Christian, a member of another faith, or an atheist. That is what happened here.

Notes

1 "Top 10 Most Outrageous Liberal Media Quotes from the Last 20 Years," *Human Events*, November 6, 2011; http://www.humanevents.com/article.php?id=23251 (accessed September 30, 2010).

2 James Carafano, "U.S. Thwarts 19 Terrorist Attacks Against America Since 9/11," *Heritage Foundation*, November 13, 2007; http://www.heritage.org/research/reports/2007/11/us-thwarts-19-terrorist-attacks-against-america-since-9-11 (accessed December 23, 2010).

3 Transcript of interview, with commentary by Lachlan Markay, "PBS's Tavis Smiley: Far More Christian Terrorists than Muslim Ones, Tea Party Comparable to Jihad," *Newsbusters*, May 28, 2010; http://www.newsbusters.org/blogs/lachlan-markay/2010/05/28/pbss-tavis-smiley-far-more-christian-terrorists-muslim-ones-tea-part (accessed November 26, 2010).

4 Steven C. Dubin, *Arresting Images: Impolitic Art and Uncivil Actions* (New York: Routledge, 1992), 242, 258.

5 "Author Christopher Hitchens in Conversation with Noah Richler, On His Jewish Grandmother, His Atheism, His Writing—and Facing His Own Mortality," *Maclean's*, December 27, 2010, 17.

6 Christopher Hitchens, *Hitch-22: A Memoir* (New York: Twelve, 2010), 107.

7 "Islamophobia," Council on American-Islamic Relations; http://www.cair.com/Issues/Islamophobia/Islamophobia.aspx (accessed November 26, 2010).

8 Ibid.

9 Bradley R. E. Wright, *Christians Are Hate-Filled Hypocrites . . . and Other Lies You've Been Told: A Sociologist Shatters Myths from the Secular and Christian Media* (Minneapolis: Bethany House, 2010), 15.

10 Ibid., 17.

11 Jerry A. Coyne, "Science and religion aren't friends," *USA Today*, October 11, 2010, 11A.

12 M. Planck, cited in Thomas Kuhn, *The Structure of Scientific Revolutions,* 2nd ed. (Chicago: University of Chicago Press, 1970), 151.

13 Leslie F. Stevenson, "Is Scientific Research Value-Neutral?" in *Environmental Ethics: Divergence and Convergence*, 2nd ed., eds. Richard G. Botzler and Susan J. Armstrong (New York: McGraw-Hill, 1998), 27–28.

14 Michael Crichton, *State of Fear* (New York: HarperCollins, 2004), 575–76.

15 James Woodward and David Goodstein, "Conduct, Misconduct, and the Structure of Science," in *Environmental Ethics: Divergence and Convergence*, 18.

16 A. N. Wilson, *Our Times: The Age of Elizabeth II* (New York: Farrar, Straus and Giroux, 2008), 398.
17 Ibid.
18 Ibid., 398–99.
19 Ibid., 399.
20 "Argument Clinic," in episode 29, *Monty Python's Flying Circus* (http://www. ibras.dk/ montypython/episode29.htm (accessed January 4, 2011).
21 Gary Greenberg, *101 Myths of the Bible* (New York: Barnes & Noble, 2000), 13, 254.
22 Lucy S. Dawidowicz, *The War Against the Jews, 1933–1945* (New York; Holt, Rinehart and Winston, 1975), 23.
23 Eric Metaxas, *Bonhoeffer: Pastor, Martyr, Prophet, Spy* (Nashville: Thomas Nelson, 2010), 92.
24 Ibid.
25 Ibid., 172.
26 Ibid., 173.
27 Doris L. Bergen, *War and Genocide: A Concise History of the Holocaust* (Lanham, MD: Rowan & Littlefield, 2003), 6.
28 Charles P. Pierce, *Idiot America: How Stupidity Became a Virtue in the Land of the Free* (New York: Random House, 2010), 141.
29 Ibid., 146.
30 Ibid., 150–51.
31 Ibid., 156.
32 Steven Naifeh and Gregory White Smith, *The Mormon Murders: A True Story of Greed, Forgery, Deceit, and Death* (New York: Weidenfeld & Nicolson, 1988), 79.
33 Ibid., 127 (italics theirs).
34 "Questions of Faith, A Conversation Between Unitarian Minister Marilyn Sewell and Infamous Atheist Christopher Hitchens," *Portland Monthly*, January 2010; http://www. portlandmonthlymag.com/arts-and-entertainment/category/book-and-talks/articles/ religion-god-0110/2 (accessed December 11, 2010).
35 Clive Foss, "Plato's American Republic," *History Today*, December 2010, 37–39.
36 John Leo, "Essay: Evil Umpires? Not in Soviet Baseball," *Time*, August 10, 1987; http:// www.time.com/time/magazine/article/0,9171,965181,00.html (accessed January 4, 2011).
37 Jim Al-Khalili, "My History Hero: Abu Rayhan Biruni (973–1048)," *BBC History Magazine* (Christmas 2010), 98.

Virtuous Apologetics: Logic and Substance

J UST AS PARTIES WHEN debating over religion can embarrass or even
disgrace themselves by their discourse, apologists can show themselves worthy of praise. This chapter examines good ways in which one might advance his
apologetic cause. The chapter will look less to the content of arguments than to
their form or context.

STATISTICAL CIRCUMSPECTION

Various men (including Mark Twain and Benjamin Disraeli) have been credited with coining and popularizing the old saw that there are "lies, damned lies,
and statistics." It may not be that bad, but statistics are notoriously misleading,
and apologists have every right and responsibility to give them a closer look.

Bradley R. E. Wright

In his book *Christians Are Hate-Filled Hypocrites . . . and Other Lies You've
Been Told*, University of Connecticut sociologist Bradley R. E. Wright shows
evidence that Protestants are less likely to commit crimes than those not affili-
ated with any church. For instance 9 percent of the former have been arrested,
compared with 15 percent of the latter. Similarly the comparisons for damaged
property (7 percent vs. 12 percent), theft of over $50 (3 percent vs. 5 percent),
and hurting someone in a fight (5 percent vs. 7 percent). But he does not leave
it at that.

Then in a qualifying statement he states that his comparisons are "bivariate" rather than "multivariate," though he has published work in the latter vein
as well. Multivariate studies are more fine grained, including such variables as
"race, social class, age, geographical region, personality characteristics, attitudes,

social ties, employment, education, and past experiences with the criminal justice system." He then uses his bivariate analysis to counter speculation that the difference was due to the fact that women were both less likely to commit crimes and more likely to go to church, for among women, the contrast is much the same.[1]

Such care brings glory to God.

Mark Driscoll

In the same book, Professor Wright has expressed appreciation for Seattle pastor Mark Driscoll's take on polls indicating a decline in church affiliation in America. While *Newsweek* ran a cover story on "The End of Christian America," Driscoll says the changes "are not discouraging, but rather clarifying." He distinguishes between active, practicing Christians and those "who simply profess Christianity without any deeper engagement." To his way of thinking, these "cultural Christians" are simply redefining themselves as "unaffiliated." And these "numerical declines are not necessarily negative." In fact, "the remaining Christians are more likely to live in accord with Christian principles and thus better represent the church."[2]

Furthermore it helps with evangelism. Since "the irreligious now face less social stigma than they have in the past," they "can now accurately identify their religious status." This "actually helps the church by reclassifying marginal, uncommitted Christians" needing the gospel.[3]

TESTIMONY

Personal testimony is a notoriously unreliable argument, in that a person can testify to all sorts of nonsense. A personal testimony is anecdotal and often contradictory, but it can be helpful if it demonstrates that otherwise respectable people have come to the convictions one is trying to advance.

It is disappointing that Zondervan Publishing House has seen fit to push feminist egalitarianism in the church through the book *How I Changed My Mind About Women in Leadership: Compelling Stories from Prominent Evangelicals.*[4] One can marvel that the contributors think they have squared their support for women pastors with Scripture. Perhaps some writers have a disorienting zeal for the happiness and affection of a spouse who has taken up this cause. But one cannot deny that this book is something to deal with, particularly since some of the writers are identified with biblical inerrancy.

That being said, one should be grateful for testimony books that rebut the claim that only dolts can be people of faith. In a day when atheists are calling themselves "brights," it is good to remind the world that some rather bright people have claimed Christ as Savior and Lord. Here are three examples, two from philosophy, one from physics, with a brief quotation from each:

- Nicholas Rescher was professor of philosophy at the University of Pittsburgh and editor of both the *American Philosophical Quarterly* and the *History of Philosophy Quarterly*. He also served as president of the American Philosophical Association, Eastern Division. "There is no doubt that two intersecting factors were operative in inducing me to make a Christian commitment: a sense of intellectual and personal solidarity with those whom I could accept as role models among believers, and a sense of estrangement from those whom I deemed naively cocksure in their rejection of belief."[5]
- William Alston was a president of the American Philosophical Association and a professor of philosophy at Rutgers, Michigan, Illinois, and Syracuse. "My way back to the faith was not primarily through philosophical reasoning, or any other form of argumentation, but through an experience of God at work in the Christian community."[6]
- Patricia H. Reiff is professor of physics and astronomy at Rice University and director of the Rice Space Institute. "Science cannot prove that God exists. If it could, then only scientists could know him. Jesus came to the children and the poor, scorning the haughty intellectuals of the day. He came to show us what God living in you really looks like. He taught with simple parables that all can understand. He died a Lamb for our sins and forever opened the throne of God to humankind."[7]

HISTORICAL SERIOUSNESS

Setting the record straight often means digging into the historical record. Skeptics love to rehearse Christian-driven horror stories, and historians need to make sure the stories are true and properly contextualized.

Alister McGrath on Michael Servetus

Referring to the execution of the heretic Michael Servetus in John Calvin's day, Christopher Hitchens says, "Calvin's Geneva was a prototypical totalitarian state, and Calvin himself a sadist and torturer and killer."[8] Alister McGrath, in his biography of Calvin, demonstrates that on this point Hitchens and those who share in his rhetoric are far off base. While McGrath makes clear that he disapproves of the execution, he puts the whole thing in context: (a) The city council, which passed down the sentence and carried out the execution, was not in Calvin's pocket. (b) Once the death penalty was assigned, Calvin argued for beheading rather than burning, a less tortuous means, but his plea was ignored. (c) It is absurdly unfair to magnify the case of the only man executed in Calvin's

Geneva when mass executions for religiopolitical offenses were typical in Calvin's day, from Germany to France to England. (d) In contrast Thomas Aquinas is never castigated for explicitly teaching that heretics should be burned. (e) Unlike today, when heresy means little more than "expression of an opinion at odds with the prevailing orthodoxy," heresy served a sociopolitical agenda in those days, including threats of anarchy or nascent communism.[9]

McGrath says that Calvin's "tacit support for the capital penalty for offences such as heresy which he (and his contemporaries) regarded as serious makes him little more than a child of his age, rather than an outrageous exception to its standards." Indeed, "to single out Calvin for particular criticism . . . suggests a selectivity approaching victimization."[10]

Rodney Stark on the Crusades

One would think that talk of the Crusades would be anathema for the Muslims, for they brought them on themselves by invading, occupying, and abusing the Holy Land. Nevertheless they get into high dudgeon over the "offense" of these military expeditions against their forebears, as if they were abused tourists in Jerusalem.

Of course there was misdirection and misbehavior on the part of some of the "Christians" who took up arms against the Islamic latecomers to the Levant, but you can say that of any army in any war in any day. Yes, much of the indignation was born of twisted theology, wherein there was some sort of special grace that fell on pilgrims to the region. And, indeed, bloodshed in the name of God is always a dicey proposition for the Christian (though it seems less troublesome for Muslims). But if you can live with expelling Saddam Hussein from Kuwait and Hitler from France, you might well have a way to see the Crusades in a new light.

Rodney Stark of Baylor University can be a great help in this connection. His book *God's Battalions* presents an admirable "case for the Crusades." For one thing he has no patience for the notion that Muslim occupiers were benign. Rather, "mass murder of monks and pilgrims were common," including 60 eighth-century pilgrims crucified in Jerusalem and 20 monks from the Monastery of Mar Saba who were burned to death in 796.[11] And these offenses continued through the centuries: "In 1040 Ulrich of Breisgau was stoned by a mob near the river Jordan; in 1064 Bishop Gunther of Bamberg and his large party of pilgrims were ambushed by Muslims near Caesarea, and two-thirds did not survive." Then there was fresh Muslim menace in the region from the rapacious Seljuk Turks who in 1048 attacked the Armenians from the east.[12]

Stark also turns his sharp focus on the battle accounts, mocking for one the report that "men rode in blood up to their knees and bridle reins." He comments,

"Surely, no sensible person will believe this."[13] Just do the math: Unless blood defies the laws of hydraulics and tends to pile up in narrow mounds around Crusaders, then this is ridiculous. Of course, there was fierce bloodshed, but even if the entire battle were waged within an Olympic-sized pool, it would take the blood of over a quarter of a million men to raise the fluid level to touch the bottom of the horses' reins. And if they are only talking about blood splatter, that can happen with the killing of a ferret.

The point is that there is a lot of nonsense written and spoken on the Crusades, and it is transmitted uncritically by friend and foe alike.

Philip Sampson on Andrew Dickson White

Proclaimed "a classic" by its admirers, Andrew Dickson White's *A History of the Warfare of Science and Theology in Christendom* is meant to insulate empirical studies from the poison of revealed faith. Never mind that Christians Isaac Newton and Gottfried Leibniz discovered the calculus, that a monk named Gregor Mendel founded genetics, and that believing Michael Faraday initiated the discipline of electromagnetics. Christianity's opponents still claim that it is at war with science.

What the book really shows is that White, at war with Christianity, is content to twist the story to suit his campaign. Philip Sampson's book *Six Modern Myths About Christianity and Western Civilization* demonstrates this to be the case and does the same with other "historical" assaults on the faith, such as the claims that Gen 1:28 has proven to be environment hostile and that missionaries have been culturally toxic.

In writing about Scottish physician James Simpson's advocacy of anesthesia to mitigate the pain of childbirth, White writes, "From pulpit after pulpit Simpson's use of chloroform was denounced as impious and contrary to Holy Writ; texts were cited abundantly, the ordinary declaration being that to use chloroform was 'to avoid one part of the primeval curse on woman.'"[14]

Philip Sampson retorts:

> This story has been investigated in detail by consulting the medical and religious literature of the period. In fact religious opposition to Simpson's use of anesthesia in childbirth was "virtually non-existent," although it was opposed on other grounds, including medical, physiological and moral. The story of Eve's curse is, however, absent. The only significant work traced by the science historian A. D. Farr that did deal specifically with the biblical point of view was by an evangelical Anglican, who defended the use of anesthesia in childbirth. Few versions of the story of Eve's curse mention Simpson's own Christian conversion.[15]

LOANING/GIVING

There are so many questions and so little time to answer them—and so many who have answered so well—that often the better part of wisdom is to simply pass along some reading. The present writer loves to give copies of C. S. Lewis's *Mere Christianity* to those who are approaching Christianity from the skeptical outside.

Of course handouts can be a mixed bag, and the loaner/giver needs to be familiar with what he is passing along, ready to offer qualifiers, disclaimers, and supplements where needed. One should read the material first himself, but sometimes reviews or annotated bibliographies, such as the one Louis Markos provides at the end of his book *Apologetics for the 21st Century*, can give one the confidence to proceed, if only to say, "Could you look this over and tell me what you think of it?"[16] And another way to introduce the literature is to give the inquirer one of Lee Strobel's *The Case for . . .* books, in which he interviews a series of apologists, whose writings can then be explored according to interest: D. A. Carson, William Lane Craig, Norman Geisler, Gary Habermas, Peter Kreeft, J. P. Moreland, and Ravi Zacharias, to name a few.[17]

Jim Parker "Plies" Mike Bryan

In 1991 writer Mike Bryan, "a lapsed Protestant on the religious *left*," enrolled in Criswell College to get a fix on conservative evangelical education. After his studies and travels with the students and faculty, he left "still a wandering soul." But he was impressed at many turns by President Paige Patterson, Dean Danny Akin, and professors Ray Clendenen and Luis Pantoja.

He took a special liking to James Parker whose apologetical teaching bothered some because of his "calm and reasoned presentation of attitudes and thoughts inimical to Christian theism." Of course Parker answered the critics, but he was fair.

Bryan recounts that Parker "was the first person at Criswell with whom I spent a good deal of time off campus, and as he began to ply me with a number of books and articles—the stack soon became unwieldy—I suspected he had been tacitly put in charge of my case."[18] "In charge" or not, Parker kept him supplied with good reading.

> One of the books provided me by Jim Parker was *Escape from Skepticism—Liberal Education as If Truth Mattered*, by Christopher Derrick, a Catholic author, teacher, and former student of C. S. Lewis. Derrick urges that we at least acknowledge that a secular education is in fact a religious education—the religion of secular humanism and atheism. His book is a more calmly argued version of some of Allan Bloom's theses in *The Closing of the American Mind*.[19]

Two Laymen Fund *The Fundamentals*

In 1909 oil magnate Lyman Stewart and his brother Milton supplied the money for publishing and distributing a dozen volumes of essays designed to counter heresy, skepticism, and incipient liberalism. Entitled *The Fundamentals: A Testimony to Truth*, these writings were distributed free of charge to 300,000 "ministers of the gospel, missionaries, Sunday School superintendents, and others engaged in aggressive Christian work throughout the English speaking world." In all, "several millions of volumes" from this collection were distributed worldwide.[20]

The word *Fundamentalist* can be traced to this event, and through the years that term has taken a beating. But the writing team featured first-rate scholars, including professors from Scotland, Canada, Germany, England, and the United States. Three were Southern Baptist seminary professors—Charles B. Williams and J. J. Reeve of Southwestern and E. Y. Mullins of Southern.

The Stewarts knew they themselves could not stand toe-to-toe in scholarship with "higher critics" who denied the historicity of Genesis or the virgin birth, but they knew who could, so theirs was an apologetic of investment.

GOD'S TRUTH, WHEREVER IT IS FOUND

The Christian apologist is debtor to many nonbelievers, for their writings are full of helpful criticisms and information. Sometimes Christians talk of "plundering the Egyptians" (see Exod 12:36) in gaining riches from cultural captors. Or in another vein one can rest in the truth expressed by Augustine and Aquinas, that "all truth is God's truth," whatever its origin. And the apologist who relies only or even chiefly on Christian writers is missing out on a wealth of material.

Christopher Hitchens on Eastern Religion

Just because atheists such as Christopher Hitchens are wrong about Christianity, that does not mean they are wrong about other faiths, and it is fair to draw on skeptics when they have something valuable to say.

Concerned that those who, like himself, are done with the Judeo-Christian perspective will turn to East Asian faiths, Hitchens pens a chapter entitled "There Is No 'Eastern' Solution" in *God Is Not Great*. He speaks of sitting under the tutelage of India's Bhagwan Sri Rajneesh, whose preaching tent bore an irritating little sign: "Shoes and minds must be left at the gate." This prompted him to image "a heap of abandoned and empty mentalities to round out this literally mindless little motto."

Hitchens then noted the way in which disciples were shaken down to help fund the Bhagwan's luxurious lifestyle, including a fleet of Rolls-Royces, and were subjected to humiliating initiation rituals should they desire to advance in the "faith."[21]

Adam Carolla on the COEXIST Bumper Sticker and Cults

When it comes to Christianity, self-avowed atheist Adam Carolla is certainly a mess. His language is often vile, but he has one advantage over many Christians in apologetics. He is utterly candid and not determined to be politically correct. For instance he is only too happy to ridicule the COEXIST bumper sticker.

> The people who tell you all religions should be respected are the same idiots with the COEXIST bumper sicker on their Prius. Who is this message for? You're pulling into the Whole Foods in West Hollywood and parking with nine other Priuses sporting COEX-IST bumper stickers. It's preaching to the choir. Actually, the gay men's chorus. The people who need to get the all-religions-are-beautiful-and-can-work-in-harmony message aren't there. Do you think Ahmadinejad is pulling his armored SUV in behind you to pick up a nine-dollar organic avocado and a wheatgrass smoothie? This would be like going to a Beverly Hills private school to deliver an important message about staying out of gangs. Your stupid bumper sticker is falling on deaf eyes. The people who really should get the "coexist" message are literally on the other side of the world. The regions that need these stickers barely have cars to put them on. And again, they wouldn't heed this coexist idea anyway. They stone you to death for having the audacity to be driving as a woman.[22]

He adds a word on cults:

> So no matter how crazy the religion is, we need to respect it. What about cults? Cults are religions, but instead of churches they have compounds, and instead of priests they have bearded weirdos with acoustic guitars. Every cult starts out as peace, love, and folk music, but eventually gives way to "bring me all the thirteen-year-old girls." All cults are about fifty-year-old white guys nailing teenage runaways.[23]

Peter Padfield on Himmler's "Showdown with Christianity"

A standard move among atheists is somehow to blame the horrible behavior of the godless on Christianity—as in the case of Hitler. To help undermine that conceit, it is helpful to check out Peter Padfield's biography of Heinrich Himmler, one of Hitler's chief henchmen. (Padfield, a distinguished naval historian, may be a believer but not conspicuously so.)

> Plans for the systematic creation of a cultural framework to replace Christianity, referred to as the "development of the Germanic heritage," were worked out between Himmler's personal staff under Wolff and academics in early 1937. A key draft obviously expressing Himmler's ideas stated that now "in the age of the final showdown with Christianity" it was one of the missions of the SS to provide the German people with "the proper ideological [*weltanschaulichen*] foundations" within which to conduct and frame their lives.[24]

Himmler pushed a "cosmic theory called the *Welteislehre*, or "world ice doctrine."

> It proposed that all events in the cosmos resulted from an eternal struggle between the heart of the sun and quantities of ice in space. This Manichaean argument of opposing forces locked in never-ending conflict fitted in with the "Darwinian" doctrine of the "struggle for existence" which Hitler had made his own—and Himmler too.[25]

Of course this was rank foolishness, but it served the Nazi worldview, which was decidedly anti-Christian.

Among the other efforts to displace Christianity were the institution of "two principal ceremonies adapted from pagan rites to replace Christian festivals—those of the summer and winter solstices—with songs of praise for the Aryan god"; funeral ceremonies "corresponding to the clan beliefs, corresponding to the family beliefs, corresponding to honoring of ancestors, the honouring of parents and our forefathers"; and the gift, from the SS, of silver beakers to couples at marriage and three things to a newborn—a silver tankard, a silver spoon, and a large band of blue silk. This silk band was wrapped around the child, with the pronouncement: "The blue band of loyalty extends itself throughout your life. Who is German and feels German must be loyal!"[26] And, in the naming, Thorisman (from the ancient Nordic god of the skies) or Adolph (from the ancient Germanic for "noble wolf") was to be preferred to a traditional Christian name such as Johann or Markus.

London *Daily Mail* on Hitler's "Christmas" Party

This is the sort of thing one finds everywhere in the "secular" press. For instance a *Daily Mail* article on Hitler's glum 1941 Christmas party (after setbacks in Russia) bears these words:

> The Nazi Christmas was far from traditional. Hitler believed religion had no place in his 1,000-year Reich, so he replaced the Christian figure of Saint Nicholas with the Norse god Odin and urged Germans to celebrate the season as a holiday of the "winter solstice," rather than Christmas. Out of sight at the top of the tree behind Hitler was a swastika instead of an angel, and many of the baubles carried runic symbols and iron cross motifs.[27]

STEWARDSHIP

In the early pages of his magisterial work *Critique of Pure Reason*, the eighteenth-century German philosopher Immanuel Kant warned against inane pursuits in philosophy.

> To know what questions we may reasonably propose is in itself a strong evidence of sagacity and intelligence. For if a question be in itself absurd and unsusceptible of a rational answer, it is attended with the danger—not to mention the shame that falls upon the

person who proposes it—of seducing the unguarded listener into making absurd answers, and we are presented with the ridiculous spectacle of one (as the ancients said) "milking the he-goat, and the other holding a sieve."[28]

Jason Lisle of *Answers in Genesis* aptly connects this with the counsel of Prov 26:4: "Don't answer a fool according to his foolishness or you'll be like him yourself."[29] And as evangelist Jay Strack once told Indiana Southern Baptist youth workers who asked about the threat of "backward masking" (the search of evil hidden messages on records run in reverse), "Don't be a dog who chases every car."

Of course the apologist is eager to pick up on the concerns and arguments of the skeptic. He is not called on to bulldoze his way through genuine questions or to deliver pontifical monologues. This is a dialogical enterprise. But there is much to be said for keeping things on track, and often that means casting or recasting the conversation in the right mode. One has only so much time and patience. Emotional capital may be frittered away on bottomless pits of conversation, and then one has not been a proper steward of himself.

William Abraham on Soft Rationalism

From the beginning Christians have denounced certain contests as not fit for participation or viewing. "In his book, *De Spectaculis*, for example, Tertullian (died c. 220), devoted an entire chapter to the [gladiatorial] games, enjoining Christians not to attend—powerful testimony to Christianity's humanitarian impulse."[30] In subsequent centuries believers at one time or another have spurned poker, boxing, and even golf as a waste of time, a threat to sanctification, or social poison.

William Abraham of Southern Methodist University's Perkins School of Theology argues that Christians should get out of another "game," namely, trying to supply airtight proofs for God's existence to the skeptics. In a piece on "soft rationalism," he argues that one really cannot formally prove the correctness of a worldview, whether of Christianity, Marxism, or existentialism. As he puts it, "Hard rationalists set the standards for rationality far too high for the subject matter."[31] Rather, one has to work at the overview level, how it hangs together, how it more or less adequately fits and serves the world.

He says that many disciplines work on a sort of informal, "cumulative case" basis—"jurisprudence, literary exegesis, history, philosophy, and science"[32]—and insists that worldviews, including Christianity, must not be held to a more exacting standard than these. In short he refuses to play the skeptic's game, by taking up a burden no one can carry in worldview disputes.

HOLY INGRATITUDE

Any number of people have a good word for Jesus, or they want to help believers' cause by suggesting a more promising line of thought than that suggested by a plain reading of Scripture. They want to "help," but the apologist needs to stick with the irreducible awkwardness of the faith.

C. S. Lewis was impatient with those who spoke well of Jesus as a moral teacher but *only* as a moral teacher. Here's his classic statement on that matter:

> You tread on my toes and I forgive you, you steal my money and I forgive you. But what should we make of a man, himself unrobed and untrodden on, who announced that he forgave you for treading on other men's toes and stealing other men's money? Asinine fatuity is the kindest description we should give his conduct. Yet this is what Jesus did. He told people that their sins were forgiven, and never waited to consult all the other people whom their sins had undoubtedly injured. He unhesitatingly behaved as if He were the party chiefly concerned, the person chiefly offended in all offences. This makes sense only if He really was the God whose laws are broken and whose love is wounded in every sin. In the mouth of any speaker who is not God, these words would imply what I can only regard as silliness and conceit unrivalled by any other character in history. . . .
>
> A man who was merely a man and said the sort of things Jesus said would not be a great moral teacher. He would either be a lunatic—on a level with the man who says he is a poached egg—or else he would be the Devil of Hell. You must make your choice. Either this man was, and is, the Son of God: or else a madman or something worse. You can shut Him up for a fool, you can spit at Him and kill Him as a demon; or you can fall at His feet and call Him Lord and God. But let us not come with any patronizing nonsense about His being a great human teacher. He has not left that open to us. He did not intend to.[33]

GRAPHICS

In an article called "Diagrams That Changed the World," the *BBC News Magazine* traced the influence of such graphics as Copernicus's sketch of the solar system, Newton's optics diagram, which showed light proceeding in a straight line, and Florence Nightingale's pie charts, which demonstrated the fact that disease and not battle was the chief cause of death in the Crimean War.[34]

They serve the old adage, "A picture is worth a thousand words." In this vein Doug Powell's illustrations in the *Holman QuickSource Guide to Christian Apologetics* are helpful. For example he reproduces the image of an eye mask just above his discussion of fideism, emphasizing its relative indifference to evidence.[35] And on the page where he introduces "integrative apologetics," he offers an imaginative construct based on the Swiss Army Knife, but in this case the turned-out tools are metallic puzzle pieces, reminders that the believer has many problem-solving tools in his philosophical kit.[36] (Earlier he presented the image of a regular knife, with folded out screwdriver, augur, punch, blades, and scissors, to demonstrate the multifarious nature of apologetics.)[37]

Later he supplied a mechanical engineering drawing of the bacterial flagellum, using machine-like components (universal joint, bushings, a drive shaft, and rotor) to advance the case for Intelligent Design. Though the microscopic bacterial elements are not colored green, blue, purple, red, and yellow, as they are in the drawing, Powell snaps the mechanism into clarity artistically. The layman would have trouble sorting things out were he to see only a photograph of the bacterium.[38] No, mask, knife, and mechanical drawings are not arguments in themselves, but they have their purpose as metaphors and interpreters.

GRANULARITY

Alvin Plantinga of Notre Dame University is the philosopher's philosopher, as adept at professional minutiae as anyone. But there is a difference. First, he uses detailed "logic chopping" to torment the skeptic (and not his poor readers), removing his wall brick by brick. Second, he does it with humor. One might even say he is toying with his opponent. It makes for quite a scene.

Alvin Plantinga versus J. L. Mackie

For instance he takes the tweezers to J. L. Mackie, who claims that the Christian God is incompatible with the wretched world as people know it. Plantinga asks how that may be. Is he saying, "Every good thing eliminates every evil state of affairs that it can eliminate"?

If so (and it seems Mackie's saying something like this), then what about the following case?

> Suppose, first of all, that your friend Paul unwisely goes for a drive on a wintry day and runs out of gas on a deserted road. The temperature dips to -10°, and a miserably cold wind comes up. You are sitting comfortably at home (twenty-five miles from Paul) roasting chestnuts in a roaring blaze. Your car is in the garage; in the trunk there is the full five-gallon can of gasoline you always keep for emergencies. Paul's discomfort and danger are certainly an evil, and one which you could eliminate. You don't do so. But presumably you don't thereby forfeit your claim to being a "good thing"—you simply didn't know of Paul's plight.[39]

OK, so it needs a tweak, something like, "Every good thing always eliminates every evil that *it knows about* and can eliminate." Perhaps with this Mackie can embarrass theism, since God is supposed to know everything. But there is another problem:

> Suppose you know that Paul is marooned as in the previous example, and you also know another friend is similarly marooned fifty miles in the opposition direction. Suppose, furthermore, that while you can rescue one or the other, you simply can't rescue both. Then each of the two evils is such that it is within your power to eliminate it: and you

know about them both. But you can't eliminate both; and you don't forfeit your claim to being a good person by eliminating only one—it wasn't within your power to do more.[40]

And so on it goes, delightfully.

Alvin Plantinga versus Judge Jones

Plantinga does the same thing with Judge Jones in the Kitzmiller case, where Intelligent Design was declared unscientific and thus unfit for mention in the classroom. According to the judge, ID is disqualified by "invoking and permitting supernatural causation" and by making statements that are not "verifiable or falsifiable." So Plantinga goes to work on the poor judge, beginning with a sample, "supernatural" statement: "God has designed 800-pound rabbits that live in Cleveland" is clearly testable, clearly falsifiable, and indeed clearly false. Testability can't be taken as a criterion for distinguishing scientific from nonscientific statements.[41]

One could liken this to water torture, the drip-drip-drip of careful analysis, which leaves the offender justly harried and befuddled.

Gleason Archer on the Second-Temple Construction Schedule

Critics of biblical inerrancy comb the text for contradictions and other errors, and inerrantists have risen to the challenge, as they should. Claiming that the Bible exhibits "verbal plenary inspiration"—that every word in the original manuscripts is "God breathed"—they take up the defense in detail. Of course, this is not just a matter of warfare with the skeptic; it also serves friends of the Bible, who might be puzzled by this or that passage. Still this is often an apologetic task.

For instance Gleason Archer's *Encyclopedia of Bible Difficulties* deals with the question, "How can we reconcile Ezra 3:8–13; 5:13–17, which say that the second temple was begun in the reign of Cyrus the Great; Ezra 4:24, which says it was begun in the second year of Darius I; and Haggai 2:15, which implies that the work had not yet begun in 520 B.C.?"[42]

Archer's answer, which takes the better part of a page, sorts it all out, noting the sequential granting, suspending, and regranting of building permits, and the ebb and flow of Israelite efforts at construction.

Some object that this sort of exacting explanation is unnecessary, that the big picture is all that is important, but they betray their misunderstanding of the Bible's nature, that it is true in *all* that it affirms. (And some might fear a Bible that speaks with such exactitude.) This is not to say that every verse is meant to be a clinical proposition; there are metaphors, round numbers, hyperboles, generalities, and so forth at play. The *Chicago Statement on Biblical Inerrancy* (1978)[43] and its sister statements on interpretation (1982) and application

(1986) spell this out. But once the verse's meaning is clear; it is defensible and properly defended to the nth degree.

Notes

1 Bradley R. E. Wright, *Christians Are Hate-Filled Hypocrites . . . and Other Lies You've Been Told* (Minneapolis: Bethany House, 2010), 231–32.
2 Ibid., 55.
3 Ibid., 219.
4 Alan F. Johnson, ed., *How I Changed My Mind About Women in Leadership: Compelling Stories from Prominent Evangelicals* (Grand Rapids: Zondervan, 2010).
5 Nicholas Rescher, "In Matters of Religion," in *Philosophers Who Believe: The Spiritual Journeys of 11 Leading Thinkers*, ed. Kelly James Clark (Downers Grove, IL: InterVarsity, 1993), 128, 131.
6 William Alston, "A Philosopher's Way Back to the Faith," in *God and the Philosophers: The Reconciliation of Faith and Reason*, ed. Thomas V. Morris (New York: Oxford, 1994), 29.
7 Patricia H. Reiff, "Three Heavens—Our Home," in *Professors Who Believe: The Spiritual Journeys of Christian Faculty*, ed. Paul M. Anderson (Downers Grove, IL: InterVarsity, 1998), 63.
8 Christopher Hitchens, *God Is Not Great: How Religion Poisons Everything* (New York: Twelve, 2007), 233.
9 Alister E. McGrath, *A Life of John Calvin* (Oxford: Blackwell, 1990), 114–20.
10 Ibid., 116.
11 Rodney Stark, *God's Battalions: The Case for the Crusades* (New York: HarperOne, 2009), 84–85.
12 Ibid., 92–93.
13 Ibid., 159.
14 Andrew Dickson White, *A History of the Warfare of Science with Theology in Christendom* (New York: Free, 1965), 346.
15 Philip J. Sampson, *6 Modern Myths About Christianity and Western Civilization* (Downers Grove, IL: InterVarsity, 2001), 116.
16 Louis Markos, *Apologetics for the 21st Century* (Wheaton, IL: Crossway, 2010), 247–71.
17 Lee Strobel, *The Case for Christ: A Journalist's Personal Investigation of the Evidence for Jesus* (Grand Rapids: Zondervan, 1998); and id., *The Case for Faith: A Journalist Investigates the Toughest Objections to Christianity* (Grand Rapids: Zondervan, 2000).
18 Mike Bryan, *Chapter and Verse: A Skeptic Revisits Christianity* (New York: Random House, 1991), 81–82.
19 Ibid., 115.
20 "Preface" and "Dedication," in *The Fundamentals: A Testimony to the Truth*, ed. R. A. Torrey et al. (Los Angeles: Bible Institute of Los Angeles, 1917; reprint, Grand Rapids: Baker, 2000), 1:5, 7.
21 Hitchens, *God Is Not Great*, 196–97.
22 Adam Carolla, *In Fifty Years We'll All Be Chicks . . . and Other Complaints from an Angry Middle-Aged White Guy* (New York: Crown, 2010), 148.
23 Ibid., 149.
24 Peter Padfield, *Himmler: Reichsführer-SS* (New York: Henry Holt, 1990), 170.
25 Ibid., 171.
26 Ibid., 173–75.

27 Allan Hall, "Hitler's Christmas Party: Rare Photographs Capture Leading Nazis Celebrating in 1941," *Mail Online*, December 24, 2010; http://www.dailymail.co.uk/news/article-1341272 Hitlers-Christmas-party-Rare-photographs-capture-leading-Nazis-celebrating-1941.html (accessed December 25, 2010).

28 Immanuel Kant, *Critique of Pure Reason*, trans. J. M. D. Micklejohn; Topic 1: Transcendental Doctrine of Elements; Part Second: Transcendental Logic; Section III: Of the Division of General Logic into Analytic and Dialectic; http://etext.lib.virginia.edu/etcbin/toccer-new2?id=KanPure.xml&images=images/modeng&data=/texts/english/modeng/parsed&tag=public&part=2&division=div2 (accessed December 25, 2010).

29 Jason Lisle, "Fool Proof Apologetics," *Answers*, April–June 2009, 69.

30 "Legatees of a Great Inheritance: How the Judeo-Christian Tradition Has Shaped the West" in *Kairos Journal* (2008): 20.

31 William Abraham, "Soft Rationalism," in *Philosophy of Religion: Selected Readings*, ed. Michael Peterson et al. (Oxford: Oxford University Press, 1996), 86.

32 Ibid., 87.

33 C. S. Lewis, *Mere Christianity* (San Francisco: HarperCollins, 2001), 51–52.

34 "Diagrams That Changed the World," *BBC Mobile News Magazine*, November 22, 2010; http://www.bbc.co.uk/news/magazine-11798317 (accessed November 24, 2010).

35 Doug Powell, *Holman QuickSource Guide to Christian Apologetics* (Nashville: Holman, 2006), 363.

36 Ibid., 370.

37 Ibid., 6.

38 Ibid., 65.

39 Alvin Plantinga, *God, Freedom, and Evil* (New York: Harper & Row, 1974), cited in Louis P. Pojman and Michael Ray, *Philosophy of Religion: An Anthology*, 5th ed. (Belmont, CA: Thomson/Wadsworth, 2008), 184.

40 Ibid., 185.

41 Alvin Plantinga, cited in "Philosopher Alvin Plantinga Demolishes Part of Kitzmiller Decision," *Discovery Institute: Evolution News and Views*; http://www.evolutionnews.org/2006/03/philosopher_alvin_plantinga_de002054.html (accessed November 23, 2010).

42 Gleason L. Archer, *Encyclopedia of Bible Difficulties* (Grand Rapids: Zondervan, 1982), 231.

43 *Chicago Statement on Biblical Inerrancy with Exposition*; http://www.bible-researcher.com/chicago1.html (accessed December 31, 2010).

Virtuous Apologetics:
Manners and Character

T HE CHRISTIAN APOLOGIST IS first of all a Christian, with standards
for demeanor. But Christians are not cookie-cut in personality. The kingdom flourishes with a range of temperaments and voices, whether in a Barnabas
or a Paul, a Peter or a Mary. But along with admirable variety, there are ideals
and limits which all should honor.

GRACE

Writing for the young-earth-creationist magazine *Answers*, Jason Lisle urges
apologists to speak "with gentleness and respect." He explains, "Our defense
should never be emotionally charged or derisive. Remember, even those who are
in rebellion against God are made in His image and deserve respect."[1]

Certainly this is a proper default position for the Christian apologist, but
when he uses the word "never," he invites some pushback. For here he seems to
present a standard which neither Christ nor Paul satisfied. For the Lord used
harsh language against enemies of the kingdom, calling Pharisees "hypocrites"
and "whitewashed tombs, which appear beautiful on the outside, but inside
are full of dead men's bones and every impurity" (Matt 23:27). Then there was
Paul, who did not shrink from sarcasm, as in 1 Cor 4:10, where he mocked his
pompous readers: "We are fools for Christ, but you are wise in Christ! We are
weak, but you are strong! You are distinguished, but we are dishonored!" Yes, it
hurt. Indeed the word "sarcasm" means "to tear the flesh," but there's a place for
being ironic in a derisive way.

Still the apologist should use as much grace as possible in getting the job done.

The Anglo-Catholic cardinal John Henry Newman, who was recently declared a saint by pope Benedict, took pains to define what it is to be a gentleman: "He is mainly occupied in merely removing the obstacles which hinder the free and unembarrassed action of those about him." He reminds one of "an easy chair or a good fire, which do their part in dispelling cold and fatigue." He "carefully avoids whatever may cause a jar or a jolt in the minds of those with whom he is cast" and "his great concern being to make every one at their ease and at home."

Unfortunately this approach would bar most biblical prophets and apostles from the ranks of the gentlemanly, but so much the worse for that designation. And he discloses an overworked delicacy when he speaks glowingly of "the gentleness and effeminacy of feeling, which is the attendant on civilization."[2]

Nevertheless his remarks on discourse are a valuable read.

> [The gentleman] has his eyes on all his company; he is tender towards the bashful, gentle towards the distant, and merciful towards the absurd; he can recollect to whom he is speaking; he guards against unseasonable allusions, or topics which may irritate; he is seldom prominent in conversation, and never wearisome. . . . He never speaks of himself except when compelled, never defends himself by a mere retort, he has no ears for slander or gossip, is scrupulous in imputing motives to those who interfere with him, and interprets every thing for the best. He is never mean or little in his disputes, never takes unfair advantage, never mistakes personalities or sharp sayings for arguments, or insinuates evil which he dare not say out. From a longsighted prudence, he observes the maxim of the ancient sage, that we should ever conduct ourselves towards our enemy as if he were one day to be our friend. He has too much good sense to be affronted at insults, he is too well employed to remember injuries, and too indolent to bear malice. . . . If he engages in controversy of any kind, his disciplined intellect preserves him from the blundering discourtesy of better, perhaps, but less educated minds; who, like blunt weapons, tear and hack instead of cutting clean, who mistake the point in argument, waste their strength on trifles, misconceive their adversary, and leave the question more involved than they find it. He may be right or wrong in his opinion, but he is too clear-headed to be unjust; he is as simple as he is forcible, and as brief as he is decisive. Nowhere shall we find greater candour, consideration, indulgence: he throws himself into the minds of his opponents, he accounts for their mistakes. He knows the weakness of human reason as well as its strength, its province and its limits.[3]

And, in a word to the Hitchenses, Dawkinses, Harrises, and Dennetts of this world, though Newman wrote this a half century before these four came to prominence,

> If he be an unbeliever, he will be too profound and large-minded to ridicule religion or to act against it; he is too wise to be a dogmatist or fanatic in his infidelity. He respects piety and devotion; he even supports institutions as venerable, beautiful, or useful, to which he

does not assent; he honours the ministers of religion, and it contents him to decline its mysteries without assailing or denouncing them.[4]

EDGE

While grace is important, so is forceful engagement. In 2 Cor 10:4–5 Paul spoke of "the weapons of our warfare," which "are not fleshly, but are powerful through God for the demolition of strongholds." With them "we demolish arguments and every high-minded thing that is raised up against the knowledge of God, taking every thought captive to the obedience Christ." This is rather aggressive talk.

C. S. Lewis on "Damned Nonsense"

C. S. Lewis made this point this way: "Confronted with a cancer or a slum the Pantheist can say, 'If you could only see it from the divine point of view, you would realize that this also is God.' The Christian replies, 'Don't talk damned nonsense.'"

At this point in the text, an asterisk takes the reader to this note: "One listener complained of the word damned as frivolous swearing. But I mean exactly what I say—nonsense that is damned is under God's curse, and will (apart from God's grace) lead those who believe it to eternal death."[5]

Then, back to the text, we read, "For Christianity is a fighting religion." And he goes on to explain that "many things have gone wrong with the world that God made and that God insists, and insists very loudly, on our putting them right again."[6]

SBC LIFE and "Edge"

When we began *SBC LIFE* magazine in the early 1990s, I traveled to New York City for a workshop held by *Folio*, the magazine about magazines. The presentations were designed to help a wide range of editors and publishers to launch or improve periodicals. One of the speakers said that each of us must make a fundamental style and content decision: Would our publication have edge or not?

Those without edge had little power to offend but were full of feel-good articles, such as those found in *Readers' Digest, Saturday Evening Post, Christmas Ideals*, and *Martha Stewart Living*. Those with edge were full of offense, laden with political, religious, or social commentary. In this connection one thinks of *The Nation* on the left and *National Review* on the right.

This was a perfect question for the magazine of a denomination embroiled in controversy over the place of biblical inerrancy in the life of its agencies, particularly the seminaries. Some church papers constrain themselves to upward-and-onward good news, "happy talk," if you will, but others inject editorial opinion and tactical news coverage on matters in keen dispute. The leaders of *SBC LIFE* chose the latter, convinced that momentous matters were in the balance and that it was their responsibility to engage the enemies of biblical authority, whether persons or ideas. They chose to play hardball, not Nerf ball, and it mattered for the good.

Of course there is a place for rosy reports, warm affirmations, cheerful announcements, and glad reflections. This is the staple for church newsletters and much of the religious press. But when it comes to apologetics, one wants more, namely, rigorous, cutting-edge engagement with the issue at hand. Thus one should expect responsible defenders of the faith to reach beyond diplomacy to invective at times.

PATIENCE

Tired of worn-out arguments against the faith and cognizant of the dire matters at stake, apologists can be tempted to snap. But that is typically counterproductive, no matter how cathartic it may be.

Bill Maher in the Truckers' Chapel

In the film *Religulous*, Bill Maher stops by a truck stop chapel. He starts asking confrontational questions about the faith, touching on such issues as original sin and the Immaculate Conception. The chaplain says it is a matter of faith, and then a big fellow in a red T-shirt says, "I don't know what this documentary is supposed to be, but you start disputin' my God, and you gotta problem. I'm outta here. You do what you gotta do, but I'm outta here."

In the commentary on the man's exit, Maher observed, "That's turning the other cheek, and that's quite a cheek he's turning." As for those who remained and engaged him in conversation, even praying for him, he said, "Loved those guys. All of them. Because they were so nice."[7]

Not everyone need be faulted who pulls out of an apologetic encounter. No one has an infinite amount of time to give those who are denigrating the gospel—as this truck driver may have been on a tight schedule, needing spiritual sustenance rather than an argument with a smug heretic. But a little more amiable patience would have helped, perhaps an exit comment, "Sorry, but I've got to go. I sure wish you'd speak more respectfully of the faith. I'll be praying that you find the Lord, sir."

Argumentum ad Huffum

Those who teach logic regularly cover such "informal fallacies" as *argumentum ad hominem, ad baculum, and ad misericordiam*. But a more disturbing

discourse poison is what may be called *argumentum ad huffum*, the ploy of getting into or going off in a huff. A person shows himself so above the other, so
refined in his sensitivities, so indignant at the proceedings that he cannot even
countenance conversation.

Certainly there are times to break off a discussion when the opponent shows
himself so evil or absurd in his thinking that reason and graciousness are fruit-
less. One does not spend the afternoon in amiable patter with an Ahmadinejad
as he rehearses his plans for annihilating Israel. But too many turn their backs
on opponents too early and then count it a sign of virtue. This may instead be
a manifestation of churlishness or even cowardice.

ACCESSIBILITY

So much academic prose is obscure, laden with jargon, belaboring points.
Professional philosophers are prone to "Chisholm" (in the style of Roderick
Chisholm), working through seemingly endless adjustments to basic propositions, alphabetized and numbered, with primes, double-primes, and such. He
finds himself several pages into a paper trying to recall whether A stood for
"Ducks have lips" or "The present king of France is bald," and he has to keep
turning back to get his bearings.

Certainly it is doable, and those who get degrees in philosophy become adept
at the style. At times it can serve to clarify things, but one wonders whether
plain speech could have done just as well. One also wonders if this represents a
certain disciplinary insecurity, whereby an essentially metaphorical enterprise (a
battle of paradigms) is mapped onto something that looks like math or physics.
Be that as it may, it is a shame that because of this writing style, philosophers
as a group are of so little help and interest to the populace they should be aim-
ing to help. (Actually this is a blessing in many cases, where society would be
harmed by better communication of misguided theories.) Certainly the Christian apologist should do everything he can to communicate important things
to the church. And while he may couch his work in the obscurities of the guild
when reading a paper to his colleagues at professional meetings, he should never
think that this is the norm.

Some of course think that academic jargon is the purest form of communication and that they are working on Olympus when they honor the canons
of academia. But there are too many counterexamples to entertain this conceit
seriously. Such philosophers as George Berkeley, David Hume, William James,
A. J. Ayer, Arthur Danto, John Rawls, and Paul Helms have done quite well
speaking clearly.

Of course Cambridge University professor C. S. Lewis is a model of accessible expression. He argued that "you must translate every bit of your Theology

into the vernacular."[8] The problem is that the man on the street thinks that a "Christian" is "a decent chap who is unselfish, etc.," the "church" is "a sacred building" or "the clergy," and "dogma" means "unproved assertion delivered in an arrogant manner."[9]

This is suggestive of a general missionary principle: "If you were sent to the Bantus you would be taught their language and traditions. You need similar teaching about the language and mental habits of your own uneducated and unbelieving fellow countrymen."[10]

Lewis mastered "Bantu" and, though he was a professor at the highest levels of British academia, he could answer with utmost clarity. To those who talked as though all Christians should be clearly superior to all non-Christians, he explained that there was no such thing as a complete Christian and a complete pagan, at least in terms of behavior.

> Christian Miss Bates may have an unkinder tongue than unbelieving Dick Firkin. That, by itself, does not tell us whether Christianity works. The question is what Miss Bates's tongue would be like if she were not a Christian and what Dick's would be like if he became one. Miss Bates and Dick, as a result of natural causes and early upbringing, have certain temperaments: Christianity professes to put both temperaments under new management if they will allow it to do so. What you have a right to ask is whether that management, if allowed to take over, improves the concern.[11]

PARODY

Whether the expression came from Martin Luther, John Wesley, William Booth, or Larry Norman, most people are familiar with the rhetorical question, "Why should the devil have all the good music?" One might also ask, "Why should the devil have all the pointed humor?" The church should have more satirists, parodists, and even comedians to jab the skeptic.

Dorothy Sayres turned her pen against modern secular culture with a parody of the Nicene Creed, "The Creed of St. Euthanasia," whose cadence mimics that of the former.

> I believe in man, maker of himself and inventor of all science. And in my self, his manifestation and captain of my psyche; and that I should not suffer anything painful or unpleasant.
>
> And in a vague, evolving deity, the future-begotten child of man; conceived by the spirit of progress, born of emergent variants; who shall kick down the ladder by which he rose and tell history to go to h _ _ _.
>
> Who shall some day take off from earth and be jet-propelled into the heavens; and sit exalted above all worlds, man the master almighty.
>
> And I believe in the spirit of progress, who spake by Shaw and the Fabians; and in a modern, administrative, ethical, and social organization; in the isolation of saints, the treatment of complexes, joy through health, and destruction of the body by cremation (with music while it burns), and then I've had it.[12]

SIMPLICITY

Someone has said that the tax code is so complex because lawyers write it, and tax payers need lawyers to deal with it. That sort of implied conflict of interest can plague any line of work, where professionals insist you need a professional to get it right. For that reason highly trained apologists have a tendency to disparage simple arguments a layman can readily understand and appreciate. This is often the counsel of pedantry, and one need not give in to it. There are too many serious thinkers who have escaped it to communicate great truths well.

C. S. Lewis

His answers are bracing in their simplicity and power. To those who say God would not be much interested in tiny earth, he retorts that if size were the issue, then an elephant would be more important than a man, "or a man's leg than his brain."[13] To those who say that Bible-times people believed in miracles "because they didn't know that they were contrary to the Laws of Nature," he answers that "the very idea of 'miracle' presupposes knowledge of the Laws of Nature; you can't have the idea of an exception until you have the idea of a rule."[14]

Elaboration may well follow, but the point is made in a sentence or two. The same goes for this observation: "The war-time posters told us that Careless Talk costs Lives. It is equally true that Careless Lives cost Talk. Our careless lives set the outer world talking; and we give them grounds for talking in a way that throws doubt on the truth of Christianity itself."[15]

Schlock?

In Thesis 15 of his "Christian Apologetics Manifesto," Denver Seminary's Douglas Groothuis insists:

> Apologetics must be carried out with the utmost intellectual integrity. All propaganda, cheap answers, caricatures of non-Christian views, and fallacious reasoning should be avoided. One should develop competent answers to searching questions about the truth and rationality of Christian faith. This demands excellence in scholarship at all intellectual levels, even the most popular.[16]

Then in Groothuis's discussion of the sixth of "Six Enemies of Apologetic Engagement," he warns against "superficial techniques or schlock apologetics."

> Some who get excited about apologetics may become content with superficial answers to difficult intellectual questions. Our culture revels in rapid responses to most anything, and technique is king. Some Christians memorize pat answers to apologetic questions—such as the problem of evil or the creation/evolution controversy—which they dispense without a proper engagement of the issues and without an empathetic concern for the soul that raises the question. I once saw a little book called something like *The Handy,*

Dandy Evolution Refuter. Yes, macro-evolution is false, and good arguments have been raised against it from both nature and Scripture, but the matter is not as simplistic as the title of that book makes it sound. Apologetics must be done with intellectual integrity.[17]

Well, yes, you don't want schlock, which is undesirable by definition. But sorting out which is trash and which is treasure sounds easier than it is. And, if we're not careful, we can slip back into the confusion that profound means complex. And we've all seen cases where the expression, "It's not as simple as that," raises a red flag of warning that unseemly compromise is afoot (as in a response to "The Bible makes no allowance for homosexual pastors" or "No one comes to the Father but by Jesus").

And it's not clear which "memorizing pat answers to apologetic questions" is shameful if the answers are devastatingly true (as when we are led to see that both ethical relativism and logical positivism self-destruct). Any substantial body of thought can be summarized in a phrase or two—whether "Existence precedes essence," "Property is theft," *"Credo ut intelligam"* ("I believe that I may understand")—and students profit from picking one up as a sort of verbal shorthand or peg for hanging more study.

As for "propaganda," there is certainly a good sense to it, namely, the effort to propagate the faith by dissemination of important information. One would hope that apologists are propagandists and not just members of a sort of intellectual chess club. And we need to be careful about tossing aside "handy dandy refuters." Handy is better than elusive, unwieldy, or occult. Dandy has its charms, if the contrast is woebegone, insipid, or soporific. And refutation is nice if the subject is grievous error.

Alvin Plantinga's "Two Dozen (or So) Theistic Arguments"[18] is a "handy dandy" denigration of the demand for proof that God exists. Even the title is flip—"You want proof? Okay, here's a batch. You happy?" Some of the "proofs" are difficult (e.g., one using Georg Cantor's set theory); others are rather simple (e.g., one appealing to the beautiful work of Mozart). But the point is not the content of the proofs; it is Plantinga's insouciance, which the novice can communicate fairly, even though he has not done the heavy lifting ("You want a proof? You might check the Alvin Plantinga article where he throws out a couple of them, if that matters to you").

But surely Plantinga has earned the right to be "handy dandy." But is not the point the strategic truth of things, not the credentials of the truth bearer? The apologetic material may come from a laminated pamphlet on a rotating kiosk in an outlet mall's Christian gift store and not from an Ivy League bookstore, but it can be good. Though the information comes in bite-sized pieces without citation, it is interesting to hear that the Sumerian king lists, discovered by archaeologists, report shorter life spans after a great flood[19] and that throughout history Christians have distinguished themselves by their care of children, whether through the orphanage-advocacy of Basil of Caesarea and Chrysostom of Constantinople (both of the fourth century) or kindergarten-founding work of the German Lutheran Friedrich Froebel (nineteenth century).[20] These facts can be helpful if you encounter someone intent on discrediting the Genesis flood or who says that Christianity "poisons everything."

Of course Groothuis is right to say "not just anything goes" in apologetics. That was the point with regard to Jack Chick's take on "IHS" in the previous chapter. And I could name other disappointments. For instance, though one can appreciate Benjamin Wiker's highly readable *10 Books that Screwed Up the World: And 5 Others That Didn't Help* (wherein he skewered Machiavelli's *The Prince* and Marx/Engel's *Manifesto of the Communist Party*, along with others), I think he abuses Descartes' *Discourse on Method*, twisting epistemology into metaphysics, for one thing. But that chapter need not be called "schlock," employing the "nuclear option" (like calling a piece of art "kitsch"). To say, "He's confused here," is more accurate. Indeed in most cases, it is simply enough to say, "He got it wrong" or "He left out a huge piece of the puzzle."

Another concern about dismissing "fallacious reasoning" and insisting on "proper engagement of the issues," "empathetic concern for the soul that raises the question," and "intellectual integrity" is that much good work is done by literary types who would not know a syllogism if it bit them on the arm. Though it is just a children's story, Hans Christian Anderson's tale "The Emperor's New Clothes" swings the sledge effectively against intellectual elitism. Furthermore one ought not sideline G. K. Chesterton simply because he had a weakness for "snappy" observations, such as these from *Orthodoxy*—"The main point of Christianity was this: that Nature is not our mother: Nature is our sister"; "For some inconceivable cause a 'broad' or 'liberal' clergyman always means a man who wishes at least to diminish the number of miracles"; "that an ape has hands is far less interesting to the philosopher than the fact that having hands he does next to nothing with them; does not play knuckle-bones or the violin; does not carve marble or carve mutton."[21]

A scholar could easily retort, "Is that really the *main* point of Christianity? Does it not share that conviction with some other religions?" "Does liberal *always* mean opposition to miracles?" "Have you studied apes sufficiently to make this dismissive judgment; if you took the time, you would find that they are quite adept at things people cannot manage." But this is to confuse genres and to miss the general point.

Of course, Groothuis, a distinguished apologist, knows all this, and, in fact, is a strong advocate of using all sorts of media, including film and letters to the editor, to "propagandize" the reasonableness of the faith. I'm simply using a couple of his statements as foils for discussion, genuinely concerned that we can lionize masters of the arcane and denigrate the offerings of nobodies simply because they are nobodies or their efforts are insufficiently nuanced.

DAUNTLESSNESS

Some charges against Christianity are so well established that the believers are apt to cede them to the enemy without a fight. When critics raise the specter of the Inquisition, the Crusades, and such, then most run for cover, granting that these were humiliating lapses in judgment, devotion, and goodness. Certainly there is a time to do this but not quite so many times as one might suppose. Those who take the time to examine the charges often find that there is good occasion for a fresh fight.

One may think of Jesus' flabbergasting remarks, when He took on the commonly accepted righteousness of the Pharisees. In one instance he pictured a "half-breed" Samaritan as their moral superiors; in another he said that people had no hope of salvation unless their righteousness exceeded that of the Pharisees.

C. S. Lewis on Witches

In Western society, where "witch hunt" is an unqualifiedly negative expression, it takes courage to say the following:

> One man said to me, "Three hundred years ago people in England were putting witches to death. Was that what you call the Rule of Human Nature or Right Conduct?" But surely the reason we do not execute witches is that we do not believe there are such things. If we did—if we really thought that there were people going about who had sold themselves to the devil and received supernatural power from him in return and were using these powers to kill their neighbours or drive them mad or bring bad weather—surely we would all agree that if anyone deserved the death penalty, then these filthy quislings did? There is no difference of moral principle here: the difference is about matter of fact.[22]

On this side of the Atlantic Arthur Miller wrote *The Crucible* about the Salem witch trials but really about Congressional attempts to root out Communism (whether through Hollywood "blacklisting" or the McCarthy inquiries into the State Department). Whatever the congressional blunders, there really were Communists and Communist-sympathizers in key cultural and political sectors and around the world. Communists were proving to be the sort who could murder over 100 million of their own people (under Stalin, Mao, and Pol Pot) and threaten the free world with nuclear annihilation. Still, it takes courage to say a good word for Whittaker Chambers (who exposed real spies, including Alger Hiss) and to stand by the jury that convicted Julius and Ethel Rosenberg (who proved to be real spies).

Lewis was writing about witches, but the principle is the same. The apologist may be called on to endure the scorn of the media and even the disdain of fellow Christians in rebutting the conventional wisdom regarding certain characters and events.

Answers in Genesis

Not inclined to wet a finger and put it in the wind (see discussion of appeasers in chap. 7), apologists are not afraid to take a strong counterculture stance, and few things could be more counterculture, even among evangelical scholars, than young-earth creationism. It is bad enough if one tries to champion Intelligent Design among the academics, but if he goes on to claim that the world is only 10,000 years old, he becomes leprous.

Of course it is no virtue per se to be counted a dolt. If that were the case, flat-earthers and phrenologists would sit in the pantheon. But when those bringing a scorned case have a rational and biblically respectful paradigm in hand, their boldness is admirable.

This came home to the author in force when he had the privilege of representing Southern Seminary on a scholars raft trip through the Grand Canyon, led by Answers in Genesis, the ones who have the Creation Museum near Cincinnati. For six days and 190 miles, they played "emperor's new clothes" as they pointed out features of the canyon that are incompatible with the old-earth gradualism touted by the cultural elites and echoed by their followers.

The author remembers from his childhood the maxim that "just as the little Colorado River could cut the mighty Grand Canyon by pluck and determination over time, we too could accomplish great things by sticking with it." But even a cursory look at the situation raised the question of how such a small river could make a miles-wide ditch. But Answers in Genesis did not stop there. They asked how the Colorado could flow uphill to make its cut, how the sedimentary layers could have such clean borders, how massive slabs of limestone could be twisted into graceful S-curves, how two-foot-long nautical creatures could be fossilized in an upright position in the sediment, and so forth.

To match the negative, they presented a plausible counter explanation—that when Noah's flood receded, massive lakes were left on the land, one of which broke through its dam, swept through the "wet concrete" of the plateau, and carved out a huge canyon in a matter of days.

In other words there was a geological catastrophe, as described in Ps 104:6–9:

> You covered [the earth] with the deep as if it were a garment;
> the waters stood above the mountains. At Your rebuke the waters fled;
> at the sound of Your thunder they hurried away—mountains rose and valleys sank—

to the place You established for them. You set a boundary they cannot cross;
they will never cover the earth again."

Geological things went "fast-forward" under God's supervision. Perhaps this involved plate tectonics or even radioactive decay and starlight speed, all as effortlessly as Noah's flood. Who says things had to proceed at the same pace as today?

And how can anyone say that he must extrapolate from current experience to be scientific, particularly when he is not in a position to verify that current regularities are eternal. After all, if a person is an old-earther, he would have to say that scientists have been making observations for only a tiny fraction of the history of the cosmos. But reliance on such a small sample seems to be as irrational as judging someone's age by his recent gain or loss of weight. If he gains a pound this year and he now weighs 200 pounds, then he must be 200 years old. Or if he gains a pound a week between Thanksgiving and New Year's Day, he must be just under four years old—a pound a week for four years.

Of course such reasoning fails to take into account such "anomalies" as adolescence and holiday binging. Of course a scientist could insist that extrapolation from one's current rate of gain or loss is the only respectable "scientific" approach but so much the worse for his stipulation.

Still to raise such questions is to find oneself outside the pale of those who say a good God would not permit the world to "look so old." The problem is, it looks only so old as one's theory makes it look. Why do so many evangelicals insist on belonging to the Church of Jesus Christ of Latter-Day Patterns?

TEAMSHIP

On his second missionary journey Paul was under fire from the Jews in Corinth. Lest he become discouraged, God came to him in a vision one night, saying, "I am with you, and no one will lay a hand on you to hurt you, because I have many people in this city" (Acts 18:10). Indeed he was able to work there for 18 months unhindered.

Christian apologists enjoy the same assurance, that there are colleagues ready to pick up where they see gaps.

Reaching Antony Flew

In one of the shocking philosophical reversals of the twentieth century, "professional atheist" Antony Flew became a theist. This did not happen overnight but was the result of decades of influence with thinkers who argued the truth, or at least the reasonableness, of belief in God.

Among the influences that nudged Flew toward acknowledging the divine were C. S. Lewis, whom he admired for his determination to "follow the argument wherever it leads";[23] Biola University professor Gary Habermas, who pressed the case for design in the universe;[24] Central Washington University professor Raeburne Heimbeck, who pressed Flew to acknowledge the difference between things problematical for belief and things incompatible with belief;[25] and Notre Dame professor Ralph McInerny, who shifted the burden of proof onto the atheist.[26] The list goes on to include professors Thomas Warren, Basil Mitchell, Richard Swinburne, William Lane Craig, and Alvin Plantinga. Through the years "Flew has faced Anglican and Baptist, Catholic and Campbellite, Dispensationalist and Orthodox, Calvinist and Arminian, all pulling together to defend the faith and to rescue a skeptic."[27]

In this respect apologetics is like evangelism in that it typically takes several if not many exposures to the gospel before conversion occurs. Those who witness understand that they may not see results but that they may well be preparing the soil, clearing out clutter, or planting a seed. Today's argument may not carry the day, but it may well lay another straw on the camel's back.

Though one may be less than enthusiastic about another's argument and feel obliged to critique it, he should do so with respect, suggesting that "some find this persuasive." The underlying conviction is that there is a brotherhood of apologetics, one which deserves a believer's grace.

Dealing with the "Four Horsemen"

In his book *The Delusion of Disbelief*, former *Time* correspondent David Aikman likens the "atheists" Sam Harris, Richard Dawkins, Daniel Dennett, and Christopher Hitchens to the Bible's four horsemen of the Apocalypse. Their "great assault upon faith was launched in 2006 against unsuspecting Americans who attend church, go to synagogue, worship in mosques, pray in temples, or otherwise live lives in which religion plays an important role."[28] Fortunately Aikman's fine response was just one of many that rose to the challenge of answering these aggressors.

Sometimes Christians lose their sense of thankfulness for the wealth of resources at hand to champion the cause of Christ. A touch of concern over publishing turf and a hint of career jealousy can rob the believer's joy at the apologetical feast set before him. For a cure he might start by considering the relative paucity of conservative, evangelical writing available in French, German, Arabic, Russian, Mandarin, Bahasa, and Swahili, to name a few languages. Bible believers in those nations are often starving for a single book in their tongue designed to combat the latest heresy plaguing their land. So believers ought not forget to celebrate what they have.

Just as many Christians pitched in to help Antony Flew see the reality of God, many have joined in the fray against resurgent atheism. Indeed this book picks up on the cause. And this writer is so grateful to be surrounded with a "cloud of other witnesses," both living and dead, who have picked up the gauntlet.

Among the living, in addition to Aikman, are Paul Copan's and William Lane Craig's *Contending with Christianity's Critics*;[29] John Haught's *God and the New Atheism*;[30] Patrick Madrid's and Kenneth Hensley's *The Godless Delusion*;[31] Gregory E. Ganssle's *A Reasonable God*;[32] Edgar Andrews's *Who Made God?*;[33] Paul Copan's *Is God a Moral Monster?*;[34] David Brog's *In Defense of Faith*;[35] Becky Garrison's *The New Atheist Crusaders and Their Unholy Grail*;[36] Timothy Keller's *The Reason for God*;[37] William Lane Craig's and Chad Meister's *God Is Great, God Is Good*;[38] and Ian S. Markham's *Against Atheism*.[39]

The list goes on and on, as should the gratitude.

MOXIE

In the midst of celebrating the apologetic riches believers enjoy today, one may easily forget the pioneering efforts of one's immediate forebears. Christians constantly and rightly rehearse the contributions of such greats as Anselm and Aquinas, Leibniz and Paley, Reid and Pascal, and more recently C. S. Lewis. And of course all believers can name professors and colleagues who instructed and inspired them in the apologetic arts. But though they were counterculture in a modernist society, they enjoyed the dignity of an academic post.

That is why one can have special affection for the likes of Francis Schaeffer and Josh McDowell, who drove their icebreakers into thick, frozen sheets of philosophical pride and specious relativism. Schaeffer had the temerity to insult Kant and Sartre, and McDowell had the "bad taste" to enthuse relentlessly over Bible connections at every turn.

Loretta Lynn, George Jones, Dolly Parton, and Porter Waggoner were said to be "country before country was cool"—before people like Patty Loveless and Rascal Flatts were invited to appear on *Late Show with David Letterman*. As much as people enjoy contemporary acts, whether at the Country Music Association Awards or in American Philosophical Association colloquia, they should give thanks for those whom a Johnny Carson or an APA would not touch with a stick in their day. But it is not just a matter of tribute. Believers need to be ready to break some ice themselves and to be willing to endure a measure of scorn from both within and without the church.

As John Adams put it,

> I must study Politicks and War that my sons may have liberty to study Mathematicks and Philosophy. My sons ought to study Mathematicks and Philosophy, Geography, natural History, Naval Architecture, navigation, Commerce and Agriculture, in order to give their Children a right to study Painting, Poetry, Musick, Architecture, Statuary, Tapestry and Porcelaine.[40]

So yes, some apologists may track mud into the drawing room from time to time, but it may well be mixed with their own blood spilled on the field of honorable battle.

Notes

1 Jason Lisle, "Fool Proof Apologetics," *Answers*, April–June 2009, 69.
2 John Henry Cardinal Newman, *The Idea of a University* (New York: Longmans, Green, 1947), 185.
3 Ibid.
4 Ibid.
5 C. S. Lewis, *Mere Christianity* (reprint, San Francisco: Harper Collins, 2001), 37. Originally published in 1952.
6 Ibid., 38.
7 Bill Maher, "Commentary with Bill Maher and Director Larry Charles," *Religulous* xlvi; http:///www.lionsgate.com/religulous (accessed January 12, 2010).
8 Lewis, "Christian Apologetics," in *God in the Dock: Essays on Theology and Ethics*, ed. Walter Hooper (Grand Rapids: Eerdmans, 1970), 98.
9 Ibid., 98–99.
10 Ibid., 94.
11 Lewis, *Mere Christianity*, 209–10.
12 Dorothy Sayres, *The Whimsical Christian* (New York: Macmillan, 1978), 10.
13 Lewis, *God in the Dock*, 100.
14 Ibid.
15 Lewis, *Mere Christianity*, 209–10.
16 Doug Groothuis, "Christian Apologetics Manifesto 2003: Sixteen Theses," http://www.ivpress.com/groothuis/doug/archives/000010.php#more (accessed December 31, 2010).
17 Doug Groothuis, "Six Enemies of Apologetic Engagement," http://www.leaderu.com/common/sixenemies.html (accessed December 31, 2010).
18 Alvin Plantinga, "Two Dozen (or So) Theistic Arguments" (lecture notes), http://philofreligion.homestead.com/files/theisticarguments.html (accessed January 1, 2011).
19 Larry McKinney, *50 Proofs for the Bible: Old Testament* (Torrance, CA: Rose, 2007), item 1.
20 Robert Velarde, *What Christianity Has Done for the World: 50 Key Contributions* (Torrance, CA: Rose, 2007), 3, 6.
21 G. K. Chesterton, *Orthodoxy* (New York: Dodd, Mead, 1908; reprint, New York: Doubleday, 2001), 115, 132, 151.
22 Lewis, *Mere Christianity*, 14–15.
23 Antony Flew with Roy Abraham Varghese, *There Is a God: How the World's Most Notorious Atheist Changed His Mind* (New York: HarperCollins, 2007), 74.
24 "My Pilgrimage from Atheism to Theism: A Discussion Between Antony Flew and Gary Habermas," Evangelical Philosophical Society Web site; http://www.epsociety.org/library/articles.asp?pid=33 (accessed August 13, 2010).
25 Flew and Varghese, *There Is a God*, 48.
26 Ibid., 55–56.
27 "Nudged by Christians, an Atheist Becomes a Theist," *Kairos Journal*; http://www.kairosjournal.org/document.aspx?QuadrantID=4&DocumentID=8999&L=1&CategoryID=10&TopicID=47 (accessed August 13, 2010).

28 David Aikman, *The Delusion of Disbelief: Why the New Atheism Is a Threat to Your Life, Liberty, and Pursuit of Happiness* (Carol Stream, IL: Tyndale, 2008), 1–2.

29 Paul Copan and William Lane Craig, *Contending with Christianity's Critics: Answering New Atheists and Other Objectors* (Nashville: B&H, 2009).

30 John F. Haught, *God and the New Atheism: A Critical Response to Dawkins, Harris, and Hitchens* (Louisville: Westminster John Knox, 2008).

31 Patrick Madrid and Kenneth Hensley, *The Godless Delusion: A Catholic Challenge to Modern Atheism* (Huntington, IN: Our Sunday Visitor, 2010).

32 Gregory E. Ganssle, *A Reasonable God: Engaging the New Face of Atheism* (Waco, TX: Baylor University Press, 2009).

33 Edgar Andrews, *Who Made God? Searching for a Theory of Everything* (Faverdale North, Darlington, OK: EP, 2009).

34 Paul Copan, *Is God a Moral Monster? Making Sense of the Old Testament God* (Grand Rapids: Baker, 2011).

35 David Brog, *In Defense of Faith: The Judeo-Christian Idea and the Struggle for Humanity* (New York: Encounter, 2010).

36 Becky Garrison, *The Atheist Crusaders and Their Unholy Grail: The Misguided Quest to Destroy Your Earth* (Nashville: Thomas Nelson, 2007).

37 Timothy Keller, *The Reason for God: Belief in an Age of Skepticism* (New York: Penguin, 2008).

38 William Lane Craig and Chad Meister, eds., *God Is Great, God Is Good: Why Believing in God Is Reasonable and Responsible* (Downers Grove, IL: IVP, 2009).

39 Ian S. Markham, *Against Atheism: Why Dawkins, Hitchens, and Harris Are Fundamentally Wrong* (Oxford: Wiley-Blackwell, 2010).

40 John Adams to Abigail Adams, *Adams Family Correspondence* [*post 12 May 1780*], 3:342; http://www.masshist.org/adams/quotes.cfm (accessed January 1, 2010).

Name Index

Subject Index

gracious speech   *67*
grain, the   *70*
granularity   *256–58*
graphics   *255*
Great Commission   *197*
Great Leap Forward   *223*
Greece   *169*
Ground-Zero mosque   *225*
Gulags   *153*
gurus   *158*

H

Hadith   *54*
hagiography   *121*
Haiti relief   *137*
Halakah Electric Institute   *56*
handy dandy refuters   *267*
Happy Arabia   *137*
harsh language   *260*
haughty intellectuals   *247*
head hunting   *186*
heaven   *73–74*
heaven and hell   *203*
hedonism   *15, 17–18, 23*
hell   *106*
helpful pagans   *133*
herd mentality of science   *235*
heresy   *248*
heroism   *133, 194*
heterodoxy   *96*
hiding Jews   *177*
hierarchicalism   *33*
higher criticism   *239*
high horse   *216*
high school dropouts   *158*
Hinduism   *49–50, 83, 147–48*
Hippocratic Oath   *207*
historical amnesia   *133*
historical travesty   *224*
Hollywood   *224*
homophobia   *233*
homosexuality   *34, 86–87, 95, 100, 155, 171, 213, 222, 229*
honor   *138*
honor killings   *140–41*
horoscopes   *220*
hubris/pride   *119*
Humanae Vitae   *34*
humanitarian activity   *176*
human sacrifice   *187*
human universals   *70*
humility   *112–13, 121*

hygiene   *186*
hypocrisy   *100, 214*

I

Ibero-Catholic   *165*
idolatry   *74, 118, 185*
illegitimacy   *185*
Immanental theocracy   *52*
immediate gratification   *156*
immoralists   *156*
impeachment of testimony   *79–80*
incest   *102*
income equality   *30*
income redistribution   *30*
incomplete Christians   *265*
Indians   *117, 125, 145, 186, 205, 226*
indulgences   *170*
inerrancy   *221, 257*
infant baptism   *118*
infanticide   *26, 186*
infant mortality   *186*
infidels   *136, 176*
Inherit the Wind   *224*
Inquisition   *269*
insult   *214, 217*
integrative apologetics   *255*
integrity   *109, 122, 125, 149*
intellectual bankruptcy   *138*
intellectuals   *84*
Intelligent Design   *256*
intuition   *70*
intuitionism   *32*
invention   *166, 195*
irreducible complexity   *60–61*
Islam   *134–42, 218, 224*
Islamization   *219*
Islamophobia   *233*

J

Jerusalem Declaration   *171*
Jesuits   *169*
Jews   *169, 171, 193*
journalism   *217–21*
journalistic selectivity   *220*
Judeo-Christian values   *175*
judgment   *126*
justice   *58*
just-war theory   *205*

K

kamikaze   *53*
karma   *147*
Katyn massacre   *154*
Keynesian economics   *156*
King's X   *98*
Kitzmiller v. Dover   *239–40*
Koran. *See* Qur'an
Koran burning   *220*
Krishna   *50*

L

laminated pamphlets   *267*
language   *196*
laymen   *167*
legalism   *55–56*
liberalism   *251*
liberation theology   *167*
lighten up hermeneutics   *76*
linguistics   *188*
literacy   *141, 167*
literature   *195, 196*
loaning/giving   *250–51*
Lord, liar, or lunatic   *255*
Lost Boys of Sudan   *189*
love   *58, 69, 110–11, 126, 175*
Love Chapter   *175*
loyalty festival   *155*
lying   *89, 95, 102*

M

machismo   *120*
mackerels in moonlight   *224*
Magna Carta   *196*
main stream media   *239*
malnutrition   *166*
marriage   *126, 164, 171*
martyrdom   *108, 123*
martyrs   *248*
Marxism   *44*
Marxist Sun Kings   *155*
Mass   *208*
medicine   *186*
meditation   *149*
Meiji movement   *151–52*
Mein Kampf   *50*
mendicant orders   *124*
mercantilism   *167*
Mere Christianity   *250*
metaethics   *8, 57*
Methodists   *189*